THE
DIAMOND RING

THE

DIAMOND RING

Business, Politics, and Precious Stones
in South Africa, 1867–1947

Colin Newbury

CLARENDON PRESS · OXFORD
1989

Oxford University Press, Walton Street, Oxford OX2 6DP
Oxford New York Toronto
Delhi Bombay Calcutta Madras Karachi
Petaling Jaya Singapore Hong Kong Tokyo
Nairobi Dar es Salaam Cape Town
Melbourne Auckland
and associated companies in
Berlin Ibadan

Oxford is a trade mark of Oxford University Press

Published in the United States
by Oxford University Press, New York

British Library Cataloguing in Publication Data
Newbury, Colin
    The diamond ring : business, politics and precious
stones in South Africa, 1867–1947.
    1. South Africa. Diamond mining industries, history
I.   Title
338.2′ 782′ 0968

ISBN 0-19-821775-7

Library of Congress Cataloging in Publication Data
Newbury, C. W. (Colin Walter), 1929–
    The diamond ring : business, politics, and precious stones in
South Africa/Colin Newbury.
        p.   cm.
    Bibliography: p.
    Includes index.
    1. Diamond industry and trade—South Africa—History. I. Title.
HD9677.S62N48   1989
338.2′ 782′ 0968—dc20   89-9230
                                                            CIP

ISBN 0-19-821775-7

Phototypeset by Dobbie Typesetting Limited, Plymouth, Devon
Printed in Great Britain by
Courier International Ltd
Tiptree, Essex

FOR TRUDY AND JACKIE

They are of no use, but as ornaments; and the merit of their beauty is greatly enhanced by their scarcity, or by the difficulty of getting them from the mine. Wages and profit accordingly make up, upon most occasions, almost the whole of their high price.

Adam Smith, *The Wealth of Nations*

ACKNOWLEDGEMENTS

I AM grateful to the administrators of the Beit Fund, the Modern History Board of Oxford University, and to the former Committee for Commonwealth Studies of Queen Elizabeth House, Oxford, for a series of travel grants which made research possible in South Africa at the outset of this project. A generous grant from the Hoover Institution on War, Revolution and Peace, Stanford University, provided a period of revision and reflection on the final text and technical support for refinement of the tables and graphs.

In the course of research, access to the records of De Beers Consolidated Mines Ltd. at Kimberley was hospitably authorized through P. J. R. Leyden, Director, and G. A. Louw, former Public Relations Manager; and I have received every assistance from the Archivist, Dr M. H. Buys, during a period when the archives were still being classified. It is to be hoped that the regrettable decision to close these archives to researchers will be reversed. It will become clearer from this study, I hope, that other public and business records throw considerable light on the company; and this complementarity of materials makes it both impossible to isolate a major mining house from scrutiny and equitable to verify the company's role in South Africa's economic and social history from its own holdings. A beginning has been made in this and other works, but it is far from complete. Supplementation to company materials exists, however, in the Central Archives Depot, Pretoria; and I am grateful for the courteous assistance provided by the Government Archives Service and the high standard of their computerized retrieval system. It has been a pleasure, too, to explore the rich, though only partially accessible, resources held by Barlow Rand Limited at Sandton, Johannesburg, under the guidance of the company Archivist, Dr Maryna Fraser. Similarly, in London, Dr Gershon A. Knight and Mrs Yvonne Moss of the N. M. Rothschild Banking and Business Archive made records available during classification of holdings. Dr R. Walker and Mrs Gwen Hoy of Charter Consolidated Limited generously provided a series of company reports; and Graham Williams of Consolidated Goldfields PLC and R. D. G. Walker of the Diamond Trading Company (Proprietary) Limited gave access and advice.

At the Hoover Institution, Karen Fung, Curator of the Africana Collection, tracked down some rare items. In Oxford, my debt to Mr A. S. Bell, Librarian of Rhodes House, and to his colleagues has grown steadily over the years. I hope this study will be some return for their unfailing help.

A number of friends have read and discussed the manuscript, and I am especially grateful for comments by Professor R. A. Davenport, Professor John Galbraith, Dr Andrew Porter, Dr William Worger, Dr Lewis Gann, and Dr Peter Duignan, and the encouragement and support of Professor S. H. Frankel. Dr Stanley Chapman of Nottingham University kindly allowed me to read extracts from the letters of Sir Carl Meyer, while Professor Robert Rotberg exchanged his own stimulating manuscript and his ideas on Cecil Rhodes. In South Africa, I owe much to the generous hospitality of Lainie and Geoff Downer of Pretoria and to Archie and Peggy Shapiro of Johannesburg. Finally, I would like to acknowledge the patience and professional skills of Mr Robert Faber, History Editor, for his assistance in the initial stages of seeing the manuscript through the press.

C. N.

Oxford, Trinity Term, 1988

Permission to reproduce illustrations is gratefully acknowledged for the following sources: De Beers Archives, Kimberley (nos. 1–8, 10–12 [Sir Julius Wernher, L. Breitmeyer], 15). Nos. 9 and 13 are from the Kimberley Africana Library, Beet MS, and no. 14 consists of items made available by the Africana Museum, Johannesburg Public Library. The photo of S. B. Joel in no. 12 is reproduced from *African World*, December 1911, by permission of the Bodleian Library.

CONTENTS

♦

LIST OF ILLUSTRATIONS

LIST OF FIGURES

◆

LIST OF TABLES

MAPS AND PLAN

LIST OF ABBREVIATIONS

AST	African Selection Trust
Bod.	Bodleian Library
BPMI	Board for the Protection of Mining Interests
BPP	British Parliamentary Papers
BRA	Barlow Rand Archives
BSA	British South Africa Company
BT	Board of Trade
BTMB	Bultfontein Mining Board
CA	Cape Archives Depot
CAD	Central Archives Depot
CAST	Consolidated African Selection Trust
CDM	Consolidated Diamond Mines of South West Africa Limited
CO	Colonial Office
COCP	Colonial Office Confidential Print
CPP	Cape Colony Parliamentary Papers
CSO	Central Selling Organisation
ct.	carat
DBCA	De Beers Consolidated Mines Archive, Kimberley
DBCM	De Beers Consolidated Mines Limited
DBMB	De Beers Mining Board
DBMC	De Beers Mining Company Ltd.
DFA	*Diamond Fields Advertiser*
DMC	Diamond Mining Company
DO	Dominions Office
DPA	Diamond Producers Association
DTC	Diamond Trading Company
DTMB	Dutoitspan Mining Board
DUSC	Despatches from United States Consuls
GLW	Griqualand West Archives, Cape Archives
GWMU	Griqualand West Miners Union
HETA	High Explosives Trade Association
HLG	High Level Gravel (Syndicate)

ICWU	Industrial and Commercial Workers Union
IDB	Illicit Diamond Buying
JCI	Johannesburg Consolidated Investments Limited
KCDM	Kimberley Central Diamond Mining Company
KMB	Kimberley Mining Board
LSAE	London and South African Exploration Company Ltd.
mt. cts.	(Note all data in carat weights of 205.304 milligrams have been converted in price and production series to metric carats of 200 milligrams.)
MEW	Ministry of Economic Warfare
MLA	Member of the Legislative Assembly
PP	Parliamentary Papers
PRO	Public Record Office
RAL	N. M. Rothschild and Sons Archive
RH	Rhodes House
SADCO	South African Diamond Cutting Organisation
SC	Select Committee
SLST	Sierra Leone Selection Trust
SPG	Society for the Propagation of the Gospel
UG	Union Government (of South Africa)

INTRODUCTION
Miners and Historians

THIS study grew from an interest in entrepreneurial and labour history in a colonial enclave which came to dominate diamond production in the late nineteenth century. The speed of industrial growth and consolidation under one company—De Beers Consolidated Mines Limited—and the impact in social and economic terms on the surrounding region left their mark on South Africa and on its historiography, which has concentrated on the origins of the industry through the biographies of its founders and the social history of the municipality, the mines, and their labour force. Much in earlier studies is a by-product of biographies of Cecil Rhodes. By contrast, the social historians of mining see the rise of De Beers as a product of the subordination of labour by organized capital. Both contributions omit a considerable body of material which can be brought to bear on diamond mining from the techniques of business history. Concentration on the origins of the industry, moreover, has led to an imbalance and relative neglect of subsequent developments in diamond mining in South Africa, except in terms of further biographical interpretation in works on Sir Ernest Oppenheimer, which is overlaid by generalized summaries of mining and marketing. The neglect is compounded by an even greater omission, namely consideration of the role of the South African state in the regulation of the industry, more particularly from the formation of the Union.

None of these objections to the current state of the difficult art of exploring entrepreneurial history detracts from the debt to one's predecessors and contemporaries who have ventilated the subject; and that debt can be repaid to some extent by surveying the achievements of those who have emphasized other aspects, or taken different views, of the development of an extractive industry in the rural heartland of the northern Cape, if only for the questions they raise which still require answers.

For convenience the main body of published sources can be grouped into historical biography, mining technology, and social and economic studies. So much in the first category is 'Rhodes-centred' that the operation of the partnerships and joint-stock corporations has been lost from sight, until dug out of original sources. Rhodes as a businessman, moreover, has received much less attention than Rhodes the imperialist and politician.[1] Indeed, there was an effort in the earliest eulogies to distance the great man from the money-makers. But it is clear that his rise to political power and international fame requires a re-evaluation of his business talents in the context of Kimberley, Rhodesia, and the Rand, if only to determine how much he owed to corporate decision-making and the talents of others. His case is relevant, too, in the wider debate on the nineteenth century entrepreneur and the growth of firms; and the questions posed by Rhodes continue through the history of De Beers into the period of reconstruction under Sir Ernest Oppenheimer. In this subsequent history there is a different order of iconography because of the detailed contribution from Theodore Gregory who made a serious effort to incorporate an economic history of diamond production and marketing into his portrait of Oppenheimer.[2] The place of corporate management is still open to investigation, however, in the 1930s and later; and I do not claim to have resolved it in this book, because the necessary records of Oppenheimer's companies after that decade have not been open to me, and I have relied on political and administrative archives.

If biography has left loose ends in the history of company decision-making, there is less excuse for not relating the technology of diamond mining to the business performance of alluvial and pipe mines. Technical sources are, in fact, surprisingly rich. But they have not been brought to bear on historical explanation for the performance of the diamond mining companies. The main reason for the primacy of engineering description over an evaluation of company enterprise lies in the work of Gardner F. Williams and his son, Alpheus Williams, as general managers of De Beers and authors of standard accounts of 'pioneering' and progress in production until the 1920s.[3] Taken together with Gardner Williams's earlier (and neglected) technical reports on Kimberley,

[1] For an enlargement on this proposition and a review of the literature see Colin Newbury, 'Out of the Pit: The Capital Accumulation of Cecil Rhodes', *Journal of Imperial and Commonwealth History*, 10/1 (1981), 25–7. A reassessment of Rhodes has been undertaken by Robert Rotberg in *The Founder: Cecil Rhodes and the Pursuit of Power* (New York, 1988).

[2] The standard chronicle on the company remains, unfortunately, H. A. Chilvers, *The Story of De Beers* (London, 1939). See too Theodore Gregory, *Ernest Oppenheimer and the Economic Development of Southern Africa* (Cape Town, 1962); and the review by K. H. Burley in *Business History*, 6/1 (1964), 72. For an overview and introduction to the industry see Timothy Green, *The World of Diamonds* (London, 1981).

[3] Gardner F. Williams, *The Diamond Mines of South Africa: Some Account of their Rise and Development* (New York, 1902); A. F. Williams, *Some Dreams Come True* (Cape Town, 1948).

these works had a great deal to say about diamond excavation and much less on the marketing of diamonds. Alpheus Williams, it is true, was less discreet in his memoir on the company, but touched on finance and distribution only to praise and vindicate Rhodes. His major contribution to the literature rests on his study of the origins of the diamond, and not on how it was sold.

The specialist insights of the engineers have been followed uncritically in two other ways. Theodore Reunert supplied a standard text on diamond and gold mining and attempted to provide the first statistical series of production and prices, which has been incorporated into later literature. Secondly the engineers took a very unsentimental and instrumentalist view of labour supply, especially in reports and articles, without, however, relating labour costs to mining profitability. This approach found its way into the influential publications of P. A. Wagner, Stafford Ransome, and Ralph S. G. Stokes (mining editor of the *Rand Daily Mail*), who extolled the value of South African mining for the British empire, without explaining how that value was produced as a return on the cost of production or the capital employed by the companies.[4]

And there the subject rested in the hands of biographers and technicians, like some vast open-cast pit to be well quarried by a host of more popular writers on diamond legend, until advances were made into Kimberley's social and economic history from very different directions by labour historians on the one hand, and a specialist study of diamond mining and business cycles on the other.

By extending the central themes of gold mining and migrancy in South Africa to diamond mining at Kimberley, urban labour historians followed the pioneer work of S. T. van der Horst and the valuable urban study made by Brian Roberts.[5] The migrant labourer has been rehabilitated from a faceless input to a member of agricultural societies which responded to the opportunities presented by cash crops and wage employment. There are serious limitations to the labour records, which have to some extent been supplemented by W. Worger's exploration of court and criminality

---

[4] Theodore Reunert, *Diamonds and Gold in South Africa* (Cape Town, 1893); P. A. Wagner, *The Diamond Fields of South Africa* (Johannesburg, 1914); Stafford Ransome, *The Engineer in South Africa* (London, 1903), ch. 6; Ralph S. G. Stokes, *Mines and Minerals of the British Empire* (London, 1908).

[5] S. T. van der Horst, *Native Labour in South Africa* (Cape Town, 1942); Brian Roberts, *Kimberley: Turbulent City* (Cape Town, 1976); William H. Worger, *South Africa's City of Diamonds: Mine Workers and Monopoly Capitalism in Kimberley, 1867–1895* (Yale University Press, New Haven and London, 1987); R. Turrell, *Capital and Labour on the Kimberley Diamond Fields, 1871–1890* (CUP, 1987).

records in order to establish the pattern of social control exercised by employers in the formative period of company operations in Griqualand West. Company records do not entirely fill the gap; and the transition to wage dependency among diamond workers over the long period of migrant recruitment for all the diamond mines and the alluvial workings in South Africa still has to be accurately charted. It is understandable, too, that the compound system has provided a central focus for more recent historical analysis, following the lead given by R. F. Siebörger and J. M. Smalberger, though I think its primary purpose has been lost from sight in favour of stressing the utility of compounding for labour management.[6] Unlike other minerals the diamond is an easily purloined commodity. There has been a tendency, moreover, to intepret the transition period from diggings to company consolidation, as in the detailed works by W. Worger and R. V. Turrell, in terms of periodic financial 'crises' or 'recessions'; and this interpretation requires support from a price and production series and an analysis of the performance of companies if the dynamics of merger and concentration are to be understood. Finally, the termination of these valuable studies in the early 1890s leaves open-ended any conclusion about the working of 'monopoly' in later and changed conditions in the South African and international diamond market. How did 'capital' face up to much bigger 'crises' of recession and over-production; and what were the results for the labour force?

The major problem faced by historians of the diamond industry, I believe, is that so much has been taken for granted on the growth of wholesaling during the construction of a production monopoly and producers' cartel. Relative scarcity of sources has aggravated the emphasis on supply rather than demand (though it is surprising just how far some earlier students of the European diamond trade were able to push their investigation).[7] But, as this study will show, I have stressed the role of the diamond merchants during company formation and have tried to unravel their relationship with the major company until the reconstruction of the industry in the 1930s brought mining houses and merchants into a single organization. A balanced account of both ends of the market has been attempted before by Godehard Lenzen, who identified control

---

[6] For earlier explorations of Kimberley's mining labour system see R. F. Siebörger, 'The Recruitment and Origins of African Labour for the Kimberley Diamond Mines, 1871–1888' MA thesis (Rhodes University, 1975); J. M. Smalberger, 'IDB and the Mining Compound System in the 1880s', *South African Journal of Economics*, 42/4 (1974), 398–414.

[7] Jean Demuth, *Der Diamantenmarkt mit besonderer Berücksichtigung der deutschsüdwestafrikanischen Ausbeute* (Karlsruhe, 1912); and for the 1880s see the well-informed study by Turrell, *Capital and Labour*, esp. ch. 5.

of production by the merchant combine as the principal factor determining the industry's response to fluctuating demand in the business cycles of the late nineteenth and twentieth centuries.[8] There are reservations to be made about the 'prices' accepted from averages of annual diamond exports; and there is a muddle over the description of the diamond syndicate and the production cartel. Nowhere is it demonstrated how the diamond contracts worked, and this limitation applies to Theodore Gregory's study which is strong on Oppenheimer's manœuvres and very guarded on the syndicate or selling organization's methods of purchase and resale.

A better understanding of the wholesalers, moreover, throws light on the nature of 'monopoly' as ownership of sources of supply or as a contractual combination subject to financial performance and open to revision. The diamond market has seen both forms of concentration, separately and acting together; and it is important to sort them out in a multinational enterprise, rather than bury the topic under the vague title of 'monopoly capitalism'.

Finally, the growth and organization of the industry must also be tackled from the viewpoint of the state in its various executive, legislative, judicial, and administrative guises. The colonial state and the successor Union government are too often seen as lending unqualified support to the capitalist entrepreneurs or acting as somewhat shadowy opponents of efforts to 'save the diamond trade' in the 1920s and 1930s. A more fundamental question to be examined, however, is how South Africa's early governments determined the ownership of rights over precious stones within their separate legislative histories, and which precedents were adopted and applied by the Union. It is an arid but important topic which displays a number of contrasts with diamond mining elsewhere.[9] Similarly, the question of taxation and the fiscal interests of the state for revenue and protection of a local cutting industry require explanation, if only to demonstrate the early weakness of Cape Colony and the later strength of the Union in this area of regulation and control.

The administration and politics of diamond mining, moreover, should help to test the challenging thesis offered by David Yudelman to South African historiography from the gold mining industry concerning

---

[8] Godehard Lenzen, *The History of Diamond Production and the Diamond Trade* (London, 1970). See too the review by Ralph Davis in *Business History Review*, 45/1 (1977), 258.

[9] See H. R. Hahlo and Ellison Khan, *The Union of South Africa: The Development of its Laws and Constitution* (London, 1960), ch. 18; and for comparisons T. F. Van Wagenen, *International Mining Law* (New York, 1918); Peter Greenhalgh, *West African Diamonds 1919–1983: An Economic History* (Manchester, 1985).

continuity in government policy, as applied through the Department of Mines and Industries, and the significance of the change of government in 1924.[10] In addition, it has to be explained why white militancy was absent from diamond mining in the 1920s and how far political patronage of the alluvial diggers in opposition to local and overseas 'monopolists' really did anything to relieve social and economic distress.

It has been assumed, too, that the South African government was master in its own house, because of increasing state supervision of the modes of mining exploration. The position of the British government in two world wars, when diamonds became a strategic commodity, has not so far been examined. In any case, South Africa was no longer the dominant producer by the 1930s, though the centralized selling organization was structured around De Beers; and it is one of the arguments of this study that considerable compromises were forced on both the government and the domestic producers in order to accommodate the interests of other African producers in contractual arrangements within the cartel.

These considerations of mining title, fiscality, labour management, and market regulation in the context of South African experience have a wider significance for other 'new states' faced with problems of internal organization and protean corporations. A beginning has been made in the history of diamond mining in West Africa; and the topic could usefully be explored for Central Africa, British Guiana, Brazil, and Australia to establish a comparative framework for assessing the social and economic results of the exploitation of a major mineral in a variety of geological and political conditions.

---

[10] David Yudelman, *The Emergence of Modern South Africa: State, Capital, and the Incorporation of Organised Labor on the South African Gold Fields, 1902–1939* (Westport, Conn., and London, 1983).

PART I
Ownership and Governance
1867–1889

◆

1

Diggers' Democracy

◆

IN the long history of mineral exploration, the nineteenth-century discoveries of gold and diamonds have been held to mark a 'new type' of rush to be rich. The concessions of kings and colonial states to proprietors were temporarily set aside by 'an initial bias in favour of individualistic, small-scale exploitation' in mining claims.[1] The rushes in the American west, British Columbia, Australia, New Zealand, South Africa, Alaska, and the Yukon marked one of the great 'adventures of the common man', before the techniques of surface mining gave way to highly capitalized corporations using the machinery of the Industrial Revolution.

Both modes of exploitation posed legal and administrative problems for the state which a thoughtful mining commission, at the end of Kimberley's first great diamond rush, divided into those arising from proprietorship of the ground containing the precious stones; and, secondly, those generated by the 'interior economy' of the mines.[2] Laws and regulations by themselves could not settle the ownership of titles to surface land and minerals, or the operations of the miner without reference to the institutions of state and local government.

Who ran these institutions was of critical importance to the thousands of adventurers, as it was to their corporate successors. The struggle to link mining interest groups with the law-makers was a common theme in the nineteenth century. The politics of mineral possession have been inseparable from the techniques of winning and marketing ores and precious stones. In the absence of any public authority or private owner, the Californian diggers set up a local government of their own in the mining camps, 1848–9. Where the colonial state asserted legal and administrative authority over mineral discoveries on Crown lands, as on the Australian and New Zealand diggings, the transition from the rules and rough justice of committees to rule by commissioners and the courts was swift, but not undisputed.

---

[1] W. P. Morrell, *The Gold Rushes* (London, 1968), 412–13; Robert Peele, *Mining Engineers' Handbook* (New York, 1918), 1468–9.

[2] CPP, G. 86-'82, 'Diamond Mining Commission, Draft Report', 90A.

For an undercurrent of resistance to government 'interference' remained part of the heritage of the digger, frequently romanticized as a defence of miners' special 'rights', and just as frequently exercised at the expense of the rights of others. In California the sturdy democratic tradition of the 'native born' cared little for the land claims of the Mexican government or the rights of Latins or Indians, except as labour. Chinese in the Australian diggings fared no better. Coloured miners were tolerated in Cape Colony, but not in the Free State or the Transvaal. The right of the state to tax individuals or claims was grudgingly admitted and frequently evaded. Everywhere on the miners' frontier, where settled government was weak, the state's exactions were contested.

Yet the need for legal title and the arbitration of disputes in the internal economy of the diggings meant that some form of local government prevailed, popular or unpopular. The diggers' committees of California which elected their own leaders won the legal backing of the United States courts; and they established a precedent followed by hundreds of diggers in Bendigo, Ballarat, Kimberley, and the Rand. Local self-government, representation in the centres of state authority, and group exclusiveness to such rights in terms of 'nationality' or European and American ethnic origins became part of the code of American, Australian, and British miners abroad.

Such exclusiveness and attitudes to authority had, in a real sense, a craft basis in the mining techniques adapted or pioneered by experienced men in alluvial gold claims and in the alluvial and deep-level diamond pipes at the outset of their exploitation. The diggers learned the hard way by luck and failure, by co-operation and working claims on shares, and by the employment of other diggers. Thousands of amateurs from all walks of life emulated their example. For the professionals who survived the early diggings and moved on, as the companies moved in, the shared experience of the self-made was not so different from a craft union.

In the early stages of commercial and mining immigration into the Cape and the Free State, this combination of skilled entrepreneurship and willingness to challenge weak or incompetent government completely altered the demographic and political balance between Boer, Briton, and African in the marchlands of the diggings on the Vaal river. There were signs that the Australian and Natal diggers who prospected on the Tati for gold in the late 1860s might spark off similar local crises for the Transvaal in Matabele territory. But the gold petered out, while diamonds did not.

Inroads by adventurers were not welcomed by the weak republics, but immigrants were not excluded, if they were white. A perceptive British officer noted that such groups of miners and traders were not loudly patriotic, however much they cultivated a display of technical expertise and emphasized the values of grass-roots democracy:

The persons who emigrate to the Free State, although many of them may be of English extraction, are nevertheless, generally speaking, but faintly impressed with the advantages arising from British citizenship. They fall easily into that method of belief so acceptable to the middle-class Anglo-Saxon, viz., a belief in universal equality, so long as that aspiration has reference only to an order of beings higher in the social scale; and of repressive superiority when the sentiment is connected with a lower or differently coloured race.[3]

CONTROL OF THE CLAIMS

The alluvial diamond diggers were from the same mould. Reports of the first rough stones picked up between the Orange and the Vaal rivers from 1867 circulated quickly throughout the region; and the sale of the 'Star of Africa'—a diamond of 83 carats—for £11,200 to Hopetown merchants in March 1869 dispelled all doubts and brought in a wave of British, Dutch, and American diggers, dealers, and property speculators. The success of the first systematic prospection by a party of Californians, Australians, and a Brazilian miner at Klipdrift on the north bank of the Vaal early in 1870 encouraged still more adventurers to invest time and savings while the strike lasted. Within the year still richer alluvial deposits were uncovered at Hebron and Pniel on the property of the Lutheran mission station. By the end of 1870, there were upwards of 5,000 diggers on the Vaal and 80 miles of tents and shanties along the banks. They had their own methods of governing the claims: 'The old diggers from the alluvial gold fields of California and Australia in the first party . . . brought with them certain rude ideas and recollections of diggers' law prevailing in the earlier days of gold-seeking in America and Australia, and many of these practices were readily adopted by the community in the Vaal.'[4]

At Klipdrift they elected a 'Mutual Protection Committee' of five who framed rules to prevent theft and illegal diamond trading, and to allow occupation of unworked claims. At Pniel, a diggers' committee conceded the right of the mission to extract a licence of 10s. per claim, which they

---

[3] COCP, *African* 83A, pt. II, Natal, Major W. F. Butler, 24 Aug. 1875.

[4] CPP. G. 86-'82, 91A. For descriptions of the early diggings see Roberts, *Kimberley*, 10–12; Worger, *South Africa's City of Diamonds*, 10–12; Turrell, *Capital and Labour*, 32–41 for early diggers' associations; F. Boyle, *To the Cape for Diamonds: A Story of Digging Experiences in South Africa* (London, 1873), ch. 6; F. Algar, *The Diamond Fields; With Notes on the Cape Colony and Natal* (London, 1872), 43–52; R. Fenton, 'Griqualand West Blunder', COCP, *African* 96, pp. 100–4.

thought was a better system than taxing a digger irrespective of the amount of ground he dug.

Well before the annexation of Griqualand there were other examples of this admission of a private rent, rather than a state impost, as a bargain between proprietors and miners. When rich discoveries were made 20 miles south of the river on the 'dry diggings', in 1870, on the Bultfontein and Dorstfontein farms, the diggers exerted a different kind of pressure: they 'rushed' the farms by mass occupation. The proprietor of Dorstfontein, Adriaan Van Wyk, made a single charge of 7s. 6d. for the right to mine each claim 'for as long as the paper on which the receipt was written held together'; and this was changed to a monthly fee when excavation began in earnest.[5] This did not prevent Van Wyk selling his Dorstfontein farm held under a Free State grant to H. B. Webb, merchant and company promoter, who sold it promptly to the London and South African Exploration Company in April 1871. The Bultfontein farm was purchased for the Hopetown Diamond Mining Company by Leopold Lilienfeld, Louis Hond, and H. B. Webb who attempted to close it and were immediately rushed and forced to allow working of claims for the usual licence fee. At Jagersfontein farm which was inside the Free State boundary prospection fees and licences were much higher, though the diggers accepted this, so long as claims were administered largely by themselves. They could not prevent speculation in whole farms: but they could occupy them in force as public diggings. Thus they pegged and rushed Old De Beers and Colesberg Kopje (Kimberley) in May and July 1871. The owners of the 17,000 acres of Vooruitzigt on which the diggings were opened up promptly sold out to the Port Elizabeth merchants, Dunell, Ebden & Co., in October 1871 for £6,300, and new rents were imposed.

The diggers, therefore, found themselves dealing with private owners at first, not state officials. But the river diggings and the farms lay on the marchlands contested since the 1850s by Griquas, Transvaalers, and Free State burghers. Possession of farms and river properties rested on a mixture of titles issued by Griqua chiefs, the Orange River Sovereignty, and the later Free State. And for none of these titles was there a clear definition of the subsoil rights for owners, contending governments, or the diggers who occupied them by a mixture of negotiation and assault in strength.

The immediate political result of the diamond discoveries, therefore, was a contest at local and state level over property and territory, inflaming

[5] Moonyean Buys, *Archives of Public Bodies, 1874–ca 1900, Instituted for the Order and Good Government of the Four Kimberley Mines* (DBCM, 1980); Roberts, *Kimberley*, 39–40; COCP, *Cape* 61 (1875). The first directors of the LSAE were: M. J. Posno, Charles Posno, Adolph Mosenthal, Joseph Mosenthal, S. Ochs, L. Ochs, Henry B. Webb, Charles Martin.

older rivalries of the Griqua and Presidents Pretorius and Brand for the Orange–Vaal lands. When negotiations broke down in August 1870, and the Vaal diggers repudiated Brand's unwise concession to a monopoly company, the Cape government was drawn in. A similar attempt to establish Free State jurisdiction at Klipdrift was countered by Acting-Governor Hay and his colonial secretary, Richard Southey, who sent in their own magistrate and took up the cause of the Griqua chief, Waterboer, who had requested British protection. In February 1871, it was agreed to submit the territorial contest to arbitration by the Governor of Natal. The new Cape governor, Sir Henry Barkly, hinted at the use of force to keep Brand's officials out of the river diggings. By May 1871, as the Bultfontein and Vooruitzigt farms were rushed, the stakes were clearly much bigger, and Barkly was determined to annex. In any case, from a sub-imperial point of view, Barkly thought it dangerous to allow the economic advantages of diamond production which was already improving the Free State's trade and currency to change the balance of economic power between the Cape and the interior: 'Should the Free State be suffered to absorb the last portion of the Diamond-Fields, as seems but too probable, it will soon rival the Eastern or Western Province in wealth and population, and it will not be content to play a secondary part, or go on paying Customs duties at the Cape ports for all manufactured goods imported for its use, without attempting retaliation.'[6] With less conviction this policy was approved by the Cape Assembly in July 1871 and by the Colonial Office and Gladstone's government for more general reasons connected with schemes for South African confederation.

Once the results of arbitration were known in October 1871, it was clear the Transvaal's claims were of no importance, and that the Griqua's northern and western boundary encompassed the diggings and kept the Free State at bay. The decision was disputed for another 5 years, but Barkly was free to annex, and Griqualand West was proclaimed British territory, 27 October 1871. Conflict had been averted by a mixture of legal bluff, intimidation, and, eventually, by token financial compensation to the Free State, after a legal decision in 1876 called in question the whole shaky basis for British occupation.[7] Unfortunately, rejection by Cape politicians of the incorporation of Griqualand into the colony in 1872 left the administration of the mining camps to a mini-autocracy in a Crown colony government which was called on to settle the property rights of owners and the interior economy of the mines without much assistance

[6] PP, C. 508, 1872, xlii, Barkly to Kimberley, 30 Aug. 1871.
[7] Eric A. Walker, *A History of Southern Africa*, 3rd edn. (London, 1957), 334–6).

from outside. For a decade, the province was separated from the elementary departmental machinery which the Cape had constructed to deal with railways, copper, lead, and coal prospection. The division of the region's most promising mineral development from its most experienced industrial and public works officials passed without comment: the consequences were soon to be felt.

By contrast with the Cape, the Free State had sought to regulate mass occupation of claims and the traffic in property by an ordinance of 2 June 1871 which laid down a pre-emptive right to purchase and throw open diggings for a monthly licence shared between government and proprietors. The incoming British adminstration ignored this compromise, though it accepted the diggers' and the Free State's limitation of claim size and the issue of miners' certificates as a source of revenue. Furthermore, the precedents established for the internal regulation of the diggings were revised or set aside. Diggers wanted both the simple system of licence fees and the adminstration of the diggings by claimholders. Both were called into question.

Nothing illustrated better the aims and organization of the diggers in the last months before British rule than the lengthy regulations drawn up by their elected committees for the Vooruitzigt and Bultfontein mining camps which were approved by the Free State in July 1871.[8] In return for registration, survey, and the monthly licence fee of 10s., the committees limited claims to two per man and reallocated any abandoned claims. With quasi-judicial authority, they imposed fines, regulated sale of spirits and gambling houses, laid out streets, and controlled sanitation and markets. In short the diggers, with the co-operation of the Free State mining inspector, acted as an elementary mining and municipal corporation, deciding access, guaranteeing pasturage and water rights, and settling disputes. They also insisted on the exclusion of Africans from the licensing system and prohibited traffic in diamonds with African servants and labourers on pain of fines and expulsion from the diggings.

The first challenge to this elementary constitution came from the proprietors of Vooruitzigt, whose agents tried to raise claim rents in September and October 1871 on the eve of annexation. The Free State allowed some increase in fees for stands, or properties adjacent to the claims, and made the Hopetown company responsible for roads and

---

[8] COCP, *African* 96, 'Rules and Regulations', encl. in Stow to Crossman, 9 Jan. 1876. For the parentage of much of this legislation and the definition of a 'miner's right' (an annual licence for parcels of land and access to water under by-laws), and for boards of elected miners with powers over mine sites in the Victoria Act of 1865, see Colony of Victoria, *Acts, Orders in Council, Notices, and Mining Board Bye-Laws Relating to the Gold Fields* (Melbourne, 1874).

sanitation. The issue of proprietors' rights was resolved in other ways by the London and South African company at Bultfontein and Dutoitspan, but the outcome was much the same. Company proprietors and the diggers exercised joint control and shared revenues, in the absence of a local inspectorate.

Whether this harmony would have lasted long is doubtful: but the annexation of October 1871 was greeted with less enthusiasm than might have been expected among the mixed community of British, American, and colonial miners, when Sir Henry Barkly sent in his commissioners in November to read their proclamations establishing Griqualand West as a territory of the Cape and to raise the flag over the three farms.[9] Within a month, the whole community was set in a turmoil by the arbitrary abolition of the diggers' committees (which were immediately re-elected) and by riots and mob justice for suspected dealers in stolen diamonds. Setting aside the committee regulations, the commissioners also allowed claim licences for coloured miners.

This they were obliged to do, because the first proclamations which brought Griqualand under a High Court also applied some Cape laws; and a second abolition of Cape African rights to licences was disallowed by Barkly who toured the camps in person in September 1872 and promised, amidst rejoicing, a form of local government with an official executive and a partly-elected legislature, as compensation.[10] But he did not retract any of the essential legislation which brought the camps under the magistrates' courts rather than under the committees. Furthermore, their most essential function—collection of licence fees—was taken over by an inspector of claims in 1872 who also controlled the allocation of abandoned diggings and supervised the roads.

More important still, none of the first proclamations which recognized the ownership of the mining properties reserved precious stones to the Crown.[11] Officials disallowed the diggers' regulations, and, at the same time, allowed great latitude to their landlords. Two further proclamations of 17 November 1871 establishing diamond fields on the farms also omitted any reservation of minerals to the state and left it unclear how far public officials would intervene to sort out inevitable disputes between proprietors and claimholders.

[9] 'Fossor', *Twelve Months in the South African Diamond Fields* (London, 1872), 63; Roberts, *Kimberley*, 62–4.

[10] *The Statute Law of Griqualand West, comprising Government Notices, Proclamations, and Ordinances together with an Appendix containing the Regulations Promulgated and Enacted from the Date of Annexation of the Province as British Territory to the Date of its Annexation to the Cape Colony* (Cape Town, 1882), 'Laws and Usages in Force', nos. 5, 7.

[11] *The Statute Law of Griqualand West*, Proclamations no. 71 (establishing diggings on Crown land); no. 72 (respecting existing titles); CPP, G. 86-'82, Buchanan, 59A–66A.

Thus, when Richard Southey took over the government of the new province as administrator (later lieutenant-governor), he inherited a truculent mining community numbering perhaps 35,000 whites and blacks to be serviced from a revenue of little more than £60,000 raised from claim licences and other fees on trade and property. He was not helped by the character and inexperience of his subordinates, particularly J. B. Currey, or by Barkly's refusal to draw on his knowledge of the Colony of Victoria and provide a department specializing in mine administration. Lacking such an institution, Southey fell back on the opinions of a narrowly-representative 'Mining Commission' which reported in June 1873 in favour of the formation of mining boards with rating powers meeting under the supervision of a government inspector.[12] Secondly (and more dangerously) he called in question the right of private landowners to a share of minerals worked on their property and, therefore, to their licences levied on diggers.

The effects of Southey's policy were felt first by the Pniel Lutheran mission which was deprived of its share of licence moneys; and this was followed by similar confiscation of the fees taken by the owners of Vooruitzigt and Dutoitspan by two ordinances of 1874 which reserved minerals on the estates to the Crown and fixed all stand rents. Both of these measures were disallowed by the Colonial Office on appeals to London from the companies. But an important proclamation defining the mining areas around the Kimberley, De Beers, Bultfontein, and Dutoitspan mines was not rescinded and became the territorial basis for legislation establishing the mining boards and the general internal working of the mines. A further proclamation of 1874 laid down the principle that these 'areas' rather than the diggings could be used for municipal purposes by the inspector of claims, the government, and the boards. In practice, however, the proprietors of the farms were able to win back control of the mine surrounds through the courts; and 'the whole territory, as it were, was forced into Chancery' until it was established in 1874 that precious stones were not reserved to the Crown on the private estates and that proprietors retained all their surface rights in the mine areas.[13] It had, at least, been demonstrated, as a result of Southey's blundering,

---

[12] CPP, G. 86-'82, 97A; COCP, *African* 96, encl. 10 for the views of George J. Lee, who had been a member of the commission. The first *Blue Book* of 1873 estimated the population at 15,000 whites and 20,000 blacks: CO, 461 (Miscellanea). For another view of the diggers, Phillida Brooke Simons (ed.), *John Blades Currey 1850 to 1900* (Johannesburg, 1987), 152–3.

[13] CPP, G. 86-'82, 95A. The case of *Ebden* vs. *Hently* in 1874 confirmed that precious stones were not reserved to the Crown on Vooruitzigt estate, and the case of *Ebden* vs. *Ling* established proprietors' surface rights.

that the pipe mines required a significant territorial space for operations, though no survey was carried out in the 1870s to assess accurately what was claimed in law.

Finally, a further ordinance—no. 10 of 1874—registered miners by a certificate, for a fee, and retained the principle of limiting claims to ten per claimholder. The duties of inspectors were closely defined, but no officials appointed were capable of undertaking the skilled supervision required. The first two mining boards, of nine claimholders each for Kimberley and De Beers, were elected in June 1874. But these bodies were required to hand over rates collected from claimholders irrespective of claim values to the provincial treasury, while they struggled with the problems of mine management in a chaotic physical environment. By 1874 the unresolved conflict between proprietors and diggers over rents was exacerbated by pressures on the internal organization of the mines in ways which revealed the inadequacy of the new government.

PRODUCTION AND MARKETING

For, like its counterparts, wherever mineral discoveries exploded into rapid social and economic transformation of existing structures, the government of Griqualand West was asked to administer the most rapidly growing enclave South Africa had yet known: an expanding population created in the space of a few years, hierarchies of immigrants, and totally new markets for imports and exports linked with the sale of diamonds. These related changes have been seen as a 'revolution' or a 'watershed' in South African history.[14]

The earliest population at the diggings was made up of transient groups of black and white fortune-hunters, traders, and labourers living in a sea of tents and galvanized-iron shacks around the four main excavation sites. Within a year the most striking developments were the vast diamond pits and the services required to keep the industry going. The camps gave way to large squares with markets, stores, eating-houses—'a circus, photographic saloons, inns and surgeries . . . mixed up with the little square tents where diamond buyers sit with their scales before them trying to make the best of bargains'.[15] Churches, synagogues, and Masonic

---

[14] Walker, *A History of South Africa*, 332–40; Kevin Shillington, 'The Impact of the Diamond Discoveries on the Kimberley Hinterland: Class Formation, Colonialism and Resistance among the Tlhaping of Griqualand West in the 1870s', in Shula Marks and Richard Rathbone (eds.), *Industrialisation and Social Change in South Africa: Class Formation, Culture and Consciousness, 1870–1930* (London, 1982), 99.

[15] RH, SPG, Orange Free State Mission, *Quarterly Papers*, 18 (1872), 9.

lodges soon appeared, together with the courts and offices, banks, and mission schools that followed the diggers from the Vaal to the veld. But the principal feature of this unusual concentration of industrial and commercial activity within an area of 3 or 4 square miles on a plateau of low rainfall and sparse vegetation was its isolation from the main centres of marketing and manufacturing. Communications by bullock-wagons and passenger carts were long and costly to Bultfontein, Colesberg, Natal, and the ports at the coast. Credit was limited by recession in the late 1860s; and the expanding networks of produce and labour supplies for the diamond fields were examples of long-distance exchanges, not integrated regional economies. Wars, drought, and rinderpest in the interior, and competition from Natal and the Cape for produce and labour services left the mines a centre for promising ventures, rather than a proven site for serious investment. Seen against the Cape economy of the 1860s, the diamond discoveries looked like dramatic salvation and were hailed as such by contemporaries: but prior to the formation of joint-stock companies in the early 1880s, 'Diamondville' was a valuable but uncertain magnet for enterprise and a vulnerable producer of a single marketable good in a colonial trade still dominated by wool, wheat, wine, hides, copper, and ostrich feathers.

It was also the scene of confused and inefficient methods of excavation. For the majority who tried their luck at the river camps and the inland quarries in the early 1870s, diamonds were not an industrial process, but a 'huge lottery'.[16] Far from bringing a 'revolution' to the economy in their ox-waggons, the diggers who dominated production till the mid-1870s used the simplest hand tools and techniques common to every mining camp in California, New South Wales, Victoria, and Otago. Descriptions of the cradles for washing diamondiferous ground and the dry separation methods show clear descent from technologies of the Sacramento, Ballarat, and Gabriel's Gully. The crowded activity of the camps gave an appearance of great progress: but the amount of coin and notes in circulation in 1873 was calculated at only £300,000. The production of diamonds took a decade to make an impact on the Cape economy in terms of export revenues; and diamonds did not overtake wool in export values till 1880.[17]

---

[16] Algar, 53.

[17] D. Hobart Houghton and Jenifer Dagut (eds.), *Source Material on the South African Economy*, vol. 1, 1860–1899 (Cape Town, 1972), 326; for diamond mining techniques see Charles A. Payton, *The Diamond Diggings of South Africa: A Personal and Practical Account* (London, 1872), 105; Boyle, ch. 9, and cf. C. M. H. Clark (ed.). *Select Documents in Australian History 1851–1900* (Sydney, 1955), sect. 1, pp. 26–7; CO, 461 (Miscellanea).

But for the peoples of the interior there were more immediate economic consequences for their pastoral and grain economies and for their marketable labour surplus. Produce and fuel from neighbouring societies became early staples of a circulatory trading system which attracted workers furnished by the Pedi, Sotho, Zulu, Nzundza Ndebele, Tsonga ('Shangaan'), and colonial societies in the Cape. Migration was widespread and accelerated commercial exchanges already functioning through a regional network. This network (it has been argued) may have been skewed towards Griqualand West, at the expense of Natal and the eastern Cape; or it may simply have been capable of distributing a greater volume of goods and services from increased domestic agricultural production, as diamonds, arms, manufactures, and labour found new outlets and raised intra-regional price and wage competition.[18] Studies of this emerging labour market have tended to emphasize the constraints imposed on the labour force. But the first mining community was more mindful of the costs arising from all kinds of inputs in industrial operations; and there is quite good evidence that, by 1875, the labour market was viewed as inseparable from the provision of 'mealies, Kaffir corn or maize' which were as much a part of local cost structures as were the periodic and seasonal absence of labourers returning to agriculture. The fact, for example, that Basutoland supplied both food and manpower was appreciated as a bonus in lowering the costs arising from the 'labour problem'.[19]

That 'problem', however, from the late 1860s lay not so much in the availability of African labour, but in its price and duration at the workplace in an industry which was harshly and inefficiently managed, dangerous to diggers and their employees, and which required a greater proportion of intermediate skills as the mines deepened. Unlike their counterparts in California and Australia, the diamond diggers also imported the Cape Masters and Servants regulations in 1872, and regarded the cost of African wages and supplies as an essential part of their investment, if they were to compete in production. Mining labourers were paid about £26 a year with food, or a scale of 1s. 6d. to 3s. 6d. per day, depending on tasks. Overseers received £120 a year and a percentage of sales. Tradesmen in

---

[18] Payton, ch. 4; Shillington, 106–7; Norman A. Etherington, 'Labour Supply and the Genesis of the South African Confederation in the 1870s', *Journal of African History*, 20/2 (1979), 235–53; Algar, 53–6; 'Fossor', 60; Siebörger; R. Turrell, 'Kimberley: Labour and Compounds, 1871–1888', in Shula Marks and Richard Rathbone (eds.), *Industrialisation and Social Change in South Africa*, 48–9; Turrell, *Capital and Labour*, 19–31; Worger, *South Africa's City of Diamonds*, ch. 2.

[19] COCP, *African* 96, Manning, 18 Dec. 1875; see too Colin Murray, *Families Divided: The Impact of Migrant Labour in Lesotho* (Cambridge, 1981), 11–12.

TABLE 1.1. *Kimberley labour registration, mine workers, and compounds, 1878–1901*

Years	Registration of contracts			Mine workers (daily averages)			Compounds[a]	
	'Old and new hands'	'New hands'	'Protectn. Passes'	Whites	Blacks	Total		
1878	63,000 (estimate)	34,095[b]						
1879	53,750[c]	22,707[d]						
1880	86,959	31,708						
1881	79,924	26,211		3,100	17,000	20,100		
1882	104,696	30,889		1,692	11,920	13,612		
1883	74,501	3,762		1,104	8,360	9,500		
1884	65,032	5,471		1,210	9,000	10,210		
1885	66,817[e]	'Return	3,427	1,900	11,300	13,200		
1886	78,407	Passes'	n/a	1,510	10,960	12,470		
1887	90,146	21,128	3,877	1,920	11,300	12,220		
1888	85,180	23,100	2,996	1,680	9,600	11,280		
1889	71,050	21,115	4,019	1,270	6,830	8,100	(13)	6,284
1890	53,624	9,824	4,473	1,409	5,840	7,249	(10)	5,231
1891	50,914	9,942	5,211	1,467	5,874	7,341	(13)	8,662
1892	44,037	9,593	6,509	1,731	7,383	9,114	(11)	n/a
1893	48,642	9,058	4,715	1,763	7,790	9,553	(9)	n/a
1894	41,242	7,626	4,891	1,581	5,915	7,496	(10)	5,826
1895	48,374	8,023	4,758	1,698	7,808	9,508	(11)	5,572
1896	47,952	7,720	5,453	1,958	7,772	9,730	(14)	6,629
1897	54,125	n/a	n/a	1,897	8,250	10,417	(18)	8,000[f]
1898	57,441	10,890	5,451	1,990	10,293	12,283	(17)	10,000
1899	52,191	n/a	n/a	1,928	10,751	12,679	(17)	n/a
1900	38,075	11,090	2,263	1,857	7,365	9,222	(18)	10,000
1901	67,988	n/a	n/a	2,085	9,145	11,230	(18)	10,000

[a] Inspector of mines reports for the end of the calendar year (including convict labour). Company compounds shown in parenthesis.
[b] Includes Dutoitspan and Bultfontein registrations.   [c] For 9 months.   [d] For 11 months.
[e] Kimberley labour registrations at the end of the calendar year including some non-mining labour.
[f] Inspector of mines estimates. There was no estimate during the Anglo-Boer war.

Sources: R. F. Siebörger, 'The Recruitment and Origins of African Labour for the Kimberley Diamond Mines 1871–1888', MA thesis (Rhodes University, 1975); *Griqualand West Government Gazette 1877–80*; R. Turrell, 'Kimberley: labour and compounds, 1871–1888' in Shula Marks and Richard Rathbone (eds.), *Industrialisation and Social Change in South Africa*; W. Worger, 'Workers as Criminals: The Rule of Law in Early Kimberley, 1870–1885' in Frederick Cooper (ed.). *Struggle for the City: Migrant Labour, Capital, and the State in Urban Africa* (Beverly Hills, California, 1988); CPP, Inspector of Mines, reports, (1879–1902); Native Affairs *Blue Books*; CPP, Police Commissioner's Reports, (1880–1902). Early registration statistics are incomplete before 1884 and, at best, crude indications of orders of magnitude for employment of black labour in the Kimberley area. Cf. Turrell, *Capital and Labour*, esp. 54, 167, 228. From 1884, nomenclature changes and they are inadequate for estimates of labour turnover. The return passes issued to departing labourers are a rough indication of discharges after the completion of the compounds; and there was a rising number of protection passes issued to Africans engaged in commerce and trades. For later

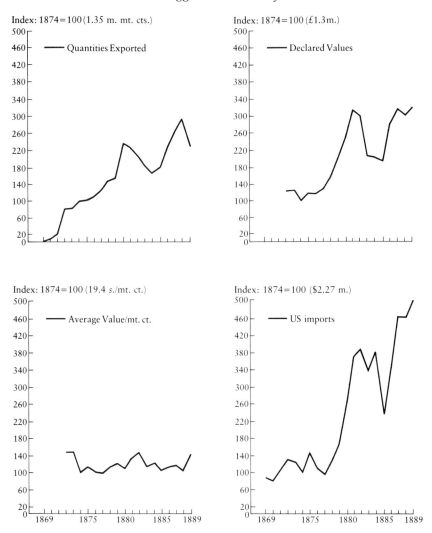

FIG. 1. Diamond exports from Griqualand West and US imports of precious stones, 1869–1889.

mine labour statistics, see Table 4.1. Registration of contracts continued at: 1902 (67,969); 1903 (66,406); 1904 (34,379); 1905 (80,130); 1906 (94,885); 1907 (94,619); 1908 (47,808). From 1902 municipal locations were allowed to house dependants of mine labourers and others (see CPP, G. 29–1903); and this addition to the resident non-mining African population is confirmed in the valuable Cape of Good Hope, *Census 1904* which gives a total black labour force of 26,582 including 7,929 domestics and 4,389 in industrial work other than mines and diggings, and 1,278 in commercial trades.

the early 1870s could ask and receive £1 to £1. 10s. per day. The gap between hand labour and semi-skilled work was established early and tended to grow wider.

Africans were regarded with a mixture of condescension and amused contempt. But diggers could not dispense with their services in small-scale operations, without diverting their own labour time away from the key operations of the sorting tables, pumping, survey, organizing supplies, and dealing with other claimholders. Mining was also an industry which easily adopted an informal colour bar, breached from time to time by the close pattern of claim ownership, debris working, and the widespread use of white paid labour and tributors 'on shares'.[20] But industrial operations quickly engendered specialists—mechanics, drivers, blasters, and labour overseers— who brought their labour with them as part of the contract arrangements which became a feature of expanded hauling and separation methods in the mid-1870s. Low contract rates also required cheap manpower at unit cost.

The industry, therefore, tended to remain labour-intensive, despite incipient mechanization and share-working by white miners. From the partial records we have of labour registration, the courts, and descriptions of the mining sites, the most striking feature of the market for men was the very high annual turnover rate.[21] For all categories of wage labour at Kimberley in which mining was predominant, totals of old and new recruits probably increased from some 50,000 to 80,000 a year throughout the 1870s with sharp falls in 1874 and 1876, because of attempts by employers to reduce wages. Recruitment of 'new hands' to keep up this flow remained on a steadily rising trend till 1880, indicating a replacement rate of some 30 per cent of the work force every year. Not all these recruits were for mining; and by 1875 the miners estimated no more than a daily average of 8,500 or 9,000 workers at the pits, subject to considerable seasonal fluctuations.

Desertion and irregular recruitment added to the cost of training a labour force. Physical violence, frequent revisions of the labour regulations making passes and penal sanctions mandatory, and appeals for more efficient police action were regular features of the diggers' programme for 'reform' of the system. A missionary sympathetic to employers reported

---

[20] Boyle, 321; Payton, ch. 4; CO 461. Even as domestics in this period, Zulus, Indians and coloureds earned up to £40 to £72 annually. Share-workers subcontracted with claimowners for a variable percentage of profits.

[21] Siebörger, apps; William Worger, 'Workers as Criminals: The Rule of Law in Early Kimberley, 1870–1885', in Frederick Cooper (ed.), *Struggle for the City: Migrant Labour, Capital, and the State in Urban Africa* (Beverly Hills, Calif., 1983), 51–90; Worger, *South Africa's City of Diamonds*, 87; Turrell, 'Kimberley'. Not all years in the official statistics were complete in their monthly totals before 1878.

in 1872 that 'a Kaffre gets on the Fields as much food as he can eat, 10*s*. a week and about 9 hours work per diem'.[22] Labour was certainly no cheaper 3 years later, when daily rates for Africans rose to 30*s*. a week, and miners complained they were spending just over £500,000 annually on their workforce for a turnover of £1.5 million in diamonds produced. They urged a general wage reduction to the levels paid to Cape railway workers, or even less, at the old rates of 10*s*. per week. Labour depots and the use of convicts, who had already been employed for road construction and, indeed, for some private contract work in the mines, were seen as additional savings at a time of decreasing profit margins.[23]

Those decreased margins can be traced to more general price rises in the early 1870s, seen by some as a major factor in the rising opposition to Southey's government.[24] The evidence is inconclusive without a retail price index, but crude comparisons with foodstuffs in Natal and the Cape indicate that the basic essentials—sorghum, mealies, and maize—were at least five times dearer than at the coastal markets. Comparisons with the Free State suggest that other supplies such as boer meal and oxen for slaughter were still plentiful and cheap. The official *Blue Book* for 1873 attributed the 'exorbitant price' to 'a series of small monopolies'. More importantly, severe cost inflation stemmed from imported foodstuffs and manufactures. The annual bill for wholesale goods in Kimberley by 1875 amounted to £440,114 and included a Cape customs duty of 12 per cent and transport costs of 25 per cent. A portion of goods—some £50,000—was destined for 'Kaffir trade' and probably much of the imports of arms and ammunition valued at £47,000. But the rest was hardware, machinery, tools, furnishings, software, and spirits, abundantly advertised in local newspapers which reflected the changing pattern of consumption in the embryonic townships that were to become Kimberley and Beaconsfield on the mine surrounds. For the claimholders engaged in producing the wealth to support their own investment and much of the service sector, the critical question was whether diamonds paid well enough to leave sufficient surplus for reconstruction within the mines' interior economy, while they were still dogged by problems of rents and the high cost of labour and stores.

[22] RH, SPG, Orange Free State Mission, *Quarterly Papers*, 20 (1874), 25.

[23] Worger, 'Workers as Criminals', 55; *The Diamond Field*, 20 Jan. 1875. Convicts were also used at Dutoitspan by the surveyor Yonge.

[24] Roberts, *Kimberley*, 117; and for local prices see *The Diamond Field*, 20 Jan. 1875; *The Diamond News*, 23 Mar. 1875; Shillington, 104–6. A load of wood fuel rose from £2 to over £10, 1872–5; and for details of goods imported to the diamond fields, COCP, *African*, 96, encl. 15.

The answer to that question lay outside South Africa. In the absence of specialized dealers, the first years of the diamond strike were marked by a concentration of sales of the finest classes of rough diamonds at Cape auctions, while lesser varieties changed hands through brokers and buyers at the mines for whatever the diggers would take. From one account of Cape and London auctions, it would seem that bi-weekly sales at Cape Town of the larger stones fetched between £2 and £5 per carat, plus a margin of £1 or £2 overseas.[25] As the industry expanded into the 'dry diggings', however, poorer grades had to be marketed along with finer stones from the river claims; and the need to find a buyer for all classes and maximize returns on production led, in turn, to selling 'in series'. This change may have been assisted by the imposition of a duty on sales by auction, which seem to have ended at Cape Town by 1873. One anonymous writer with experience of diamond valuation pin-pointed a fall in local prices from the opening of the Kimberley mine in 1871 and connected this with changes in buying techniques. The convention of squaring the weight of a stone and finding its value by applying a notional carat price derived from auctions, gave way to a 'running carat system' without any 'squaring', in which a notional average price from overseas sales was applied to the total weight of a mixed parcel of stones. Thereafter, a mixture of diamonds was traded in all the camps—'rough and smooth, chipped and sound, big and little were all popped into the scale together and purchased at so much a carat, and to this undignified process had the river stones also to submit'.[26]

The men who handled the diamonds during this transition period have attracted more romantic description than serious accounts of how they worked. The 'kopje-walloper' with long boots, a courier bag of cash, and a good horse left his legend.[27] But after an increase in licence fees for brokers and dealers to £25 and £50 a year, and restriction of legitimate sales to recognized offices, many of the more flamboyant characters gave way to agents acting for colonial mercantile companies and London diamond wholesalers. There were 185 dealers and 81 brokers registered at Kimberley in 1875; and while occasional large finds still made news, the more usual transaction through these buyers was a pillbox or a bag of unsorted stones under one carat in weight. Some storekeepers and

[25] Payton, 24–6, 116–21, 124–6; COCP, *African 89*, (1876), 38; *The Diamond Field*, 20 Jan. 1875. Local trades were administered under Ordinance 21 of 1874.

[26] 'Fossor', 57; and for 19th-c. methods of evaluation see H. Emmanuel, *Diamonds and Precious Stones* (London, 1865).

[27] Gustav Saron and Louis Hotz, *The Jews in South Africa: A History* (Cape Town, 1955), ch. 6.

canteen owners were still permitted to purchase and sell for a licence fee, though gambling houses were excluded from the market. On the fringes of the trade, the poorer brokers scoured the legal and illegal outlets, backed by their well-funded principals, for a small commission, in order to set up on their own account.

Without knowledge, such independent ventures were a dangerous path into diamond dealing. As the scale of transactions increased and the quality of South African stones decreased into cheaper varieties, purchase of unassorted diamonds carried great risks for the inexperienced 'walloper' and a profit for the man who could recognize potential for cutting and the likely demand for different varieties and colours. The general result of the trend towards greater volume is, however, clear enough in the moderate fall in the average carat price from the late 1860s, as the local market absorbed larger quantities of smaller stones and as the London and European wholesaling and cutting industry reorganized to deal with the 'Cape flood'.[28]

The price fall is imperfectly measured in the early declarations of diamonds passing through the Kimberley Post Office and the Cape Customs (see Fig. 1), from about £2 or £3 per carat in the late 1860s to about 30s. by 1872. This is supported by more general descriptions of the trade at the European end, where cutting had already expanded to deal with Brazilian imports in the 1840s and encountered a shortage and high prices, before Cape diamonds reduced the price of brilliants by about 150 per cent by 1873. The imports which crowded out the highly valued, small, white Brazilian stones included, it is true, a greater number of larger stones. But many of these were 'yellow' diamonds, and there was a growing unwillingness in London to pass these on to Amsterdam and Antwerp from 1871. From this date, yellow diamonds 'which before 1870 were worth some thousands apiece are now worth only as many hundreds, and smaller yellow diamonds, formerly sold at 100s. per carat, now only fetch about 40s.'[29] Although this observation from Ochs Bros. to Lord Rothschild applies to a longer time-scale, there was relatively little change in the price index for Cape diamonds after 1872, but striking changes in volume. The biggest change in price had come about well before the date of the Ochs' commentary and had reduced the average value of imported stones by about 50 per cent between the 1860s and the early 1870s, though the cutting price of small brilliants 'which forms a portion

---

[28] Lenzen, 141–3; H. Heertje, *De Diamantbewergers van Amsterdam* (Amsterdam, 1936); Turrell, *Capital and Labour*, 77–8.

[29] Bod., Harcourt MS 120, Ochs to Rothschild, 9 Jan. 1893.

ILL. 1. Diamond buyers and offices, Kimberley, early 1870s

of their value [was not] greatly diminished'. From the mid-1870s, moreover, these smaller varieties began to sell in great quantities to an expanding retail market, 'owing to the growing prosperity of the United States which absorbs the greater portion of the supply of white diamonds'. India also took a very large quantity, possibly the bulk of yellow diamonds coming from the Cape at this early period.

It took roughly a decade for this international market to become well-established and to cope with the classification and the finance required to handle bulk imports and to fund purchases and resales to cutters. The reorganization brought merchants to London from the Continent and from South Africa, where local houses had been prominent from the beginning in learning the art of diamond buying as well as more usual speculation in land and property which determined the proprietorship of the mines. The London Post Office directories indicate that there was a shift from bullion and jewellery to pearls and diamonds among the merchants concentrated in the Hatton Garden, Ely Place, Holborn Circus, and Holborn Viaduct area of the City during the 1860s and the 1870s.[30]

---

[30] Caroline M. Barron, *The Parish of St. Andrew Holborn* (London, 1979); W. A. Aronheim, 'The Development of Diamond Industry and Trade in Peace and War', M. Social Science thesis, Research (New York, 1943), 71–4).

Similarly, the number of diamond cutters and setters doubled between 1865 and 1890, though this does not compare with the much larger investment and increase in wages in factories in Antwerp, Amsterdam, and Paris. It has been argued that already, in the 1860s, merchant importers of roughs were anxious about the increased supply and feared a depression in the early 1870s, and that considerable funds were required 'to carry the stocks'.[31] There were, however, only three merchant houses listed as specialists in this import in 1875 out of the thirty-two diamond merchants listed for the Hatton Garden area; and it is perhaps anachronistic to regard the London diamond market as internally stable and well-organized at that date. The rapid increase in merchants and brokers suggests, rather, they were able to deal with South African production (which did not all go to London) by making their purchases at the Kimberley end and leaving the local sellers to hold unsold varieties in the banks.

They were enabled to do this without bulk sales and special pooling arrangements in London, by using the expertise of some South African mercantile firms and by establishing their own agents to negotiate directly at Kimberley. Conversely, a few of the South African firms established themselves as importers in London in the 1870s, notably A. Mosenthal, Von Ronn, William Dunn, Hamilton, Ross & Co., Savage & Hill, J. Searight. The London house of the Port Elizabeth firm of Blaine & Co. set up as Blaine, Macdonald and Co. in 1876 to finance diamond buying.[32] Harry Mosenthal's London branch opened as Joseph Mosenthal & Co., run by the three sons of Adolph Mosenthal. Anton Dunkelsbuhler who had gone out as agent for Mosenthal in 1872 founded his own firm in London in 1875 and specialized in diamonds. The Hopetown firm of Lilienfeld Bros., prominent in the earliest land syndicates, sent Martin Lilienfeld to found a second import agency at Hatton Garden in 1875. The soldier and businessman Julius Wernher moved the other way as a buyer for the Paris and London financier and diamond merchant Jules Porges, in 1870, along with David Harris and a score of lesser men who stayed to invest in claims and company shares. V. A. and E. M. Litkie of Hatton Garden also moved to the diamond fields and were among the first buyers to advertise in the local press.

---

[31] Theodore Gregory, 'The History of the Diamond Syndicate' (MS, DBCA, 1964), 21; Turrell, *Capital and Labour*, 74–6. I can find no support for a decline in rate of profit among merchants at this period.

[32] Port Elizabeth Chamber of Commerce, *Reports* (1874–7); COCP, *Cape* 74, Cotton to CO, 16 June 1874 (for commercial interests in the diamond fields).

As yet, the diamond business and mining attracted remarkably little investment from the London or Continental capital markets. *The Mining Magazine*, which deplored the heavy subscription of 'Home' capital into the 'railway mania' of the mid-century, took a very poor view of the diamond fields as an object of speculation and gave a bad press to the enthusiastic literature on the diggings.[33] Ventures like the London and South African Exploration Company were rare and directed essentially at improved land values and rents. This was also true of promotions from a better-informed centre of colonial trade and banking at Port Elizabeth, where the forty-four companies of the chamber of commerce were represented in the diamond fields by L. Dreyfus & Co., Dunnell, Ebden & Co., Blaine & Co., Lilienfeld, and Mosenthal. The chamber deplored the lack of accurate statistics on diamond exports and pressed for annexation to the Cape in order to secure better legal and administrative services for the 'surplus' money thought to be seeking a safe investment.

South Africa's twenty-three banks were not so eager, however, under their articles of association to provide long-term funding for diamond production. The seven leaders, headed by the Standard Bank, were ready enough to branch into Griqualand West in the early 1870s, acting as insurance agencies, making short-term loans and forwarding parcels of diamonds to London. Such agency work was equally involved with the trading sector of the diamond fields and with limited investment in land, stores, and transport, rather than mining claims which were not well secured by survey and title. For the moment, the expansion of trade stimulated by diamonds was a readier source of interest, as indicated by the steep rise in discounted bills 1872–5, required for the 'high pressure speed' of business with the new centre of commerce in the interior.[34]

So, while the merchants prospered, there was a shortage of working capital for the mines. It was commonplace for claimholders like C. D. Rudd, Paddon Bros., Baring-Gould, Lewis & Marks, and Isaac Sonnenberg to double their mining activities with more certain returns from business in hardware, foodstuffs, pumping and hauling contracts, and property deals. It was the business community, not the miners, who felt the injustice of high rents on stands sufficiently to fund the administration's purchase of Vooruitzigt from its proprietors in 1875.

[33] *The Mining Magazine and Review* (1872), 372; see *The Economist*, 'Commercial History and Review', 10 Mar. 1877 for comment on the increase in 'accumulated and realised capital' seeking an outlet, but not finding it in South Africa yet.

[34] Port Elizabeth Chamber of Commerce, *Reports* (1875), 8, 16, 26. Discounted bills rose to over £1 million at the height of the trade boom, 1874–5. For the reluctance of the banks to invest see J. A. Henry, *The First Hundred Years of the Standard Bank* (London, 1963), 65; S. D. Chapman, 'Rhodes and the City of London: Another View of Imperialism', *Historical Journal*, 28/3 (1985), 662.

TECHNOLOGY AND GOVERNMENT

The main characteristic of the diggings at this period was technological crisis, rather than confidence for investment. When Barkly visited the mines in 1872, they were open quarries worked by some 2,500 miners with 10,000 labourers. Already De Beers was riddled with pits from 50 to 100 feet in depth. Kimberley accounted for about half the claimholders, while there was little development of Dutoitspan and Bultfontein. Alluvial techniques adapted from experience elsewhere allowed the greatest possible number of surface claims and fractions of claims and produced the maximum of confusion and waste, as in the Kimberley mine where

for a space of about half-a-mile men are ascending and descending the deep chasms which have been excavated, passing on foot or driving carts along the narrow roads between the claims. There are twelve of these roads, each about one hundred and fifty yards long by twenty feet wide. On either side of each road are deep gullies, in many places one hundred feet deep, and some sixty feet wide. In these gullies the mining is carried on. The scene is perfectly dazzling. It looks and is a monster danger. Weak ladders, the very picture of insecurity, are used for ascent and descent, sometimes only a rope and foot-holes in the sides of the gullies. The ground dug out from the bottoms of the gullies is conveyed to the top in galvanized-iron buckets passed along ropes or stout wires worked with pullies . . . accidents are frequent. Carts and mules have fallen from the roads into the pits. But the worst danger to be apprehended is a landslip from one of the roads.[35]

This pattern dominated the development of Kimberley and De Beers as the deepest mines, where the softer and more friable surface ground yielded diamonds easily and was worked most rapidly by diggers who expected to encounter bed-rock. Only gradually did it become clear that they were excavating a pipe whose oval perimeter of a dozen acres held riches that were novel, untested, and concentrated to great depths. The configuration of Dutoitspan and Bultfontein was much the same, though they differed in surface area and contained intrusive masses of shales or igneous rocks ('floating reef') over diamond-bearing ground. Uncontrolled exploitation of their poorer surface levels filled many of the claims with debris, as these two quarries were quickly divided into easily flooded gullies and carried relatively limited numbers of claim workers before the late 1870s. De Beers mine was not much richer on the surface, and it was excavated

[35] RH, SPG, Orange Free State Mission, *Quarterly Papers*, 18 (1872) 8; Theodore Reunert, 'Diamond Mining at the Cape', in J. Noble (ed.), *Official Handbook, History, Productions, and Resources of the Cape of Good Hope* (Cape Town, 1886), 177–219; Reunert, *Diamonds and Gold*; PP, C. 508, 1872, Barkly to Kimberley, 29 Oct. 1872; cf. Boyle, 235.

TABLE 1.2. *Distribution of claims and claimholders by mine, 1875*

Claims and fractions per claimholder	Kimberley		De Beers		Dutoitspan		Bultfontein	
	Frequency	Claimholders	Frequency	Claimholders	Frequency	Claimholders	Frequency	Claimholders
Under one full claim:	117	256 (67%)	33	62 (43%)	0	0	2.25	5 (4%)
One/Under two:	112	80 (21%)	46	42 (29%)	43.5	43 (38%)	59	59 (45%)
Two/Under three:	60	24 (6%)	28	14 (10%)	44	22 (19%)	60	30 (24%)
Three/Under four:	30	8 (2%)	15	5 (3%)	24	8 (7%)	33	11 (9%)
Four/Under five:	18	4	24	6	52	13	44.5	11
Five/Under six:	23	4	20	4	30	6	10	2
Six/Under seven:	0	0	24	4	24	4	12	2
Seven/Under eight:	7.5	1	7	1	14	2	0	0
Eight/Under nine:	8.5	1 (3.4%)	16	2 (16%)	8	1 (35%)	16	2 (16%)
Nine/Under ten:	9	1	9	1	18	2	18	2
Ten full claims:	20	2	50	5	20	10	10	1
Over ten in two names:	0	0	0	0	24	2	0	0
TOTAL	405a	381	272	146	301.5	113	264.75	125

Sources: COCP, *African*, 96, Crossman report, 1 May 1875; F. Oats, 9 March 1876. Crossman's return from the inspector of claims is probably an underestimate. Registration for 1875 excluded abandoned claims. Oats gave higher totals in his report for early 1876: Kimberley (400); De Beers (585); Dutoitspan (1,450); Bultfontein (1,070). Larger claim holdings have been grouped together to calculate the percentage of holders.

at a slower rate than Kimberley, leaving poor ground to the west side and a very large bank of floating reef and dikes of rock around and across the central claims till the 1880s.

Kimberley mine, therefore, was the most intensively worked, and had reached 190 feet by 1875—three times the depth of De Beers and Dutoitspan. To some extent progress had been assisted by the intervention of a Free State inspector who insisted on roadways across the claims; but these had begun to collapse by 1872. Diggers turned to other techniques and constructed a system of hauling wires and ropes suspended from machinery at the rim of the mine on elevated staging, creating a vast web of aerial conveyors. Hand capstans used to haul up buckets were replaced by 'whims', or large-diameter timber wheels which shifted heavier loads. By 1875 the first steam-engines were employed in this long-distance haulage. The constant seepage of water through the porous shales required similar power technology in the form of a double-action pump which cleared some 50,000 to 60,000 gallons a day by contract with the mining board. The board too entered into contracts to clear debris and fallen shales from claims. Very boldly, it also paid to drive a vertical shaft into the north-east corner of Kimberley mine 200 yards outside the perimeter to a depth of 286 feet. But it lacked the money and the courage to drive tunnels into the mine.

Indeed, it is not certain whose claims would have benefited from this initiative which outpaced the conditions of ownership and investment inside the mine. The numbers of claims worked in each mine and their physical distribution changed fairly rapidly through the early 1870s. From the registration lists for 1875 (see Table 1.2), it can be seen that Kimberley mine contained by far the largest proportion of fractioned holdings under one full claim of 31 × 31 feet; and these crowded sites were worked by a large percentage of the total number of claimholders. To a lesser extent this was also true of the De Beers mine: most claimholders held fractions under two claims in size. At Bultfontein and Dutoitspan, by contrast, there were evidently very few small fractions held and a greater holding of larger sites, though it is also clear that fewer than half of the registered claims were actually worked.[36]

At the other end of the scale of claim ownership there were few sites of more than two claims held by single owners in the Kimberley mine. In the other mines there was a higher proportion of multiple claimholding, sometimes in two names, to get round the ten-claim limit of the mining

[36] COCP, *African 96*, Oats, encl. 12; CPP, G. 34-'83; DBCA, *Landlords of the Kimberley Diamond Fields, 1870–1889*.

ILL. 2. Rotary washing, 1874

legislation under Ordinance No. 10 of 1874. A good third of Dutoitspan claimholders held multiple claims, and Bultfontein was noted as a site for African and coloured diggers—perhaps as many as 120—though many of these were bought out after 1875.

The impression left by the claim records is one of social differentiation within the mining community, rather than a united workforce of diggers. Some were eager to expand their investment still further and fretted at the limitations imposed by the regulations and the technology of the crowded mine sites. Others—perhaps the majority by 1875—were hard pressed to make a living from digging in encumbered claims, on shares, taxed by the mining boards and by the administration and the proprietors of land surrounding the mine sites. Evidence collected at a public enquiry 1875–6 tended to reflect the views of those who spoke at the noisy public meetings, and these were mostly multiple claimholders who were agreed on the need for reforms, but divided on the measures to be taken. There was a measure of agreement that the boards, especially in the Kimberley mine, had failed to cope with drainage and reef falls and had become an instrument for improving the claims of a small coterie. There were accusations of jobbery on tenders, insufficient supervision of contractors who used board labourers for private work, and monopoly of pumping contracts for benefit of board members. The significance of the accusation made against the young Cecil Rhodes at a public meeting in January 1876 (from which he was cleared in dubious circumstances) was that he attempted to sabotage the Kimberley board's service to particular claim areas and could supply a lucrative pumping contract of his own.[37]

Because the technology of the mines could be so easily disrupted by competing entrepreneurs, some claimholders thought the boards should be only partly-elected and subject to more official control. Others, such as W. Ling and Henry Tucker, wanted complete autonomy, control of mine rates, and the replacement of officials who made no survey and whose claim records were incomplete. Far from presenting a united front to authority, the diggers had been stratified, like the pits they dug, by 5 years of success and failure. The old levellers of the diggers' committees still had a loud voice in the chorus of complaints; but the substance of their difficulties lay in their earlier success in occupying the mines in strength and digging in disunity. The paradox of the most fragmented holdings in Kimberley and De Beers, where there was most reason for concerted political action, was that less than half of the claimholders bothered to vote in board elections; and many were disenfranchised because they held less than one full claim. In these circumstances, board powers were exercised by the wealthier activists, wielding two or three votes, and work tendered out was performed in their interest.

Complaints from Bultfontein and Dutoitspan miners exposed similar technical problems. The rating levies imposed by officials, which made 'debris-covered claims pay for relieving a few claims of water', were unjust; labour and funds could be directed towards favoured diggers. Officials, for their part, found it impossible to order diggers in these quarries to clear claims or end the traditional 'right' dating from the first occupation to sort ground for diamonds on the spot and leave spoil in unworked pits. For challenging this 'right' an early diggers' committee had been burned in effigy and gave up. Again, as at Kimberley and De Beers, there was a division between those advocating more government supervision and outright purchase of the mine areas from the proprietors of the farm, and those who simply wanted a speedier system of settling disputes through a magistrate or mine warden, without recourse to expensive litigation in the civil courts.

At both camps, therefore, the evidence of the 1875 enquiry revealed that mining at deeper levels and in conditions of multiple claimholding could no longer be dealt with by appeals to 'diggers' democracy'. As an aggrieved Dutoitspan claimholder put it:

---

[37] COCP, *African* 96 for evidence taken at public meetings at Kimberley and Dutoitspan mines, Dec. 1875, Jan. 1876; for comments on Rhodes's actions see Roberts, *Kimberley*, 142.

I have always been in favour of self-government, and advocate the control of the mine by the claimholders, but the terrible experience of the last 18 months has taught me quite differently. If men who have never been trained for business; men who have been living with humble pursuits and occupations; men who never in their lives had £500—I say if such persons are suddenly placed in control of large financial matters they are apt to be recklessly extravagant with the money of other people, and to look after their own interests, to the detriment of the interests of the public. We never have a statement of expenditure and receipts from the Mining Board.[38]

But could the government of Griqualand West offer any remedy? The problems of the mining industry, on which its own finances ultimately rested, lay in the inability of the diggers to increase volume of production much more, without a radical restructuring of the conditions of ownership in the claims. The basic difficulty for Southey's administration, 1873–5, was that its sources of revenue were not sufficient to undertake any major reforms of proprietorship or mine management, without cutting itself off from the vested interests required to support, politically and financially, the cost of such an undertaking. Already subsidies from the Cape were required to help meet the legal and police services provided for the mercantile and mining community. Much had been hoped for from the survey and sale of farms in Griqualand West. But this policy fell apart, because of difficulties in determining ownership in conditions of extensive African usufruct, the failure of irrigation schemes, and general lack of confidence among white settlers. Revenue from land sales which brought in £2,000 in 1872 dwindled to nothing.[39]

Having failed in a 'Crown lands' settlement scheme, the government fell back on the market and the mines as sources of direct taxation. The diggers contributed some 26 per cent of revenue, 1872–5, totalling £315,205, from their registration and claims certificates, transfer fees, and sales of forfeited claims and tickets to sort through heaps of debris for diamonds. These fees had increased in variety rather than severity. Added to labour registration fees and the hated hospital tax of 1875, they amounted to no more than 1.3 per cent of the declared value of diamond output (some £6 million) over the same period.

Like miners' licences elsewhere, of course, they fell on the rich and insolvent alike; and there was no possibility, as on the Australian gold fields, of reducing direct taxes in favour of an export duty, without risking widespread smuggling and evasion. Direct taxes may have been the last

---

[38] COCP, *African* 96, Burkner, 5 Jan. 1876.
[39] COCP, *Cape* 61, 1875 (land claims); Shillington, 108–9; CPP, G. 63-'77, App. E; A. 64-'80; cf. Worger, *South Africa's City of Diamonds*, 28–9.

straw for many diggers who had abandoned working their claims, but still paid for registration and the right to sell out their interest. There was a notable increase in transfer and 'hypothecation' (or mortgaging) fees connected with the sale of new claims in 1875, and this may well have been evidence of a concentration in the more workable and richer ground by fewer claimholders, particularly as it is paralleled by a decline in diggers' registration licences, 1872–5. Some diggers were ready to expand their holdings; others hung on hoping that an improvement in prices would enable them to realize their stake at a profit.

By contrast, licences in the commercial sector from the retail and wholesale trades and stamp duty on business transactions increased steadily, and were the major staple of the provincial chest. This sector was also a source of profit from rents for the proprietors of the mine areas on which the growing township stood amid heaps of spoil in a jumble of stands, roads, and drains technically owned by absentee landlords, but serviced by the government.

This common factor of rising rents united many of the diggers with the tradespeople of the camps; and it was coupled with suspicions of financial irresponsibility on the part of the government and the unrepresentative legislative council, compounded by the frustrations of mining in an increasingly difficult environment. There was enough tinder to spark off the 'revolt' of March and April 1875 against Southey's administration.[40]

There were many other grievances listed in the newspaper warfare and in petitions from public meetings, including control of illicit diamond buying (IDB), the issue of licences to African diggers and debris workers, and slow settlements in the courts. There was, too, an undercurrent of dissatisfaction at the working of Crown colony government in place of the freedom of assembly allowed to the diggers' committees by the Free State. Official investigation of the colony's finances at the end of 1875 provoked rancorous accusations of mismanagement and revealed a sense of lost power in the interior economy of the mines which were run by the few for the benefit of the many.

Indeed, Lieutenant-Colonel Crossman, who carried out this investigation, put control of the mines and insecurity of title in expensive working

---

[40] Roberts, *Kimberley*, ch. 8; Turrell, 'The 1875 Black Flag Revolt on the Kimberley Diamond Fields', *Journal of Southern African Studies*, 7/2 (1981), 194–235; I. B. Sutton, 'The Diggers' Revolt in Griqualand West, 1875', *International Journal of African Historical Studies*, 12/1 (1979), 40–61; for detailed sources see COCP, *Cape* 76 (1875) and *Cape* 78 (1875) esp. for London pressure groups; Simons, ch. 12; see too Turrell, *Capital and Labour*, 49–71 for another assessment of the rebellion.

conditions at the top of his list of general points of disorder. The frustration was easily exploited by a hard core of diamond-fields politicians led by William Ling, Henry Tucker, and others who had formed a 'Committee of Public Safety', in August 1874, to repeal the mining ordinance, extend board powers, end IDB, and bring government finances under close scrutiny. Outside these rational requests lay the less rational aims and oratory of a wilder fringe of anti-British malcontents and revolutionaries, such as the Fenian Alfred Aylward, who sought their solution in armed force.

Even so, the verdict that the anti-government movement of 1875 aimed at a 'white proletarian republic' hardly squares with the considerable property holdings of those who attended the mass meetings of March in support of Ling, who refused to pay back-rent for his half-acre stand on Ebden's Vooruitzigt farm. The common bond of diggers, shopkeepers, and assorted tenants lay in fears of even higher fees after the court case, which Ebden lost. The mining camps combined against 'proprietors' encroachments' by forming a Diggers' Protection Association, and for a time they found themselves in passionate agreement with Aylward's simple assertion that past sale of the farm to a land syndicate made no difference to miners' rights to 'free encampment and sorting grounds'. They were eagerly convinced by the misleading parallels drawn by Albany Paddon from the Australian gold fields where, it was claimed, an annual fee of £1 allowed digging 'anywhere'. Some, too, may have believed that if Ling lost his case, 'the monopolists may have the whole of the kopjes to themselves'. But there were many others, like Ling, who held nine portions of claims in the Kimberley mine, who feared that higher rents would 'depreciate the value of claim property' by making it more expensive to work. They agreed with the respectable and quite unrevolutionary G. R. Blanch and Fred English that sorting ground on the mine surround was a reward for 'labour, virtue and patience'.[41] They listened with a certain respect to Ebden's attorney, who braved the assemblies and blamed the government for failing to take over the farms on which the mines were worked. In the end, many of the popular resolutions passed were not for war on constituted authority, but for lower taxes and better facilities for the small entrepreneurs, who hoped for a rise in claim values.

---

[41] COCP, *Cape* 61 (1875), encls. in Southey to Barkly, 5 Sept. 1874; *The Diamond Field*, 6 Mar. 1875 (For Kimberley Hall meeting); 31 Mar. 1875; 14 Apr. 1875; *The Diamond News*, 15 Apr. 1875; *The Mining Gazette*, 13 Apr. 1875 (for meetings of 'Bankers, Professional Men, Merchants &c.'). Southey did consider enrolling coloureds from the Cape Mounted Riflemen, and had 250 volunteers who certainly included Cape Africans and possibly Fingos and Zulus; see 'Arming the Blacks', *The Diamond Field*, 14 Apr. 1875.

Such reasoning clearly bored Aylward who wearied of the meetings and, thirsting for action, ordered assembly under arms, if he and his volunteers raised a black flag 'as a sign of mourning, desolation and unity'. By the end of March 1875 'Adjutant' Aylward was illegally drilling his men. Deputations to Southey and newspaper polemic kept things on the boil and brought the mining boards into the fray, when it was suggested by Tucker's *Diamond Field* that control of licences, IDB, and disputed claims be added to their functions.[42] In truth, the Kimberley board had its own reasons for a fight with Ebden's agents over water rights which the board had been selling illegally; and it had a private battle with the surveyor of claims over dangerous reef which it hoped to resolve by assuming greater legal powers. In April, the board came out openly in support of the Protection Association, while denying it was 'political'. It was immediately joined by the De Beers mining board, which met to petition against 'licences to natives', suggesting respectfully that if 'class legislation' was not allowed, 'the difficulty might be met by placing the issue of diggers' certificates in the hands of the Mining Boards'.

These moves to recover powers lost by the abolition of the old committee system were submerged, however, in the more dramatic events surrounding the arrest and trial of William Cowie for sale of arms to Aylward, and the aggravation of public feelings by rumours of 'black squads' enrolled and armed to keep order. When Cowie was fined, the black flag was raised over the tailings and bloodshed was barely avoided. The fine was paid; more fiery speeches were made; and the armed white squads and a crowd of some 3,000 which laid siege to the court house dispersed.

The 'rebellion', such as it was, brought in troops from the Cape and cost the province an extra £21,000 in public debt. The ringleaders either fled, or were tried and acquitted. The issues were more complex than a mere confrontation between rowdy miners and officials, though Kimberley's riotous few months do have some parallels with Victoria's 'Eureka stockade' at Ballarat in 1854, when twenty diggers were killed. In Australia, diggers resisted government licences on Crown land. At Kimberley they resisted the land companies. In Victoria they demanded representation without property qualifications in the state legislature of a self-governing colony, while the Griqualand franchise was open to all white males who troubled to register as voters (and not more than about 1,500 did) in a system of very restricted representation. Australian diggers obtained an end to arbitrary decisions by government commissioners and

---

[42] *The Diamond Field*, 31 Mar. 1875.

the establishment of wardens' courts for mining disputes, while Kimberley retained the unspecialized verdicts of the ordinary civil courts. At the end of the day, the mining boards survived to win greater control for their sectional interests. They were joined late in the 'rebellion' by another pressure group of forty merchants and businessmen headed by J. B. Robinson, Isaac Sonenberg, the auctioneer A. A. Rothschild, and diamond dealers such as Anton Dunkelsbuhler who regarded rioting as bad for trade, and sought help from the Cape government. Under the surface agitation these groups of vested interests asserted themselves not to entrench diggers' 'rights', but to reform an incompetent administration in ways that would safeguard commerce and the mining industry.

For, it was this commercial and mining combination which helped fund Southey's last important act before his removal from office. To end the continual wrangle between diggers and proprietors on the most crowded and valuable mine sites they took up the provincial government's issue of £100,000 of debenture stock at 5 per cent to pay for state purchase of the 17,000 acres of Vooruitzigt estate from Ebden, as urged by the diggers' committees in 1873 and negotiated by Governor Barkly at Cape Town in May 1875. Most of the mine area's 734 stands were snapped up by their holders as valuable properties in a growing township, and the rest were auctioned off for £117,897 for the government, less interest and the cost of convict labour employed to level sites and clean up the streets. No move was made, however, to purchase the estate of the London and South African Exploration Company. It might well have asked more for its 15,500 acres, and was not so susceptible to colonial government pressures; or it may simply be that the mine surrounds of Dutoitspan and Bultfontein did not, as yet, promise to attract speculators south of the main centre of trade near to the Kimberley and De Beers mines. Without such support, the government could not afford to make a second guaranteed loan to underwrite state proprietorship for the benefit of local entrepreneurs.

With the main source of contention settled for the moment, Lord Carnarvon and the Colonial Office decided in August 1875 that the province could be run by a less expensive administrator and advised Barkly to recall Southey and Currey. In November, Major W. D. Lanyon and an acting colonial secretary replaced them, and the searching enquiry by Crossman got under way.

To some extent this enquiry kept agitation alive at the thought of more public meetings and a post mortem on Southey's rule. A committee of miners was elected and reported at length on the extension of board powers, limitation of government controls, and reduction of taxes on the transfer of claims. More significantly, it recommended compulsory registration of labour at a depot, enforcement of passes, confinement of workers to employers' camps and compounds, penal sanctions with lashes and fines to prevent desertion, and locations (designated residence) outside the camps to hold unregistered workers. Purchases of firearms in the gun trade were to be made subject to labour services by African buyers. The police were to be expanded by including a department specializing in prevention of IDB with strict control of canteens to divide trade in diamonds from trade in drink.[43]

This catalogue of employers' intentions pointed the way to future organization of the mines. For the moment, the industry was still at a stage of transition from ownership by multiple claimholding to concentration and amalgamation. Diggers were still divided on whether to retain or abolish the ten-claims limitation. Six years of frenzied exploitation had created a market. But the volume of production required to meet lower prices implied the need for restructuring the outmoded technology and partnerships which had served well enough to open up Kimberley to the world and which now constrained its development.

[43] COCP, *African* 96 (1876), encl. 3, 19 Feb. 1876; Baxter, 7 Jan. 1876; Cole, 1 Sept. 1875; Oats, encl. 12.

2
Miners' Oligarchy

♦

ONCE the dust had settled on Kimberley's 'revolt', it was left to Governor Barkly and Carnarvon's special commissioner, Lieutenant-Colonel Crossman of the Royal Engineers, to find ways of reforming the administration of the province. Lord Carnarvon insisted on an end to financial deficit, and ordered cuts. Southey, in his own defence, insisted that the root of all his trouble lay in 'the uncertainty of tenure and of rent charges of claims in the mines and plots of ground for stands around and in the vicinity of the mines'.[1] Sir Henry Barkly went to investigate.

He found, as Crossman was to do, that mining at Kimberley and De Beers had advanced to the stage where interests were divided on the fundamental issues as much as they were united in opposition to exactions by proprietors or to undue 'interference' by government. The Kimberley mining board and most of the De Beers claimholders wanted repeal of the mining ordinance of 1874. Others saw the ten-claims limit as the only obstacle to progress. Still more wanted this retained, but with a different method of electing mining board members according to the value and not the number of claims worked. Barkly sympathized with the larger claimholders and promised yet more freedom from control so as not to disrupt 'the ordinary principles of commerce in respect to the buying and selling of claims'.[2] The details were left to the new officials to implement.

Such free market 'principles' could not operate, however, unless the legalities of proprietorship, the Crown reserve of minerals, and the spread of leaseholding on the mine surrounds were settled. Barkly took steps to speed up this process through a land court set up to examine all disputed titles to farms, against the protests of the LSAE; and he reformed the licencing system for debris-working on the Vooruitzigt estate which the government now owned, against the protests of claimholders, by promising to use the income for pumping machinery.

---

[1] COCP, *African*, 83, Southey to Barkly, 30 June 1875.
[2] Ibid., Barkly to Carnarvon, 20 Oct. 1875.

When Crossman arrived, therefore, he found two different systems of mining tenure in operation. One, which was settled by the purchase of Vooruitzigt, assumed that minerals were reserved to the Crown, but gave the diggers a property right through claim registration. The other, derived from Free State titles and subsequent legislation, excluded Crown reserve of minerals and applied the mining ordinances to registration of claims at Dutoitspan and Bultfontein, guaranteeing individual tenure in return for licence fees. The basis for these assumptions had yet to be tested by the courts. Also to be tested was Southey's assertion that government could participate in the claim licences levied by the LSAE.

At the end of his investigations in 1875 and 1876, Crossman appreciated that security of tenure was linked to the management of the mines under a common set of regulations and that other grievances over IDB, definition of the mining area, and limits to claim ownership could be resolved with the participation of the claimholders. Lacking a legal brief, he saw the problem as one of local government, rather than proprietorial rights, because a small population of perhaps 30,000 to 40,000 did not justify the expenditure of over £80,000 in 1875, and because the province could not pay for a second purchase of farms from a wealthier and more determined owner in the shape of the LSAE. Consequently, he concentrated in his reports of February and May 1876 on important, but fundamentally secondary issues, and recommended economies and management of the mines within the framework of current laws and institutions created by Barkly and Southey. It was easy enough to condemn the lack of value for moneys expended since 1871 which had increased the secretariat and reduced the police to a dozen men and a small mounted force. Official buildings looked like much of the mining camps—temporary structures of wood and galvanized iron. The legislative council met in a hut. The gaol could be cut through 'with a penknife'; the hospital held twenty whites, while African patients were treated in a tent outside. For all the expenditure on a surveyor-general's department, there was no proper survey of mines or farms.[3]

But after all the calculations were made, Crossman and the new administrator, Major Owen Lanyon, could lop only £3,000 off expenditure, after allowing for increased spending on the police. Loans were clearly required from Cape Colony to cover the cost of new surveys. Crossman made out a strong case for a share of the Cape's currency and customs duties; but that was not an argument likely to appeal to Cape politicians, particularly as the mining community was so lightly taxed.

---

[3] Ibid., Crossman to Carnarvon, 5 Feb. 1876.

For the moment, the diggers could not be pressed for more (the political risk was too great). The way out, perhaps, concluded Crossman, was to work the mines by large companies, paying royalties on their profits.

For this to happen, the limitation on claimholding had to be lifted, even at the risk of an exodus of diggers and a decline in trade. Moreover, the technical arguments presented by Francis Oats, the Cornish mining engineer, clearly impressed on Crossman the need to consolidate interests, especially in the Kimberley and De Beers mines:

Were joint companies to be formed, Government would be relieved of great difficulty, mines would be worked more economically, means might be adopted for regulating the supply of diamonds according to the requirements of the market, better prices and more profit in the long run being thereby obtained. Illicit diamond dealing would be more easily checked and thus fewer stolen diamonds would find their way to the Continental markets and there sold at comparatively low prices, so keeping down the price of those obtained in a legitimate manner; proper steps could be taken for the examination of workmen leaving the mines, fewer workmen would be required under an improved system of working, and many of the great difficulties as regards native labour, such as desertion from one employer to another would be obviated.[4]

This blueprint for amalgamation, monopoly supply, and control of labour echoed some of the more far-sighted miners and dealers. It was a direction of intention, rather than a legislative programme for industrial investment.

More immediately, as much responsibility as possible was shifted to the mining boards. This tactic was limited by the need to keep an official surveyor and perhaps a mining magistrate to settle disputes, and by the recognition that restricted development of Bultfontein and Dutoitspan precluded fully autonomous boards for all claimholders. But for Kimberley and De Beers mines, the boards were seen as a step towards companies:

The mines should be looked on partly as a municipality and partly as a trading corporation, and Government should interfere with them as little as possible. Beyond specific power retained for the safety of life, a power especially necessary in mines where every man works on his own account and the race for wealth is so keen that they think little about endangering their own lives or those of their neighbours, the Government after collecting such dues on royalties as may be necessary for the purpose of the administration, should leave nearly everything to the diggers themselves.[5]

Crossman approved of the idea of a licensing body made up of miners. Indeed, he went further than many of the claimholders by recommending

---

[4] COCP, *African*, 83, Crossman to Carnarvon, 1 May 1876.   [5] Ibid.

that the votes exercised in board elections should depend on the rateable value of an individual's claims, 'as it is a board for the management, as it were, of a commercial speculation, and not a political organization'. If this were done, mining officials could be reduced to two commissioners. As for control of labour, he approved the idea of depots to receive and register workers issued with passes and badges ('like London cabmen'), and their confinement to camps and compounds overnight.

In the wider context of South African political and economic development in the 1870s, Crossman also pointed the way to incorporation into the Cape. But a few months after his departure, the province was saddled with an unexpected burden of £90,000 in compensation for the Free State, when Barkly's land court disputed the basis for Waterboer's 'grants' between the Modder and the Vaal which were part of the justification for British annexation. A squeeze on mining credit and a fall in claim values added to the financial undesirability of a constitutional merger. By October 1876, Carnarvon deplored the 'failure of mining' to save one of the pieces on the grand mosaic of federation; and a deputation of merchants with mining and mercantile interests met with the secretary of state to express their fears about impending frontier wars and the delay in implementing constitutional reform.[6]

Unfortunately, the land court also upheld the LSAE's claims to Dorstfontein and Bultfontein farms, and no appeal for mineral rights was lodged by the Griqualand West government. A judgement of the Griqualand High Court, 10 August 1876, confirmed that the title to Dutoitspan reserved nothing to the Crown; and so most of the licence money held by government had to be paid back. Appeals to the Privy Council upheld this decision and similar unrestricted company rights over Bultfontein. By 1879, some £33,000, or 5 per cent of total revenue 1872–9, was refunded to the proprietors.[7]

TOWARDS INCORPORATION

Annexation to the Cape was postponed, along with the necessary legislation for company investment. When a bill for annexation was presented to the Cape Parliament in June 1877, a committee headed by

---

[6] COCP, *African*, 105 Carnarvon to Molteno, 5 Aug., 30 Sept. 1876. For another view of the 'depressions' of the 1870s see Worger, *South Africa's City of Diamonds*, 34–5, 118; and cf. fig. 1; and for the beginnings of private company investment see Turrell, *Capital and Labour*, 79–82.

[7] CPP, G. 86-'82, Buchanan, 'Memorandum', 30 Dec. 1881.

Richard Southey looked hard at the resources of his former seat of office. After taking evidence on the value of farms and mines, and on future estimates of revenue, the committee reported that the province had a total debt of £260,317. On the other hand, it was favourably impressed by assurances from Francis Oats that the annual production of £2 million of diamonds would be sustained, as the mines went deeper. Property values would soar, if the mines 'were all bought up by a company or companies.[8] There was still the position of the LSAE to be considered; and a well-informed speculator like John X. Merriman believed that the decisions of the courts were a significant bar to investment on its properties. But he saw in the 'capitalization' of the stand licences on Vooruitzigt a major source of taxation and a way of discharging debts, if the province was taken over.[9]

Equally significantly, there was also a swing in favour of annexation among the largest claimholders such as J. B. Robinson, who sent a petition from Kimberley businessmen and his own memorandum to the premier, Molteno, recommending incorporation, because of his 'large stake in the Province'.[10]

Even so, Cape politicians were wary of taking in a mining enclave which demanded up to six representatives in the Assembly; and when they agreed to pass the Griqualand West Annexation Act of 1877, only four were allowed. The Kimberley Legislative Council was no more enthusiastic at this stage. Divided in their views on federation, and preoccupied with the effects of British annexation in the Transvaal, risings in the interior of Griqualand, and disasters in Zululand, Kimberley politicians, Governor Bartle Frere, and the Cape ministry postponed implementing the measure for 3 years.

During the delay, the claimholders, the mining boards, and diamond merchants improved their managerial autonomy and their commercial stake, while waiting for the legislation to guarantee tenure for company development.

Lanyon supported them by taking up the issue of unregulated recruitment of labour. A commission of miners and the surveyor-general reported in June 1876 on the ways and means.[11] A central depot and other reception points on the Vaal and Basutoland routes were required to receive workers and direct them to the mines. The system of occasionally auctioning Africans on the market square at £1 a head (witnessed by

[8] CPP, A.1,-'77; RH, Molteno Papers, Lanyon to Frere, 19 Apr. 1877.
[9] RH, Molteno Papers, Merriman, memorandum, 9 Apr. 1877.
[10] Ibid., Robinson to Molteno, 26 Apr. 1877 (and encl.).
[11] PP, C. 2220, 1879, Frere to CO, 30 Aug. 1878; Worger, 'Workers as Criminals', 63–5.

Crossman) was to end. Labour was to be signed on and off at the beginning and the end of a contract period. Employers were to provide food and lodgings, in order to end 'board' wages in the town and the temptations of clandestine trade in diamonds. Greater penalties were recommended to stop poaching of labour and to ensure that vagrants were caught in the recruitment net.

Before any of this could be implemented, employers responded to a short recession in June 1876 by cutting wages and lost about half of the mining workforce of 12,000 men. Wages were raised again, as demand picked up. Lanyon accepted all of the commission's proposals except the cost of extra depots, in a new labour ordinance of 6 November 1876 which provided for registration and direction of recruits for 1 to 12 month periods of service. He had already acted to toughen conditions in the gaol (compared unfavourably with the mines because prisoners were given 'too much food') by introducing unpaid brick-making, wood-cutting, and a treadmill. Now, he increased the numbers of police, speeded up court cases, and set up a special magistrate's court to deal with infractions of the pass regulations and with absconders.

The general effect of the 1876 legislation was to increase conviction rates for vagrancy, desertion, and 'neglect of duty'. But new laws did not improve the labour supply at cheaper rates of pay or ensure longer periods in the mines.[12] While the courts certainly heard more cases, there was also a rising recruitment of new hands, fairly steady monthly averages, and a greater turnover in numbers employed, indicating a highly mobile labour force intent on short-term employment.

Secondly, Lanyon supported the wealthier claimholders by pushing through the repeal of the ten-claims limitation in November 1876. Protests from the Port Elizabeth Chamber of Commerce alleged that 'speculators' had prevailed in the legislative council, 'the effect of which must be the creation of a monopoly of the diamond mines, lessen their productions, depress labour, cripple business, reduce the value of landed property, destroy a great centre of industry'.[13]

The immediately verifiable result was a rapid turnover in claims, as measured by the steep rise in transfer fees, 1876–9, from £400 to just over £5,000. From other evidence, it would seem that Lanyon's legislation happened to follow a recession arising from a shortage of working capital, 'when in consequence of the tightness of the money market, mining properties were almost valueless, many diggers who were forced to sell

---

[12] Worger, 'Workers as Criminals', 76–7, for tables of arrests.
[13] Port Elizabeth Chamber of Commerce, *Reports* (1878), 44.

their claims during that period were ruined, or much reduced in circumstances'. This is supported by other sources which attributed the beginnings of large-scale claim amalgamation to 'sales effected during a time of great depression', especially in the Bultfontein mine, where 'many of the claims belonged to natives who did not know their value when they sold them'.[14]

The depth and severity of this 'depression' should not be exaggerated, however. There was a fall in the annual total of discounted bills circulated by the banks by some 30 per cent in 1876, a slight fall in diamond prices, but little decrease in the volume and value of diamond exports (see Fig. 1). The 'crisis' was mainly the result of an end to the easy credit of earlier years and the high rate of interest 'sometimes as much as five per cent per month' which brought down the unwary in the commercial and mining sectors of Griqualand's inflated market economy, and gave to those with resources the chance to buy out the insolvent.[15]

But because of this burst of claim speculation, Crossman's recommendations for extending mining board functions and decreasing official supervision were modified by Lanyon. The mining engineer or surveyor (also termed an 'inspector') retained his powers under the 1874 Ordinance for the working and safety of the mines. The mining inspector was empowered to nominate half of the eight-member boards for Kimberley and De Beers and to chair their meetings.[16] No new board was elected or appointed for Dutoitspan, after 1875, or for Bultfontein (technically a 'diggings'), until 1883; and both remained firmly in the charge of Captain H. J. Yonge, as inspector. The rest of the mining establishment was thin on the ground. Ward doubled as surveyor under the surveyor-general, F. H. Orpen, but only the boards produced any plans for the mines. Indeed, it may be doubted whether the board members were greatly troubled by these officials. A registrar recorded labour recruitment, but not desertions; and an inspector of native locations with magisterial powers enforced pass controls on all servants employed in the local labour market, so far as he could keep a trace of workers whose indifference to the complex formalities of different classifications of

[14] *Reports of the Cases Decided in the High Court of Griqualand West*, vol. 17 (1882–83), 56.

[15] CPP, A. 6-'77, App. For a commentary on the Cape's internal debt and its part in the recession see DUSC, 12, Consul Siler, 25 Aug. 1883. The Standard Bank did not attribute this recession to diamond mining either: Alan Mabin and Barbara Conradie (eds.), *The Confidence of the Whole Country: Standard Bank Reports on Economic Conditions in Southern Africa 1865–1902* (Johannesburg, 1987), 58–9, 87–8.

[16] *The Statute Law of Griqualand West*, App. 1, 437. At mine elections, voters had 1 vote per claim, 2 for 5 claims, and 1 extra for every additional set of 5 claims to a maximum of 10 votes.

employment and residence was matched by employers' willingness to avoid registration fees.

Finally, miners were not given the authority they claimed to determine the issue of licences. More seriously, a projected warden's court for mining cases lapsed in 1877 in favour of the tortuous litigation of the province's civil courts. But on the whole, it is arguable that the modified status of the boards made little difference to their functions in the late 1870s, as claim consolidation progressed. From the lists of their elected and nominated members and from reports of their meetings in the press, it is evident that in the Kimberley and De Beers mines the major claimholders retained, in practice, a measure of autonomy over reef clearances, pumping, blasting regulations, sanitation, and the disposal of abandoned claims. They determined the rising scale of claim assessments on which rates were paid for general administration, and they set the special rates for pumping, hauling, and clearing debris through the boards. They ordered machinery on credit through the Crown Agents. There was a fair turnover of board members, though a few, such as H. W. Dunsmure, T. Shiels, and R. Baxter, served almost continuously from 1874 for the De Beers mine; and, like a number on the Kimberley board, they were future company directors.[17] A source of their power lay in the ineffectiveness of officials (Walter Ward was treated with contempt by claimholders), and in their direction of contracts arranged by tender with the board.

Already there were important differences between the two mines. The scale of board charges remained high in the Kimberley mine at 4s. per load for clearing dead ground, compared with 2s. 6d. at De Beers, over and above the annual rates. The burden discouraged some of the less successful diggers in claims vulnerable to falls and flooding, and remained a high cost well into the 1880s. De Beers mine with shallower levels, dikes of igneous rock, and little working at all in the 'west end' beyond the main gullies of the central claims was able to avoid some of this extra cost. There was a steady haulage of reef in De Beers 1877–81, amounting to some 600,000 loads. But this clearance over 5 years was less than a third of the unprofitable extra tonnage hauled out of the Kimberley mine in 1 year. So important was this function that the Kimberley board operated like a small company with four locomotives, two hauling engines, trucks, tramways, and contracted overseers and labour. By 1882, the

---

[17] DBCA, KMB/2, loose minutes, 1879–1881; claim valuations; KMB/4, ledger, Jan.–Nov. 1878; DBMB/2, ledger, 1880; reports in *DFA*, 1878–80; see too Moonyean Buys, *Archives of Companies on the Diamond Fields of Southern Africa, 1878–1889. Absorbed in the Big Amalgamation*, (DBCM, 1979), 16, 27; Worger, *South Africa's City of Diamonds*, 41.

board had spent £1.5 million on reef removal, compared with a mere £150,000 paid out by the De Beers board.

These operational requirements exceeded the capacities of many of the partnerships in the claims. The technology required to operate at deeper levels was not new, but it was expensive and had to be supplemented by equally expensive labour. The advent of steam-power from 1875, when applied to hauling, effectively tripled the capacity of the capstans on the surround to bring up tubs of blue clay and reef. This in turn required more labour to clear treated ground at the mine perimeter, heavier overhead wires, more tramways, waggons, and more semi-skilled workers and overseers. Many white diggers displaced from the claims found employment in these jobs. Because basic hauling tonnages increased, there was also a necessary improvement in diamond-recovery techniques with the introduction of rotary washing machines from 1875, hand-powered, horse-powered, and finally steam-powered. Moreover, as the mine deepened and diamondiferous ground became harder, blasting became more frequent. 'Lumps' solid as stone damaged the blades in the rotary pans, and the conglomerate required a period of exposure to the atmosphere and some mechanical crushing before washing treatment. By the late 1870s, much of the Kimberley mine was nearing the 400 feet level, and encountered this problem first, followed by De Beers in the early 1880s. The remedy adopted was to lay out the clay on 'floors' at the mine surround; and that process, too, required more supervised labour and considerable reorganization of surface working methods, as well as expansion of the surface area available to claimholders.

At the same time, total labour charges for all four mines, estimated at about £500,000 by the diggers in 1875, were judged by Francis Oats in 1877 to vary between £600,000 and £1,600,000 over a period of 16 months, revealing fluctuations in the monthly and seasonal supply of men, and perhaps a greater demand for labour at Dutoitspan and Bultfontein from 1876. For at those mines, Inspector Yonge had managed to stop debris-sorting in the claims, and there is evidence of rising claim prices and some consolidation from 1878, in conjunction with rapid mechanization. Yonge also used convict labour to lay out roads between claims and obtained an agreement, in 1881, from the LSAE proprietors for companies to lease land for floors at the rate of £1 an acre for every claim worked.

At all four mines, then, there was an increase in working costs by the end of the decade, as well as an overall rise in production and sales. The mechanization foreseen by Oats and others as an answer to geological difficulties had only partly solved the problems of reef fall and flooding.

Cecil Rhodes, who knew at first hand the very high delivery charges on engines ordered in England, had been right to assert that 'the application of machinery to diamonds will lick depreciation in prices'. But he seriously underestimated the gross working costs of mining which, in Oats's view of 'well conducted mines' required some 30 to 50 per cent of outlay to be spent on general purposes, including plant installation and water and reef removal, before the calculation of direct charges—labour, stores, and administration—for hauling ground, recovering diamonds, and selling them.[18]

We do not have the working records of miners at this period, only fragments suggesting how the 'interior economy' of the mines operated. But it is likely that these lessons in capitalization were learned the hard way in the late 1870s, through bankruptcies, some amalgamations, pooled experience, and running arguments with the boards and the inspectors. There was clearly a move away from working on 'shares' towards partnerships employing overseers among the 300 claimholders who held 392 claims in the Kimberley mine in 1877, assessed at £940,000. The largest partnerships and private companies—J. B. Robinson and Co., Paddon Bros., Baring-Gould Bros. and Atkins, Francis and Tarry, Green and Paton, and the Kimberley Mining Company had obviously made some progress on consolidation of claims in different parts of the mine. There was a similar configuration in De Beers, assessed at only £273,000 for 612 claims, while the 2,400 claims in Bultfontein and Dutoitspan were given the low valuation of £76,403, based on sales. By 1879, after further reduction of claimholders to 130 in Kimberley mine, the assessed value rose to £1,313,487. One or two more private companies had appeared, but the general impression of all four mines is still one of fragmentation of effort, despite the pace of technological change.

The pressure for legislation to secure new sources of capital and end fragmentation came first from those who wanted to expand operations on the mine surrounds. A meeting of joint committees of claimholders from De Beers and Kimberley framed new regulations, in April 1879, for complete control over the mine area, not just the claims, leaving only safety matters to the inspectors. More specifically, it was proposed that any person or joint-stock company should register a fixed area of 'depositing, sorting, or washing ground' to be determined by the boards' by-laws.[19] In a sense, this was to return to the powers approved by

[18] For development of the mines, CPP, G. 86-'82; G. 27-'82; G. 34-'83; Reunert, 'Diamond Mining at the Cape', 190–1; *Statistical Register of the Cape of Good Hope* (1878–85); RH, Rhodes Papers T 14, Rhodes to Rudd, 1 June 1876; COCP, *African*, 96, Oats, provincial engineer's report, 78. [19] CPP, G. 86-'82.

Crossman, and exercised within the mines by the part-nominated boards, which had a direct interest in improving production techniques. It also opened the way to new operations on a scale not possible in the 1870s.

The initiative had a favourable reception. Governor Bartle Frere visited the diamond fields and concluded that their wealth was not likely to be quickly exhausted and that the commercial and industrial development of the province could be usefully added to the Cape without much financial risk. Lanyon and the acting-administrator, Rose Innes, began to make both boards and mines ready for the corporate investment required by the larger claimholders, in a last burst of legislation before Griqualand was taken over in October 1880.

Such investment depended on the confidence of a new entrepreneurial section of Kimberley's community—the diamond merchants, dealers, and brokers who had flocked to the mines in the 1870s. There had been a number of schemes aired by these men for company promotion, but little money invested other than in land. W. A. ('Tramway') Hall, manager of Walsh and Co., tried to pressure the Legislative Council into making mining concessions; and Thomas Lynch, backed by the London firm of Blaine, Macdonald and Co., aimed at amalgamating half the claims in the Kimberley mine in 1876. All this foundered on insecurity of tenure and restrictive legislation. Lynch was also listed as a diamond dealer, claimowner, and company promoter; and this pattern of local investment out of profits and speculative capital by unspecialized entrepreneurs was repeated many times.

From 1877 too, company and diamond men moved into municipal government. Kimberley's first town council contained three or four claimholders, and the first mayor, John Birbeck, was a diamond dealer, and was followed by the even more notable B. I. Barnato and J. B. Robinson in 1879 and 1880. Having captured the municipality, dealers and miners were ready to turn their attention to the politics of large-scale management through the boards and through the Cape legislature.

In this, they were favoured by the high level of production and exports after 1876. For the index of imports of precious stones into the United States held firm; and towards the end of the 1870s this indicator of demand for cut diamonds moved up sharply towards a 200 per cent rise over 1874 values (Fig. 1). In London, *The Economist* concluded that the increase in 'surplus' capital by 1877 would follow improved communications and investment opportunities. The same issue also carried advertisements for the Robey and Lincoln engines which were transforming methods of production at the diamond fields.[20] There are indications, too, that merchants and local dealers were ready to respond to the growing volume of diamond sales by direct cash transfers and by bills on London houses, just as they began to invest in local properties and shares. Measured by the licences issued for buyers, their numbers probably peaked at just over 200 in 1879, and then declined throughout the 1880s, as more specialized agents commanding more capital traded with the producers.[21] A diamond trade ordinance of 1877 which limited casual brokerage meant that most diamond buyers had to hold two kinds of certification, which divided them further from the producers; and other legislation in 1880 limited diamond trading by companies to the banks and to those individuals who were principals or agents with increasingly elaborate registers of sales. In 1878 almost anyone who was a claimholder could take out a diamond dealer's licence. By 1880, considerable capital was needed to set up as a buyer and exporter, and even the form and size of notices advertising the profession were strictly laid down. By then, those merchants who did not have claims were willing to finance men who did and entered into company promotion, using London, Continental and local mercantile capital on a totally new scale.

Several necessary conditions had to be met, before this wave of company investment was possible. Mining legislation, mine boundaries, and mine boards were overhauled in order to allow companies greater scope in managing and protecting their stake.[22] Dutoitspan and Bultfontein were brought into line with the amendments proposed for Kimberley and De Beers, by making claimholders pay rates to small nominated boards under the inspector. To allay the anxieties of proprietors and investors a little-noticed ordinance on 'Fixity of Tenure' gave a perpetual quitrent title to those digging on Crown lands 'in free and undisturbed possession' and empowered the mining boards to allot 'machinery stands' on the mine surround. Rose Innes who as administrator framed the measure argued it was needed 'in order to induce capitalists to invest, as it was represented that this could not be done so long as the claims were held on a monthly tenure'. Indeed, he went further and attributed the whole change in the

[20] *The Economist*, 10 Mar. 1877; Port Elizabeth Chamber of Commerce, *Reports* (1877), 19.

[21] *The Diamond News*, 1877; CPP, G. 3-'88, App. J; G. 86-'82, 73A; Turner's Guides, 1878, 1884. Brokers' licences were frequently taken out by buyers and exporters to cover their operations for principals in the local market: Ordinance 4 (26 Mar. 1877); Ordinance 8 (16 July 1880).

[22] The legislation is contained in Ordinances no. 15 (26 Nov. 1879) [Mining]; 6 (1 June 1880) [Fixity of Tenure Mines and Diggings]; 11 (28 July 1880) [Prevention of Diamond Thefts]; 16 (22 Sept. 1880) [Registration of Leases]; 21 (30 Sept. 1880) [Mining Areas, Vooruitzigt]; 17 (22 Sept. 1880) [Government of Diamond Mines]; CO, 107/9, Frere to CO, 10 Sept. 1879 and encls.; Innes to Frere, 22 July 1880.

scale of investment at Kimberley to this simple ordinance alone which marked the end of the first phase of mining 'by causing companies to be established'. Lanyon also gave it his support, though he thought the government did not get enough from it, because the licence could not be raised under quitrent from diggers who were 'the lightest taxed people in the world'. The Colonial Office agreed, but allowed this 'handsome present to the licensees' to pass.[23]

But to allow the miners to 'capitalize' claims was not enough. They had to be protected against loss through IDB. Again, it was Rose Innes who set about overhauling the local detective force and prepared a defence of the searching and 'trapping' system which were the basis for control of theft, against the misgivings of the Colonial Office.[24] An ordinance to search workers required the boards to enforce it and organize the detectives to control IDB on the mine sites. In September 1880, legislation was passed allowing the leasehold of claims with provision for registration of mortgages, thus making amalgamations more likely in the Dutoitspan and Bultfontein mines by agreement with the LSAE. Finally, a new ordinance and regulations prescribed for the general government of diggings, mines, and the powers of the boards. This was a major revision of a decade of laws and proclamations, and returned the interior management to elected boards of twelve in the two deeper mines. The boards now had total control of the depositing floors in areas that could be enlarged, if necessary, by executive action of the governor-in-council. Electoral rules allowed multiple votes for claimholders with high rateable values and ensured that the managers and directors of the greatest numbers of claims would retain these powers.

With the ground prepared in law, one last and vital requirement was a survey. This was made by Leo Marquard, sent by Merriman from the Cape as 'Special Commissioner in Land Matters'. And for the first time claims were measured 'with accuracy and refinement' and the depositing sites were laid out under difficult conditions on the estates.[25] Further surveys in 1882 continued Marquard's work, making over huge floors to the miners and eating into the area controlled by the borough council and occupied formerly by standholders on the Vooruitzigt estate.

At Dutoitspan and Bultfontein the 'radiating floors' were not so easily allocated, where they involved cancellation of the leases of standholders who formed a 'league' to defend their interests, and the history of the properties moved into a new phase of intensive litigation. From this phase,

[23] CO, 107/9, Lanyon to Frere, memorandum, 25 July 1880, and minutes.
[24] CO, 107/9, Innes to Frere, 22 July 1880.
[25] CPP, G. 50-'82; G. 62-'83; C. 3-'85; A. 27-'85.

the LSAE emerged victorious over the colonial government's attempts to control fees levied on private land; but it lost its case for squeezing the diggers by an *ad valorem* tax on production. Both sides, by 1880, were anxious for a compromise. LSAE licence fees were raised from 10s. to 27s. 6d. per claim per month, but 'radiating floors' were included, and a 'fixity of tenure' was held to apply in Bultfontein and Dutoitspan.[26]

COMPANY INVESTMENT

The rush of joint-stock company investment at Kimberley from April 1880 marked the beginning of a long period of mining development in South Africa through public subscription. Much of this capital was locally-generated with considerable reinvestment through inflation at the Cape, followed by speculation in rising share values and a collapse of the market in December 1881 and early 1882, until measures were taken to decrease bank advances against scrip and to enforce commercial laws on directors' liabilities.[27] The initial joint-stock ventures of 1880 which resulted in a subscribed capital of £2.5 million took contemporaries by surprise as 'a new feature in the commercial history of the country' marked by over-allotment of shares for small returns.[28] The young Rhodes, like others, was euphoric over the changes wrought and the possibilities for advancement of the companies by political representation and railways:

To shew the change since you came here, De Beers was almost abandoned in your time [1874] and yet now is valued at nearly a million and you must remember these are now fictitious figures, but ground changes hands readily at the values marked on the valuation plans, in fact claims here sell much more readily than land in the Colony . . . what I want to impress on you is the fact that this is now the richest community in the world for its size and that it shews every sign of permanency. The present proved depths of our mines alone would take our present rate of working a 100 years to work out and of course we cannot tell how much deeper they may go.[29]

[26] CO, 108/8, 'Memorandum of Suggestions' [1880].
[27] S. H. Frankel, *Capital Investment in Africa: Its Course and Effects* (London, 1938),63–4; Houghton and Dagut, i. 276–7; Turrell, *Capital and Labour*, 106–121 for a careful analysis of the local share market and company promotion; and for a different view of investment see Worger, *South Africa's City of Diamonds*, 45–6. For the part played by diamond stocks in the short recession see DUSC, 12, Consul Siler, 10 Nov. 1882; Mabin and Conradie, 101.
[28] Port Elizabeth Chamber of Commerce, *Reports* (1881), 27; J. W. Matthews *Incwadi Yami, or Twenty Years' Personal Experience in South Africa* (London, 1887), 246.
[29] Rhodes to Merriman, 16 May 1880, in RH, T. W. Baxter (ed.), 'Yrs C. J. Rhodes, The Letters of an Imperialist', [transcripts]; and for an abridged version, Phyllis Lewsen (ed.), *Selections from the Correspondence of J. X. Merriman, 1870–1890* (Cape Town, 1960), 81.

However intense the public excitement, closer analysis of the pattern of company formation at Kimberley does not entirely support the view that over-capitalization was widespread, though there was certainly a predominance of vendors' and promoters' scrip over subscribed working capital. For example, Rhodes, Rudd, R. D. Graham, W. Alderson, H. W. Dunsmure, and three smaller claimholders pooled their ninety claims, valued in scrip of £100 shares and issued only a few to the public, when De Beers Mining Company Ltd. was registered in May 1880. Similarly, in the Kimberley mine the Central company was registered with a capital of £149,000 mainly in the hands of the twenty-six founders.[30] The temptation for vendors to sell when premiums rose was great, but the share registers for the earliest period do not show a wild series of transfers or a watering-down of stock. For the whole period of the 1880s, 136 private and public mining companies have been traced, and their boards, articles, and initial capital structures are known. More detailed records of twenty companies which survived the period of consolidation by mergers have also survived. With two exceptions, the main cluster of registrations at Kimberley and in London was concentrated in the first 3 years producing some seventy-seven companies as joint-stock or limited partnerships under the Cape Acts of 1861 with a nominal capital of £8.6 million.[31] It is possible the total of registered companies represented a capital of £10 or £11 million. This estimate would agree with the lists published by Kimberley sharebrokers in April 1881 to impress on the public that, by then, the companies were nearly fully subscribed. In the majority of cases, amalgamated claims at incorporation were valued in ways which bore a direct relationship to the yield and worth of the ground; and often founder-directors were obliged to put up cash as well.

But given the unwillingness of founders to go on raising capital by subscription, even the better-managed companies soon ran into problems over working capital. 'Ready money' was not available when required; and Rhodes complained to Merriman in 1882 that the mines were 'worked

---

[30] Buys, *Archives of Companies*. Joint-stock companies were registered under Cape Acts 23 and 24 of 1861 as partnerships in which capital was divided into shares 'so as to be transferable without the express consent of all the partners'. Act 24 allowed limited liability to apply to partnerships. For the British Companies Act of 1862 (25 & 26 Vic., c. 89) and its significance for limited liability see A. B. Levy, *Private Corporations and their Control* (London, 1950), vol. 1, p. 82. For estimated capital values for mines, Turrell, *Capital and Labour*, Apps. 2–6, based on company prospectuses. And for a warning about distinctions to be made on 'Capital' outlays in mining between ore-bearing land ('claims') and man-made capital which otherwise inflate estimated company valuations see S. H. Frankel, *Investment and the Return to Equity Capital in the South African Gold Mining Industry 1887–1965: An International Comparison* (London, 1967), 4.

[31] *DFA*, 11 Apr. 1881.

so unprofitably that the results are all distributed in the country in return for labour, fuel, food, etc., and nothing is left to be remitted to home shareholders or shared by bankrupt colonial ones'.[32] On the other hand, neither the De Beers Mining Company (DBMC) nor the Kimberley Central which eventually came to dominate their respective mines, was greatly troubled by the temporary fall in share values late in 1881, and continued to pay small dividends. The founders remained tightly in control. Twelve of them still owned 52 per cent of DBMC capital raised to £755,120 by small take-overs 3 years later, when there were only 245 shareholders in all. If more money was required, they would have to earn it.[33]

Their principal source of earnings lay in the local diamond dealers. Very few companies, perhaps a dozen, were registered in London and Paris, and none were listed on the London Exchange till after 1885. That did not prevent share-dealings, of course, and Kimberley Central opened a share registry office and had a committee of London shareholders in 1883. But capital and direction were predominantly South African, although about half of the boards of 103 companies had representation from overseas and local buyers.

To understand the position and influence of the merchant principals and their agents in the early 1880s is to classify those who were most numerous immediately before the period of company flotations. Out of the hundred or so diamond dealers listed in the Kimberley trade directories for 1878, there were eighteen who were principals or partners in London wholesale firms formed in the 1880s. Some of these private companies remained active in the London and Kimberley diamond trade for the rest of the century, and many were expanded by taking in experienced dealers who returned from the diamond fields (see Table 2.1). All provided a solid core of expertise and capital, based on experience and their holdings in the mines. They were particularly strong in Dutoitspan and Bultfontein. In all, some thirty-nine of the buyers listed in 1878 became directors of mining companies and had shares in forty-six of the seventy-seven companies that can be analysed in this way.

The significance of this association should not be exaggerated. Directorships were not always a guide to predominant ownership of the company's equity. Kimberley Central had no identifiable merchant interest before later amalgamations brought in Barnato. DBMC too did not start off with merchant investors, and local dealers held only 3 per cent of subscribed capital in 1881.[34] Continental capitalists, moreover, were

---

[32] RH, Rhodes Papers, T. 5, f. 37; Newbury, 'Out of the Pit'; 29.

[33] DBCA, DBMC/11, 12 journals; KCDM/22, *Reports*; cf. Turrell, *Capital and Labour*, 119.   [34] DBCA, DBMC/11, Dec. 1881.

TABLE 2.1. *Mining company boards with diamond merchant directors at formation, 1880–1882*

London and Kimberley diamond merchants	Kimberley mine (of 28 companies)	De Beers mine (of 18 companies)	Dutoitspan mine (of 38 companies)	Bultfontein mine (of 21 companies)
Jules Porges and Co.	2		1	
Lewis and Marks Snr.	2		3	
Lewis and Marks Jnr.	1			1
Martin Lilienfeld and Co.	1		1	1
F. T. Gervers	1			1
Barnato Bros.	2	3	2	
J. B. Robinson and Co.	5		2	1
V. A. Litkie	1		1	1
J. Walter	1	1		
Herz, Rosenfeld and Co.	1	2		
Paddon Bros.	1	2		
Mosenthal, Sons and Co.		2	1	2
M. J. Posno		1	1	1
J. B. Finlason			1	
L. and A. Abrahams		1	2	
Ochs Bros.				2
Joseph Bros.				1
J. Birbeck		1		
A. Dunkelsbuhler and Co.	2	1	2	1
TOTAL	20	10	21	12

Note: In all, there were 63 company boards with diamond merchant directors out of 105 registered companies that can be traced.

Sources: Moonyean Buys. *Archives of Companies on the Diamond Fields of Southern Africa, 1878–1889, Absorbed in the Big Amalgamation* (DBCM, 1979); *The Daily Independent* (1880–2); *The Diamond News* (1878–82); DBC Archives, Ledgers 11, 12.

concentrated in London-registered companies—Anglo-African, Phoenix DMC in Dutoitspan, Victoria DMC in De Beers, Bultfontein Mining Company, and in the Paris-registered Compagnie Française des Mines de Diamant. In all these, Continental and London bankers held shares, headed by L. and E. Erlanger (Frankfort), Baron Schroeder (London), the Rothschilds, L. Goldschmidt (Paris and Berlin), and Grunebaums (London and Paris). But they are not typical of the pattern of shareholding at this stage. That pattern was set in Kimberley by claimholders' flotations, assisted by the 'Kimberley Share Exchange and Broking and General Agency Company', formed in 1880 by Graham, Tarry, Wallis, Lynch, and managed by the diamond dealer D. J. Skill. For a time share broking by dealers of all kinds became a popular sport around Market Square, led by Barnato who started a small 'Stock Exchange' of his own. But once the investment bubble burst at the end of 1881, speculation was overtaken by the more serious business of keeping up share values by production and sales.

The influence of the merchants and dealers was more gradually exerted in ways which helped solve the cash-flow problems of the companies and radically reduced the numbers of the buyers. From Table 2.1 it is clear that the diamond merchants had a major stake in company management and were represented on well over half of the early boards. J. B. Robinson is a special case as a local entrepreneur with interests in seven mining companies: it is not certain which of the diamond houses he dealt with. Like A. Goldschmidt and other merchants he was also a sharebroker, along with A. A. Rothschild the auctioneer, and sundry other dealers and property 'evaluators' who flourished in the heady atmosphere of speculation in tramways, waterworks, theatres, and hotels on the crest of the mining boom. Outside the inner circle of nineteen merchant exporters there were a further twenty-three accredited dealers and brokers with seats on boards at the period of incorporation. Many of these continued to operate in the dual role of company director and diamond dealer, and some (Michaelis, Harris, Phillips, Neumann) became partners in merchant firms.

Secondly, the very large numbers of unspecialized dealers and brokers were levelled down after 1882. Listed buyers number only seventy-five in 1884 and forty-seven in 1887; and they were reduced to forty-two merchants, dealers, and brokers, as distinct from share dealers, in 1889. In short, company sales were handled by fewer diamond buyers. As in the mines, amalgamation of interests to meet new capital requirements reduced the number of independent entrepreneurs.

From the process of joint-stock incorporation, then, there arose an investment and managerial constituency in Kimberley representing buyers and sellers, merchants and miners. And from the incorporation of Griqualand into the Cape, this constituency created a small but effective political lobby in the Cape Assembly, with the election of Rhodes and Robinson as two of the four members for Kimberley and Barkly. Its effectiveness lay not in numbers, but in the support the members could muster through Merriman in his long tenure of office as commissioner of the sprawling department of Crown lands and public works which embraced everything from convict stations to railways, telegraphs to mines. Merriman understood the miners' requirements from his own experience. He was a close political friend of Rhodes. It was fitting, therefore, he should head a commission of six mining directors and diamond dealers, plus the manager of the LSAE and the Crown Prosecutor, which reported on the structure of the industry, 1881–2.

After taking evidence from six leading companies, the mining boards, and some of the river diggers, the commission set a sub-committee to work on commercial aspects of the industry and pronounced on the new 'interior economy' of the mines. Their general recommendations looked back to the diggers for their views on the abolition of direct taxation by certificates, the reduction of transfer fees, and their opposition to officials. They were critical of the boards, but they shied away from substituting them by a warden's court to hear disputes, and they resisted suggestions for different regulations for the LSAE estate and mines, in case these made later amalgamations more difficult. For the time being, the boards still looked like the best institutions for keeping officials at bay, for administering company rates, and for allocating abandoned claims. Commissioners keenly supported their powers to police the mines and organize a search system. Their electoral rules were changed to allow plural votes based on the value of claim assessments; and they were enabled to revise their by-laws to cover their quasi-governmental and judicial functions in the mines and on the mine surround. At the insistence of Rhodes, it was recognized the boards might have to be abolished, if the mines came under one owner. Big changes were in the air: 'Rules which were framed for the government of a community of several hundred individual miners, have now to be applied to a handful of trading corporations, among which two or three bid fair, like Aaron's rod, to swallow up their weaker brethren.'[35] In anticipation of this event the commission prepared draft legislation in order to maintain the boards under the dominant mine owners, until replaced by amalgamated companies in each mine. In no other colony did miners have such a free rein.

The committee which reported on the diamond trade also prepared new measures which were supported by testimony collected by Rhodes. That testimony of diggers, directors, and officials stressed the losses through IDB—as much as 30 to 40 per cent of company production, it was claimed. Companies floated in the recent boom had few reserves; banks were wary of lending against scrip; and overseas capital would not come to Kimberley, argued Sammy Marks (director of three companies), if producers were robbed by their employees. Remedies

---

[35] CPP, G. 86-'82. Members of the commission were J. X. Merriman, Rhodes, Leigh Hoskyns, J. H. Lange, J. B. Robinson, F. Baring-Gould, Walter Ward, Anthony Goldschmidt, George Kilgour (LSAE), J. C. E. d'Esterre.

proposed included more rigorous enforcement of the 1880 regulations, extended use of 'trap' diamonds, special police courts to avoid unreliable juries, and better registration of sales by dealers. A cable from thirteen diamond mining companies with London offices urged control of canteens, and punishment by lash and expulsion.[36]

Much of this had been said before. But the committee organized contributions from companies and the boards to fund the detective force required to improve on Kimberley police methods, which were designed to mobilize labour rather than ferret out clandestine traders. It was admitted, in any case, that registration and the pass system had largely failed to control labour mobility: 'as many natives register themselves to Companies for three to six months, simply for the sake of the pass. Having obtained this, they desert, and are allowed to wander under its protection, and, in a majority of cases, to act as middlemen between the white illicit buyer and the raw native.' Isolation was seen as the ultimate solution: 'it would be necessary that all natives in the mines and on the floors should be kept in compounds away from the townships'. That remedy had been favoured by three of the six companies giving evidence, though they preferred that compulsory quarters should be paid for by government.[37]

These reports provided the basis for the draft legislation and the arguments of the mining lobby to the Cape Assembly in April 1882. Rhodes, Robinson, and Merriman were able to push through a miners' and merchants' charter in the shape of the Diamond Trade Act of June 1882 and the Precious Stones and Minerals Mining Act of September 1883.[38]

The first measure consolidated regulations for licencing, recording, and restricting trade in diamonds under the detective department, supervised by the mining boards and an employers' organization—the 'Board for the Protection of Mining Interests'. For the first time, reasonably accurate statistics were forwarded through the protection board to government departments at the Cape. A special court was established to hear IDB cases; penalties were increased, and powers of entry and arrest were defined. As in the past, labourers found with stones were presumed to have stolen them.

The mining act of 1883, by its definition of prospection rights and public and private mines, became the foundation of subsequent Cape legislation.

---

[36] CPP, A. 9-'82, Giddy to Rhodes, [1882].

[37] CPP, 82-'82; G. 86-'82, App. 3.

[38] Acts 48 of 1882 and 19 of 1883; for an analysis of the social effects of the Diamond Trade Act see Turrell, *Capital and Labour*, ch. 9.

Its immediate importance was to reconstitute the mining boards and (as Rhodes had intended) to ensure their abolition, when nine-tenths of the mine became the property of a single firm.

Having reinforced their powers of governance, the companies continued to use these instruments to remove dead ground, to drain sites, to blast out 'dangerous and injurious claims', and to appropriate depositing floors.[39] They moved with ease on the Vooruitzigt estate to expand the mining area. Standholders with mining rights avoided government and municipal taxes within that area. And they ignored blasting regulations, risking the destruction of Kimberley by storing 'vast quantities of dynamite, gunpowder, explosive caps . . . without the supervision of any responsible officer' in nineteen magazines in close proximity to the town.[40] On the estates of the LSAE, the boards colluded with the company against non-mining standholders in a complex readjustment of leases and access to depositing sites, after a select committee under Rhodes and Robinson and a representative for the standholders had refused compensation for the dispossessed.

From 1882 too, by-laws provided for a system of 'searching-houses', special uniforms for all employees, guards at strategic points, and complete enclosure of the mine sites with fences. The new detective force under John Fry was in action from October 1882, with ten inquisitors (left anonymous in the official lists) and a searching branch under Walter Ward with three inspectors and forty-five searchers recruited from the local IDB underworld as the eyes and ears of the force. Initial expenditure was over £30,000 a year; but some £20,000 was earned from the sale of captured diamonds in 1883, and salaries were paid at first by the Protection Board and the companies. Trap diamonds were supplied through the boards, and had to be accounted for when sold.

Thus primed, Fry's men laboured to flush out diamond fences from their list of twenty-six 'Kaffir Eating Houses' and to set trap stones to catch the criminal and the naïve. Cases were heard without benefit of a jury, and from the abstract of convictions 1881–2, it would seem the delinquents were mainly storekeepers and traders, and not African labourers. All received stiff sentences of up to 5 years hard labour, or large fines (little of which was ever paid).

The companies were not pleased with the results. The whole detective department was judged to produce little return 'on an almost useless

[39] DBCA, DBMB/1, 1882–4; KMB/1, 3, 1879–89; DTMB/1, 1883–7; DTMB/11 (sanitation, searching); BTMB/3, 1883–5 (searching). There was also a separate depositing sites committee for Bultfontein, 1881–5; see too CPP, G. 62'-83; G. 29-'84 (Vooruitzigt).
[40] CPP, G. 62-'83, Hutton, 3.

outlay', after 3 years of effort.[41] But the criminal records indicate a gradual decline in both convictions and acquittals from 1882 for cases heard under the act, though there was a rise in cases in the Cape circuit courts and the appeal courts. The trend was downwards, however, in the rate of convictions, from 179 in 1882 to 68 in 1890, with only a score or so annually during the 1890s.

Public reaction was hostile to 'trapping' methods among canteen owners and the network of minor brokers and dealers on the fringes of the market. An amendment to include a section on prohibition of liquor sales to African workers, on the grounds that the spirits trade, like the gun trade, encouraged illicit dealing, had no more success than measures to reform the arms traffic. The most immediate result of employers' dissatisfaction and the unpopularity of the service was a high turnover of detectives and informants, including John Fry, dismissed for an excess of zeal against Isaac Joel, nephew of Barnato. After that, there was a shift of responsibility to the companies for stopping theft at source.

More ominously, the extension of the searching system into the mines provoked a different kind of opposition in 1883, when overseers, mechanics, and drivers refused to comply with regulations on 'stripping', and went on strike. Some companies compromised and did not enforce the regulations. Others did, and the smouldering discontent of mechanics and overseers against physical searches and compulsory uniforms exploded again in April 1884 into lock-outs and stoppages which threatened the operations of Kimberley Central and the French Company. Clashes with the police and their special constables resulted in the death of eight miners.

It is easy to find an early example of 'worker solidarity' in this grim little episode; and there is ample evidence of organization behind the protest. It is less certain the solidarity extended to black workers. The most straightforward explanation is the one given by the craftsmen and overseers in their petitions: they objected bitterly to loss of status under the law by treatment similar to the Africans they managed. And for their part, immigrant African workers kept out of the affair, though they ceased work in the absence of overseers. They were a cast of silent thousands in a minor drama played out between mine-owners and their mechanics. Only the outer locations and shanties in the dusty backstreets were theirs,

---

[41] DBCA, BPMI/1, minutes, 24 Nov. 1884. For the Protection Board's record of convictions see 'Our Diamond Industry', May 1885 (circular); and CPP, C. 1-'94; G. 3-'88 for IDB cases; CPP, Police Commissioner's Reports, 1884. For an analysis of the white labour force, Worger, *South Africa's City of Diamonds*, 158–77; and for the strikes, Turrell, *Capital and Labour*, 122–45. The general trend in the ratio of black to white workers moved downwards in the 1880s to 4/5:1, despite greater employment of blacks in the early years of the decade.

for the duration of periodic contracts. For, with the foundation of the municipalities of Kimberley and Beaconsfield and the advent of piped water, electricity, and solid colonial-style buildings during the mining boom, the social and economic lines were more sharply drawn than in the days of the camps and the diggings. But the workforce was still too itinerant with a base in rural societies to be thought of as a 'proletariat'; and the white minority which depended on mining employment expected special consideration from the company owners, not support in a common cause from a population of transients. If there existed a 'worker consciousness' at Kimberley in 1883, it was to be found in the ranks of a small labour aristocracy on the make.

As regulatory agencies, the mining boards and the companies were jolted into recognizing this growing social division at the workplace. Contracts of service for whites were changed to permit less rigorous inspection of clothing, and not bodies, in return for information on illicit dealing. The mining boards never quite recovered from the opposition to their organization of 'searching-houses' at Kimberley and De Beers; and the companies began to seek a different solution from 1883 through the compounding of black workers.

Before they could finance this kind of social control, they had to prove themselves in the first years of incorporation. Joint-stock limited liability was not an onerous constraint on directors in commercial law in the 1880s, but it exposed their ventures to regular audit, questions from shareholders (many of whom were also claimholders), and the ever-present possibility of litigation with contractors, the mining boards, and the municipalities of Kimberley and Beaconsfield. They were defended by the courts against accusations of misleading prospectuses, when there was a 'rage for shares'; their mining areas were held sacred against the town councils, which could not cut so much as a drain without permission. But they could not escape liability for short-term debts to the banks.[42]

The mining boards had a different function, as semi-public bodies, and served to protect the companies against the full costs of keeping the mines working. With a quarter of all claims covered by fallen ground, the Kimberley board paid out £1.9 million to 1884 to ease the burden on the miners. By then, it had given up paying contractors in cash and had recourse to bills. Many of the smaller companies, in any case, defaulted on their rates, and as the board's bills became overdue, the local banks refused to discount any further. By 1884, the Kimberley board owed

---

[42] *Reports of the Cases Decided in the High Court of Griqualand West*, vol. 1 (1882–83), esp. Frere DMC, 56, Atlas DMC vs. Poole, 27.

£245,885 to creditors, and when the bank of Africa tried to sequestrate properties in the mine, the Griqualand High Court held that normal insolvency laws did not apply. Once more, the Kimberley mining lobby succeeded in passing a special act to legalize the borrowing powers of the boards, without raising rates over a low maximum, and the debt was covered by a government loan.[43]

Companies and boards were favoured too by a lack of company taxation. As a proportion of Griqualand provincial revenues, moneys from licences, sales, and registrations from the biggest industry in the country amounted to no more than 25 per cent—hardly more than in the days of Southey and Lanyon. And a proposed tax on exports was quickly turned down by the 1882 commission. Added to Cape revenues, the contribution of the mining companies was swallowed up at just over 1 per cent, comparable to sales of cheap land and court fines.

The first companies, then, enjoyed a tax-free holiday. They paid heavy duties on imports of stores, machinery, and blasting powder, though there were special concessions for work undertaken for the boards. It is not surprising, therefore, that out of the thirty members of the Kimberley mining board 1882–90, twelve were directors of Kimberley Central and four were diamond dealer-directors. All thirteen members of the De Beers mining board 1883–7, with three exceptions, were directors or employees of DBMC. For the defence of company interests entailed control of the machinery for running the mines. They had won some outstanding legal, as well as political and financial, concessions. They possessed as leasehold or freehold some 126 acres of open-cast mines, reputed to be the richest in the world, along with a variety of private claimholders who were unrepresented on the mining boards. They had access to hundreds of acres of floors on the mine surround under government licence and private rental agreements, to the detriment of other standholders and the municipalities. The fact that Vooruitzigt was legally Crown land made little difference to private ownership of minerals, in the absence of legislation specifying a Crown reserve; and the companies were free to acquire other areas of this estate. The 33,000 acres of the LSAE estates were a different matter. In time, lessees of the company in the two mines would be regarded (as they are referred to in the 1883 Act) as 'owners', though it was also held by the courts that this meant they owned 'the right to dig for and keep the diamonds and precious stones found', and little else.[44]

[43] CPP, G. 107-'83; Act 22 of 1885.
[44] CPP, A. 64-'80; A. 7-'91; LSAE vs. Rouliot, *Cape Times Law Reports*, vol. 1 (1891).

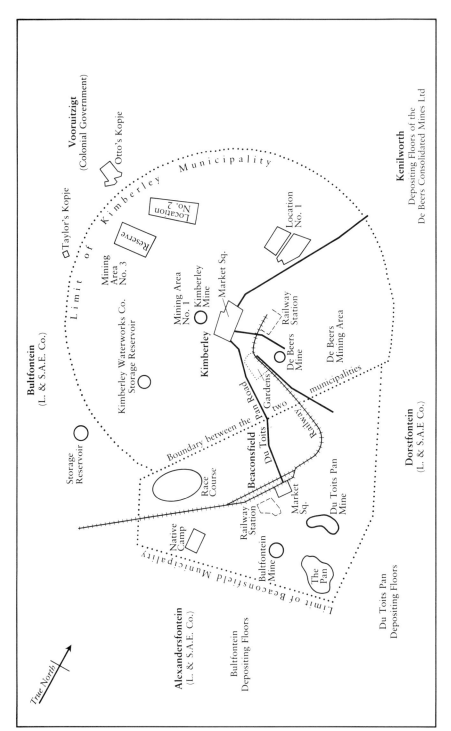

MAP 1. Kimberley: municipalities and mines, 1888

The oligarchy of merchants and company directors who ran the town councils, lobbied the Cape Assembly, and exercised power through the mining boards and the protection board were the true heirs and successors to the minerals licenced by Free State grants on the farms of the diamond fields. The dramatic period 1877–83 marked a transition from ownership by claims to ownership as a state or land company concession, without, however, disturbing the indefeasible right of claimholders turned mine-owners to the possession of precious stones. On this basis, merchants and miners were socially and economically structured in a dominant hierarchy which outgrew the rules and regulations made for the diggings a decade earlier which the 1882 commission set about removing because:

The anomalies arising from this development meet us at every turn. The wealthy capitalist who has a quarter of a million invested in the mine, is still called a digger; while the property from which he draws his wealth is still supposed to be marked out into arbitrary divisions called claims, each of which, though it may be worth ten thousand pounds, is of the same size, goes by the same name, and pays the same licence as the little patch of gravel on the river side, which was possibly not worth ten shillings.[45]

The courts had undone attempts to reserve minerals to the Crown; expropriation was ruled out in 1875; titles on the Vooruitzigt estate were carefully guaranteed by other legislation in 1879, as a basis for company formation. On all important counts the oligarchs who replaced the diggers had triumphed. The barons were strong where the Crown was weak. As a preliminary to cutting costs and restructuring their fiefs, they turned their attention to closer management of the serfs.

[45] CPP, G. 86-'82.

3

Company Consolidation

THE decade of exploitation by joint stock and private companies in the 1880s began with a multitude of entrepreneurial ventures and ended with the dominance of one firm, De Beers Consolidated Mines Ltd. Scores of corporate holdings and small partnerships were winnowed and sifted by failure, merger, and competitive success. In 1885, half-way through this process, all four mines still had forty-two companies and fifty-six private claimholdings.[1] But already in the De Beers and Kimberley mines a handful of firms possessed much of the workable ground, and the pattern of consolidation was firmly established.

Interpretation of the reasons for this relative progression have been strong on biography and weak on business history, focusing on rival personalities engaged in the share 'battles' of the late 1880s, when De Beers Mining began to acquire Kimberley Central, but neglected the production records and debt financing essential to company growth. This approach has been challenged by more detailed exploration of the conditions of labour management, state legislation, and company investment in industrial technology, though it is not always demonstrated precisely how some companies rather than others improved on this conjunction of social, political, and financial factors. One extension of the argument of control of the means of production by a few dominant men is to regard the whole decade as a purposeful capitalist contest which prefaced the main event—the organization of all the diamond and gold industries under monopolies by an assault on the working class. Ironically, this interpretation is reinforced by the excellence of some of the older works by S. Herbert Frankel and others on capital investment in South Africa which treated diamond discoveries as a miraculous source of internally-generated funds, attractive to overseas financiers, without explaining how the most successful company managed such resources

---

[1] Reunert, 'Diamond Mining at the Cape', 41–2; and for other estimates, CPP, G. 27.-'82, 35; cf. Paul Emden, *Randlords* (London, 1935), 225.

'from within itself'.[2] The only common feature of the historiography is the seeming inevitability of the outcome.

The first technical studies of diamond mining in the Kimberley area were less sure who would win, though they strongly advocated concentration of effort through company mergers. Theodore Reunert and Gardner F. Williams, while informative on the geological and economic reasons for technological change, pass quickly in their standard works over the turbulent transition period that drew them to Kimberley, without an analysis of the herculean task of amalgamation. For them, the figure of Rhodes was Hercules enough. Even those few who have looked to marketing, rather than production, for their main theme are equally brief on the implications of merchant participation from the demand side for management and debt financing, also looking to the character of Rhodes as the 'personification' of 'centralisation', in their prefaces to the later history of the diamond trade.[3]

The approach adopted here is closer to the technical studies and the labour historians than to the biographers, but looks to the comparative performance of the companies for an explanation of consolidation, rather than single factors of production. In the last count, the historical explanation must rest on these factors in combination within each mine, before some of the busy entrepreneurs of the 1880s became 'monopoly' magnates.

It is easy, however, to be influenced by the outcome of the story in entrepreneurial studies, when the winner takes all and the losers are relegated to the archives. But it is important to recognize that the late 1870s and 1880s in Kimberley saw the formation of a pool of talented and ruthless miners, merchants, and politicians whose functions overlapped and who were no more destined, as individuals, to succeed than the diggers who had tried their luck a decade earlier. One can be certain, however, that those who had the direction of small companies and partnerships

[2] Esp. Chilvers; and the biographies in Geoffrey Wheatcroft, *The Randlords: The Men who Made South Africa* (London, 1985), 92–110; R. Turrell, 'Rhodes, De Beers, and Monopoly', *Journal of Imperial and Commonwealth History*, 10/3 (1982), 311–45; Turrell, *Capital and Labour*, ch. 10 for a different 'structuralist' analysis; Worger, 'Workers as Criminals', 51–90; Duncan Innes, *Anglo: Anglo American and the Rise of Modern South Africa* (Johannesburg, 1984), 21–44; Frankel, *Capital Investment*, 52–9, 61–3. I am grateful for the permission of the President and Fellows of Harvard College and the editors of *Business History Review* to revise and reproduce material which appeared originally in 'Technology, Capital and Consolidation: The Performance of De Beers Mining Company Limited, 1880–1889', *Business History Review*, 61/1 (1987), 1–42.

[3] Reunert, *Diamonds and Gold*; Williams, *The Diamond Mines of South Africa*; Wagner, *The Diamond Fields of South Africa*; and cf. Gardner F. Williams, 'The Diamond Mines of South Africa', *Transactions of the American Institute of Mining Engineers*, 15 (1887), 392–417; and the inspector of mines W. C. C. Erskine in CPP, G. 34-'83; Lenzen.

by 1883 had secured the basis for production at low rent, in their titles to land and claims, and they were favoured by a steady labour supply which was cheap at unit cost and subject to controls designed to reduce theft. They were also favoured by an overseas demand for diamonds and an evolving marketing structure which could handle the volume and variety of South African stones. Those who effectively managed the De Beers and Kimberley mining boards, the protection board, and the miners' union were set fair to deciding the ways in which capital could be applied to production in larger and more efficient units. The same conditions did not apply, however, to Dutoitspan and Bultfontein, where the ground landlords in the shape of the LSAE lived on their rents and were a power to be reckoned with.

WINNERS AND LOSERS

Companies in the two sets of mines were also differentiated by the ways in which they weathered the short recession in diamond prices after 1882. Much has been made of this set-back in accounting for the takeover of the financially weak by the strong in the early phase of amalgamations up to 1885, when there was a recovery in both price and volume. The general pattern of mergers in the mines, unfortunately, does not support such a simple explanation, because the majority of company purchases were spread over the whole period in De Beers, and were 'bunched' towards the end of the decade in Kimberley mine.[4] Secondly, prices and yields were extremely varied in the mines, and generalizations about returns to companies from annual 'averages' or from aggregates of production are open to the objection that some firms remained well above average, while quite large ones, such as Kimberley Central, suffered from other financial disabilities which allowed only one take-over, 1882–4, while DBMC acquired four smaller firms in that period.

Why some companies made the progress they did, measured in quite conventional terms of investment and profitability, must be explained before the larger question of consolidation strategies can be answered. And the most fundamental factors which help to account for company

---

[4] Cf. Worger, 'Workers' 73, 78, for a 'collapse' of the European diamond market; Turrell, *Capital and Labour*, ch. 7 for a different view of 'profits'; and Innes, 34–5, where the wrong date is given to the recession. Basically, there is a failure to consider the volume traded at this period and relative performance by companies in conditions of restricted credit and a fall in commodity prices resulting in 1,102 insolvencies at the Cape in 1883 and 842 in 1884: DUSC, 13, Consul Siler, 23 Jan. 1885; Mabin and Conradie, 110, 123, 161.

performance lay in the physical topography and the technology applied in the four mines. Kimberley and De Beers had the advantage of richer claims and the penalty of deeper levels than the shallower and broader workings of Dutoitspan and Bultfontein in the 1880s. In the latter quarries, small claims actually increased in numbers as the mine areas expanded. Many of these were not worked, because of reef falls, as the shallow mines went down to the 300 and 400 feet level from 1885. Altogether Dutoitspan and Bultfontein, on average, accounted for some 45.6 per cent by weight and 46.5 per cent by value of the output of the Kimberley group in the 1880s. In the two deeper mines companies concentrated on the areas of richest yield, producing over 50 per cent of diamonds by weight and value.

More significantly, the relative output of the two leaders changed markedly, as De Beers mine production expanded from a modest 16.4 per cent of the group's total output to just over a third in both value and volume, as Kimberley's early domination vanished under reef falls. On the whole, there was little reason to suppose that companies in De Beers mine would lead moves towards group amalgamation from the early 1880s. But there was every reason to suppose that the lead would be given from somewhere in the two deepest mines, rather than in the less profitable quarries on inferior ground burdened with the heavier claim licences extracted by the LSAE.

Consequently, much turned on company management and performance within these two mines. In Kimberley mine, the advantage of higher carat yields per load was considerably offset by the need to haul greater quantities of dead ground, and the percentage of diamondiferous blue in total haulage and excavation was much lower than in De Beers. In short, it cost the mining board and the Kimberley companies about twice the financial effort to recover a decreasing quantity of carats, before 1886, while the De Beers companies wasted less money, machinery, and manpower on dead ground in return for a rising carat yield. A more detailed picture of this advantage can be grasped from the production series of DBMC which operated in richer ground than the average and managed to haul some 50 per cent of blue ground in total excavation work till 1888, when the company ceased hauling any unprofitable surface reef at all.

Compared with other companies and particularly with its principal rival, Kimberley Central, De Beers Mining paid close attention to comparative costs and yields in board minutes from 1883. The directors concluded that although they had a higher percentage of working expenses to carat yield than some other companies, they were in richer claims and could afford the difference, provided contractors' charges and direct labour costs

ILL. 3. Open surface workings, Kimberley mine, 1886

for basic operations were reduced.[5] Their investigation of comparative performance throughout the mine was made, moreover, at the critical period of white labour resistance to the searching rules enforced through the detective department, and at a period of heavy investment in hauling and washing machinery to clear reef and improve recovery rates from processing blue clay left to weather on the floors. Both of these factors— labour management and mechanization—featured too in reports and debates within the mining board, and surfaced more publicly in the reports of the mining inspectors and at annual shareholders' meetings. They were coupled, moreover, with two specific aspects of labour control and mechanization common to both of the deeper mines: namely provision of barracks and compounds to check IDB, and the extension of operations underground. In the case of DBMC, the board decisions to compound black workers and invest in shafts were made in May 1884, immediately after the climax of white labour unrest.[6]

There was more to labour management, however, than simply deciding to house workers at company expense in order to force the searching regulations on the bulk of the workforce. In practice, DBMC had not been dissatisfied with the system as it operated in the 'searching-houses' set up in March 1883 for the examination of labourers coming off the work sites in the pits and on the floors. Monthly 'finds' suddenly increased to some 7,000 carats (about £75,000), brought forward by men who would no longer risk smuggling stones out of the mine area. Undoubtedly more finds were not reported—just how much more was a matter for speculation, ranging from 12 to 30 per cent of total production. But other companies in the mine and in Kimberley decided to take over responsibility from the detective department by centralizing the numerous camps, yards, stores, and 'kaffir houses' already used for resident workers.[7]

The DBMC board was willing enough to follow, because of the need to overhaul the contract system in 1884 in which almost all operations for hauling were tendered out to private contractors or to company employees from the ranks of the overseers. Work was performed at piece rates, and the labour was either supplied from the company's general workforce or brought in from outside. After the end of the strike in April, DBMC recontracted only 80 of their 200 white workers, and the company

---

[5] DBMC, *Annual Report* (1883), 10–12; DBCA, DBMC/2, minutes, 7 May 1883.

[6] DBCA, DBMC/2, minutes, 7 May 1884; BPMI/2.

[7] DBCA, DBMC/3, minutes, 3 and 5 Nov. 1884, 20 Jan., 4 and 11 Aug. 1885; 26 Apr., 5 May, 1886 (for estimates of expenses for convicts); see too Smalberger, 'IDB and the Mining Compound System in the 1880s', 398–414; Van der Horst; Turrell, *Capital and Labour*, ch. 8; and for estimates of IDB see Gardner F. Williams, 'The Diamond Mines of South Africa', 410–12 with analysis of recovery weights.

took the opportunity to try to end a separate costly and long-standing dispute by enforcing minimum loads at new contracted rates for piece work. Henceforth, for hauling to the floors at 2s. per load, the minimum was raised to at least 1,000 loads per day. Recovery rates improved; working costs in terms of labour charges declined; and the production costs per load of 16 cubic feet of blue clay fell from 10s. to 8s. and remained there for the next 3 years. There was also a temporary fall in weekly wages for black and white workers 1883–5, which was general throughout the mines.[8] But the essential feature of the new contract system was that all labour was supplied through the company to end the presence of casual outsiders.

Furthermore, to keep contractors' labour out of the critical area of theft at the final recovery stages of diamonds, when concentrates were washed and sorted, DBMC turned to convict labour through the good offices of the civil commissioner, E. A. Judge, and his minister, John Merriman. Supplies of convicts were irregular at first, no more than 200 annually, after a compound for them was constructed in 1884, and the company paid for rations, clothing, guards, and a visiting magistrate. Dearer per man than 'free' compound labour, convicts were employed uniquely in the most sensitive areas of the floors and washing sites, and their extra cost was repeatedly justified in terms of the prevention of IDB.

Following these changes, there was no hesitation in investing in compounds for the rest of the African workforce, after a lead was given by Kimberley Central and the French Company from January 1885. DBMC constructed two new central compounds that year, as amalgamations continued and more labour was taken over from other companies. They were not enclosed till the following year, but residence was compulsory for periods of 2 months, and later this was lengthened to the whole period of the contract. Access to the mine sites from the compounds was strictly controlled by a member of the detective department, appointed as compound manager; and labour for contractors was supplied only from this source.

The compounds attracted a good deal of attention from contemporary critics who saw in them a system of company 'truck' which denied labour its spending power in the canteens and stores, thereby reducing the retail trade of Kimberley's commercial sector. And they have been regarded by historians since then as symbols of a rigorously-controlled industrial system. In fact, they took some years to become established, and there

---

[8] DBMC records show a rising production per working day in early *Annual Reports* to 1,300 loads by 1884/5 in blue ground and 1,349 for reef. By 1888, the company, after mergers, was producing 3,000 loads of blue and no dead ground per day.

were still many smaller locations on the mine sites for surface and other workers. Their facilities—baths, hospitals, and shops—were approved by company boards only towards the end of 1886, when enclosure by fences and overhead netting was completed. With a few exceptions, companies provided no free rations. Beer was allowed, but no spirits, at least in theory. (There were complaints that Cape brandy and wine had been introduced into De Beers West End compound at Christmas 1886). Only then, too, were regulations tightened up to exclude strangers and to refuse numerous permits to attend funerals, when these rites developed into a clandestine market.[9] By then, DBMC had appointed a medical officer, less as a preventive measure than as a way of investigating an immediate problem of deaths from dynamite fumes in the mine.

Opposition to the compounds from the Kimberley Chamber of Commerce and the Cape Assembly was countered by public meetings with representatives of the protection board and the miners' (employers') union, led by Rhodes and Baring-Gould. A compromise which ensured purchase of compound stores from local wholesalers and deferred any similar control of white workers was embodied in legislation on the truck system. A new commission was appointed to look into the working of the Diamond Trade Act and the incarceration of workers. But the system was not really in doubt. For, as a member of the miners' union concluded: 'the Compounds and the Diamond Trade Act, as it stood, went hand in hand'.[10]

That double purpose has sometimes been lost from sight by defenders and critics. In the rather benign view of the inspector of mines the extension of the closed compound system to other mines by 1887 resulted in great park-like areas where

The Kafir labourers are lodged in comfortable, clean, and well-aired dormitories; food and clothing and smaller necessaries are supplied at a regular tariff within the compound to any employé who chooses to purchase at these stores. Employés are not compelled however to purchase within the compound if they prefer buying in the town. Neither clothing or food is given in lieu of wages or on account of wages due; the wages are all paid in cash, and any food, clothing, or other articles purchased in the compound stores must be paid for in cash. Swimming baths, hospitals, and recreation and instruction rooms are all provided, and medical attendance and medicine are supplied free.[11]

---

[9] DBCA, DBMC/3, minutes, 11 Jan. 1887. There were some free rations at Bultfontein and Dutoitspan, for example. For later evidence of conditions in the compounds, see below, ch. 4.

[10] DBCA, BPMI/3, A. W. Davis (member for Bultfontein mine); and BPMI/1 for minutes of meetings; Act 23, 1887 (Labourers Wages Regulation); CPP, G. 3-'88 (Diamond Laws Commission).

[11] CPP, G. 28-'88, W. C. C. Erskine, 14.

ILL. 4. An early labour compound (1885?): enclosed but without overhead netting

Unlike the De Beers and Kimberley compounds, where labour at the end of contract was purged of any swallowed diamonds in a detention room, Dutoitspan and Bultfontein still had searching-rooms run by each company. There is some evidence that compounding may have lengthened the average contract period in the Kimberley mine, where companies undertook to pay labourers' fees for pass registration. But the annual recruitment rates suggest that labour turnover was still high in the 1880s. Certainly there was no shortage of workers.

A different judgement on the compounds can be made, however, in conjunction with the increased stringency of police action from 1883, when there was a dramatic rise in arrests and summary convictions.[12]

---

[12] Worger, 74-8; and more generally, Turrell, 'Kimberley'. It is to be noted, however, that arrests declined steadily after 1886 from over 16,000 to under 5,000 a year, and the police force was reduced when most locations were closed at Kimberley until 1904; CPP, Police Commissioner's reports (1886–90). There was a rise in return passes and labour turnover, before further reductions in the early 1890s in the recruitment of mining labour: see Table 1.1.; Cape of Good Hope, *Census, 1891* (Cape Town, 1892); *Census, 1904* (Cape Town, 1905). Not all later registrations were for mining labour: cf. Turrell, *Capital and Labour*, 167–8, where the evidence for recontracting in the statistics to 1885 is extended to the statement that 'most' Africans were recontracted later in the decade.

This may have been a way of encouraging 'old hands' to re-recruit, though most convictions seem to have been for breaches of the peace and drunkenness, rather than breaches of the Masters and Servants regulations. For those who lingered in Kimberley gaol, after Lanyon's 'reforms', recompounding may have looked like a welcome release. On the other hand, there is no evidence that employers used the compound system to reduce wages, which rose from weekly averages of 25*s*. to 30*s*. for African labourers 1885–9; and it is doubtful whether periods of contract lengthened much beyond the usual 2 to 3 months.[13] It is equally difficult at this early period to attribute high death rates to the compounds in the absence of general and specific morbidity and mortality rates for disease in the 1880s.[14] Moreover, the idea of using compounded Africans for labour substitution, or 'deskilling', does not stand up against close examination of the white to black ratios for surface and underground work from 1883.

What is more certain is that the compounds were used immediately to provide a ready supply of on-site labour, especially for underground workings, which took about half the daily averages in the case of DBMC, as a result of the changes in the contract system, as outlined by the De Beers Mining general manager in 1888:

Nearly all the underground work is done under the contract system. Contracts are given to experienced miners at set prices per foot or per load. The average number of white men employed in the mine is 214, and the number of natives is 1,350. The Company provides the native labourers who are paid by the contractors. In order to insure a constant supply of labourers we have increased the accommodations of the compounds, so that at the present time we have 2,300 in the West End Compound, which covers about five acres of ground. Within this area the natives are confined during their time of service and closely guarded so as to materially reduce the stealing of diamonds. Too much cannot be said of the advantages of the compound system. By it we are able to keep a constant supply of labourers. No alcoholic liquors are allowed inside the Compound, and the natives are consequently always fit for work, a great contrast to those who are allowed their freedom. Our natives are better housed and better fed than the uncompounded natives, and are better paid than the miners in many of the European countries. Those unfit for work either through sickness or an account of injuries received in the Mine are taken care of free of cost in the Company's

[13] Detailed records for workers' contract periods do not exist for the 1880s; but see DBMC, *Annual Reports* (1888, 1889); and especially DBCA, DBMC/6 (general manager's letter-book, 1887–8).

[14] Turrell, 'Kimberley', 58–9, 65–6. DBCA, DBMC/3 for short reports by Dr Otto on compound mortality and Kimberley hospital mortality. General mortality rates for males were probably very high in the 1880s in Kimberley district at over 90/1,000, according to the earliest district health reports and crude population estimates. See too Fig. 4 below.

ILL. 5. Kimberley Central DMC: first outside shaft, 1884

hospital, which adjoins the Compound. There are fewer accidents under the present system than there were in the open workings. A very large majority of the accidents are due either to the carelessness or the stupidity of the natives themselves. A large percentage of the deaths in the Compounds has been caused by receiving natives who come in companies from the countries north of the Transvaal, many of them so starved and emaciated as to be beyond help.[15]

In time, other evidence would wear some of the complacent gloss off this statement. In one respect, it was grimly contradicted by an underground fire later in the year. But the main intention was clear enough, and just as it had been in 1884: the compound system was to control IDB and avoid using outside labour for the contractors, just as no outside labour substituted for De Beers Mining convicts on the floors. Incarceration made a vice out of a necessity.

The spread of contracting into underground work was the second major decision taken by De Beers and Kimberley companies in 1884, because

---

[15] DBMC, *Annual Report* (1888), Gardner F. Williams, 11.

excavation work in both mines had passed the point where open quarrying could be carried on without continuous falls of reef. Their deepest claims at 300 to 500 feet lay in pits which merged at the upper levels into the sloping sides of a crater of debris and bituminous shales, dangerously cut back, precipitous, and very expensive to remove. The effort had led to bankruptcy of the Kimberley mining board. The earliest attempt at underground working by a vertical shaft from claim 320, owned by Kimberley Central, was buried by reef in September 1884.

Both mines had also reached the layers of hard rock surrounding the diamond pipes. Opinions were divided on the strength of this rock wall if it were to be exposed by excavation from within the mine, but they were unanimous on the difficulty and cost of drilling shafts outside the mine perimeter and tunnelling into the blue at the current stage of local mining technology. The French Company and Kimberley Central experimented with two outside shafts on the north and south sides of the Kimberley mine, using drifts to remove shales just above the rock surround, in an effort to cut back the dangerous overhang above their claims. At great expense they continued this system vertically into the hard rock outside the mine and began to cut horizontal tunnels to join up with a second system of vertical shafts sunk from the mine interior. There were six of these worked by different companies when Gardner Williams visited the mine in 1885. Unlike the outside shafts, they were all constructed at relatively little cost by burrowing downwards 'on the "coffer-dam" principle of gradually lowering a square timber box, through the loose stuff, shovelling out the reef from the inside, and fixing on box after box, till it had sunk right through the bottom of the fallen reef, forming a strong timbered shaft'.[16] Once into the blue, this simple application of imported technology by the engineer Edward Jones paid its way by hauling out diamondiferous ground.

In his later published work, Williams dismissed much of the innovation in a few lines, before devoting many pages to his own 'systematic mining'. But in his earlier published commentary of 1886, he had perceived, more generously, that the 'Jones system' and the outside shafts which led to underground 'chambering' of the blue were a product of improvisation, designed to maximize production, because of the high cost of imported Baltic and American timbers.[17] Consequently, the companies with tunnels under their claims resorted to stopes, or breasts, every thirty feet, leaving pillars 12 feet thick, as these chambers were carried upwards to another

[16] Reunert, 'Diamond Mining at the Cape', 198.
[17] Gardner F. Williams, 'The Diamond Mines of South Africa', 402.

tunnel and the blue ground was removed through the main shaft. At a critical point, the 'pillars' were judged to have been 'so much weakened as to be unsafe for further working' and were blasted out, causing the mass between the two levels to cave in and feed the shaft with further loads.[18] There were other perilous variations on this technique of 'overhead stoping' which entailed opening the chambers to loose shale, as fast as the blue was removed. In the De Beers mine, a similar 'Jones system' was applied through five shafts in the central claims. Victoria DMC ventured to sink an outside shaft and a drift into its two claims in 1885. De Beers Mining started a very original circular shaft through the rock well outside the northern perimeter, but abandoned it for an incline shaft on the western margin which drove through softer shales and basalt and into the claims at 200 feet. The same honeycomb of chambers and pillars kept the endless lines of tubs filled and moving up the incline.

This unprecedented adaptation of Continental and Cornish mining techniques to the excavation of diamonds from deep underground was ingenious, rapid, and economically sounder than trying to remove surface reef and shales. The policy was applied more single-mindedly in De Beers than in Kimberley. For in the latter mine the Central company tried to maintain two systems from the outside and the surface interior, with the result that overhangs at the 500 and 600 feet levels gradually caved in giving rise in November 1888 'to the greatest fall of reef which has ever taken place in Kimberley' and covering three-quarters of the excavations; 'waggons, the haulageways, the foundations of the hauling machinery, nearly all came down with the reef'.[19] These techniques had been condemned by the mining inspector by 1889. They were totally abandoned in Kimberley mine, in favour of the incline and underground shafts pioneered within the De Beers claims.

The advance underground, therefore, gave the De Beers companies a considerable edge over their rivals. There were other factors too which had a bearing on their profitability and their competition for control of the claims.

First, it was assumed by early company directors that cheaper fuel, machinery, explosives, and supplies of water would lead to more efficient exploitation of the mines. Despite fairly low working costs for these items in the accounts before 1885–no more than 17 per cent compared with

---

[18] Reunert, 'Diamond Mining at the Cape', 199–201; Gardner F. Williams, 'The Diamond Mines of South Africa', 403.

[19] E. Boutan, 'On the Actual State of the Cape Diamond Mines', *South Africa*, 30 Mar. 1889; CPP, G. 11-'90. For the open workings, see ill. 3 above.

50 per cent for wages and salaries—there was an enormous devotion to improving sources of energy and transportation.[20] Costly and scarce fuel was seen as the major obstacle to mechanization. And at the Cape, Rhodes and Merriman speeded through a bill to extend the railway system to Hopetown and beyond. Indeed Rhodes, as government treasurer, would have taxed the mining industry to pay for completion. But a loan from the imperial government removed the need for this politically risky sacrifice, and the last 24 miles to Kimberley and the 'North' were opened for traffic in November 1885. The diamond fields became a customer for British coal delivered from the Cape at £6. 5s. a ton and for Indwe coal at cheaper rates and less steam-power. The result was a dramatic rise in machinery imports for 'mining and sawing' from £24,000 in 1885 to nearly £200,000 by 1888. In company accounts the lists of pumping engines, winding engines, boilers, headgear, and pitwork from London, Durham, and Cornwall grew longer, together with investment in machine shops, locomotives, tramways, and artisans to service the hardware of industry.

But the tools of this investment were frequently idle, and much was written off to join the vast graveyard of industrial dinosaurs in the mine area, as improved machines replaced older models, and wood-burning gave way to coal and electricity. There was, therefore, a startling regression in the levels of mining mechanization at Kimberley, as measured by the numbers of machines and their nominal horsepower (Table 3.1). Also at this period of the 1880s, there is an equally surprising increase in the ratio of daily averages of hand labour to the number and power of machines employed. It is true that the horsepower rating of the average machine rose from about 11 to 15. But this does not account for the disparities between mines engaged in surface and underground working, and those producing solely from surface claims. Compared with the highly-mechanized Dutoitspan, the De Beers mine was underpowered with only half the engines; and Kimberley mine was little better until late in the decade, when it rated the highest nominal horsepower on the fields and suffered the greatest disasters from reef falls.

The explanation for this absence of correlation between production and machinery may lie, quite simply, in an enormous wastage, financed from high levels of gross profits, and in duplication of effort by the numerous companies of the early 1880s. It would be inaccurate, therefore,

[20] DBCA, DBMC/2 and KCDMC, 1881-3; RH, Baxter [transcripts], 106, Rhodes to Merriman, 16 May 1880. For the railway see A. J. Purkis, 'The Politics, Capital and Labour of Railway-Building in the Cape Colony, 1870–1885' D.Phil. thesis (Oxford, 1978), ch. 5, esp. p. 255; Cape of Good Hope, *Statistical Register* (1888–9).

TABLE 3.1. *Mechanization, power, and labour ratios, 1882–1889*

Year	Kimberley	De Beers	Dutoitspan	Bultfontein	Totals
1882					
Engines	96	65	133	82	376
Nominal hp	1,252	641	1,343	798	4,032
Engines/labourers (daily averages)	1:50	1:35	1:27	1:36	
1884					
Engines	81	61	122	72	336
Nominal hp	1,015	639	1,266	714	3,634
Engines/labourers (daily averages)	1:22	1:32	1:30	1:38	
1887					
Engines	39	22	69	33	163
Nominal hp	640	355	889	554	2,439
Engines/labourers (daily averages)	1:83	1:159	1:52	1:86	
1889					
Engines	29	15	29	3	89
Nominal hp	609	375	386	157	1,592
Engines/labourers (daily averages)	1:91	1:180	1:74	1:202	

Sources: CPP, inspector of mines reports (1882–9) [machinery totals not given every year]; *Statistical Register of the Cape of Good Hope* (1882–9); Williams, 'The Diamond Mines of South Africa', *Transactions of the American Institute of Mining Engineers*, 15 (1887), 392–417. Both black and white workers, overseers and mechanics, are included in the daily averages on which the totals are based.

to regard diamond mining as 'capital-intensive' at this stage of development, bearing in mind the continuation, indeed the increase, in the labour force till 1887 and 1888, when there was some reduction of daily averages. At a more humble level of 'prime movers', the use of hand labour in a partially mechanized industry was paralleled by the continued employment of thousands of horses, mules, and oxen in the daily operations of companies which experimented with technology, but relied on more elementary inputs to make it work.

Like fuel, water was also seen as a vital requirement for raising steam and for washing the conglomerate at the recovery stage of production. Some of this could be supplied, as it always had, by pumping the claims free of natural drainage; but more had to come from the Vaal and the Kimberley Waterworks Company set up by Thomas Lynch in 1881. This enterprise grew out of a defunct railway project to take diamondiferous ground to be washed and sorted at the river and was applied, instead, to remedying the frequent shortage and lack of purity in a municipal supply 'saturated with dead cats, Kafirs, or dogs'.[21] The water monopoly provided the supply through 17 miles of pipe at 1*s*. 3*d*. per 100 gallons, mainly to the mines which doubled their total consumption 1884–7 to some 200 million gallons a year. As the companies consolidated, De Beers Mining purchased a concession of its own from a Beaconsfield water company and arranged for legislation in 1888 to sanction this new supply. The Kimberley Waterworks Company came to terms by purchasing the new concession from De Beers for £10,000, by reducing the price to 8*d*. per 100 gallons, and by obtaining a monopoly for at least 25 years.

Compared with the politics of transport and water, the labour supply required little new legislation and was taken for granted. All the companies were careless of life and limb in their failure to enforce safety regulations on the contractors. Dangerous storage of explosives and accidents from 'abuse of dynamite' were frequently criticized by mining inspectors, but there were few prosecutions for negligence.[22] As had been foreseen, sixteen dynamite magazines in the south-east corner of the De Beers mining area exploded in January 1884 at a cost of £17,000 and three African labourers, but no enquiry was ever held. In the worst disaster of the period, a fire at De Beers Mining's no. 1 shaft in 1888 killed at least 24 whites and 178 blacks, because of limited ventilation and lack of escape shafts. The company was not exonerated by a cursory official enquiry, but it was not prosecuted either.[23]

Such events were the more spectacular episodes in a longer and mundane catalogue of industrial accidents which were part of the price paid for rapid development. The partial records of the 1880s indicate a general upward trend in accidents and deaths at all mines both absolutely and as a percentage of black and white labour employed (Fig. 2). The mean rate for three mines is remarkably consistent, suggesting common causes, while that for Bultfontein is lower, because it is incomplete, and labour was laid off at the end of the period. The comparison also indicates that underground working was not the principal cause of this overall increase in fatalities: reef falls remained the biggest single cause of all accidents, until mining went underground at De Beers from 1888. Even so, surface

---

[21] Roberts, *Kimberley*, 190. Act 12, 1880 (Kimberley Waterworks Company); CPP, C. 4-'88; A. 4-1906.

[22] CPP, G. 28-'88, (inspector of explosives).

[23] CPP, G. 66-'88; cf. Boutan in *South Africa*, 13 Apr. 1889, for a different account of the fire at 'Friggin's shaft' starting in an underground engine room killing 42 whites and 360–80 blacks.

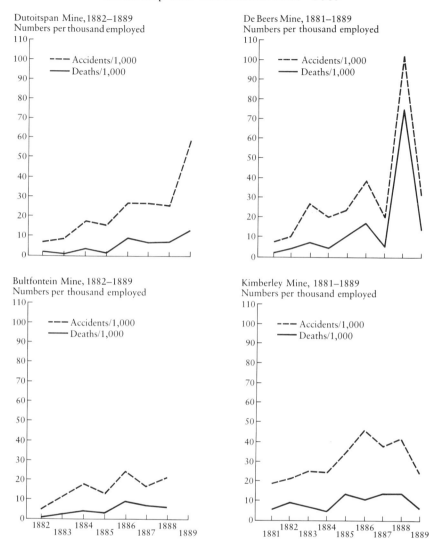

FIG. 2. Accidents and deaths in Kimberley mines, 1881–1889

workers still made up well over a third of the average daily totals at De Beers and Kimberley and all the workers at Dutoitspan and Bultfontein, where there was a high percentage of accidents from machinery on open sites. The mortality rates, moreover, take no account of diseases contracted at the compounds. The general impression is one of haste and improvisation to raise contractors' production rates, while labour received flat rates

ILL. 6. Fire at De Beers no. 1 shaft, 12 July 1888

of pay, at this time, and ran greater risks from lack of training and supervision as the mines deepened.

The picture of reckless and costly progress is confirmed by an application of the labour records to the hauling and washing records for the Kimberley and De Beers mines so as to yield a crude index of 'efficiency' in terms of man/days and production.[24] It would seem that more loads were hauled and washed at the rate of about 5 per man/day in De Beers than in the Kimberley mine which had a rate of 3.5 in the early 1880s, when much time and energy was devoted to reef clearance. The problem did not entirely disappear. But it is surprising that greater mechanization did not improve labour efficiency, which declined slightly at De Beers to

[24] An estimate of labour productivity is hampered by lack of a data on the allocation of work time by contractors to different mining operations. Some labour was also allocated by the company to machine shops and other surface tasks. DBMC records indicate a working year of 280 to 300 days, and the mean has been used as a basis for estimates of man/days in conjunction with the annual averages of workers employed. Rates for Dutoitspan and Bultfontein 1884–5, when there were very full data, yield 3.8 and 3.2 loads per man/day, suggesting efficiency comparable with the deeper mines'.

4 loads per man/day and to 2.5 loads in Kimberley mine in the late 1880s. The downward trend is confirmed, moreover, by the first detailed report on mining operations for DBMC, 1887–8, which yields a rate of 3.9 loads for all hauling and washing; and this fell still further, after amalgamation with Kimberley mine, to just over 2 loads in the first full working year of De Beers Consolidated Mines. The companies could claim, with some reason, that they had increased the amount of diamondiferous ground at lower cost. But they had done so not through any great advance in the application of scientific knowledge to the means of production, but by utilizing larger numbers of hand labourers within the contract system which speeded up the process of excavation.

This mixture of imperfect technology and expanded labour, nevertheless, achieved results which are reflected in the companies' indexes of production, yields, costs, and profits.[25] Two points were important for merger strategies in the mines. Loads of blue ground accumulated on the floors were part of a deliberate policy to render the conglomerate more friable. The total accumulation of part-processed 'stock' also became a valuable asset, a source of 'capital' for mergers, a reserve listed at cost of production, and a factor influencing the amount of diamonds available at short notice for merchant buyers. Secondly, company dependence on local buyers was emphasized by the 1882 Diamond Trading Act, which limited sale by corporations, a provision not changed till the Act was amended in 1887. In the interval, only very small percentages of diamond production were forwarded to the London market directly by the companies. De Beers Mining used the banks for shipping some of their stock to Rudd and Co., their director's agency at Queen Victoria Street, leaving the responsibility for clearing this export to London directors. But like its rivals, the company came to rely on a select group of buyers acting for the London merchants with an interest in the mines.

The sales ledgers of DBMC confirm the evidence of the trade directories that there was a steady reduction in the numbers of this group. Of the seventy-nine buyers recorded, 1881–7, only seven bought diamonds every year, and they took the largest purchases by volume.[26] The remainder made only occasional purchases and were gradually eliminated from the company's sights. By 1886, all of the annual sights (sales of diamond assortments) were for twenty-nine buyers, most of whom had been in

---

[25] These results are discussed in greater detail in Newbury, 'Technology, Capital and Consolidation', 12–16.
[26] Ibid., 26.

TABLE 3.2. *Buyers, principals, and sales by De Beers Mining Company, November 1881–1886*

Recorded buyers	Carats	Principals	% of total sales
F. T. Gervers	109,022		
F. W. Felkin	76,348	F. T. Gervers	15.4
D. Symonds	123,392		
C. and A. Moses	37,366	Barnato Bros.	13.5
A. Beit	122,164		
J. Wernher	11,675	Jules Porges & Co.	11.0
S. Neumann	64,018		
[M. Michaelis][a]	38,400	Martin Lilienfeld & Co.	8.6
B. Lewis	65,950		
I. Lewis	15,854	Lewis & Marks Snr. 6.9	8.3
J. Lewis	16,459	Lewis & Marks Jnr. 1.4	
W. Dettlebach	67,243	W. Dettlebach	5.7
P. Dreyfus	41,458	Mosenthal, Sons & Co.	
I. Dreyfus	17,212	T. Dreyfus Ltd.[b]	4.9
Woolf Joel	35,111		
Barnato Bros.	5,121	Barnato Bros.	3.4
H. Abrahams	21,933		
N. Abrahams	2,235	J. Walter, J. & A. Abrahams	1.9
G. Imroth	21,761	[A. Dunkelsbuhler ?]	1.8
M. Joseph	3,843		
H. Joseph	12,742	Joseph Bros.	1.4
J. E. Abrahams	15,703	A. Dunkelsbuhler	1.3

In all total sales = 1,188,456 carats. Sales to these recorded buyers at Kimberley represent 77.2% of total sales by DBMC at Kimberley and in London, 1881–86.

[a] Michaelis probably bought for Wernher and Porges, though he partnered S. Neumann, who bought for Lilienfeld.

[b] It is not certain when T. Dreyfus was established in London to take purchases from P. and I. Dreyfus.

Source: DBCA, DBMC/11, 15.

the game since the late 1870s, and whose purchases were destined for about a dozen London houses (Table 3.2). A related trend was towards larger weights in the size of parcels. By the same date, lots of 5,000 and 6,000 carats were quite common, and parcels as heavy as 10,000 to 11,000 carats were bought by Alfred Beit and by Symonds and Moses for Jules Porges and Co. F. T. Gervers who purchased the largest number of parcels from DBMC over the period, occasionally took similar large weights, though the low valuation prices suggest inferior-quality stones.[27]

FINANCING CONCENTRATION

The pace of production and the general rise in turnover among the exporters in association with companies facilitated the cash flow necessary to maintain full working capacity. The evidence lies in the records of company profitability in the 1880s, and, more particularly, in the record of those firms which competed at the end of the amalgamation period.

In the case of De Beers Mining, trading profits on sales were remarkably stable throughout the decade, despite the brief recession of 1882–3 and extensive flooding in the mine. Both sales and trading profit, moreover, display an upward trend in relation to capital employed. Kimberley Central, by contrast, had a lower turnover and ratio of sales to capital employed till 1885, when there was little difference between the two companies.[28] DBMC paid a modest dividend regularly in the early years, rising to 20 per cent of shareholders' equity. This, too, contrasts with Central which paid high dividends of 22 to 36 per cent in some years, and nothing at all in 1884–6. Neither company was burdened by tax.

There were much greater contrasts in the ways in which companies managed their current liabilities and raised money. Because of the peculiarities of the diamond trade in which returns from sales were spread over the year and delayed if shipments were made to London directly, all the companies had problems building up reserves and were pressed for working capital. Indeed, the item 'reserves' is absent from the accounts, except for blue on the floors and diamonds in the safe, and much of the annual surplus was on paper. Bank borrowing against diamonds as collateral was frequent; and blue ground featured in transactions between companies. In general, directors were unwilling to raise capital by the issue of new shares and preferred, in the case of DBMC, to rely on working

---

[27] DBCA, DBMC Journals, 11, 12, 13; DBMC/15 (diamond ledger). Some 19 purchasers in the ledgers do not feature in contemporary lists of licensed buyers. These are probably incomplete (it is hard to believe H. Hirsche or Isidore and Paul Dreyfus were not licensed). W. Joel and others may have been licensed in the name of their principals (Barnatos Bros.). There are also occasional sales to directors—Rhodes, Robinow, English—who did not hold licences. The problem of merchants' agents is discussed in evidence to the commission on the diamond trade in 1887; CPP, G. 3-'88, esp. statements by A. W. Davis, 128; Hyam Abrahams, 142.

[28] DBCA, KCDMC/22. Both companies had higher gross profits than the estimated general average of 35% on a capital of £2 million: Reunert, 'Diamond Mining at the Cape', 197.

profits and advances from diamond merchants, as the cost of mergers and current liabilities grew.

Backing from the merchants could not be taken for granted, however, and all companies used a variety of techniques to fund expansion of assets during the first phase of amalgamation in the mines. These were simply based on purchase of claims in return for company shares, a process which brought in five companies to DBMC 1883–4, but was delayed in Central's case by its liability for part of Kimberley mining board debts. The price of amalgamated claims was based not on the share value of the company's total assets, but on the estimated yield and potential value of the ground taken over, less any debts and the cost of clearing reef. Variations on this technique in the first 6 years of the decade resulted too in direct payments out of profits by DBMC for a small number of claims in Australian Gully and in Eagle Company in 1885, an exchange of depositing floors as part of a bargain with Elma Mining, and payment of compensation to United Mining for stoppage of work, when it was acquired in 1886.[29] By 1886, De Beers Mining and Kimberley Central had the bulk of claims in their respective mines. But Central was still blocked by the French Company, Standard, and Kimberley United from complete control, while De Beers still had the Oriental and Victoria companies to contend with. The first serious attempt to amalgamate throughout all four mines was led by the financier and company director C. J. Posno, who had interests in Dutoitspan and Bultfontein. He issued a prospectus for a 'Unified Diamond Mines Company' in 1885 with a projected capital of £10 million, backed by Paris banks.[30] This scheme was turned down by the major companies, but the plan contained the germ of several important ideas for the control of all production and sales by pooling diamonds and for raising mortgage bonds to at least £2 million, some of which was to be traded for shares in amalgamated companies.

Rhodes and his board immediately brought forward proposals of their own, in February 1886, for unification with leading companies in the other three mines, based on the well-tried formula of share exchanges at a price determined by claim valuations. Only ground of the highest value was considered; and Rhodes laid considerable emphasis on his own company's underground workings and debt-free position in regard to the De Beers mining board compared with Kimberley Central.

---

[29] DBCA, DBMC/2, minutes, 1883–6; and for the pattern of amalgamation in each mine, Newbury, 'Technology, Capital and Consolidation', table 2.

[30] DBCA, DBMC/3, minutes, Jan.–Feb. 1886 for a printed version of Rhodes's alternative scheme; Lewsen, 202; and for earlier schemes, Turrell, *Capital and Labour*, 207, 209–10.

There were a lot of imponderables in this proposal which other directors pointed out, not least the market value of shares at the date of merger; the estimate of the company's net worth; the issue of very large capital sums without consultation of shareholders; and the statutory powers of companies to complete mergers outside their own mines. If successful, DBMC would gain very large holdings, conservatively valued, in other companies and 'a voice in their management' to influence production. Furthermore, total production at Kimberley could be 'steadied . . . to give European buyers greater confidence than is now possible'.[31]

The objectives were retained, but the scheme was premature, because of the need to change the company's articles of association and to organize an agency in London to deal with banks and stockbrokers directly. Rhodes and Stow may also have engineered an important change in the Cape's joint-stock legislation on warrant dividends, passed later by the Assembly, which enabled drafts to be issued to overseas shareholders.[32] In the meantime, Elma Mining was taken over in April 1886 by issue of ordinary scrip and an exchange of loads of blue ground from DBMC workings. At the general meeting of shareholders in May 1886, Rudd gave a hint of what was coming by seeking authority and a change of articles to set up the 'Home' share registry, to increase the number of directors, and to allow Rudd's son and the diamond merchant Julius Wernher to stand as directors' alternates at meetings of board members in London.[33]

In early 1887, two additional techniques were used for mergers. Completion of the purchase of Gem Mining was carried through by using buyers who registered shares in their own names with funds provided through the company; and a mortgage bond was arranged for Gem by Alfred Beit, who loaned that company £20,000 in return for an option on shares. DBMC immediately drove tunnels to test Gem's blue ground and found it worth keeping out of the hands of rivals. The clandestine purchase of shares prevented their price rising inordinately, and DBMC got thirty good claims when the takeover was completed through Beit's option for the sum of £53,000. A similar method of share purchases through nominees initiated the acquisition of Victoria DMC, when Stow and Jules Porges and Co. provided the money in London and began quietly buying throughout early 1887. In addition, terms for an open merger were worked out in Kimberley for payment in scrip and cash. Meanwhile, Oriental DMC was bought out in March 1887 for £64,000 in scrip plus a £4,000 commission to Beit who negotiated the deal. When this was

[31] DBCA, DBMC/3, minutes, 1886.   [32] DBCA, DBMC/3, minutes, 3 Feb. 1887.
[33] DBMC, *Annual Report* (1886), 10–11.

completed, Victoria directors were informed that DBMC owned most of its share capital, purchased for £57,000, and that its claims were surrounded by other mergers. The company yielded in April 1887, and two of Victoria's directors, R. Hinrichsen and Francis Oats, were taken on to the board of DBMC. The final amalgamations within the De Beers mine were accomplished by purchase of claims in small properties at the end of 1887.

Similar amalgamations had been completed in Kimberley mine which made the Central company predominant in 1887, but without a monopoly of claims, so long as the French company remained independent. In both DBMC and Central there were, too, considerable changes in the pattern of share ownership and board control, important for subsequent merger negotiations. The most significant for Central was the backing of Barnato Bros., after a merger with Standard DMC, which brought Barney's nephew, Woolf Joel, on to the board and to the position of acting-chairman, from 1888, when Francis Baring-Gould was in England. Apart from Joel and L. Breitmeyer, Central's board had little merchant representation. The nominal capital of the company which stood at £1.4 million in November 1887 included Barnato's important holding of £85,000, and the stake of the shipping magnate Sir Donald Currie, which amounted to £76,560. Diamond merchant and dealer holdings, including the Barnatos, were under 10 per cent of ordinary shares, held for the most part by the British and South African directors.[34] This division was reflected, too, in the double registration of the company in Kimberley and London and in a London section of the directorship (though no minutes have survived) to exercise control of share dealings and diamond sales through their agency in Holborn Viaduct.

De Beers Mining had also divided its board by 1887 with F. S. Philipson-Stow and Robert English in England at the London transfer office to supervise bank loans, capital equipment orders, and sales, while the Kimberley board under Rhodes or Rudd as chairman brought in six new directors by mergers and elections. The expanded board of twelve included four diamond dealers and merchants' representatives—Beit, Hinrichsen, Harry Mosenthal, and (briefly) E. Bruch, as agent for Jules Porges, and (less certainly) Charles Nind. In 1887, the nominal share capital of £1,265,620 was still predominantly in the hands of fifty-four shareholders holding over 1,000 shares each. Of these eighteen were dealers or merchants holding some 60 per cent of ordinary shares—notably, Joel, Mosenthal, and Beit. Barnato held 1,218 shares in DBMC when the

---

[34] DBCA, KCDM/19, 20 (share registers).

register was made up in 1887, though it is clear from transfers he was continually trading on his own behalf, just as Beit was trading on behalf of the company. They were joined by Lord Nathaniel Rothschild and Leopold de Rothschild who took up 5,745 shares in October and November 1887. But, on the whole, there were few British or Continental banks and finance houses represented on the share lists at this stage, though there was a large number of small lots of under fifty shares held by the public in Hamburg, Paris, and Anvers. The holdings of Rhodes or Rudd—4,000 to 5,000 shares each—were slightly above average for dealers and directors, though much less than the holding of W. Alderson and his son in Sheffield who still had over 10,000 founder shares. Other new directors such as John Morrogh and Thomas Shiels, who came on to the board through mergers, or G. W. Compton, who had been a large shareholder since 1881, were also in this select group, though none of them quite matched Stow's holding of 5,567 shares.

The analysis suggests that in the case of DBMC there had been a marked shift in share ownership, reflected in company direction, towards the diamond merchants on whom sales operations largely depended. Company management at Kimberley, however, was in the hands of the founders, reinforced by Francis Oats and by the appointment of the American mining engineer Gardner F. Williams as general manager in May 1887. The lines of communication to London were through Stow and English, neither of whom had close connections with the diamond trade (indeed Stow, ex-digger and successful attorney, was opposed to merchant influence within the company); and the frequent absences of Beit and Mosenthal from Kimberley make it less certain that power was exercised solely in the interests of a few merchant houses. What is more certain from the board minutes is that their advice and services in financial matters became indispensable.

Their support was particularly valuable from May 1887, when amalgamation with companies in other mines was initiated in Kimberley. Few of the details had been settled before the board decided Rhodes should go to London in July to sort out the division of responsibilities with the London section, and take advice on alterations to the articles of association before seeking any new debenture issue. Before his departure, he outlined the general strategy to the shareholders, using the method of mortgaging DBMC assets to acquire Victoria as an example; and he dwelt at length on the respective capital values and yields of the Kimberley and De Beers mines, as a basis for share exchanges.[35]

---

[35] DBMC, *Annual Report* (1887), 12.

The appointment of Williams, moreover, brought in a man who had made two visits to assess the mines in 1884 and 1885 as part of his consultancy in mining matters for N. M. Rothschild and Sons. It is quite likely, as he claims, that he suggested an introduction to this merchant bank which had experience of Kimberley mining to further the cause of amalgamation.[36] Rhodes had already expressed a wish for such an introduction, after meeting Williams on the Rand in February 1887.

Once in London at the end of July, Rhodes found that rumours of amalgamations were reflected in a steady climb in the shares of DBMC, Central, and the French Company. The danger of consolidation within the Kimberley mine and the formation of a rival block able to compete for holdings in Dutoitspan and Bultfontein called for countermeasures. A plan to purchase the French Company seems to have been hatched immediately Rhodes and Stow had been interviewed by Lord Rothschild, though Rhodes was still suspicious of what he termed the 'speculator's view', fearing the banker would take advanatage of the share rise and sell out, before purchase was complete.[37] A loan of £750,000 and a new issue of £250,000 debentures organized by Beit, Porges, and Wernher were underwritten by Rothschilds; and 50,000 new DBMC shares destined for French shareholders were lodged with the bank.[38] The Kimberley board approved this initiative at once and a syndicate was formed in London to use the cash to buy up shares in the French Company. Rothschild's share broker, Ludwig Lippert, Rhodes, and the engineer De Crano went to Paris to make a provisional agreement with the French directors on 10 August 1887; and this was finalized in September as a share exchange on the basis of 162 De Beers Mining for 100 French shares with a special option for the French shareholders on a block of new De Beers ordinaries.

Kimberley Central took alarm, and directors and major shareholders with interests in the French Company, such as Currie, tried to force better terms from Rhodes and even outbid DBMC. Rhodes and the London directors resisted, using the well-tried technique of buying up shares on borrowed money, as an insurance to control proxy votes in Paris, 'so that in case the Central break the French agreement they are equally

---

[36] Gardner F. Williams, *The Diamond Mines of South Africa*, 286; RH, Baxter [transcripts], Rhodes to Rudd, 5 Feb. 1887. For Rothschilds' interest in the Anglo-African company in Dutoitspan mine in 1882 see Chapman.

[37] RH, Baxter [transcripts], Rhodes to Stow [July] 1887 'Private'; RAL, XI/121/19 (Sundry).

[38] For details see Newbury, 'Technology, Capital, and Consolidation'; and for a different interpretation, Turrell, *Capital and Labour*, 217–18.

unable to carry on amalgamation of the Kimberley Mines separate from ourselves'. Lippert also used his influence with the French directors to keep their 'loyalty'; and Stow went to Paris 'to defeat any new offers from Kimberley Mine'.[39] By early October 1887, Stow's syndicate had secured 4,505 French shares, and he had cornered Currie's votes with Lord Rothschild's help, to be used as proxies in Paris. By then the London and Kimberley directors of Central had come to terms on 3 October and agreed to buy back the French company from DBMC, pending the approval of the sale by French shareholders on 6 October. On 1 November the French company contract was made over to Central in return for 35,600 Central shares and £200,000 in Central debenture stock.

DBMC now had a big stake in the Kimberley mine through its holding in Central; and this expansive strategy was extended to the other mines in the group. For, Rhodes announced to Stow, after his return to the Cape in October 1887, that he had reached an 'understanding' with the chairman of Central, Baring-Gould, and with Barnato and Beit that purchase of stock and companies in Dutoitspan and Bultfontein would continue, so as to bring the main producers into a single leaseholding arrangement with the LSAE, financed by a single parent company—De Beers Mining. This would be restructured under the name of 'De Beers and South African DM Ltd.' with a capital of £3.5 million and some £2 million in debenture stock. De Beers £10 shares would then rise to £40 or £50; ordinary share capital could be kept low; and output would be increased for a secure diamond market. The whole thing was to take 'about nine months'.[40]

The grand plan ran into difficulties arising from the terms of the lease, the registration of French company claims transfers in Kimberley, and from a new debenture issue for DBMC to finance 'fusion' of the deep-level mines. Baring-Gould and his directors held out for a higher price than a straight share-for-share merger. Barnato, it would seem, agreed in November to throw in his lot with Rhodes and make over his Central shares, in return for a life governorship in the new company. Nevertheless, there was a 'share battle' in the sense that there were heavy purchases for DBMC by nominees in Kimberley and in London. Rothschilds' confidential advisers, Smith and De Crano, inspected the mines in November 1887 and concluded that De Beers had better reserves and organization, and was worth backing. It was essential, they reported, that Rhodes should buy up Central shares; and De Crano recommended

---

[39] RH, Baxter [transcripts], Rhodes to Stow [Sept.] 1887 (from Lisbon); RAL, B 17 Rh., Meyer to De Beers Mining, 2 Sept. 1887; Meyer to Stow, 13 and 30 Sept. 1887.
[40] RH, Baxter [transcripts], Rhodes to Stow, 22 Oct. 1887.

a new loan of £300,000 for that purpose. By the end of 1887, the share registers show, as Rhodes claimed, that his company held 9,250 Centrals; and Beit and Gold Fields of South Africa purchased more 'to give us the voting power in respect thereto'.[41] This policy continued throughout early 1888 by using funds from the debenture issues on the security of the De Beers mine.

With the take-over firmly in hand, the directors were able to register De Beers Consolidated Mines Ltd. (DBCM) in Kimberley, 13 March 1888, and announced a capital of £3.1 million in £5 shares and £1.5 million in debenture stock. The shareholders of DBMC approved the projected 'fusion' in April on the basis of eleven old shares for ten Centrals, plus a cash payment to persuade a reluctant minority of Central shareholders who wanted more. It was still not certain, however, the agreement would be given a smooth passage at a Central general meeting. Rhodes, therefore, urged purchase of shares in all three remaining mines, as a basis for the 'consolidated' company. Rothschild also took a hand by appointing the diamond merchant Paul Dreyfus as his agent at Kimberley to speed up the mortage bond on the security of the mines and by the issue of £2,250,000 first-debenture stock to cover old debts and leaseholding in Dutoitspan and Bultfontein. It was Rothschild, too, who urged Barnato to influence Baring-Gould and other directors to come to terms, or risk wrecking the amalgamation.[42] The amalgamation agreement between Central and De Beers was finally signed, 28 June 1888, for a joint capital of £3,950,000, after share exchange and payments in cash: ten shares of Central were given against twenty-two £5 De Beers with a bonus of 48s.

Central recalcitrants, therefore, made trouble and persuaded a Kimberley court to interdict the transfer of Central. The Cape Supreme Court upheld their interpretation of Central's articles of association. Julius Wernher angrily urged Rhodes to liquidate Central on the strength of De Beers controlling interest and to threaten the directors with exclusion from the new board.[43]

Rhodes was very willing to carry out this manoeuvre. The articles of the new consolidated company issued in March 1888 stood for much more than a restructured mining merger. They envisaged a corporation with powers to undertake any commercial or industrial venture 'in Africa or elsewhere', and to treat with rulers and governments for concessions, loans, and privileges in the grand manner of chartered companies in India,

---

[41] DBCA, DBMC/3, minutes, 30 Dec. 1887.

[42] RAL, 116/16 (Dreyfus correspondence), 1888; RAL, T43/23 Rothschild to Barnato 12 May 1888.

[43] RH, Rhodes Papers 9 (Finance), Wernher to Rhodes, 10 Aug. 1888.

Borneo, and West Africa. As he confided to Stow, Rhodes wanted a close brotherhood of men committed to his expansive views. For this reason he rejected Rothschild's advice to reward his directors with founders' shares, and chose instead to appoint life governors—Barnato, Stow, and Beit—along with himself, with the right to nominate directors and alternates and to share profits in excess of 30 per cent of dividends. Such men would be in an extraordinary position of patronage and privilege. Mere representatives of shareholders were not enough for 'a Company that will be worth as much as the balance of Africa'.[44]

It was certain, therefore, that those who arrived as victorious amalgamators and members of the charmed circle would not tolerate directors who had made their task difficult. From April 1888, a special committee of DBCM set about allocating the massive share purchases to its own nominees, in order to influence 'voting power' at general meetings to determine the new directorate. The disastrous fire of 11 July 1888 was seen by Rhodes as giving Central a temporary production advantage, blunting his ability to 'force terms' on the recalcitrants.[45] There was a last burst of share purchases to cover all shareholder votes; and by November 1888 it was possible to buy out the objectors. In any case, Rothschild, too, had lost patience and insisted on an end to delays. At a shareholders' meeting of 29 January 1889, liquidation of Central was voted through. The minority caved in and gave up legal action.[46] The whole of the Kimberley mine was then 'bought' by a DBCM tender for £5,300,000 (which was £40,000 less than Rhodes had calculated in October 1888). Fusion was formally complete by 25 February, though the transfer of property and other details of the 'great Hypothecation' dragged on into July.

As the power-play came to an end, the DBCM men were in no mood to receive Central directors. A fifth life-governorship, reserved, perhaps, for Baring-Gould, remained unfilled, though he took a lesser seat on the board in which only five ex-Central directors retained places alongside fifteen DBCM nominees. Barnato received his reward; five other diamond merchants were represented; and Carl Meyer who stood for Rothschilds' (though he retired from the bank) became one of the most influential directors of the London section of the board.

[44] DBCA, Board 1/1/1, Articles of Association, 1888; Baxter [transcripts], Rhodes to Stow, 14 Apr. 1888.

[45] DBCA, DBMC/3, minutes, 28 Apr., 12 June 1888; the committee consisted of Morrogh, Compton, Shiels, and Nind; RH, Baxter [transcripts], Rhodes to Stow, 9 Nov. 1888.

[46] The objectors got 11 old De Beers shares (£10) or 22 (£5) for 10 Centrals plus 51s. cash: *South Africa*, 23 and 30 Mar. 1889.

The victors were still left with the task of absorbing Bultfontein and Dutoitspan. A few lesser figures, such as Joseph Mylchreest, could be bought out for cash, and retired home to live in style. In other cases, DBCM already had very large holdings in Griqualand West DMC and Bultfontein Consolidated. But massive funding to transfer leases owned by all the companies was needed. Rhodes had boasted in March 1888 that he would crush outstanding companies 'by making the price of diamonds fall to 14*s*.' But he was really in no position to start a production and price war; and the French engineer Boutan could see no reason why the companies on LSAE ground should not hold out indefinitely in a market which he thought had been 'rigged' by late 1888 to keep diamond prices up.[47]

Rhodes and his board chose, instead, to 'wait for the reef to fall' in the two shallow mines and purchase them as cheaply as possible, without burdening the consolidated company with too great a charge, as he confided to Rothschild:

You can see clearly that they have reached a depth at which the reef is bound soon to fall, and that with their low yield they can neither haul out the reef nor work underground at a profit, and therefore they must arrange settling. At present we should have to pay them about £300,000 a year, if the reef fell we should get them for half. Meantime, no one can form them in antagonism to us as we hold the control of the Griqualand West and the Bultfontein Consolidated. If I had looked on the De Beers Consolidated as an ordinary mine, liable to work out, I should not mind, but with the ore [sic] we have in sight we may say the Mines are simply perpetual, and I do not like to permanently burden our capital too severely. In addition to this we have now got the powers we required, and with the enormous task back country daily developing we have every chance of making it another East India Company, and the great thing is to keep our capital as low as possible.[48]

This close attention to tactics for larger ends in the 'interior' took Rhodes back to London in April 1889, where he and Beit continued to buy up shares of the Anglo-African DMC to increase their range of holdings in Dutoitspan. By 17 April, with additional buying by Jules Porges and Co., DBCM had sufficient voting power on the Anglo-African board to arrange an offer of sale; and this was accepted by the London board. In April and May, too, came the glad news that large reef falls were bringing down shales on to claims in the two quarries, reducing share values and lowering

---

[47] Mylchreest was paid £115,000 plus 6 months' production of loads of blue: *South Africa*, 27 Apr. 1889; Boutan in *South Africa*, 4 May 1889.
[48] RH, Baxter [transcripts], Rhodes to Rothschild, 29 Oct. 1888.

the price all round. Bultfontein Consolidated and Griqualand West agreed to purchase of their leases 'in perpetuity' for 7½ and 4 per cent of their capital in annual payments. Terms for Bultfontein Mining Company were arranged by arbitration through a committee headed by Sir Hercules Robinson, which awarded an annual rent of £41,000 for title. Sir Donald Currie was delegated to negotiate with Anglo-African and the smaller companies which fell into line by accepting total payment of £1,450,000 for purchase of leases. Only North-East Bultfontein and Gordon DMC run by C. J. Posno and Julius Pam held out, encouraged by new finds and the backing of the LSAE. In the end, the total purchase price, including annual 'obligations' to shareholders of Bultfontein Mining, came to £2,564,000.[49]

To meet this sum and other charges, it was confidently announced by Barnato, who chaired the first general meeting of DBCM in July 1889, that Rhodes had gone 'home' to raise a second debenture loan 'in a manner similar to the Cape Loan at 5½%' through the house of Rothschild. This meant that the company would be saddled with further redemption charges on £1,750,000 as well as the first mortgage loan of £2,250,000, contracted in 1888 to finance the Kimberley mine purchase. Calls for a new subscription were made in December 1889, when diamonds were reported to be selling at 40s. per carat and DBCM £5 shares were up to £23.

The debenture loans were offered to investors in early 1890, and the pattern of purchases reflected the widespread financial interest and confidence in amalgamation. DBCM shares were now listed in London, Paris, and Berlin. But the principal investors were British banks and a few foreign banks, which all took just over half of the debenture stock (56.6 per cent), including Rothschilds of London which took 17.8 per cent. Smaller finance houses and fifteen diamond merchants took a significant share (15.5 per cent), and so did a few of the London directors.[50]

When such loans were equivalent to over half of its equity from 1888, clearly De Beers Consolidated bore little relation to the company which had operated on an employed capital of £700,000 in the early 1880s. Capital employed, including debt, amounted to £6.2 million at the end of the decade. In return for this enormous expansion of assets, the company owned four mines valued collectively at about £23 million. Monopoly through ownership was not entirely complete. Some very small

---

[49] DBCA, Board 2/7/1, minutes, 17 Apr., 1 and 3 May, and meetings through June and July 1889; RAL, 116/17A, Dreyfus to Rothschild, 29 Apr., 1 May 1889.
[50] *South Africa*, 21 Dec. 1889; and for the debenture stock issue, DBCA, 11/1/2 (share ledgers); and RH, Central Mining and Finance, DBCM ledgers.

enterprises in the vicinity of Kimberley at Otto's Koppie and St Augustine hauled blue but washed very little. The Vaal River DMC, registered in London in 1889, began to revive some of the 140 alluvial claims at Gong Gong for high quality but low yield. More significantly, in the Free State, New Jagersfontein, formed in 1887 with a capital of £1 million and five diamond merchants on its board, and the Jagersfontein United Mining Company, run by Pam, began to exploit systematically the 1,114 claims owned by the Jagersfontein Mine and Estate Company in Fauresmith district. Buoyed by the discovery of the 'Pam' diamond of 241½ carats (the largest found in South Africa by 1889), neither company showed any desire for amalgamation. They ran the danger, however, that the Free State government might exercise greater control than was possible in Cape territory by making the Estate Company mine other land in its possession; and this threat late in 1889 led to the overthrow of the company's board, by Rhodes, Beit, and others keen to present a united front and buy into New Jagersfontein to control production.

But for the moment these were secondary issues beside the major achievement of uniting production management in the diamond mines, after 20 years of fairly unsystematic and occasionally damaging competition. Competition had been reduced and eliminated by the mobilization of retained profits made within the industry, and by the finance available on the security of claims and raised through merchants and brokers intimately connected with marketing the industry's product. The reasons why De Beers Mining had come to the top lay primarily in the company's strategic location in a relatively rich endowment, steady profitability ratios, and sound management by a board in which Rhodes was an occasional inspiration, rather than a dominant personality, until he learned to understand the financial side of his business. Like Rhodes, the board as a whole learned a good deal from mistakes made in the Kimberley mine and from its merchant participants. It has been forgotten how much it owed to other sources of group management in the 'interior economy' from the mining boards on which all directors had served, or from the defensive organization of the protection board which supervised novel police methods and labour registration. The structure of labour management and the compounds also derived from the shared experience of miners and merchants in organizing to prevent theft and control supply for the contractors. In addition, De Beers Mining had its own supply of servile convict labour at sensitive points in the recovery process as an additional defence and method of control.

Company governance in the mines and the mining area was favoured too by the politics of incorporation, which allowed Rhodes, Rudd, and

Robinson and others a voice at the Cape, backed by the evident wealth and power of the new industry. The early legislation which was the product of the miners' commission of 1882 confirmed this power by amendments, freed companies from mining board debts, and improved their capacity to attract overseas investment in their shares in 1888. The miners' lobby refined its organization through the Griqualand West Miners Union under Rhodes in 1888 to put up three candidates for election to the Assembly, including Barnato, calculating that it could muster 2,350 votes on the Kimberley rolls against 1,200 'anti-mining' votes from the commercial sector.[51] The success of this electoral campaign which made Barnato an MLA by the 'largest majority ever' confirmed the status of mining leadership at the level of government, just as Rhodes and Rudd had begun to prove it for different and wider purposes at the level of imperial government through the chartered British South Africa Company in 1889.

Rhodes's chairmanship during the period leading to reconstruction was, however, intermittent and strategic, rather than tactically close to everyday operations. He was not always present at important board meetings in Kimberley; and as the board expanded to twenty in 1889, divided between Kimberley and London, he exercised his undoubted authority, charm, and political influence at long range and in concentrated bursts of advocacy and manipulation. Even the articles of association of DBCM, for example, which bear the unequivocal stamp of his purpose, were not all his work and owed much to the back-room drafting of a committee consisting of Currie, Atkinson, Mosenthal, and the company lawyer Hawksley, as well as the founder.[52] His correspondence with Lord Rothschild illustrates his grasp of detail and accuracy of prediction concerning the course of amalgamation from the summer of 1888. But so much of that complex orchestration took place in London at the hands of Stow, Meyer, and Beit and the forgotten men of the Central, Bultfontein, and Dutoitspan boards that it is impossible to attribute the sequence of events simply to his direction. For it was the London board with constant reference to Kimberley which carried through the final stages of amalgamation from the beginning of May 1889, following 'a desultory discussion . . . started by Mr. C. J. Rhodes as to the future policy of this Company', as the minutes impiously and laconically record. The chairman was there when obstacles needed removing. It was undoubtedly Rhodes who initiated the usual raid on the shares of targeted companies in the final phases; and

[51] DBCA, GWMU/1, minutes, 25 Sept. 1888 (and voters' rolls); *South Africa*, 6 Apr. 1889. The miners' ticket included Barnato, J. H. Lange, T. Lynch—all elected, and W. S. Lord QC for Kimberley, Rhodes and G. Paton for Barkly.
[52] DBCA, Board 2/7/1, minutes, 10 July 1889.

it was Rhodes who characteristically secured the 'arbitration' of prices for leases by squaring Sir Hercules Robinson (for 200 guineas), when companies in Dutoitspan and Bultfontein hung fire. But by then he was already launched into even bolder ventures and impatient with the end-game of amalgamation. At Kimberley, by 1889, he had much less to do with the essential details of the Central acquisition than Paul Dreyfus, Rothschild's agent.

The founder company, then, was not the work of one man, but essentially a corporate body run by an executive which delegated a lot of its functions to small committees, and participated in the wider government of the mines. The details—machinery, labour, sales of diamonds, tenders to contractors—were settled by these committees, frequently chaired by Rudd and Stow, 1883–5. Rhodes asserted himself by 1886 with his plan for general amalgamation (borrowed from Posno and moved in a board meeting by Mosenthal); and he was very active in company mergers till 1887, together with Nind, Beit, Morrogh, and Hinrichsen. From 1888, when many at Kimberley turned to gold prospection on the Rand, interests diversified. Rhodes became absorbed in other ventures, but mastered the terms of amalgamation discussed by an expanding collective of miners, merchants, lawyers, and engineers who redesigned mining as it was known at Kimberley. In a sense the so-called 'amalgamator', who was not the unique architect of his company's structure was made by the decade of company consolidation at Kimberley which enabled him to indulge his greater ambitions outside the mines.

PART II

From Monopoly to Cartel
1890–1919

4

Production and Marketing

De Beers Consolidated Mines and the Diamond Syndicate

WITH the amalgamation of Kimberley companies in sight at the end of 1889, it was confidently predicted that the new 'De Beers combination' would keep up prices by cutting production from four to two million carats a year.[1] The company's shares were worth four times their nominal price and accumulated stocks of rough stones were still fetching 35*s*. to 40*s*. at Kimberley. There were good grounds for believing in the carefully publicized accounts of controlled output and centralized marketing through London merchants. The corporate interests of producer and merchant-investors implied a profitable monopoly.

Rothschilds' consultants had emphasized this functional complementarity as a reason for financial backing. Jules Porges, diamond merchant and financier, while on a tour of Kimberley and the Rand in 1889, outlined for his partners the ways in which a syndicate of buyers or a marketing company might handle the £3 million worth of stones still in the vaults of London importers, as a result of the feverish period of production during the previous 3 years. Rhodes, he revealed, had the example of the great copper corner by the Société des Métaux in mind.[2]

In fact, the market began to decline at the end of the year and was further depressed by the onset of the Baring crisis in 1890, when half the value was wiped off Transvaal gold shares and three Cape banks collapsed. Mere 'combination' could not save the day. All production at Bultfontein and Dutoitspan ceased from April 1890; investment in new shafts was postponed; and blue ground taken over from amalgamated companies was left to weather longer on the floors. Black labour was paid off, and left in large numbers, and most whites were made redundant or permitted to scratch a living from sorting through the debris heaps,

---

[1] 'The Price of Diamonds', *South Africa*, 14 Dec. 1889; 'Dear Diamonds', *DFA*, 21 Jan. 1890.

[2] Charter Consolidated Archives (unclassified MSS), Porges to Wernher, 7 Jan. 1889.

for a licence fee and small returns. For a decade, the closed mines were held in reserve.

But would command of resources ensure a profit from supply? Rhodes clearly thought so, even in the midst of financial uncertainty. And to make sure that lesser mines did not upset this control of output, the Kimberley section of the board sanctioned the purchase of sufficient shares to nominate their own directors for Koffyfontein and Jagersfontein mines in the Free State. 'This action', Rhodes confided to Stow, 'has to be kept most profoundly secret, it could not be communicated to the Home Board, as Mosenthal is one of the largest shareholders in Jagersfontein, and I believe several others of the Board.'[3] Production in those mines was cut too. Enquiries from intrigued shareholders for details of the £101,800 listed against these (anonymous) investments in the balance sheets drew a blank at the annual general meeting.

The board was more alarmed by the news of discoveries on Wessels's farm, 4 miles from Kimberley, which precipitated a 'rush' for 4,000 claims in April 1891, and an uncontrolled production which threatened to escape the vigilance of the detective department. The reluctant proprietors sold out to Henry A. Ward, and the board took an option on his 50,000 acres on 27 August 1891. Against the opposition of the London section, the local directors pushed through purchase of the farm for £460,000, tolerating Ward's right to excavate and wash diamonds for 5 years as the only way of securing control. For the same reason, they paid £194,000 for Pam's New Gordon Company, which was at once shut down.[4]

This insistence on total ownership, at whatever cost, in a period of financial difficulty, resulted in the first serious signs of strain in the structure of the company's executive. Several different objectives were being pursued at once in London and Kimberley. Company viability in the early 1890s depended on steady redemption of the mortgage loans raised to cover the amalgamation, plus regular dividends to keep up the value of the De Beers shares. Confidence in the monopoly firm was confidence in the trade, argued the merchant directors. But in addition to normal business profits, Rhodes and the Kimberley board intended to use the company as a source of investment in his other schemes for mining and chartered administration in Mashonaland and Matabeleland. A financial reserve to cover this programme and expansion into railways and coal was planned; and in 1890 the first of a series of loans was made

---

[3] RH, Baxter [transcripts], Rhodes to Stow, 22 Nov. 1890.
[4] CPP, A.1–'91; DBCA, Board 2/2/2, minutes, 27 Dec. 1890. For details of the Wesselton rush, Worger, *South Africa's City of Diamonds*, 275–9.

to the British South Africa Company. The unemployed white miners laid off by closures were recruited for the Mashonaland trek. As premier of the Cape from June 1890, the chairman supervised at a distance, initiating policies which the two sections of the board were asked to carry out.

Rhodes could expect loyal, but not unwavering, support from the eight or so permanent directors at Kimberley. Most of them, like Compton, Robinow, Nind, Oats, and Morrogh, were old mining hands and co-founders. Williams, as general manager, was his appointee and his alternate on the board. Less certainly, Barnato and Woolf Joel could be relied on to promote sales, but not to sacrifice them to schemes for 'the interior'. None of this loyalty made them 'Rhodes's men' (though Carl Meyer in London thought them too subservient). They were all collectively responsible to the shareholders, and not simply the acolytes of their famous chairman. In any case, Rhodes rarely attended board meetings from 1894, and worked through the company secretary, W. H. Craven, who was in a key position as well-informed co-ordinator of the two sections of the board, keeper of the company's minutes and correspondence, and principal executor of company business.

He was also a permanent member (as Rhodes was not) of the company's diamond committee. From 1889 this body negotiated sales with the buyers, with Oats, Robinow, Compton, or Nind in charge, along with Williams, and occasionally Barnato and Joel. Rhodes attended some meetings during 1889–91, and not again till 1896. The usual diamond buyers for London principals were Breitmeyer, Harris, Hirsche, and Dreyfus, who were also alternates for merchant-directors. But it was not a cabal of producers and buyers operating by unanimous agreement. Buyers left when decisions were taken on company sales, and this rule applied to directors such as Barnato or Beit. Later, after Rhodes's death, the young Ernest Oppenheimer would gain an insight into the intricate and often acrimonious negotiations of the committee.

The chairman could expect much less support, however, from the overseas section of the board. By the articles of association, at least four directors had to reside in London. For most of the 1890s, the minutes show that over half of the full board of twenty were in the metropolis, occasionally reinforced by visitors from Kimberley. Only four could be classified as strongly beholden to Rhodes (Beit, Robinow, Stow, and English) in an executive usually chaired by Sir Donald Currie, and with a solid core of four or five merchant and banking representatives who spoke for the diamond trade, the banks, and Continental investors. For 3 years, like their counterparts in Kimberley, they also had a 'diamond committee' where the same rules of confidentiality applied, but were difficult to enforce. Merchants on the board were required to leave during votes on diamond sales. But they can be regarded as 'inside traders' with privileged access to information about the condition of production.

To bring some order into this division of functions a small committee of the London board was pressured by Stow, when chairman in 1890, into defining the responsibilities of the two sections in company by-laws. In principle, all technical management and decisions on methods of production lay with the Kimberley directors. London would look after investment and sales. But there was an overlap, because of the primary role of the Kimberley diamond committee and Rhodes's propensity to make investments of his own. Accordingly, it was laid down that all expenditure over £20,000, purchase of property, stores, the disposal of diamonds, declaration of dividends, and elections to the board itself had to be decided jointly, with the chairman exercising a casting vote.[5]

But in practice, the early 1890s were full of contradictions and improvisations, as conflicting interests made themselves felt. Failure to work out a selling policy in London was matched by independent initiatives in Kimberley to get rid of an unsold surplus in a weak market. Thus, from December 1891, the Kimberley board resolved to strengthen prices by limiting total monthly production to 160,000 carats. But at the same time, Wesselton (Premier) mine was allowed by Rhodes to wash over a million loads a year till 1896, producing diamonds which the lessee, Ward, had to market through De Beers and London channels. In time, many of these difficulties were ironed out, as production and marketing techniques were learned and applied to create the working monopoly which is characteristic of the later period of Rhodes's chairmanship. But the company was commissioned by its articles, though not by its more conservative directors, to serve as one of the cornerstones of Rhodes's expansive policies, as well as South African mining. Its first decade of growth, therefore, depended on co-operative adjustment of production, sales, and investment through managerial technicians in Kimberley, buyers and merchants in London, and by the less predictable chairman and those who supported his views on diversification.

The principal technician of company production was Gardner F. Williams, who took over the running of the whole group of mines from 1889. Already in his early fifties, taciturn, huge, and physically courageous (he had played his part in rescuing miners from the fire of 1888), Williams earned his salary of £3,000 by ensuring that diamonds would be supplied

---

[5] DCBA, Board 2/7/1, minutes, 18 Mar. 1890. Company growth and investment are treated below in ch. 5.

as cheaply as possible from a variety of dangerous geological conditions to meet the requirements of world demand. As the older mines of Kimberley and De Beers deepened and their yield decreased, the conglomerate of blue ground contained more hard rock. For a time, this suited the contemporary practice of 'weathering' for six months or longer on the floors, thus reducing the loss of small diamonds and building up a stock of partly processed ground ready for final washing, concentration, and diamond recovery. But sooner or later, the company had to decide when to bring Bultfontein and Dutoitspan back into production. In the meantime, Wesselton could be relied on to yield more, cheaply, by open-cast methods than the expensive deep level mines, though these could not be abandoned, because of the high quality of their stones.

MACHINES AND MEN

The art of 'winning' diamonds, then, involved considerable planning and organization to ensure a balanced recovery rate of assortments acceptable to the merchants, economical to the company, and co-ordinated by the application of large-scale hauling and washing techniques. To carry out this heavy responsibility, Williams had under him managers for each of the mines who supervised the safety and efficiency of operations, untrammelled by government inspectors. Officials approved his regulations and methods: they did not interfere. Under the managers were the overmen, who saw to blasting and all contracted work. On the surface, floor managers organized concentration and recovery at the washing plants, and compound managers supervised the registration and discipline of labour.[6] Outside the immediate hierarchy of senior management, two outstanding engineers of great talent, George Labram and Louis Seymour, designed powerful winding engines and pumping plant. And Labram and the engineer Fred. Kirsten revolutionized recovery techniques by their invention of the 'grease table', which exploited the diamond's physical affinity with oily matter.

Williams's demesne which he ruled till his retirement in 1905 lay in 17 square miles of mines and open pits, vast floors, and tailings heaps held together by a complex network of railways, tramways, hauling lines, and roadways. It was a small industrial city with its compounds, workshops, machine shops, water and electricity supply, and a population

[6] Moonyean Buys, *Archives of the General Manager 1888–ca 1949 and Department* (DBCM, 1981), 8–9.

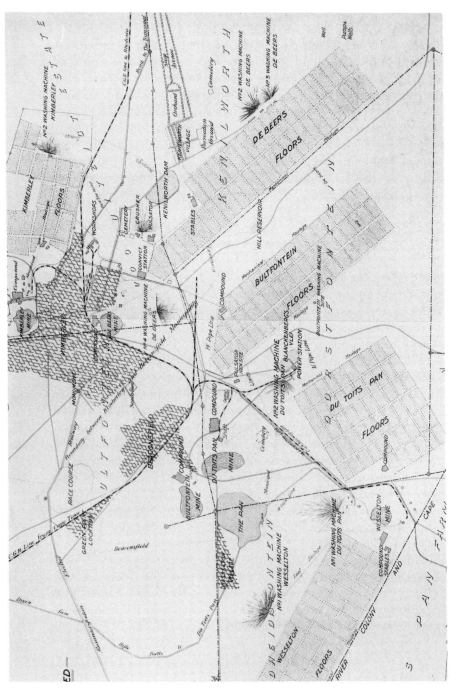

2. General plan of De Beers Consolidated Mines Ltd., 1906

of between 15,000 and 20,000, when at full stretch. The railway line to Kimberley was obligingly routed to unload coal, timber, machinery, and stores at the mine area. Eventually, the floors were all surrounded by double wire fences, like the compounds. As the period of the siege proved, the Kimberley mines could be stocked and provisioned like an armed camp.

But at the beginning of his general managership, Williams had to accept much of his technological inheritance as he found it. With Bultfontein and Dutoitspan shut down, he directed his efforts to restoring and deepening the system of shafts and tunnels which had collapsed or had been put out of action by the fire. Williams proceeded more carefully, hoping to avoid further collapse by driving only a few galleries at a time on each level, and allowing the 'pillars' a wider base of solid blue to rest on. As the roof of the galleries was dug out, new ones were excavated; and as the upper levels were worked out, others were started lower down. From a rock shaft in the De Beers mine three levels of tunnels were constructed, crossed by the galleries, to join up with the old incline shafts. A similar plan was followed in the Kimberley mine from 1890. In both mines the lesson of the fire was learned, and bare flames were replaced by incandescent lighting run from two electric plants.

To minimize recovery costs the surface floors were extended to allow for longer pulverization of the blue ground: 'The heat of the sun and moisture soon have a wonderful effect upon it. Large pieces which were as hard as ordinary sandstone when taken from the mine soon begin to crumble. At this stage of the work the winning of the diamonds assumes more the nature of farming than mining. The ground is continually harrowed to assist pulverization by exposing the larger pieces to the action of the sun.'[7] This proven technique was combined with more imaginative use of available traction power by installing an endless wire rope haulage 5½ miles long to dump the blue ground automatically. Secondly, Williams installed improved washing pans and brought all the deposit on the floors to three 'pulsators' housed on the De Beers floors. There, it was passed through a series of cylinder screens, and the diamonds and heavy concentrates were drawn off to the sorting tables. From every 240 loads of blue washed by this method, only one concentrated load of 16 cubic feet of gravel and diamonds passed to the sorters. This delicate end processing of the concentrates was carried out 'first, while wet by white men, and then, when dry, by native convicts'. The deposit was gone over

---

[7] DBCM, General manager's report, *Annual Report* (1890), 19.

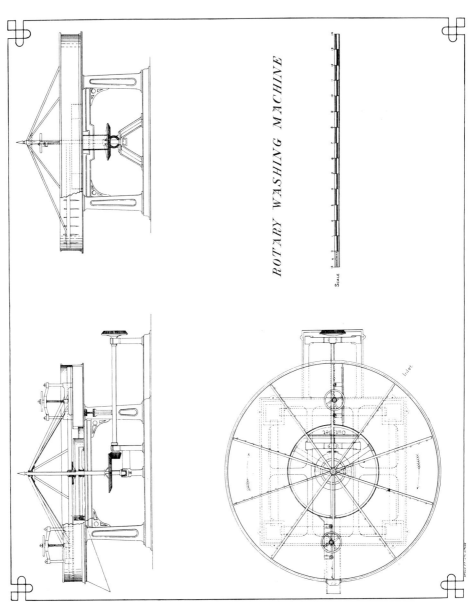

ROTARY WASHING MACHINE

Fig. 3a.

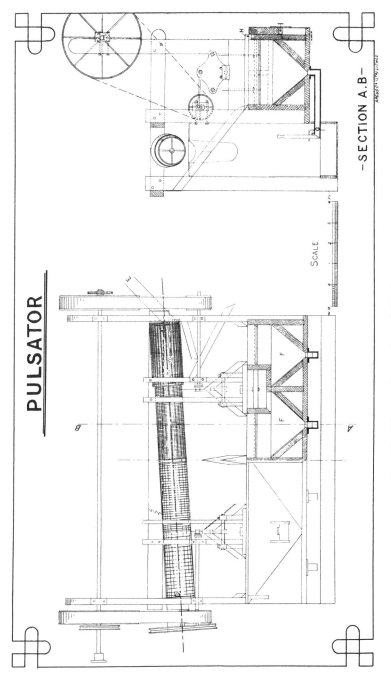

FIG. 3b. The mechanization of Kimberley mines, 1890

ILL. 7. Rotary diamond washing machines, 1894

as often as diamonds could still be found 'sufficient in quantity to repay the cost of convict labour'.[8]

Two important innovations improved the recovery process. From 1895, hard lumps were crushed in a huge plant—'the largest of its kind in the world having a capacity of about 1,000 tons in ten hours'—following a tour by Williams to works in Montana and Germany. And from 1898, the 'grease' table made sorting fully automatic, reducing the number of sorters from 195 to 32.

The lessons learned from reorganizing the older mines and the inventions and adaptations of the early 1890s were applied to production at Wesselton from 1897, and to Bultfontein and Dutoitspan after 1901. All blue ground was trammed to a central pulsator, after washing on the floors, on a single endless line with fully automatic tipping. Regarded solely in terms of applied technology, therefore, production from all five mines neared a peak of mechanical efficiency shortly after Williams's retirement in 1905, when the main shaft at Kimberley mine reached 3,000 feet and an output of over 10,000 loads a year was being processed. That was Williams's principal achievement, which his son took over as general manager. Alpheus Williams continued the industrial complex by hauling from six rock shafts along 155 miles of track and endless steel ropes to the floors which held nine million loads of blue and served two pulsators through scores of washing machines and the crushing mill. A central power-station, completed in 1904, supplied cheap electricity to the company and the municipality.

---

[8] DBCM, General manager's report, *Annual Report* (1890), 20.

In all, the index of total loads of ground processed annually by this mammoth application of mining technology increased by 300 per cent between 1890 and 1914, and the index of diamond recoveries rose by 60 per cent and more over the same period. What is more remarkable is the relatively slow rise in charges and direct mining costs until after the Anglo-Boer war (Appendix A.1). The cost of production was spread very unevenly, however, throughout the group of mines. After an initial success at the period of amalgamation, Gardner Williams was unable to reduce the expense of working the De Beers and Kimberley mines. Average costs per load remained stubbornly at about 6s., rising steeply in 1913, as Kimberley's 'great hole' neared the end of its useful life. This expense was offset to a large extent by Wesselton, where loads could be raised and processed for 2s. to 3s. in the 1890s, rising to 4s. and 5s. as the mine deepened. When Bultfontein and Dutoitspan were brought back into production, there was a steady fall in costs to 3s. per load by 1914. Thereafter, all mining production was subject to considerable wartime inflation till 1920. Nevertheless, the first 10 years of consolidated production displayed little or no increase in direct costs (mainly wages), followed by steep rises and a generally high index till 1920.

Much of the explanation lies in the relatively steady levels of compounded labour, before 1898, followed by an expansion of a more expensive work force to keep pace with the operation of all five mines in the group. The poor quality of the labour statistics precludes a satisfactory series, though it is clear enough (see Table 4.1) that daily averages and end-of-year totals for the compounds were fairly flat for much of the 1890s, and then doubled before 1914, as the mines reached their maximum production. Increased mechanization brought higher manning levels again.

The detailed reasons for the allocation of labour to particular tasks are not discussed in the technical reports of management, because for much of the period the labour supply was taken for granted. The annual recruitment and registration of workers at Kimberley continued to feature the usual high rate of turnover for short-term employment, rising from 40,000 or 50,000 to 80,000 and 90,000 after 1900. Some of this total registration included non-mining labour and pass registrations for Cape coloured residents, but the general trends are confirmed from the DBMC records, as the major employer. Overall, the company's black and white labour force trebled between 1890 and 1914. 80 per cent or more were African workers on 3- to 6-month contracts. There were seasonal fluctuations in the strength of this force up to 30 and 40 per cent of the annual average. The market for mine labour, commented Williams in 1904, remained

TABLE 4.1. *Kimberley district mine workers,*
1902–1920

Years	Whites	Blacks	Total
1902	2,107	9,949	12,056
1903	2,281	10,362	12,643
1904	2,755	11,407	14,162
1905	2,974	15,333	18,307
1906	3,708	20,176	23,884
1907	3,583	18,190	21,773
1908	2,031	21,685	23,716[a]
1909	*1,876*	*11,119*	*12,995*
1910	*2,207*	*16,904*	*19,111*
1911	*2,361*	*17,654*	*20,165*
1912	2,550	12,416	14,075[b]
1913	2,741	13,482	16,223
1914	2,289	9,088	11,377
1915	771	1,307	2,078
1916	*1,306*	*6,656*	*7,926*
1917	*1,926*	*10,548*	*12,474*
1918	2,013	9,217	11,230
1919	*2,537*	*13,083*	*15,620*
1920	2,630	10,882	13,512

[a] Registrar of natives averages which take no account of the massive lay-off at the end of 1908.
[b] For calendar years from Department of Mines, *Reports*. Kimberley district mines included alluvial companies, but not alluvial diggings, in these totals.

Sources: CPP, inspector of mines reports; DBCM, *Annual Reports* 1902–1921, Department of Mines, *Annual Reports*, 1912–1921. Early official statistics are 'daily averages' for calendar years. These are not consistent in later years and De Beers totals which are averages for financial years have been given (in italic); DBCA, GM 1/2/2; 7/9/2 for weekly averages.

'peculiar, owing to the fact that as soon as the rains come a large percentage of the natives wish to return home to plough their lands'; and there was usually another exodus, when crops were ready to harvest.[9] When the compounded work force reached its highest monthly average at some

---

[9] DBCM, General manager's report, *Annual Report* (1904), 11.

20,000 in 1906, there was a total intake of 52,708 contracted men and a discharge of 48,208 during the year—a turnover of 220 per cent, suggesting most of the labourers were short-term workers. Undoubtedly many recontracted after an absence of several weeks; and some stayed on the compound managers' books for years. But the managers' reports stress the flow of 'raw' and partly-trained workers, not an experienced cadre of semi-skilled and skilled Africans. This factor of short-term recruitment, rather than absolute shortage, occasioned most complaint before 1900. DBCM did not recruit labour until after that date, in response to a specific crisis, and the more usual comment in reports, when the crisis was over, was that labour was available, when required, at the compound gates.

A less obvious reason for the parallel rise in hand labour, as the mines mechanized, lay not so much in supply 'surplus' as in the work practices which were extended by greater production. Although hauling and washing rates were improved by the application of greater power for larger machines, mining at the work face made very little use of machine drills, except for developing rock shafts, and there was no room in the galleries for mechanical excavation. The standard methods hardly changed at all and were the same as in the 1880s—blasting, hand drilling, loading, and tramming to the hoisting shafts by contractors' gangs of up to thirty men. As the galleries proliferated at new levels, over half of the total labour force was employed underground, in the ratio of one white to about eight blacks, compared with one to three for surface work.

Moreover, development work underground and constant repairs and timbering, following mud rushes, diverted labour away from surface work after 1894, as levels in Kimberley and De Beers went below 800 and 900 feet.[10] The first indication that output in any mine might be restricted by labour shortage was in 1896, when there was a general reluctance to face the risk of mud rushes in the De Beers galleries, and strenuous efforts were made to encircle the mine with a tunnel 300 feet from the surface to drain water away from the pipe and its porous shales. The opening of Wesselton to underground work repeated the usual cycle of increases in hand labour in conjunction with mechanical hoisting.

Indeed, the only two developments in technique which might be said to have saved on manual labour were the mechanical sorting table and three 'Little Giant' steam shovels imported in 1901 to load lumps, tailings,

[10] Ibid. (1896), 4. The problem was not really solved (see *Annual Reports* for 1901, 1911, 1919). From 1910, too, bituminous shales caught fire in Bultfontein mine creating 'hot' mud rushes.

and debris directly into hoppers bound for the washing plant. There were indications, by 1911, that blue ground from the deep mines had become so hard as to require to be 'treated direct without flooring' in mechanical crushers. After some initial experiments in 1913, lack of development work during the World War postponed this major change entailing the elimination of a whole stage in the production process which would have cut back on surface labour.[11]

A final reason for the long reliance on hand labour was its availability at low unit cost. Managers were complacent about the 'excellent supply of labour' most years, occasionally attributing this abundance to drought, loss of cattle by rinderpest, and other failures in subsistence, so that 'the natives have been compelled by starvation to seek work'.[12] Sources of supply remained principally Tswana, north and south Sotho, and large contingents of Xhosa from Ciskei and Transkei prior to 1914. The 'British' Basotho were valued as a permanent source, as their self-sufficiency in agriculture failed from about 1898. Wages at the diamond mines, between £3 and £5 per month, were more than twice the average for wages in the gold mines and well above the minimum necessary to attract these workers.[13]

The discipline of industrial production was enforced through the compound, which prevented desertion for the duration of a contract and simplified enforcement of penalties for breaches of regulations (disobedience and theft were the most usual) under the Griqualand variants of Cape Masters and Servants Acts. A variety of defensive descriptions of the compounds continued to be published: which did not touch on the main point, namely that an institution designed to prevent theft was readily adapted to service the requirement of the mines for direction of labour when and where it was needed most. Condemned as temporary prisons or extolled as salutary open-air cantonments for an army of migrants, the compounds became part of the production line sited on the mine floors or connected by underground passages to the shafts.

Part of the difficulty in fully assessing them as industrial and social institutions lay in their number and variety. Gardner Williams and others concentrated on the largest show pieces, such as the vast barracks of sixty-four huts for 2,000 workers at Bultfontein with 'the usual Church, butcher's shop, supply stores, guards' quarters, counting-house

---

[11] DBCM, *Annual Report* (1911), 19.   [12] Ibid. (1898), 3.
[13] Murray, 13–14. The company kept few records of ethnic origins. For 1910, 1911, 1912, labour averages were 40% Tswana, 25% Sotho, 20% Cape, 15% 'Shangaan' (Tsonga), Ndebele Zulu, etc.: DBCA, GM 1/2/2.

. . . hospital'.[14] But there were many more—at least eight or ten in the early 1890s, rising to over twenty at the period of maximum employment. The earliest examples were little more than crude dormitories consisting of an enclosed square of 'rows of one storey buildings constructed of corrugated iron . . . divided into rooms holding about twenty natives each'.[15] Wood and water were supplied, but not rations, with the exception of provision of soup for underground workers from 1896, in defiance of the Kimberley retailers. There were searching rooms and detention rooms for end-of-service purging of any swallowed diamonds, and a few had open-air baths. By 1906, a monthly average of 12,000 underground workers were housed in seven compounds communicating directly with the five producing mines, including a Dutoitspan compound for 2,900 men. There were a further eleven for floors and surface sites with contingents of a few hundreds to a thousand. Three compounds made up the De Beers convict station, housing 1,113 prisoners for work at the washing and sorting plant and for compound sanitation.

The convict station which had been gradually expanded from the 1880s was a more rigorous adaptation of the compound system to the needs of the company for complete security in the final stages of diamond recovery, as well as investment in the training of a long-term captive force. The cost per man, including officials, guards, and stores, increased from £28 a year to £50 which was, in fact, slightly less than the annual wage for contracted Africans. Convicts were worked for longer hours, and they were selected as 'long-sentence' men (usually for stock theft), paid no wages, easily directed, and totally subject to searching techniques.[16]

The convicts, in short, were a special case of a more general direction of labour through the compounds to assigned tasks in the production process. The utility of daily shift workers close at hand far outweighed any initial costs in compound construction and maintenance. This was particularly evident in the 1890s, when there was a large amount of night work to build up stocks of blue on the floors, as well as development work. Prior to 1893, the company employed a good third of the supervisory grades of miners as 'contractors' on 10- to 10½-hour shifts underground. Their gangs were supplied from the nearest compound and paid on a ticket system at a flat rate per shift from the earnings of the

[14] DBCM, *Annual Report* (1890), 23; (1903), 13; Williams, *The Diamond Mines of South Africa*, 13 (plates) and 421, 440–8.

[15] Ibid. For occasional rationing at the Kimberley floor and stable compounds see DBCA, S. 1, 1896; CPP, 6. 48–'96, p. 76.

[16] DBCM, *Annual Report* (1906), 25; CPP, C. 4–'05; G. 5–'07; G. 5–'07; G. 4–'08; 6. 8–'09; DBCA, S. 1. 1900.

ILL. 8. After the siege: some De Beers directors and shareholders at Kimberley for the eleventh annual general meeting, 23 February 1900. *Standing:* D. J. Haarhoff (company lawyer, director 1907–1917); Gardner F. Williams (general manager); Dr Thomas Smartt MLA (shareholder); Alpheus F. Williams (assistant general manager); William Pickering (company secretary, director 1917–1933); Capt. T. G. Tyson (shareholder, director 1902–1912). *Seated:* Isidore Dreyfus (diamond merchant, alternate director for Sir Julius Wernher); Lt. Col. David Harris MLA (director 1897–1931); The Right Hon. C. J. Rhodes PC, MLA (director and life governor 1888–1902); George W. Compton (director 1888–1923); Louis Reyersbach (diamond merchant, alternate director for Alfred Beit).

contractors. Those who were not engaged in drilling, tramming, and loading were paid at a flat weekly rate: 'The natives on entering the compound are contracted to the compound managers for 4 months, the contract wages are 15s. per week paid fortnightly, then the compound manager again sub-contracts them to the mining contractor for whom they work and from whom they receive their wages.'[17]

With earnings from special tasks, a labourer might make 18s. to 20s. on six tickets per week, but the average was less at about 15s. In 1893, Williams agreed with the contractors to change to three shorter shifts of 8 hours for underground work, providing there was no decrease in

[17] CPP, G. 5-'96.

output from the combination of day and night work, and that labour was still paid fortnightly.[18] In practice, this led to greater differentiation between compound averages and wages received by workers engaged on shift work or at flat weekly rates. Average earnings on the surface stayed at 18s. to 19s. per week for 10-hour shifts with wood and water provided. For underground workers on 2 to 4 months contracts earnings ranged from 15s. to 24s. per week (at 3s. or 4s. per shift), plus medical care at the mines' hospitals constructed from the mid-1890s. Shift work continued on this basis till the Anglo-Boer war. The company secretary of Gold Fields of South Africa wrote in 1895 to learn how the compound model operated and what the scale of rations for convicts was, as a guide to 'a uniform system of rations' on the Rand.[19] The convict scale of rations was cited as evidence that these workers were adequately fed on bread, mealies, meat, and vegetables: but DBCM provided no such largesse for other workers, in deference to pressures from the Kimberley commercial sector. Contract workers had to purchase provisions and clothing from compound stores, at an estimated cost of 1s. per day. The profits on the transaction were a source of funds for charities selected by the company chairman.

For the workers, lack of free rations was an effective deduction from wages of some 20 to 30 per cent, and the health of the work force may well have suffered because of unwillingness to purchase expensive vegetables instead of cheaper mealies and meat. Despite screening for infectious diseases, inoculation against smallpox, and occasional quarantines, notification of diseases was commonplace, including cases of scurvy and leprosy. The compounds may well have aggravated periodic outbreaks of dysentery, 'enteric' fever, influenza, and the all-embracing 'pneumonia' which debilitated and killed. Data for mortality rates before the mid-1890s are far from perfect and not entirely satisfactory thereafter. It would seem that deaths from industrial accidents declined over the period from 1890 till 1914. Qualitative evidence of general mortality among contract workers and convicts suggests periodic crises in workers' health consistent with epidemics and underlying malnutrition, against a falling trend in male mortality rates for Kimberley District (in which mine labour predominated). There were outbreaks of 'pneumonia' in the compounds in 1892, 1893, and a severe outbreak in 1897. A medical report attributed the causes to 'the clothing of the boys and the soil of the flooring' in conditions of severe overcrowding.[20] A change to concrete flooring,

[18] DBCA, Board 5/1/1, Williams to Craven, 3 Mar. 1892; S. 1 (1896) [compound manager's reports].
[19] DBCA, S. 1 (1895), Gold Fields to DBCM, 17 Aug. 1895.
[20] DBCA, S. 1 (1897), 'Departments', Arthur Fuller, report, 22 Dec. 1897; S. 1 (1900),

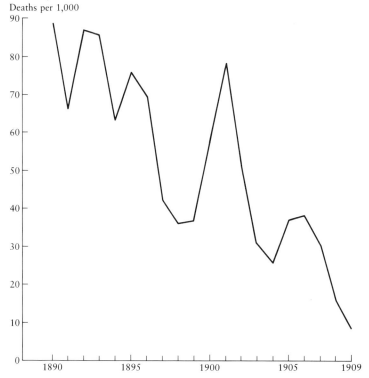

Deaths per 1,000

FIG. 4. Mortality rates for black and coloured males: Kimberley District, 1890–1909

regular disinfection, and a space of at least 400 cubic feet per worker were recommended. Williams went some way to meet this requirement in the new compounds for Dutoitspan and Bultfontein, but convicts and

Scott to Williams, 15 Aug. 1900. Convict huts measured 30 × 30 × 10 feet for 30 men. For health conditions see *Blue Books on Native Affairs*; *Annual Reports* of DBCM; see too CPP, G. 4-'1908 (for convicts); *Dominions Royal Commission. Minutes of Evidence*, pt. II, Cd. 7707 (1914), 93; and more generally, CPP, District Health Reports; Reports on Hospitals and Asylums; Medical Officer of Health Reports; and the Cape *Statistical Register*. Kimberley Africans had a mortality rate of 41 per thousand by 1896 which was generally lower than 27 other towns surveyed in the Cape; cf. too the high rate for recruits for the Rand from tropical areas, 1906–13, 40 to 75 per thousand: COCP, *Africa* (South), 1033 (1913), 1042 (1914). Turrell, *Capital and Labour*, 163, provides rates for the worst period 1896–1905, including the siege, which exclude Wesselton labour from the calculation although these workers were treated at Beaconsfield mine hospital. Causes of death were listed under respiratory diseases, zymotic diseases, and 'violence' (accidents) in that order, and the mortality rate from all causes fell sharply after 1907, possibly as a result of inoculations and greater care in selection of recruits. Deaths from accidents fell from about 5 to under 1 per thousand, 1890–1914. The very full health records for the Cape would repay closer study to establish general morbidity among all sections of the population and work-related conditions of health.

others on the old sites were still housed in huts allowing half this space. Whatever the good intentions, the siege of Kimberley swept them aside, when typhoid and dysentery killed 1,500 blacks, raising the mortality rate again to a crisis level which was only exceeded by the loss of 22 pe. cent of the labour force in 1918, when 2,500 black workers were killed by influenza.

These were exceptional losses, shared by whites as well. The more general average mortality rate from all causes at Kimberley mines, 1890–1913, was 23.8 per thousand black and white workers employed monthly, which was comparable to the rate for Premier diamond mine in the Transvaal, and it is confirmed to some extent by the mortality rate for convicts (24.1 per thousand) for the shorter period 1896–1904. The trend was down, but it is likely (on current research) that the mortality rate for African males at Kimberley in the 1880s and early 1890s was very high (at a mean of 95 per thousand 1886–96), while the mine-specific rates for 1897–1909 yield a mean of 38 per thousand. The period of amalgamation took the greatest toll, followed by a slow and spasmodic improvement in measures to save lives at an industrial enclave.

Apart from more immediate cause of suffering, the siege of Kimberley and the Boer war precipitated a major crisis in labour supply for the company. By the end of 1899, the work force of 12,000 Africans had been kept at the mines up to 12 months, employed on defences, road-building, and the usual tasks of hauling and washing. An effort was made to send some contingents through the Boer lines, to reduce the number of mouths to feed; and there is some evidence that Rhodes cut African rations to induce more to leave.[21] When the siege was raised in February 1900, those who had survived refused even the shortest contracts and fled. New sources of labour either preferred better-paid work carrying, driving, or producing food for the army, or were unable to reach Kimberley from the north. The shortage was aggravated by a decline in the number of convicts allocated by the government to 600 or 700 a year.

From March 1900, therefore, Rhodes and his management displayed anxiety about the ability of the company to return to pre-war levels of production. Coal and timber were in short supply, as were foodstuffs for the workers available at 30 per cent under strength. At the end of the year it was uncertain whether DBCM would be able to make its deliveries to the London merchants which weakened Rhodes's bargaining position during negotiations for a new contract. Surplus revenue might

---

[21] Rotberg ch. 21; Peter Warwick, *Black People and the South African War, 1899–1902* (Cambridge, 1983), 129–30; for other aspects of the siege see ch. 5 below.

ILL. 9. Merchants, buyers, and directors at De Beers, 1904. Not all present are identifiable. *Front row, left to right:* Arend Brink, Ernest Oppenheimer, B. Horkheimer, Alpheus Williams, W. Harris, C. E. Hertog. *Second row, left to right:* D. J. Haarhoff, C. E. Nind, J. H. Lange, Sir Lewis Michell, David Harris, T. Tyson, (unidentified). *Third row standing, left to right:* William Pickering, J. C. Minnie, G. H. Bonas, (three unidentified), H. P. Rudd, H. Hirsche, F. Hirschhorn. At the back row, top left is L. Breitmeyer?

not cover investments in cold storage and dynamite ventures. Rhodes ordered the company secretary to put up the price of provisions at compound stores, hoping to make £20,000 a year in profits 'on our sales to the natives'.[22] To tap alternative sources, W. D. Fynn, a Kimberley manager and labour broker was sent to the Transkei. With haulage and washing rates threatened, Rhodes urged hiring drill boys 'at any price or even employ white men'.

Gardner Williams responded to the crisis by sending his own expeditions to Barotseland and Zululand, but failed to find enough men. He had better luck in the more usual area of supply through agents sent to recruiting centres in Basutoland, and he was optimistic that the additional scheme for tapping Cape labour would restore numbers. 6-month contracts for

[22] RH, Rhodes Papers, telegrams, Rhodes to DBCM, 1548 (14 Nov. 1900); RH, MSS Afr. s. 227, Rhodes to Beit, 6 Nov. 1900; Rhodes to Pickering, 4 Aug. 1900. Rhodes also sent Williams to Indwe to improve the quality of coal, because dirty coal increased the amount of labour required to clean and fire the boilers.

a flat rate of 15s. per week with wood and water, paid passages, and a bonus for recruiters stimulated the recruiting drive in Transkei and Ciskei with some help from local magistrates.

But the rates of pay were no better than before the war, and average annual numbers remained insufficient to meet the need for expanded output required by the purchase of LSAE lands in 1899 and the reopening of Bultfontein and Dutoitspan. At the end of 1901, Williams reported:

It is now with great difficulty that the 'boys' are induced to take out 'passes' (contracts for work) for more than three months. This arrangement has been most unsatisfactory, for just as a 'boy' has been trained to do good work, his 'pass' expires, and he leaves the compound. Agents have been employed collecting labour in all parts of Cape Colony, Basutoland, Bechuanaland, Rhodesia and such parts of the Transvaal as are free from the enemy. By this method a large number of 'floor' boys and underground 'shovel boys' have been obtained, but not the class of labour that can be trained for drilling. The scarcity of drill boys has greatly handicapped the output and the underground development work.[23]

Numbers were eventually made good by the recruiters, and up to £20,000 or £30,000 had to be spent on this service annually till 1908, raising the costs for mining to unprecedented levels. For the first time too, the company set up its own labour employment bureau to monitor and record annual intake and separate the large numbers of Cape Xhosa, kept at the Bultfontein compounds, from Pedi and Sotho. Those from British Bechuanaland had been reluctant to return, after a strike at the West End compound was suppressed by force in 1901. Improved rates for drilling brought them back; and a higher rate for contractors was allowed to pay the new scale. The company also turned to Natal to supplement the convict force with an extra '250 Natal prisoners' in 1906, who promptly attempted to escape and were repatriated by a relieved superintendent 2 years later.[24] With one exception, the new piece rates established in 1901 remained unaltered till the First World War and longer (see Table 4.2).

The company's evidence to the Dominions Royal Commission in 1913 confirmed that wages for blacks had been static, despite increased costs for foodstuffs and clothing at the compound stores. White workers' wages, on the other hand, rose from an average of 16s. to 22s. 6d. per shift, during the period of general labour conflict at the South African mines after 1900. Little of the conflict touched DBCM, where even unskilled workers by 1914 earned four times the shift rate for blacks.

[23] DBCM, General manager's report, *Annual Report* (1901), 4.
[24] DBCA, S. 1. 1901, Williams to contractors, 26 Sept. 1901; 'The worst class of criminals I ever had to deal with', E. C. Dyason in CPP, G. 8–'1909.

TABLE 4.2. *Wage rates for surface and underground workers, De Beers Consolidated Mines, 1901, 1914*

		1901	1914
Underground (eight hours)	Drilling	3s. to 5s. per shift	5s. per shift
	Machine drills	n/a	4s. per 30 feet
	Loading	3s. 6d. to 4s. 6d. (45–65 trucks) = 7s. per 100 loads	22s. 6d. per 100 loads
Surface (10 hours)	General hands	2s. 6d. to 3s. 6d. per shift	2s. 6d. per shift
	Loading	3s. 6d. to 4s. per shift	12s. per 100 loads

Source: DBCA S.1; *Dominions Royal Commission, Minutes of Evidence,* Part II, Cd. 7707 (1914).

When asked to explain the lack of upward movement in African wages, the assistant general manager, I. R. Grimmer, fell back on the conventional (and not disproven) notion of 'target work':

The native comes here with the idea of making so much money. For instance he does not look at it quite in the same way as a white man. He would not take into consideration the number of hours he has to work in the week, but he would calculate how much money he would get at the end of the week, and he would make up his mind that he would take so much money home, and would feed himself accordingly. So I would not like to say that there is any relation between the rise or fall in wages and the cost of living.[25]

In the absence of 'any movement towards combination', and evidence of some recontracting, continued Grimmer, company wage levels and the differential between whites and blacks were justified in comparison with agriculture and other industrial rates.

But there was, in fact, periodic unrest over compound conditions and changes in work practices and wages. The protector of natives, G. W. Barnes, who was usually enthusiastic about the compound system, published his disquiet, in 1895, about cases of physical abuse by overmen and contractors which appeared in the records as 'cruel cases' and resulted in warnings rather than prosecutions. When this mild criticism appeared

[25] *Dominions Royal Commission* (1914), 17.

in the Native Affairs *Blue Book* for 1896, along with confirmation from the civil commissioner, DBCM issued an angry protest at the implied 'slur on the Compound Manager of this Company'.[26] But this did not stop Barnes raising other cases of abuse by Zulu guards and criticizing the indeterminate responsibility for labour discipline in the management hierarchy. More usually, though, discipline was enforced by fines and loss of earnings, with occasional reference to the magistrates' courts.

After the strike by the Basotho over ticket rates, there were few examples of resistance. In 1910, grievances were channelled into fighting among Sotho at the Wesselton compounds which led to two deaths, police intervention, and the dismissal of 700 men who refused to work. The following year, a cut in wages led to an outright strike at Wesselton, mass arrest of 1,600 workers, trials, fines, and more dismissals. The attention of the Native Affairs Department, which monitored, rather than investigated, these events turned instead to a series of disturbances, assaults, and illegal punishments in the cramped compounds of Jagersfontein which had led to the shooting of black workers who rioted over the murder of one of their number in 1914.[27] Conditions at the Free State mine were probably worse than any other diamond mines and were roundly condemned by Union mine inspectors 1912–14. But there were no prosecutions of managers or overseers.

A more measured protest was received, however, from fifty-one DBCM workers at Green Point Location, Beaconsfield, who requested an end to detention houses and their searching procedures, the adjustment upwards of flat rates in line with contract prices, more official control of compounds, and an end to employment of convicts 'in Competition with free labour'.[28] The Native Affairs Department branch at Kimberley was inclined to dismiss this literate and thoughtful document as 'not influentially signed', but agreed that the detention centres were 'humiliating'. Asked to clarify the issue, Inspector Barrett analysed in some detail the end-of-contract search methods for the enlightenment of his superiors:

Articles like boots, sewing machines, or bicycles, which cannot be effectually searched without destruction, are not allowed to leave the compounds. Boys are permitted to introduce such articles only on this clear understanding. When a

[26] CPP, G. 5-'96, 34; DBCA, S. 1, 1895, DBCM to Native Affairs, 2 Apr. 1895.
[27] CAD, NTS 2065 121/280, Cook to Debell (New Jagersfontein), 10 Mar. 1914; Terence Ranger, 'Faction Fighting, Race Consciousness and Worker Consciousness: A Note on the Jagersfontein Riots of 1914', *South African Labour Bulletin*, 4/5 (1978), 66–74.
[28] CAD, NTS 2044 60/80, petition by Soga Mgikela and others to Botha, 22 Oct. 1915.

boy owning any such article wishes to leave, he has to dispose of his rights to someone who is remaining, or if he intends to return, he may leave it in safe keeping with the compound Manager.

Detention parades are held once a week or once a fortnight according to the number of boys about to be discharged.

Having divested himself of prohibited articles, each boy taking his discharge, first of all hands any cash on his person to the compound manager, who keeps a careful record, and returns it at the close of the detention period.

He then enters the first room, carrying everything which he wishes to take away. His kit is searched in his presence. He strips and his clothing after being searched is made into a bundle with the rest of his kit, and locked away. His person is carefully searched, attention being devoted to any suspicious cuts, protuberances or open sores, in all of which at different times, diamonds have been found concealed.

In exchange for his clothing he is next allotted a liberal supply of the company's blankets; whereupon he enters a large room, or sometimes a courtyard partly roofed and partly open to the sun, in which together with the rest of the current batch of discharges he is destined to pass in eating, sleeping, smoking, or basking in the sun, a period sufficient to frustrate any attempt to leave the Company's employ with swallowed diamonds.

Each hand is enclosed in a stiff fingerless leather glove locked round the wrist by means of a light chain. The glove has a niche or recess in the palm, useful for filling a pipe or handling a porridge spoon. The purpose of the glove is to prevent a Native from regaining possession of stones swallowed or otherwise introduced into the rectum, keeping them concealed about his person during the detention period, and swallowing them afresh when about to be discharged. There is no doubt that this used to take place before the gloves were introduced, and to a less extent when the gloves were not sufficiently stiff.

I shall forward as soon as I can obtain it a photograph of a parcel of stones swallowed by a single boy, and passed by him without any apparent injury. The value of the parcel at rates prevailing shortly before the war would be about four thousand pounds. The boy in question must have represented some sort of combine; for it is inconceivable that he had found all the stones himself; but his willingness to risk so much, seems to indicate some previous success in evading all precautions.

A grey-headed suspect who can no longer obtain employment in the compounds once said to me with a twinkle: 'There is no difficulty created by the wit of men that cannot in time be overcome by the wit of other men.'

During detention, a chart is kept of each boy's motions; there is a device by means of which each stool is tipped onto a screen and washed under a jet, the process being watched for the appearance of previously swallowed diamonds. No boy is discharged from detention until his evacuations are deemed sufficient in character and number. The period is usually five or six days. When the boys have been duly passed they again parade before the Compound Manager, and receive back their money, kit and clothing. White guards only are employed in connection with the detention house.[29]

Statistics of total recoveries by these means are unavailable. But purging and search resulted in 190,000 carats in 1897 and 1898, and the annual recovery rate remained at about 100,000 carats till 1901, especially from the West End compound, the convicts, and the stable compounds. Investigators blamed the 'leakage' on labour from the locations—'the scum of Kimberley'—employed on the floors, whence they established a channel through the military hospital which attended to black workers after the siege. This partial evidence of the recovery rate, if at all typical, is very significant of a potential clandestine trade amounting to about a month's recovery, or £150,000 at current values.[30]

Using less drastic means, DBCM also continued to pay for 'finds' at the rate of 5s. per carat, plus 2.5 per cent of estimated value, which resulted in a fairly steady surrender of some 40,000 to 50,000 carats a year, especially by the convicts who were allowed to accumulate savings in this way. White workers who surrendered diamonds earned about £3,000 a year in bonuses, compared with £11,000 for blacks. Taken together with rates of pay that were higher than on the Rand mines, this inducement and the searching system were considered by management to have cut down internal IDB to perhaps 10 per cent of total diamond production.

Such were the basic methods of mechanization and old-fashioned worker regimentation which Williams and his son applied to an industrial process whose special problems entailed special solutions. At one level, the technology of the company proved adaptable enough to meet the production requirements of the market for diamonds. It was further tested during the Anglo-Boer war, when the machine shops were diverted to armaments and fabricated 'Long Cecil' from a 'solid piece of hammered steel, ten feet long, ten-and-a-half inches in diameter' which fired 28 lb. projectiles up to five miles.[31] At another level, the migrant labour system permitted great flexibility when it was necessary to shut down plant, or divert labour through the compounds to new development work. The complementarity between mechanization in an ordered sequence and variable supply of hand labour met the need for regular inputs at low unit costs, though the assumptions of management about fixed market

---

[29] CAD, NTS 2044 60/80, A. L. Barrett (inspector and protector of natives) to director of native labour, Johannesburg, 11 Nov. 1915; BRA, HE 230 (1908–9), for the minutes of the joint IDB committee for De Beers and Premier: estimated levels of loss and trapping methods.

[30] DBCA, S. 1, 1901, acting compound manager's report, 26 Mar. 1901; general manager, report: 'diamonds recovered from various compounds, January 1897–31 December 1901'.

[31] Buys, *Archives of the General Manager*, 15.

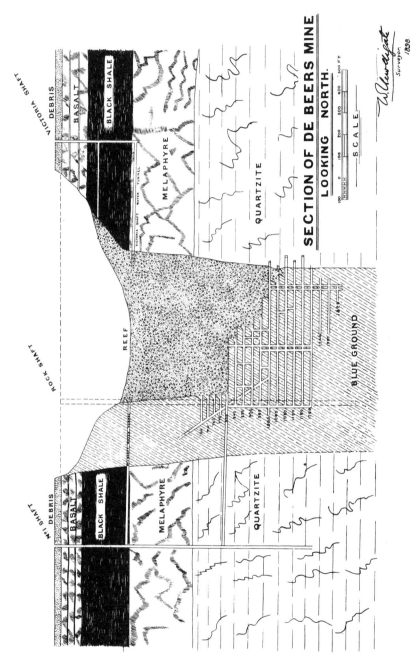

FIG. 5a.

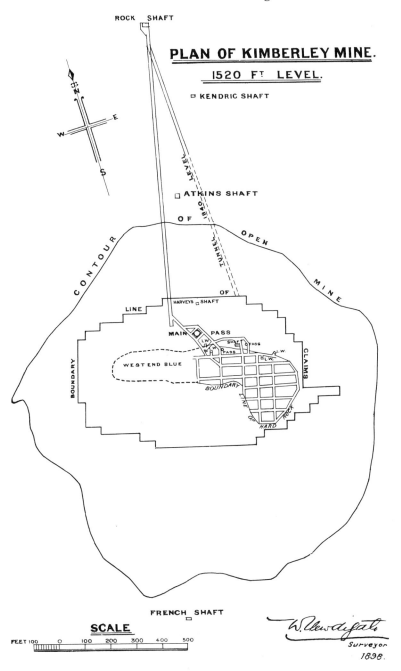

FIG. 5b. The development of underground mining at Kimberley, 1898

TABLE 4.3. *Evolution of the London Diamond Syndicate, 1889–1930*

Participation by:	1889 Sept.–Dec.	1890 –1 %	1892 –4	1895 –1900	1901 –6 %	1908	1909 –12 %	1913 –14 %	1915 –19 %	1920 –3 %	1924 %	1925 –30
Wernher, Beit and Co.	X	X 23	X	X	X 34	X	X					
L. Breitmeyer and Co.							X 30	X 30	X	X 30	X 20	X.
Barnato Bros.	X	X 20	X	X	X 27½	X	X 30	X 37½	X	X 30	X 35	X.
A. Dunkelsbuhler and Co.	X	X 10	X	X	X 12	X	X 12½	X 10	X	X 12½	X 11	
Mosenthal, Sons and Co.	X	X 15	X	X	X 12	X	X 12½	X 12½	X	X 12½	X 11	
Joseph Bros.		X 7			X 9							
F. T. Gervers		X 8			X 1							
I. Cohen and Co.		X 5										
M. Lilienfeld and Co.		X 5										
S. Neumann and Co.		X 5										
Feldenheimer and Co.		X 2										
V. A. Litkie and Co.			X		X 4½							
Central Mining and Investment Corporation							X 15	X 10	X	X 15	X 15	
N. M. Rothschild and Sons						X						
Anglo American Corporation											X 8	X.
Johannesburg Consolidated Investment Co.												X

Sources: DBCA, Diamond Committee 2/5/1–4; Rough Minute Books; London Board Minutes (1889–1900); Diamond Syndicate 6/1/1–6; BRA, WB Letter Books; CAD, MNW, and TES series. % participation is not available for all years.

rates were severely tested by the Boer War. Recruiting met the demand, without raising wage rates, except for drilling, and there was no alteration in white to black ratios. These methods did not change till the 1920s. From 1903, the management held about a year's production on the floors. What weight of diamonds should be fed to the market from this reserve was for others to determine.

DIAMOND CONTRACTS

By their investment in the industry, the principal London merchants were clearly in a position to influence the way in which the company was run. Whether they could regulate production policy was still an open question in the early 1890s. In practice, it took the merchants about 4 years to arrive at a regular working agreement among themselves on how to fund consignments purchased from DBCM at Kimberley, or shipped separately for sale through the company's London office. During that period, separate sales to lesser buyers outside the series of 'combines' resulted in a dual price structure with discounts for the fortunate, in return for bulk orders and options on future production. The first half of the decade, moreover, was one of depression in sales of finished goods and constriction of the banking credit essential to Amsterdam and Antwerp buyers and manufacturers. The high hopes of a settled market after the great amalgamation gave way to an intense rivalry for access to stocks under discount agreements.

The merchant directors on the DBCM board were not in a position in London or in Kimberley to outvote the representatives of other shareholding groups. Of the twenty-one directors who attended meetings from November 1888 to the end of 1890, only Harry Mosenthal made regular appearances; and Beit came more occasionally. They were not reinforced until the arrival of Paul Dreyfus, Barnato, and Woolf Joel in 1890 and by Julius Wernher (who replaced Dreyfus), as the hard core of importers of rough stones at the metropolitan end. At Kimberley, they were considerably outnumbered by directors who manned the diamond committee. Numbers were not, of course, conclusive evidence of the strength or weakness of the merchant lobby, and there were critical board meetings when Beit, Wernher, and Meyer got their way on company policy, more usually by arguments from their position as financiers and share brokers than from a direct interest in the trade.

The first indication that amalgamation might lead to a merchant corner of production came towards the end of 1889, when the London board minuted the rumour 'that this Company are to sell all their diamonds to a syndicate for two years'. No director present admitted to knowledge of this deal, which originated in Kimberley with Barnato, Bernheim, and Max Michaelis (for Wernher, Beit and Co.), 'the De Beers Company undertaking to the buyers to keep the sale secret', with options on fixed monthly quantities at a rising price.[32] Michaelis arranged another 3 months of purchases on behalf of Mosenthals, Barnatos, Dunkelsbuhler, and Wernher, Beit and Co. for early 1890, in return for advances of up to £200,000 to meet DBCM's cash requirements. Again, there was a pledge not to sell to 'outsiders' under contract prices. Other firms were admitted into the syndicate early in 1890 (see Table 4.3) for a share in the costs and the reassortment of stocks for sales to the Continental buyers.

The expansion of the combine was made necessary by the need to clear the very large accumulation of one and a half million carats arising from the amalgamation period, when rival mines had produced hard for good prices. While the ten participants laboured to sell this stock to the Dutch and Belgians, prices slipped from 43s. to 30s. per carat at Kimberley. In March 1890 the syndicate declined to take up any options, and the company in the midst of financial gloom had to rely on separate sales through merchant directors and the smaller dealers. Indeed, Wernher was not really in favour of any more 'combinations' at this stage, preferring to see a cut in production and few sales on a poor market.

Strapped for investment funds, Rhodes worked out a method of building up a stock in London from May 1890 for clandestine sales through F. Philipson Stow and the merchant F. T. Gervers outside the syndicate. The private 'reserve' did not reach the projected £1 million to fund expansion; and it did not remain 'secret' for much longer than May 1891, when Wernher and a few other directors had to be enlisted to help clear the extra stock. In any case, the Kimberley board had to agree to limit sales through its ordinary channels to 160,000 carats a month from the beginning of 1891. Stow fulminated at this evidence of pressure from the 'Holborn Viaduct contingent' and threatened to withdraw, leaving Rhodes 'under the Jews in free and undisturbed possession of everything'.[33] He regretted 'this damn secret reserve' and planned to sell direct to Dutch buyers. By July 1891, with Stow's faith and patience weakening, Rhodes suggested Rothschild should be informed about the

---

[32] DBCA, Board 2/7/1, minutes, 4 Sept. 1889; Board 6/6/1, Barnato Bros. to DBCM, 27 Sept. 1889 (for monthly options up to 182,000 carats at 34s. to 36s. per carat).

[33] DBCA, Board 5/1/1, Stow to Craven, 14 Jan., 13 May 1891; BRA, WB Cape 1, Wernher to Breitmeyer, 27 May 1891. For a fuller account, Colin Newbury, 'The Origins and Function of the London Diamond Syndicate, 1889–1914', *Business History*, 29/1 (1987), 5–26.

main objective of the subterfuge, as a gesture of personal loyalty, rather than a matter of strict company policy: 'If you ask me why not do it with the knowledge of the whole Board, you know yourself that such a course must fail. In the first place the buyers on the Board would reduce their offers, and in the second place the natural greed of the shareholders would not allow the accumulation.'[34] The argument was unimpressive and the policy extremely divisive, as Rhodes continued to run two sales operations with negotiated prices for Kimberley buyers and direct shipments to London, where lots were disposed of for whatever they would fetch 'as so much wool'.[35]

Great exception was taken to the 'secret reserve' policy when all the board was informed, though some of the indignation was ritual, as, in the end, Wernher, Beit and Co. had assisted in clearing Stow's stocks. The reserve was made official 'in trust for the company' from January 1892 at about £500,000, and securities in the form of British consols were purchased out of ordinary retained profits to make up the fund to nearly the figure Rhodes had intended, though it was not at his disposal. Garbled accounts appeared in the Kimberley press with the false information that 'Mr. Rhodes, the Chairman of the Company, was quite unaware of the circumstances'. Stow despaired of liberating his chief from 'the hands of the Chosen'.[36]

A modified form of the syndicate operated during the last half of 1891, encouraged by Lord Rothschild, to boost sales and enable the company to meet its high debenture and interest payments, as well as the additional burden of Wesselton production. The term 'syndicate' is used in correspondence from September, when merchants agreed to take 'pool' (or mixed) stocks at a discount from the De Beers and Kimberley mines. Throughout 1892, parcels continued to be sold to syndicate members— Wernher, Beit and Co., Barnato Bros., Dunkelsbuhler, Joseph Bros., Mosenthals, and Litkies—'at a nominal price higher than the actual sale price in order to keep up the market rate'. There were also sales by members of the Kimberley diamond committee to 'outsiders' under nominal, or 'basis valuation, which gave rise to angry correspondence from Wernher's agent, Ludwig Breitmeyer.'[37]

---

[34] RH, Baxter [transcripts], Rhodes to Stow, 19 July 1891.
[35] DBCA, Board 5/1/1, Stow to Craven, 17 July 1891.
[36] *DFA*, 26 Mar. 1892; DBCA, Board 5/1/1, Stow to Craven, 5 Feb. 1892.
[37] DBCA, Board 2/5/1 (Diamond Committee), 21 Oct. 1892. By 1893 the terms 'basis' valuation for parcels delivered in the first contract month and 'par' valuation including an additional percentage on 'basis', according to sales, effectively raising the price of deliveries, were current; DBCA, Board 6/1/1, note, 17 February 1893.

But time was on the side of those who could help fund the company regularly. The trend was towards sales on 2- or 3-month options from April 1892 and through 1893, as smaller buyers were squeezed out. By 1894, Breitmeyer was negotiating on behalf of the syndicate for all goods produced on 3-month options. The Kimberley diamond committee, with no buyers present, turned down an offer by an Antwerp syndicate for Belgian and Dutch cutters 'as a very dangerous policy to adopt, especially as this Company has in the past had the experience that they can expect no support from them in the event of any collapse in the market'.[38] The dependence of merchants and monopoly was mutual.

As arrangements with the syndicate acquired some of the characteristics of single-channel selling, the discount worked out with the diamond committee became a standard feature of bulk transactions at between 10 and 15 per cent of the basis price. Breitmeyer instituted the practice of sample parcels for a run of production from company mines, early in 1894, which served as a check on quality control and valuation in later years. The method of raising valuation periodically and so increasing the purchase price dated from Wernher's belated enthusiasm for 'combination' in 1892, as he conceded that the merchants could organize resales to Continental dealers in a measured and appreciating volume and restore confidence that cut stones would also rise in price. The experience of sustaining prices in a poor market till the middle of 1894 began to pay off and yielded a high rate of return on syndicate resales at 30 per cent on a turnover of just over £1 million in May and June, when demand picked up. Even Rhodes had been brought round to accepting the idea of very large secret deals at discounts on nominal prices published for the benefit of the outside world, and had retreated from his proclaimed policy of supporting smaller buyers.

The syndicate also ensured, in its early years, that surplus roughs were held at the point of production in blue ground, or in the company safe, particularly when prices were at their lowest in 1894 at 24s. to 25s. per carat, to allow the past surplus in London to be cleared. It was important, advised Wernher, 'that goods are not allowed to come over all at once, and that is what people are most afraid of, for there would be a serious fall'.[39] And to that extent the merchant buyers exercised a constraint on the producer by setting a ceiling on periodic deliveries.

What was true of the recession period in 1890–3 remained true for syndicate policy over the next 2 decades. From 1895, the valuation price

[38] DBCA, Board 2/5/1 (Diamond Committee), 24 Dec. 1894.
[39] RH, Rhodes Papers, C 24, Wernher to Rhodes, 11 July 1891.

index of sales began to improve for DBCM and moved on a long upward trend, disrupted temporarily by the sharp recession in the American market, during 1908–9, and by the outbreak of the First World War (see Fig. 6). Prices for production from New Jagersfontein and Koffyfontein, owned largely by DBCM and the Barnatos, followed this trend, though it is not certain all their diamonds were marketed through the syndicate prior to 1895.

From 1895, too, the syndicate had a monopoly of production from DBCM and agreed to take a whole year's output at 200,000 carats per month over two periods of half-yearly options at a fixed price. Deliveries were spread evenly 'to provide us with cash regularly', explained Meyer. And the syndicate also had an option on the reserve stock of 450,000 carats held by the company.[40] With much tighter control over Kimberley buying and a strict practice of allowing dealers at home to acquire diamonds only 'in series' at fixed resale prices, the syndicate was able to continue the pattern of 6-month options down to 1900 for the benefit of the five principals, the company, and (it was argued) the trade at large. Forward options undercut sales by negotiation; and the establishment of a 'buyers' list' in London gave the syndicate a further means of persuading independent dealers to accept the system without argument, as F. T. Gervers complained in 1893: 'I had previously held over me a sort of threat that if I never bought my name would not be kept on the list of buyers, & I should get no sight at all. I was practically compelled to buy a much larger quantity than I wanted, but I did so under a personal promise from Rhodes to Felkin that I should not be undersold [at Kimberley].'[41] Such promises were worthless as relations with the syndicate took precedence for essential long-term provision of income. Gervers and others had to be content with a small 'sub-participation' in the combine and specialize in grades the principals did not want.

Two problems threatened this growing harmony of interests between producer and merchant. As mine production developed and changed, there were complaints about deterioration in the 'average' quality of parcels sorted first at Kimberley by the company valuator, Arend Brink, 'which, if continued, would result in loss for the syndicate, besides disorganising the whole of our business in London', argued Wernher's agent.[42] Various causes were blamed, from hard 'lumps', the use of convicts for sorting,

---

[40] RH, Rhodes Papers, C 27, Meyer to Rhodes, 25 Dec. 1895.
[41] RH, Rhodes Papers, C 7, Gervers to Stow, 8 Dec. 1893. F. W. Felkin was Gervers's buyer at Kimberley.
[42] DBCA, Board 6/1/1, Hirsche to DBCM, 4 Sept. 1896; Robinow, 'Report for the Diamond Committee', 28 Nov. 1896.

and faulty production records, which the buyers insisted on inspecting. The company was asked to accept contract clauses on 'fair average quality' and fixed percentages from each of its three operating mines.

Rhodes took strong exception to these new conditions, and Gardner Williams warned that any exclusion of 'fine sand' diamonds would entail an expensive loss on recoveries. In the end, agreements from 1897 contained provision for quality control and special price reductions for excess percentages of 'inferior goods' and 'fine sand'.[43] But the quality problem would not go away and was exacerbated by increased production from Wesselton mine, where costs were cheaper and were taken into account by the syndicate which priced Wesselton goods lower than 'pool' goods from Kimberley and De Beers. So strained were relations between the syndicate and the 'Home' board in 1898 that Rhodes and Oats announced they were going to England 'to discuss the whole question of the future sale of diamonds', on the grounds that Wesselton had to compensate by a higher price for deterioration in yields from the older mines.[44]

Furthermore, Rhodes was turning over in his mind a different pricing system for annual purchases, claiming that 'private sources' indicated that the syndicate was preparing to raise its own resale values, without benefiting DBCM. These sources were letters from James Rochfort Maguire, close friend and a director of the Chartered company, who had been despatched to Antwerp to inspect records of syndicate resales, and the diamond merchants R. Levy and Nephews excluded from the combine.[45] The private intelligence provided enough evidence of a very high mark-up for Rhodes to confront the London board early in 1899 with a proposal to raise basis valuation prices at Kimberley and to take a 50 per cent share of the syndicate's profits. Such a participation, he argued, would give DBCM 'inside knowledge' of the trade and open the way to separate sales through their own or other agents.[46]

This was dangerous territory. The innovation was hotly opposed by merchant members of the board. For the moment, less favourable terms

---

[43] DBCA, Board 6/1/1, Syndicate to DBCM, 4 Jan. 1897. Even so, the company valuator found it was advantageous to use a mesh size insisted on by Wernher, Beit and Co., and that small goods had been sold at full rates in the company's favour 'and against the Syndicate': S. 1 (1898), Brink, 'Report on the present Position of the Diamond Contract', 28 June 1898. The company owned up to this oversight.

[44] DBCA, Board 2/5/1 (Diamond Committee), 17 Nov. 1898.

[45] RH, Rhodes Papers, C 78, Maguire to Tymms, 7 Nov. 1898; Levy and Nephews to Rhodes, 1 Feb., 27 Apr., 15 May 1899; Newbury, 'The Origins', 16.

[46] RH, Rhodes Papers, C 24, Rhodes to Beit, 17 Jan. 1899; DBCA, Board 2/7/1, minutes, 20 Apr.–28 June 1899.

had to be accepted for a year's production from June 1899, because the support of the merchants and Rothschilds was required for the purchase of LSAE lands at Kimberley. The proposal also brought to a head other contentious matters concerning Rhodes's investment policies and the profits of the life governors. With Kimberley under siege from October 1899 to February 1900, the company was in no position to bargain.

But in April 1900 Rhodes was back at the Burlington Hotel in London, threatening to revive his old practice of separate shipments. Wernher offered to take delivery of 975,000 carats of 'pool' and Wesselton goods for the syndicate over 5 months at increased prices; and the contract was linked with assistance in the sale of debentures to cover the purchase of the sites of Bultfontein and Dutoitspan from their ground landlord, in order to bring them into production again.[47] Although a contract was agreed, the argument continued into September 1901, when Rhodes was nearly excluded altogether from negotiations, and output was threatened by the labour crisis. Lord Rothschild intervened to caution the chairman against the use of commission sales through dealers, who could not sustain prices in bad times by holding unsold stock. Sales to the highest bidder would only lead to 'confusion' and introduce an element of 'almost suicidal' speculation. Moreover, any attempt to centre company sales on London would attract the attention of the Inland Revenue, which might claim tax on all DBCM's profits.[48]

In addition to this sobering thought, there were indications from within the syndicate that the company, in all equity, might have to be given a share of the 'huge profits' made in the current market when American demand was so strong. In any case, Rhodes stuck doggedly to his contention that the company was hobbled by the long-term options, when 'there is a profit of at least 20s. per carat or over £400,000 at present market price [20 per cent]; but the extraordinary thing is that in return for this we are tied up for a further six months on options', without the possibility of raising the basis price immediately on a further million carats in deliveries.[49] Julius Wernher, who had succeeded to Stow's life governorship in 1898, was slowly won over to the idea of profit-sharing, in return for Rhodes's agreement to commute the life governors' interests by a share distribution, after capital reconstruction of DBCM. Carl Meyer too who had led the opposition was brought to see some of the force of Rhodes's case, recognizing that the alternatives of sales to the highest

[47] DBCA, Board 2/7/1, 9 and 18 Apr. 1900.
[48] RH, Rhodes Papers, C 7B, Rothschild to Rhodes, 29 Aug. 1901.
[49] BRA, WB Cape 17, Reyersbach to Hirschhorn, 25 June 1901; RH, MSS Afr. s. 227, Rhodes to DBCM, 16 Aug. 1901.

bidder or sales through one firm on commission might damage DBCM's ability to pay a regular dividend, in the absence of occasional help from the syndicate at the end of a financial year.

A new contract with an expanded syndicate, dated 2 December, 1901, ran for 5 years and was renewed for a further 5 to the end of 1910. The syndicate agreed to purchase an annual quantity of diamonds up to £4 million in valuation at 6-month options to be made up of deliveries of 'pool', Wesselton, and debris stock at prices which were only slightly better than those objected to by Rhodes. To meet the company's point about lack of price flexibility on long-term deliveries, a formula was applied to periodic basis valuations to take into account the 'total average prices' realized in London and allow for syndicate expenses and a discount of 12 per cent. Equal profit-sharing, after an initial 5 per cent to the syndicate, was allowed on resales. The company also shared any losses and bore the cost of any future export duties.[50]

Rhodes's persistence and the expertise of his diamond committee changed the relationship with the merchants in time to take advantage of a boom in sales till 1908. There were further debates about the percentages of 'rubbish' and 'sand' allowable in deliveries, but the company had won the right to determine the ways in which classes of rough stones from different mines were included in parcels to keep up the total agreed value of annual deliveries. In time, this became an important variable in the producer's choice of production strategies, as all five mines were worked by DBCM. By 1901, the average price for the company's output had recovered to its 1890 level, while the value of sales had increased by 75 per cent. Over the next decade, under the terms of the 1901 contract and its revision in 1906, some five million metric carats annually—nearly the total of world production—passed from the company to the syndicate, valued at £13 million by 1913.

The revision of terms in 1906 slightly reduced the syndicate's discount to 11 per cent of basis valuation and the initial commission before profit-sharing to 4 per cent. There were other difficulties, as contracted prices got out of line with real prices for stones from different mines, necessitating more frequent valuations than every six months. But the syndicate preferred the relative simplicity of a fixed price per carat based on average resales during the previous year, and this became established practice as part of the pricing and delivery formula. For its part, the Kimberley diamond committee insisted on knowing the business dealings of the

---

[50] RH, Rhodes Papers, C 7B, 315, 317; Hawksley 11, Hawksley to Rhodes, 2 Feb. 1902 (for the 1901 contract).

ILL. 10. Premier (Transvaal) Diamond Mine, early operations, 1903. Incline shaft at mine one with head gear, machine shop and sorting house.

syndicate with other mines, as the industry passed into a new phase of competitive development.[51] Less obviously, the move towards closer association with the syndicate in 1901 was also the beginning of a shift in responsibility for holding unsold stock in London, rather than in Kimberley, as the company was able to plan output to make up values delivered on a long-term contract.

This change was accelerated by the short crisis of 1908–9, when company production was stopped, and the syndicate was split and reconstructed in order to handle stocks from De Beers and New Jagersfontein. To rescue the company for the purpose of paying an annual dividend, a 'No. 2 Syndicate' was hastily put together to buy £400,000 of goods per month at 25 per cent below valuation. When the main syndicate revived to take new options in early 1909, much of the 'sub-participation' by financially weak merchants was eliminated, and there was an increase in the capital subscribed by the five principals—Barnatos, Wernher, Beit and Co., Mosenthals, Dunkelsbuhlers, and the Central Mining and Investment Corporation (which handled much of Wernher, Beit and Co.'s Rand interests).[52] The

[51] DBCA, Board 6/1/2 (Diamond Committee), 24 Jan. 1906.

[52] BRA, WB Inland 30. Central Mining was created by Wernher, Beit and Co. in 1895 to take over the assets of the African Ventures Syndicate. In 1911–12 the company acquired much of the holdings of its parent company and H. Eckstein and Company. Principal shareholders were the partners in the private companies with some French and German interests. RH, 18A/2.

Syndicate emerged from the recession with sales suspended or reduced and profits on resales down to 4 per cent in the last half of 1909. Before the contract came up for renewal, it was clear that DBCM was skilfully adjusting its assortments to include higher proportions of Bultfontein stones which the syndicate had difficulty in selling, but which fetched a better price at Kimberley, because of weight and quality, and enabled the company to meet contracted delivery values more easily.

Consequently, the reconstructed syndicate was more favourable to frequent adjustments of purchase price, based on sales, after 1910. The company, for its part, had a decade of experience of profit-sharing and wanted further changes. For during seven of the financial years 1901/2 to 1908/9, the syndicate made a net profit on resales of £5,092,736, or 15.7 per cent on a total turnover to dealers of £37.6 million. In 1907/8 there was a net loss of £209,606, borne equally by the syndicate and the company. In the profitable years, however, it was found that although 'equal participation is real concerning the losses, it is not applied in the case of profits. In such cases it is greatly affected by the commission of 4% that the Syndicate is authorised to take on the amount of sales before the participation in profits.'[53] This commission together with other charges reduced the company's share disproportionately in years when there was only a small net profit, so that the total division, 1901–9, left £1,562,847 for the company, compared with £3,320,283 for the syndicate.

More frequent adjustment of valuation, therefore, was linked in the 1910 contract with a sliding scale for profit-sharing (worked out by Arend Brink) at protracted negotiations in Kimberley. After an initial 4 per cent to the syndicate, the company would take roughly two-thirds of profits, if these were between 10 and 12 per cent, on resales. Brink also won the company's battle to exclude a quality clause which sooner or later would leave DBCM holding 'rubbish' as unsold goods. 'It had always been the policy of the Board and of Mr. Rhodes that the diamonds should be sold on a fixed prices basis', he argued, whatever change in average values resulted from deterioration of the Kimberley mine, or from the crushing and washing of 'lumps'.[54] Like dealers in London, syndicate agents would have to take parcels 'in series', including the good with the bad, at agreed valuations for the whole parcel. By 1913, with higher prices than ever under the new contract, the balance of profits on resales went to the

---

[53] DBCA, 6/1/3, internal memorandum, 20 Apr. 1910; RAL, 111/27, Viallate to Rothschild and Sons, 11 Apr. 1910.
[54] DBCA, Board 2/5/2 (Diamond Committee), 25 June 1910.

company. But by then too, the world market had changed and quite different strategies were required all round.

For the initial purpose of the selling organization formed by merchants who had participated directly in the growth of the diamond market, and in the mining investment of the 1880s was to stabilize output and restore price levels that had fallen in the early 1890s. The theory of restricting production and distribution of what was essentially a luxury good at that date was well understood. Controlled marketing, as Porges had foreseen, could not be left to the consolidated company: diamonds were not copper, and required enormous 'management of the diamond market', both in the physical sorting of imports and in discounting on bulk sales; finance to purchase a whole year's production with options on further periods at rising prices; and a say in the running of the company itself.[55] This was all the more necessary in the case of DBCM under a chairman with wider objectives, divided in its corporate management, and saddled with a high level of debt.

Once the mines were under a single producer, Gardner Williams and his technicians had demonstrated that output could be curtailed or expanded by co-ordinated underground and surface operations in a planned sequence, serviced by the required amount of labour through the compound system. The labour crisis after 1900 also demonstrated that this combination of mechanization and labour-intensive methods was vulnerable, but not really in question, when maintained by extra investment in recruiting in order to meet a new demand on expanded production.

It was not so easily demonstrated however, that the moderate efficiency and great flexibility of the mines could be matched by a merchants' combine in the depressed conditions of the early 1890s, when there was more than one channel for sales. Rhodes's secret reserve and the continuation of sales to smaller dealers at first hampered efforts by the principal London houses to organize their series of *ad hoc* buyers' agreements. Despite merchant representation on the DBCM board, there was little co-ordination of production and sales before 1894. Much of the responsibility for maintaining the 'combine' at all lay with Wernher, Beit and Co. which bought consistently, even at a loss, keeping up a modest resales price, 'altho' half the directors were out of their wits about the accumulation'.[56] As the investments of this finance house increased in South Africa and world-wide, it served as the sheet-anchor to hold the

---

[55] Charter Consolidated Archives (unclassified MSS), Porges to Wernher, 7 Jan. 1889.
[56] BRA, WB Cape 5, Wernher to Breitmeyer, 7 July 1892.

syndicate in place. From 1894, Rhodes and his directors came to rely on the sheer expertise of the merchants in clearing stocks by long-term contracts. The relationship between producer and wholesaler took on the appearance of an integrated 'monopoly' which characterized operations till 1902.

Some of this harmonization and discipline can be attributed to the return of Breitmeyer from Kimberley in 1895. He had little faith in Rhodes's direction, displaying great sarcasm in his private correspondence about 'the mastermind in Cape Town', and exercising a personal control of the diamond section of Wernher, Beit and Co. At Wernher's death in 1912, Ludwig Breitmeyer, as senior partner, was the natural successor, and formed his own company to lead the syndicate. Far more than Alfred Beit, who had little to do with DBCM's diamonds and concentrated on gold, Breitmeyer administered syndicate policies. Where Wernher advised and persuaded, Breitmeyer regulated for the same ends until the 1920s.[57]

Sensing a more positive direction in London and aware that the market after 1895 showed great promise, Rhodes and his Kimberley directors—especially Oats—won important concessions on profit-sharing and control of assortments which became standard features of subsequent contracts. The crisis of 1908 underlined this complementarity by increasing the burden of unsold stocks in London, restructuring the syndicate, and rescuing the company from short-term liabilities. The lesson of 1908 was that the syndicate was essential to uphold prices for goods passing to Amsterdam and Antwerp 'almost exclusively on credit', in order to give dealers time to sell to manufacturers 'without the fear of cheaper goods coming into competition, and thus causing indiscriminate selling on the part of the weaker holders, which in a very short time would lead to the complete demoralization of the market and prevent any sales'.[58]

These points were stressed, at the same date, by Wernher's rival in the trade, Adolphe Wagner, who estimated the 'enormous stocks' carried in rough and cut goods at over £100 million. A whole industry had expanded rapidly at the old Continental centres to manufacture the series purchased for cash by buyers in London and resold on credit for cleaving, rounding, and polishing by some 15,000 workers in factories owned by dealers.[59] Much of the work on steam-driven diamond mills was put out to 'cutters' who with their workmen and apprentices contracted to transform a buyer's stock into gem stones, minimizing the large material loss involved in

[57] For some of his pithy comments, BRA, WB, Cape Inland; and DBCA, Board 5/1/1.
[58] BRA, WB Inland 29, Wernher to Solomon, 10 Mar. 1908.
[59] BRA, HE 230, Wagner, notes [1909]; Heertje, 212.

'handling' roughs. Polished gems were then sold through specialized wholesalers for the European and American jewellery trade at over 100 per cent mark-up to the final purchaser. The trade in brilliants was also financed by long-term credits from 3 to 18 months by wholesalers and banks specializing in diamonds—a point which made it difficult for overseas producers to break into the widespread distribution chain by manufacturing at source and selling directly to Paris, Amsterdam, and Antwerp. For the moment, the merchants in roughs were the nexus of the long series of transactions. Advertising had not yet taken over; though there was more than a touch of salesmanship in the articles inspired by London dealers for the *Pall Mall Gazette* in the early 1890s which extolled the brilliant as an item of female dress and as a mark of respectability among the middle classes. Diamonds were not yet regarded, perhaps, as a 'store of value' against inflation. But the proliferation of cheaper gem stones made it possible for greater numbers of men and women to emulate their social superiors by purchase of a luxury good at firm prices.[60]

Gradually the lessons inherent in the delicate credit structure of the manufacturing and distributing ends of the industry were absorbed by the producers and the syndicate merchants: volume was to be regulated; and all varieties, even small stones, could be sold in series. After 1908, sales contracts were further adjusted to meet the need for more frequent valuation of changing sources of production at Kimberley, and to counter the more assertive policies adopted by the company under the chairmanship of Francis Oats. But by then the producer's 'monopoly' of the 1890s had ended.

[60] *DFA*, 21 June 1890.

5

A Colonial Company

Growth and Diversification

BUT what kind of business enterprise did the early directors combine to create? From the above, it is clear that De Beers could not simply act as a vehicle for the ambitions of Cecil Rhodes. Interpretations of Rhodes's career, and the standard work on the company itself by Hedley Chilvers, which sketch in mining development as a background to a central portrait of the founder, miss much of the point of the technological organization and market combine in the 1890s. The first duty of the directors was not to further the ambitions of one of their number but to make a profit, and decide how that profit was to be used. The directors who chaired the first three annual general meetings of shareholders—Barnato, Robinow, and Oats—in the absence of Rhodes stressed that this would be done by building up reserves of blue, keeping as much employment as possible, and by meeting heavy redemption charges, dividends, and working costs out of the surplus from sales, without increasing capital. Compromises had to be made almost at once. Promises of full employment at Kimberley had to be cancelled, when Bultfontein and Dutoitspan were closed on a weak market in 1890 and 1891. Failure to negotiate a continuous contract with the early syndicate almost led to the suspension of any dividend, until advances were arranged through Rothschilds in 1890, in order to avoid making excessive demands on the South African banks. In all, the company had a poor start, and the first decade of its performance began in crisis and a certain amount of confusion about lines of responsibility between Kimberley and London. Rhodes, however, set the tone of his long chairmanship by brashly making loans of £20,000 to the Paarl and Western Province Banks, and by planning his secret 'reserve' of diamonds and cash.

After 4 years of experiment and argument, the selling agency enforced a certain discipline on the company. The policy of establishing a reserve for investments was changed to a reserve for meeting emergencies. Excessive secrecy about establishing control over Koffyfontein, New Jagersfontein, and Wesselton through purchase of shares changed to approval by the London board for limitation of sources of supply. Rhodes's initial suspicion of his merchant-directors and his fear that the 'natural greed of the shareholders' would not permit large and openly-audited accumulations gave way to dependence on the merchants' skills in clearing stock, and acceptance all round of the need for substantial assets held in consols which were not available for distribution.[1]

It was established, too, that lobbying to elect more merchant-directors in London could be stopped by the company secretary, William Craven, who organized a counter-lobby from Kimberley, and it was Craven who successfully prevented individual merchants from borrowing against diamonds held by the company.[2] Sounder heads, such as Wernher, simply accepted 'cash diamonds' and a reserve as a way of paying off interest and debentures. For it was the annual interest charge of £300,000 to £400,000 on the first and second mortgage debentures, issued to secure control of the mines, which limited Rhodes's room for financial manœuvres. With the help of Rothschild and with loans from the Standard Bank, in return for half the company's account, this liability was managed in 1891 and 1892. And as the reserve was legitimately approved by the board, it was agreed in April 1892 that the company might borrow from it, if equivalent diamonds were set aside to cover the advance. An important vote of the London section recorded that responsibility for diamond securities rested with the directors as a whole and not any faction in Kimberley or London. The merchants present won an equally important proviso that such security in stones was not to be unloaded on to the market at a price below current valuations.[3] Stow disagreed with this condition, which to some extent called in question his chairmanship of the London section and his handling of the early 'reserve' sales. He resigned his seat on the board, though not his directorship, and was replaced by Sir Hercules Robinson.[4] But this loss of an ally only weakened Rhodes's position in London, where the business of the board was increasingly handled through subcommittees.

At the end of this short period of in-fighting, it had emerged that Rhodes could not get his way in the face of the company's financial difficulties,

---

[1] RH, Baxter [transcripts], Rhodes to Stow, 19 July 1891.

[2] RH, Rhodes Papers, C7, Mosenthal to Rhodes, 14 May 1891; Craven to Rhodes, 3 Mar. 1892.

[3] DBCA, Board 2/7/1, 20 April, 30 May 1892.

[4] RH, Rhodes Papers, C7, Stow to Rhodes, 18 July 1891. In effect, Rhodes, Beit, and Barnato, as life governors, would share 25% of profits after a dividend of 36%, and Stow's share was divided between Rhodes and Beit: Beit to Rhodes, 1 July 1893. Stow did not resign his life governorship till May 1898, but took no part in company management.

Sales on Diamond Account
Index 1890=100 (£2,641,600)

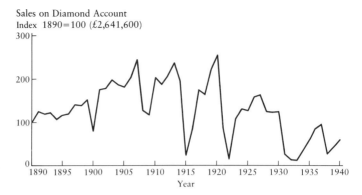

Working Costs of Mining
Index 1890=100 (£1,012,200)

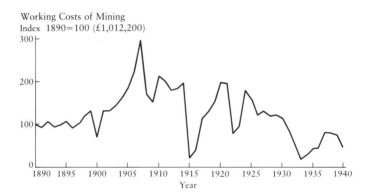

Other Charges and Distribution Costs
Index 1890=100 (£70,400)

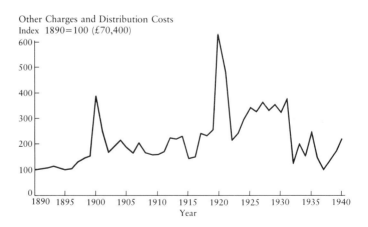

FIG. 6. De Beers Consolidated Mines: sales and working costs, 1890–1940

and that those who looked on De Beers simply as a source of dividends for British and foreign investors would have to reckon with the Kimberley section of the board, where there was more sympathy for regional use of funds. For Barnato, the company was a source of 'the mining consols of the world' and a corner stone of Cape Colony's credit.[5] A more measured assessment by the company's London secretary, E. R. Tymms, discerned a metropolitan–colonial struggle to frame policy between Currie and Meyer on the one hand, and Rhodes, Oats, and Williams on the other. The London section he observed 'will not remember that ours is a Colonial Company and ought to remain so'.[6]

THE PROFITS OF MONOPOLY

Evidence for the soundness of this colonial mining company lay in the financial statements and annual reports. With certain exceptions concerning investments and false returns of the value of diamond output in the early 1890s, these gave a well-audited presentation of profitability and progress, particularly in the mechanics of production. There was much less information on marketing, until the channel through the London diamond syndicate was regularly established in 1895. Even so, the method of recording 'sales' in the 'Diamond Account' obscured the practice of discounts to the merchants and included a valuation of diamond stocks on hand at the beginning and end of each financial year.[7] This was never questioned. The annual general meetings held at the company's offices in Kimberley with fifty or so directors, alternates, and buyers present reads like a small directory of *diamantaires*; and they understood how the system worked.

They were more interested in the underlying trends and the immediate returns from processing a natural endowment of minerals. For the 1890s, during the period of 'monopoly', the trends were steadily upwards in terms of production and sales values, until the recession of 1907 and increasing competition. This progression was not clearly discernible, however, till 1895. Thereafter, sales values increased by over 100 per cent before 1907, and the company was helped by Williams's strict control of working costs, which did not rise significantly in line with general charges and distribution costs until the Anglo-Boer war. After that crisis, general charges too were

---

[5] DBCM, *Annual Report* (1891), 20–4.
[6] RH, Rhodes Papers, C7, Tymms to Craven, 4 Sept. 1890.
[7] Ibid., Stow to Rhodes, 17 June 1891, for evidence of false returns.

ILL. 11. Premier (Transvaal) Diamond Mine, western face of the mine, 1905

brought down, while working costs which threatened to get out of hand, because of a shortage of labour, were gradually adjusted to meet production requirements in parallel with sales by bringing new mines into production and phasing out Kimberley and De Beers (Appendix A.2).

After working costs and charges, very large figures were listed annually for 'depreciation' on machinery, plant, shafts, offices, and stand properties, usually as a lump sum along with other major items of expenditure, such as interest for leased companies and mortgage debentures. Details of how this lump sum was spent by writing off against profits were never supplied and the distinction from 'working costs' or new capital investment was left obscure. Shareholders had no complaint, however, about 'general charges' (including directors' fees of about £600 each) which were hardly more than 7 per cent of working costs, though they rose steeply to meet the extra expenses of the war and the public charities subscribed to at Kimberley in periods of recession.

The company could well afford to be less than precise about 'depreciation', because, in the absence of any taxation, gross profits left such a wide margin between the return from diamond sales and the costs of production. The two yardsticks of profitability on trading capital (all assets less current liabilities) and on overall capital employed (trading capital plus other investments) demonstrate that there was ample room, over the whole period before 1914, for the company to adopt investment strategies which fell into two broad sectors. Purchase or lease of mines and lands associated with mineral production, particularly in South Africa, served to reinforce the company's position as the major world producer in the 'Rhodes period', and was accepted by all the directors as necessary, even if it meant locking up capital in undeveloped estates. The rising value of such investments in the 1890s, particularly after the purchase of Wesselton and LSAE lands, served to 'dilute' the company's profitability ratio on overall capital. Secondly, there was a more debatable selection of investments in coal, railways, cold storage, dynamite, agriculture, and other companies associated with Rhodes's ventures which could be judged as a proper use of funds only by their profitability.

Directors were divided about the worth of this selection. Some were content with the high return on trading capital and a large reserve in low-yielding consols; and others expected the company to play a major role in the development of southern African communications and resources. But both sections of the board were agreed on the need for steady dividends. They were not agreed on the amount of 'venture capital' available outside their annual obligations to redeem debentures and pay those dividends at between 20 and 40 per cent on ordinary shares. Nor did they get much advice from either Rothschilds or Wernher, Beit and Co. on investment selections.[8]

The Company's profitability ratio shows an average return of 13.7 per cent on capital employed to 1894 in all assets, including stocks of blue on the floors, after considerable writing down of machinery and plant. This ratio did not advance much until all mines were in production from 1902, and then it was sharply reduced by taxation, incurred for the first time in the United Kingdom and at the Cape. There was little danger that De Beers could not meet its liabilities from earnings or reserves after the early 1890s, when the current ratio was very low (below 0.25).[9] But

---

[8] The evidence for this lies in BRA, WB which shows that the main business of the partnership lay less in diamonds and the syndicate than in gold by the end of the 1890s and expanded into Johannesburg utilities, coal, cement, railways, and ventures outside Africa.

[9] Statements on investments as assets changed in the published balance sheets, esp. after 1905, when current assets included large items from Cape Explosives.

for much of that period the company remained highly 'geared' by the size of debt in relation to capital employed, starting from a level of 54 per cent, after the cost of amalgamation had been settled. As redemption charges reduced the size of the debt, this ratio was first lowered, and then raised sharply by the debenture loans issued for the purchase of the LSAE estates in 1899. By the period of the First World War, total debt which had been as high as £5 million was reduced to £3.8 million, or 30 per cent of capital employed. The company's largest investment was in itself and the properties surrounding Kimberley, and there were those on the board who were content that this should remain so, after they had surrendered their shares in Dutoitspan mines and in United Bultfontein Consolidated, Griqualand West, and New Gordon, and had bought full possession of Wesselton by 1896.

Rhodes was not content with pre-emptive purchases of mines and control of supply. He was careful to keep De Beers separate, however, from what he regarded as 'speculations', such as his early Gold Fields partnership with Rudd or the United Concessions and the Chartered Company in its formative years.[10] He formally asked the permission of the directors to promote the shares of the British South Africa Company and his Great Namaqualand Syndicate for copper in July 1890. De Beers purchased 210,000 ordinary £1 BSA shares; and Beit, Michaelis, and Barnato were allotted blocks in the general subscription for one million 'Chartereds'. The De Beers holding was distributed to shareholders as a bonus in 1891, at a reduced value, less a thousand or so held in the names of Rhodes and Beit. Barnato emphasized to the shareholders that they had been bought out of profits and incurred no liabilities. The London board agreed to pay for the recruitment of men for the Mashonaland expedition (it was not informed that the company also armed these 'pioneers'); and on the security of the shares held by Rhodes and Beit, De Beers allowed the BSA drawing rights up to £3,500 monthly to help found the new colony.[11] Further advances were made through 1892 at 6 per cent interest, and the Kimberley board agreed to underwrite an issue of £750,000 debentures, taking £297,909 of these to cover future loans. The London directors reluctantly approved and insisted that De Beers

---

[10] John Flint, *Cecil Rhodes* (London, 1976); John S. Galbraith, *Crown and Charter: The Early Days of the British South Africa Company* (Los Angeles, 1974); Newbury, 'Out of the Pit', 33–4.

[11] DBCA, Board 2/7/2, 27 Jan., 12 May 1891; 5/1/1, Beit to Craven, 6 Jan. 1891; and for agreements with the 'pioneers', 5/1/1, 1891; 5 applied for farms in Mashonaland and 4 abandoned them; Board 2/2/2, 23 Mar. 1892. The board sold 53,500 BSA shares at 17s., 1892–3.

would have 'the absolute right to and cession of all diamond mines now or hereafter discovered within the sphere of the Chartered Company's operations'. This formula was embodied in a contract when Rhodes was present, in April 1892, to give a glowing forecast of the BSA's prospects.

None of that prospectus from the chairman prevented De Beers selling off BSA ordinary stock from July 1892 at less than nominal values, as pressure mounted to find cash for dividends and interest at the end of the financial year. The London section listened cautiously to Rhodes when he returned in 1893 full of the advantages of his new Bechuanaland Railway Company's proposed extension between Vryburg and Mafeking to link Kimberley with Gaberones. It was agreed to advance £100,000 on the security of BSA debentures, in return for low freight charges for company fuel and stores, and with a lien on any diamond discoveries in Bechuanaland. De Beers was also drawn into Rhodes's wider railway strategies which turned on the 'Sivewright agreement' with the Transvaal to complete a line from Bloemfontein to the Vaal and Johannesburg by a loan secured at the Cape to which the company subscribed £150,000 at 3½ per cent.[12]

But support for these ventures was lukewarm. De Beers could not be used as a holding company, like Gold Fields, though the minerals concessions were arguably consistent with the policy of taking options on potential sources of diamonds. There were signs that even loyal members of the board, such as Barnato, were restless at this involvement in sub-imperial designs. They would have nothing to do with Rhodes's African Transcontinental Telegraph Company formed at the end of 1892. And as it became clear that Rhodesia was not going to be a second Rand, and Gold Fields was reconstructed as a trust company with the help of Wernher, Beit and Co. and on the strength of its large and valuable investment in De Beers, there was little possibility of drawing on the £1 million reserve which Rhodes had initiated for the cause of 'Zambesia'. As Lord Rothschild warned:

It is quite possible that the Articles of Association may give you a loophole; but nowadays people are disposed to construe all articles of association more severely than they used to do, and if it became known that the De Beers Company lent money to the Chartered Company some of De Beers shareholders might move for an injunction, and get up an agitation to turn out the Board and put in their own nominees, which would be most undesirable.[13]

---

[12] Wilburn, 'The Climax of Railway Competition', 81–3.
[13] RH, Rhodes Papers, Charters 3A, Rothschild to Rhodes, 15 Jan. 1892.

Nevertheless, railways and land had their special attraction, and in 1894 the board was persuaded to take up 2,000 Bechuanaland Railways shares, in repayment for advances already made; and it was resolved to continue monthly subsidies to the BSA in return for 200,000 acres in Matabeleland and five million acres 'of the best land in Bechuanaland'.[14] And that was as far as close association with schemes in 'the North' went. Subsidies stopped in July 1895, well before the Raid. At the same time, De Beers sold off its only Rand holdings in the Robinson Gold Mining Company and Robinson Diamond Mining Company to some of its directors for £70,000. Thankful to have distanced itself from the political fiasco, the Kimberley board willingly cleared Gardner Williams of a 'technical' offence, after a case had been brought against him for storing arms and ammunition for the BSA Company.[15]

Prospection and investment in cheaper supplies of fuel were of a different order. Williams carried out a survey of coal mining at Indwe in 1893 for the company, and a block of debentures in the Indwe Collieries and Land Company was taken up by Rhodes and distributed to friends and directors in March 1895. These were then sold to De Beers for £75,000, which Rhodes justified to shareholders as 'a good public act' (which led to other such acts later in Natal).[16]

By the date of the Raid, then, the company had £423,000 in stocks and shares and a further £643,736 in Wesselton estate and mine, Kenilworth estate and village, and other lands around Kimberley (excluding the company's mammoth mortgages for Bultfontein and Dutoitspan). From its investments, De Beers could reckon to make about £100,000 annually, contributing only 5 or 6 per cent to annual revenue, or 9 per cent if all rents from land and stands are included. In other words, the main contribution from a measure of diversification came from close to the centre of the company's main activity. Rhodes made much of the BSA and Bechuanaland at annual meetings. But by 1898, the only serious company holding in 'the North', after discreet sales of shares, was £106,000 of Mashonaland Railway stock which was expanded into Rhodesian Railway Trust shares, plus the token 1,622 BSA shares. The entitlement to lands and minerals in Rhodesia remained, but De Beers concentrated on what it knew best and preserved its reserve in consols paying only 2½ per cent as a more accessible fund than investment in an 'African East India Company'.[17]

---

[14] DBCA, S. 1 (1895), BSA to DBCM, 26 Jan. 1895; Board 11/1/2.
[15] DBCA, Board 2/2/5, 21 May 1896. In 1895 Williams offered to resign, but was persuaded to stay with an increased salary.
[16] DBCM, *Annual Report* (1896), 14.
[17] RH, Rhodes Papers, C7, Stow to Rhodes, 18 July 1891; the phrase is Stow's.

If Rhodes did not get his way with company surplus, he could at least claim with some justification that De Beers was 'half partners with the Colony', when it produced half the Cape's exports by value, and he vigorously defended it from any attempt to tax diamond mining. In return, funds were provided to help the Progressives, particularly in the close election of 1898 which might have brought Rhodes back into the premiership. Voters' rolls were carefully scrutinized for municipal and national elections, and care was taken to incorporate casual white labour into the list of permanent company employees who were instructed how to vote.[18] For as long as Rhodes was regularly returned to the Assembly for Barkly West, there was a solid block of six supporters from Kimberley which eventually included David Harris and L. S. Jameson. In 1903 the company had five of its directors in the Assembly from Kimberley and other constituencies. In the end, this representation could not stave off attacks on the industry, but it afforded a remarkable period of grace throughout the 1890s.

A further consideration which determined cautious and conservative financial management was the position of De Beers in the constellation of mining companies whose performance affected overseas confidence in the great investment boom of the Rand. Beit reminded Rhodes as early as 1894, when there was a threat of import duties on diamonds in the American market, that regular payment of first charges and dividends depended on the closest co-operation with the syndicate and the limitation of production on request from London:

There is a fear in the market that the De Beers will not be able to keep up its present dividend, and I must say that unless you succeed in further reducing working expenses, I cannot see how we can in the near future pay more than 20/- p.a. Such a reduction would have a very bad effect not only on De Beers shares, but would generally effect South African securities, particularly shares connected with our group like Charters, Goldfields etc. I think therefore it is most necessary to make a tremendous effort to maintain present dividends.[19]

Rhodes heeded this advice and moved closer to Beit, when they agreed to co-operate in future policy by purchasing Stow's life governorship with its possibility of participation in 'super profits' at a certain level of company performance, which was not reached till 1896. The first sign that the

---

[18] For an attempt at taxation see DBC, *Annual Report* (1891); voters' rolls, DBCA, S. 1 (1897), 1898.

[19] RH, Rhodes Papers, C24, Beit to Rhodes, 14 July 1894. Identity of shareholders cannot be fully analysed. But in 1903 some 24.7% of preference and deferred shares were held in Europe and 22.8% in South Africa; bearer shares, however, amounted to 44.7% of equity and are untraceable: DBCA, S. 1 (1903).

company's relationship with the syndicate promised long-term profitability came, indeed, the year before (despite the Raid), when an improved financial market enabled De Beers to convert its 5 per cent issue of £3.5 million first mortgage debentures redeemable by 1915. Holders of old debenture stock received a bonus of 3 per cent; and by lengthening the term of redemption there was a considerable reduction in annual charges.[20] Total long-term debt was reduced over the following 5 years, as trading profits reached higher levels and the undistributed pre-tax profit, as a percentage of shareholders' equity, rose above 36 per cent, and net profits of 36 per cent were paid in dividends to shareholders. In a sense, 'natural greed' triumphed over Rhodes's idea of 'public acts'.

There were moves in London to make use of this evident profitability by financially restructuring the company and ridding it of redemption charges altogether. When Carl Meyer became chairman of the London section, representing City institutions and Continental shareholders, there was even more resistance to African investments and more attention was given to the ways in which profits were divided (though it cannot be assumed that South African shareholders were an unimportant minority). In September 1895, Meyer proposed reducing the obligations paid for Bultfontein and hoped for a 40s. dividend the following year. This was to be done by increasing capital from nearly £4 million to £8 million, 'the 4 millions thus obtained to be used to pay off all the Debentures at 105'.[21] He recognized, of course, that such a restructuring would effectively reduce the real percentage paid in dividends, and, therefore, any share of net profits over and above the 36 per cent required to pay a dividend, before the life governors took their cut. Meyer thought this 'loss' for Rhodes, Beit, and Barnato might be made good by allowing them their share of undivided profits first, before any other major charges.

Two years earlier, when Rhodes had feared that declaration of a high 40 per cent dividend would stir up 'agitation' at the Cape for income tax, he might well have agreed to increased capitalization.[22] But for the moment he had his hands full on the eve of the Raid. By 1896 neither he nor Beit and Barnato were willing to alter the Trust Deed in such a way as to reduce their share of profits, particularly as Rhodes and Beit were agreed there was a strong possibility of funds from this source to

---

[20] RH, Rhodes House, Central Mining and Investment Company ledgers, 'De B.C.M. Ltd. 5 per cent First Mortgage Debentures Delivered against Scrip November 1895'.

[21] DBCM, *Annual Report* (1896); esp. in the lists of those holding large blocks of shares: see Newbury, 'Out of the Pit', 45; and 5. n. 19.

[22] RH, Baxter [transcripts], Rhodes to DBCM, 6 Apr. 1893.

make good the investments the directors refused. Moreover, after the suicide of Barnato in July 1897, the two remaining governors stood to share the 25 per cent of post-dividend profits between them. When Sir Julius Wernher was appointed to Stow's vacant governorship (without profits) in 1898, the purpose of this high office in the company was to further Rhodes's 'idea', embodied in his will, as much as to secure continuity of direction between the syndicate and the mining company. The position of a governor was, in the view of the founder, 'a trust for public purposes after death, and [I] shall use what I can spare for that purpose during life'.[23]

To ensure there would be plenty to spare for these 'purposes', Rhodes and Beit came to terms with the London section of the board in May 1898 as the sole participants in excess profits. In return for agreeing that the redemption of debenture debt should be made as a first charge, the life governors secured that income from investments was brought into the revenue account and included in the total profits in which they participated.[24] This was considered to entail a magnanimous 'sacrifice' on the part of the governors by their agreement to share in redemption payments. Whether they were right to maintain that such charges should not be entered into profit and loss, but paid out of a special reserve fund was not tested in law. But Oats ably defended Beit and Rhodes for their contribution to 'the development of the country', without questioning too closely just how 'public acts' had been funded in the past.

At the London board meeting in May, however, Rhodes had extended the terms of the bargain to include an acceptance of his belief that the company should become less dependent on mining by diversifying into other investment projects for 'public purposes'.[25] The test of this verbal agreement came at the end of 1898, when Beit submitted a proposal to buy a holding in the South West Africa Company founded with British and German capital in 1892 to develop extensive concessions in Damaraland and Ovamboland (in the central and northern areas of the German territory). The board agreed to take up 10,000 £1 shares (out of a flotation of £2 million), and paid £5,000 for mineral rights in the Kaokofeld, but

---

[23] For Barnato's death see Wheatcroft, 193–4. David Harris was not appointed as a governor, but elected as a director; RH, Rhodes Papers, C7, Stow to Rhodes, 15 Mar. 1898; Rhodes to Stow, 16 Mar. 1898. For this (and older) reasons, F. Baring-Gould was overlooked in favour of Wernher.

[24] DBCM, *Annual Report*, and general meeting (1898), 2, 18.

[25] DBCA, Board 2/7/1, 4 and 11 May 1898; present were Meyer, Baring-Gould, Atkinson, English, Morrogh, Shiels, Mosenthal, Wernher, Currie, Beit, and Rhodes, plus the company lawyer, Hawksley.

refused a further offer of 106,000 shares from Rhodes and Beit, after considerable prevarication.[26]

Rhodes boiled over. From the Burlington Hotel he dictated a long indictment of the board's persistent opposition to his investment negotiations. Wesselton had been purchased against their wishes. An offer of a half interest in Rand Mines by Wernher, Beit and Co. had been rejected in 1892; and participation in Gold Fields and Wernher, Beit and Co.'s Deep Levels on the Rand had been dismissed in 1896, losing the company millions, though individual directors thought these were risks worth taking.[27] The reserve, he claimed, had been his creation; and he had been rewarded by ingratitude and the sale of BSA shares well below par, while the board made grudging advances for railway development— 'like selling the house for nothing over which the seller held a mortgage'. This 'unkind and unfriendly act' made without reference to Rhodes was a mean response to the free gift of land in Bechuanaland and Rhodesia. The board had opposed the valuable Indwe railway construction with its promise of cheaper coal. They had gone back on the agreement to consider more favourably his outside investments, in return for sacrificing a part of the life governors' profits.

I then pointed out to Mr. Beit that I thought at a low rate if we could acquire a considerable interest in German South West Africa [sic], it would be advisable in the interests of the Company. The area of their mineral rights represents a country almost as big as France and the formation is similar to ours and undoubtedly rich in copper deposits. We were in my absence offered an interest of about one-tenth for about £15,000, a mere bagatelle. It amazed me to learn that not only was the offer abruptly refused but no reference was made to me in my capacity as Chairman after such an offer had been submitted. It is not necessary for me to point out that the cable rates to South Africa have been greatly reduced and I do not think the question of cable expenses should have been considered in connection with this matter.

When I arrived at Home and found out the situation I claimed from Mr. Wernher a repetition of the offer on the grounds that I had negotiated this matter with Mr. Beit in the interests of the Company many months previously. Messrs Wernher, Beit and Company, with great liberality agreed to repeat the offer. The result is that we possess a further 80,000 South West African shares which taking the difference on cost at present price represent a profit of about £100,000. But apart from this I consider it was a distinctly wise investment. The land lies contingent to us, the cost was a mere bagatelle and we have every chance

---

[26] DBCA, Board 2/7/1, 5 Dec. 1898; BRA, WB (for reports on the South West Africa Company).

[27] RH, Rhodes House, MSS Afr. s. 227, Rhodes to DBCM (Lombard Street), 19 Apr. 1899.

in the future of getting a handsome return. I claim at any rate that before an absolute refusal was given the Chairman and members of the Kimberley Board were entitled to have their opinion asked. This purchase also included the acquisition of the sole right to diamonds which through dilatory action in London was absolutely lost. In Berlin I was enabled to obtain a renewal of the offer though at an increased price and the loss of the right to 10,000 shares at par which in the first agreement covered the right to diamonds.

To avoid any misunderstanding as to the matters I have raised, as I said before, I wish it to be distinctly understood that I do not claim that De Beers should embark in undertakings other than diamonds entailing the expenditure of enormous sums of money, but in view of the fact that the Trust Deed was changed with the unanimous approval of the shareholders for the purpose of enabling the Company, when it is deemed advisable, to take an interest in other ventures as well; in view of the enormous expansion going on in Africa and the special opportunities that I have for wise and judicious investment; and considering the limit of life which every one must agree is the fate of all mines and the risk of discovery at any moment of diamond pipes equally rich or fairly rich; I feel that it is most essential that we should gradually, with wisdom and care, make investments in undertakings other than diamonds, so that in case our mines, through unforseen circumstances, are rendered less valuable, we should be in a position to say to our shareholders that we have not all our eggs in one basket.

In this matter I feel I should have the support of the shareholders, if not the majority of the De Beers Board, if those resident in South Africa are added to those resident here. However if my forecast is a mistaken one and the Board resolves to continue this persistent opposition to myself, then I propose to submit the whole situation to my shareholders and if they don't support me to retire from the active management of De Beers and leave it in the hands of those whose wisdom in managing the affairs of the Company I hope will prove as satisfactory as I claim my record has been, since the amalgamation of the Mines.

This mixture of commercial testament and ultimatum was considered by a chastened board at a special meeting the following day and a reply upholding their views but declining to vote against Rhodes was prepared by Meyer and signed by six directors. Their case was that the shareholders of De Beers were more numerous in Europe than in South Africa, and that the Trust Deed was not a licence to use company funds. In any event the Kimberley board was free to invest up to £75,000 annually, without London approval. And they were frightened off ventures in the Transvaal by the policy of Rhodes in his confrontation with Kruger. Lord Rothschild, whose bank held some 31,000 shares, also entered the controversy, claiming to speak for the Continental shareholders, who considered the life governors too well rewarded from retained profits. This Rhodes dealt with deftly by offering to take the whole matter to court.[28]

In May 1899, with Rhodes present at London meetings, tempers were cooled. Beit testified to the offer of participation in Rand gold mines (denied by Meyer), but he agreed with the general stand taken by the directors and was supported by Francis Oats. No one was really willing to take the controversy to the shareholders. A compromise was worked out by which it was agreed to use any balance over the £1 million in reserve (currently some £179,000) for other investments, and the Kimberley section was permitted to spend up to £100,000 independently. Mashonaland railway debentures were to be sold off and replaced by new Trust shares in the reconstruction of Rhodesian Railways. Rhodes dropped his request for a contribution towards a railway to Lake Tanganyika. After a meeting with Dr Sharlach and Edmund Davis of the South West Africa Company, a De Beers director, C. E. Atkinson, was taken on to their board with a watching brief on mineral exploration. More important, it was decided to end the position of the London and South African Exploration Company as landlord of half of De Beers mines by offering to buy them out, using Baron Emile d'Erlanger as intermediary for a commission of £10,000.

This was by far the biggest investment the company had made since amalgamation. By June 1899, the LSAE agreement for a transfer of land and other properties was signed and the shareholders authorized a new issue of £1,750,000 in debenture stock at 4½ per cent, repayable over 30 years, to cover the cost. As the political climate deteriorated in South Africa, it proved difficult to persuade institutions or the public to take up this issue. Towards the end of 1899 the company was borrowing heavily from Wernher, Beit and Co., the Bank of England, Rothschilds, and even from the South Africa Company, as the export of diamonds was cut off by the siege of Kimberley.

Although he may have expected a short war, Rhodes rushed by train to the source of his wealth on 10 October, as the Boer ultimatum was about to expire and when half a million of the debentures were still unsold.[29] His primary concern was to organize supplies to keep the mines operating and furnishing diamonds. But from 14 October rail and telegraph communications were cut and the Boers took over the Waterworks Company at the Vaal. The Kimberley Waterworks reservoir which was linked to the town through Wesselton and the considerable

---

[28] RH, Rhodes Papers, C7B, Board, 26 Apr. 1899; Rothschild to Rhodes, 19 Apr. 1899.
[29] RH, Rhodes House, MSS Afr. s. 227, Rhodes to Pickering, 13 Nov. 1900.

stocks of coal, dynamite, and foodstuffs helped to sustain the resistance by 500 imperial troops and armed volunteers. The De Beers and Kimberley shafts were used to shelter white civilians from shelling, while frontal assault was countered by using the tailing heaps as defences, reinforced with locally manufactured mines. Through Boer indecision as much as through improvisation the town survived and production continued into December, two months before the relief, with little real damage to plant, but heavy mortality from disease.

There were other costs which the company found hard to justify. When the accounts were drawn up and published in the *Annual Report* for 1903, claims on the imperial government were estimated at £272,904, including damage to farms. In the face of hostile criticism, the company reduced this claim by £147,395 for relief work, wages, the town guard, and arms for company employees. Rhodes warned the company secretary not to damage their case by detailing too much including the cost of a wreath for a trooper's grave, an item which aroused public indignation.[30] In the end, a claim for only £54,641 was submitted and was reduced by the War Office to £30,000 which the company had to accept along with the suspension of any dividend for 1899/1900. By forgoing £1.5 million the shareholders covered the most expensive of their chairman's 'public acts'.

The short crisis over war losses and the longer aftermath of difficulties over labour and fuel increased the company's dependence on the contract with the syndicate. With no dividend to pay, the directors relied on Wernher's offer of new options on diamond production in April 1900 and purchase of £300,000 in unsold debentures to restore confidence in De Beers shares. Rhodes pressed other syndicate members to take up all the unsold debentures, and agreed to slightly reduced prices in the contract signed in June.

Lord Rothschild was still worried, however, by the reactions of French shareholders to substantial writing off in the form of 'depreciation', while the great reserve and balances of up to £1.5 million were not represented in cash and were hard to explain away as mine 'assets' or investments. The company would have to pay a bonus from such a large book surplus in excess of a dividend of 40s. per share. Revenue would have to be debited openly for all mine expenditure and purchase of outside interests which Continental shareholders might not approve

before a division of profits with the Life Governors is arrived at. It is not enough to write a certain amount every year off the machinery & plant. Every pound expended on these items and on other matters should be debited to Profit & Loss

---

[30] DBCM, *Annual Report* (1903), 2–3 for a statement of costs.

account. It will never do for the Life Governors to draw say from £200,000 to £250,000 in hard cash and for the shareholders not to get any advantage from the marvellous prosperity of the Company.[31]

A dividend was paid again in 1901. But as negotiations over profit-sharing with the syndicate came to a head, Carl Meyer threw his weight against the chairman's policies, which threatened a return to commission sales and exposure of the company to British taxation. Shareholders, he argued, deserved better because they had lost some £1.2 million in dividends since 1896, because of the method of calculating the amounts due to the life governors; and in 1900, on Rhodes's insistence, they had written off nearly all the accumulated profit as not represented in cash. The way out was a capital reconstruction by which the governors could commute their interest and compensate the shareholders in deferred shares. Above all, he was opposed to further South African ventures which would make De Beers 'into a kind of General Finance and Exploration Company'.[32]

Rhodes found time while resting at Rannoch Lodge in Scotland, in August 1901, to make some calculations with Beit on the costs and benefits of a commutation. From 1896, when for the first time the level of dividends to shareholders had risen to the point where the governors shared 25 per cent of the balance of net profits, increasing amounts were paid annually to Rhodes and Beit, with the exception of 1900. But 1901 had been a bumper year, when they took £316,593 and a very large balance remained unappropriated. In all, they had made some £800,000 after the death of Barnato, apart from whatever ordinary shares they held. Depending on the size of the commutation, they decided it was no bad thing to give way. Rothschild added 'a few lines from New Court' counselling a continuation of past selling methods and warning against setting up a company outlet in London. When Rhodes appeared at London board meetings in September, the policy of juggling with the accounts so as to decrease the visible surplus coveted by shareholders was thrashed out, and reconstruction was decided. At Kimberley, it was left to Sir David Harris to steer the plan through the annual general meeting in December 1901.[33] In effect, the company's capital was increased to £4.5 million by a split of the £5 ordinary shares into preference shares, paying a dividend of 40 per cent, and deferred shares, which were expected to pay their usual high yield. The life governors surrendered their special interest

[31] RH, Rhodes Papers, C7B, Rothschild to Rhodes, 2 Nov. 1900.
[32] Ibid., Meyer to DBCM, 20 Sept. 1901.
[33] Ibid., C7B f.235 (misplaced), Beit to Rhodes [Aug. 1900]; Rothschild to Rhodes, 20 Aug. 1901.

in return for 160,000 deferred shares, which they agreed to hold for five years. In his struggle to improve the terms of the diamond contracts and to use surplus profits on outside investments Rhodes had really got his own way: that was how he interpreted the outcome of the argument, when surveying his projects in agriculture, cold storage, and dynamite manufacture for the benefit of Beit in November 1900.

FARMS, BEEF, AND DYNAMITE

Much in these schemes was experimental, and some of it was politically motivated, in order to combine development with a secure British presence in the rural heartland of Afrikanerdom. Rhodes enlisted De Beers as a joint investor in the purchase of fourteen farms in Groot Drakenstein Valley to grow fruit and settle skilled British immigrants in the western Cape. The scheme was expanded with the guidance of Californian managers into the Paarl and Stellenbosch and financed by £160,000 from Rhodes, De Beers, and Wernher, Beit and Co. The investment also contained the germ of his plan to settle yeomen and ex-soldiers in the Transvaal and the Free State:

In a small way I have tried to encourage fruit cultivation in the Cape Colony and possess some twenty or thirty farms in the Paarl and Stellenbosch districts. Owing to their special knowledge the men in charge of these farms are almost entirely English who have studied fruit cultivation in California, and for the first time we have a number of English upon the land in these districts. At first they were looked upon with suspicion by their neighbours. This feeling has now totally altered.[34]

Rhodes thought group settlements of this kind would keep the Uitlanders out of the towns, 'to heal up the division' between Dutch and English. One of his last acts was to float 'Rhodes Fruit Farms' as a limited company in 1902, with a capital of £300,000 shared with De Beers and Wernher, Beit and Co., and directed by Sir Charles Metcalfe, Edward Syfret, and the ubiquitous Dr Jameson.

At the same period, research into rinderpest by Sir Robert Koch was supported by De Beers. Rhodes planned to remedy the widespread shortage of fresh meat by scientific stock breeding on lands around Kimberley and by breaking the monopoly of cold storage held by the Graaff family's

---

[34] RH, Rhodes House, MSS Afr s. 227, Rhodes, 7 May 1900; Moonyean Buys, *De Beers' Administrative Records Pertaining to the Rhodes Fruit Farms Limited, 1899–1937* (DBCM, 1982).

Combrink and Company at Cape Town. With financial backing from De Beers a rival plant was constructed in April 1900; and with a contract for carcasses from Australia, De Beers Cold Storage was managed by the politician T. E. Fuller, promoted to the board specifically for this task. Refrigerated railway cars ensured distribution to branches in Kimberley, Johannesburg, and Durban. With the backing of Johannesburg Consolidated Investments, Barnato Bros., and Lewis and Marks, De Beers came to terms with Combrink and took a half share in the amalgamated Imperial Cold Storage and Supply Company in February 1902, in time to take over lucrative contracts with the mines and the army. Opposition from some directors led to a reduction of De Beers financial interest, but the company provided the chairmen for the cold storage firm into the 1920s, though few dividends were ever paid, and Sir David Graaff resumed total control in 1924.

De Beers major diversification into the manufacture of dynamite arose from the high costs of supplies from Nobel's Modderfontein factory run by the British and South African Explosives Co. Ltd., which had the main concession for the Rand and Kimberley. The Kimberley board investigated alternative sources through Gardner Williams, who toured Europe and America in 1898 and was in touch with W. R. Quinan, manager of the California Powder Works at Pinole, who provided estimates of production costs. Even the London board approved of this initiative 'to offset the high cost of present supplies'.[35] In July 1898 Williams presented them with a modest plan for an investment of £40,000 to £50,000 in a factory which would supply dynamite at 20s. a case of 50 lbs., against 50s. to 60s. a case from the Transvaal. Even so, the London directors moved cautiously, and Mosenthal secured a new tender from the Nobel Dynamite Trust Company for a 2-year contract at the higher price.

In October 1898 Rhodes received Quinan's estimates which specified a site of 200 acres, railway transport, drainage to the sea 'to carry off waste and acid waters' from a factory with a capacity of 10,000 cases a month. Invited to manage the enterprise, Quinan asked for a salary of $20,000 over 2 years and permission to hire his own engineers. The Kimberley board, without reference to London, accepted these terms and promised a 'free hand', leaving details of the contract vague.

[35] RH, Rhodes Papers, C7B, Williams to Rhodes, 16 Apr. 1898; DBCA, Board 2/7/1, 4 May 1898; MSS Afr. s. 218, W. R. Quinan, 'South African Explosives'; see too A. P. Cartwright, *The Dynamite Company: The Story of African Explosives and Chemical Industries Limited* (Johannesburg, 1964), esp. for the establishment of Kynoch and Company Ltd. in Natal in 1909, 115–16.

As so much was left unsaid, Quinan chartered a vessel on his own initiative to transport heavy equipment from the United States to produce nitric and sulphuric acid, and ordered other essentials from France and England. When he arrived in July 1899, he personally selected the only suitable site in the Stellenbosch division along the shores of False Bay at Somerset West, and this choice was approved by the government inspector of explosives, J. E. Foakes. The area was sufficiently populated, however, to push up the purchase price of the 1,440 morgen of land acquired, and coloured smallholders on the Gordon estate received £4,000 for the sale of freehold and quitrent titles. An application to construct the factory was opposed by Stellenbosch council and Bond supporters prevented the sale of government land, but an appeal to Schreiner's ministry in its last days resulted in official approval. In all, the Bond managed to delay the project for a year, and Quinan had to pay an extra £10,000 to 'Blackmailers' from among the Somerset West petitioners and proprietors. The cost of land and construction to the end of 1899 stood at £250,000. Despite the alarm of the London board, a small clique of Rhodes's friends from among the Kimberley directors—Fuller, Harris, Jameson, Oats, and Williams— sanctioned the bills. Once the American cargo arrived in September, the scheme rolled forward, and the government provided a new railway siding at Helderberg station and extended the line as far as the works.

The economic advantages of the project now turned on the outcome of the war and the fate of the dynamite monopoly which had been one of the mineowners' grievances. Hoping for its abolition, Quinan planned to produce 1,000 cases a day. Instead of one factory, there were really to be four in the Cape sand hills, plus an unapproved power plant, lavishly equipped with machinery from all over the world. Only in the choice of a sulphuric acid process did the London board exercise some control by selecting a German patent from the Badische Anilin and Soda Factory at Oberhausen (which Quinan admitted was 'the highest stage of development'). But by November 1900, it was clear De Beers would have to face the costs alone, as Wernher, Beit and Co. and the chartered company refused to participate. Beit nervously advised Rhodes and Quinan to 'mark time' till the question of Nobel's Transvaal monopoly was cleared up in November, when the British government decided it could not be renewed. Once this was known, the London directors assured a suspicious Quinan that there was no 'Nobel influence' among their number to prevent large-scale production for an open market.[36]

[36] RH, Rhodes Papers, C7B, Quinan, Report, 10 Oct. 1901; MSS Afr. s. 227, Rhodes to Beit, 6 Nov. 1900; Tymms to Rhodes, 20 Nov. 1900.

Indeed, Rhodes hoped that the Transvaal could be made to pay through a duty levied on 'foreign' explosives 'in our favour'.[37] A steady demand from the Rand for 1,000 cases a day would cost some £500,000 a year to produce. But perhaps favourable freight rates between the Cape and the Transvaal could also be organized to justify such a heavy outlay. When Milner abolished the old dynamite monopoly in August 1902, he was anxious not to tax mine stores too heavily through an excise duty, in order to assist the recovery of the industry. Joseph Chamberlain took a less compassionate view of the excise on dynamite, to make it clear to the world that the mining companies would not profit excessively 'by the war which was in part due to their existence'. But he did not want any local protective duty to fall on imports of British manufacture to assist a South African De Beers or Nobel's factory at Modderfontein 'whose exactions in the shape of extortionate profit were one of the principal grievances before the war'.[38] The De Beers' venture, therefore, would have to stand or fall in open competition with its rival.

Once the Transvaal was admitted to the new customs union at Bloemfontein, the excise was abolished and the general import duty on manufactured dynamite was halved to 6s. 3d. per case. This removed at a stroke the tariff advantage which lay behind many of Quinan's calculations. Somerset West works were now on the same footing as the Modderfontein factory run by the Explosives Company for Nobels. As Quinan now showed, there was very little to be gained by processing imported raw materials at the Cape, and it was likely that dynamite could be delivered more cheaply from Europe to Johannesburg through Delagoa Bay than dynamite with high freight charges between Somerset West and the Rand.

The dream of a new monopoly faded. Capital costs for the factory mounted in the De Beers accounts to £929,659 by June 1903, with very little to show in return. Beit hastily arranged a contract with some of the principal Rand mining groups, in return for financial cover of the cost of production, plus 6 per cent of the capital required to run the explosive works. But this did not come about until the new company was floated, 6 April 1906, with a capital of £500,000 and £750,000 in debentures. In the meantime, the price of dynamite supplied to the Rand mines and settlement of their financial underwriting was fixed by an 'Adjustment Board' (on which De Beers had no representatives). But none

---

[37] RH, Rhodes House, MSS Afr. s. 227, Rhodes to Tymms, 23 Oct. 1900.
[38] COCP, *Africa South*, 705, Milner to Chamberlain, 6 Aug. 1902; Chamberlain to Milner, 22 Aug. 1902, Milner to Lyttleton, 27 June 1904 (with enclosures from Quinan).

of this arrangement by a trusting Quinan helped repay the initial cost of starting the project.[39]

Worse, Quinan's production schedule was disrupted by two explosions in March and July 1904 in the nitro-glycerine separation plant and in the gelatine mixing house. Three white and five black workers were blown to pieces or died of burns. A third accident in March 1905 resulted in a fire in the gun-cotton house and the drying house which killed eight workers. A commission which enquired into the sixteen deaths was divided in its verdict, generally accepting the explanation of Quinan and his son, who blamed the 'inexperience' of the workers, but noting that no compensation laws applied to the factory. One member wrote a special report criticizing employment of 'raw kaffirs' who could not read instructions and warnings instead of 'missionary kaffirs and coloured men' to whom Quinan was averse.[40] Fortunately, the works were free of such disasters from 1906, though there were disquieting reports from a government inspector on defective nitro-glycerine batches which had important consequences for the reception of De Beers explosives in Australia.

With the factory in production from 1905, Rand contracts were continued on a cost-plus basis for about half of the Rand's annual supply at 50s. a case for blasting gelatine and 37s. for gelignite. By 1907, the explosive works was turning out 30,000 cases a month. Savings were made on the cost of imported materials, but there was nothing in the accounts to indicate that sufficient profit was made from Rhodesian or Rand contracts to pay back the initial outlay, as increases in freight rates narrowed the margins over working expenses. The Nobel Trust began to ship dynamite from Europe to Rhodesia at cut prices to take over an expanding market. There was resistance from miners on the Rand to the quality and type of De Beers explosives. And although the Rand contract was renewed in 1908 for 9 years, the factory still operated at less than full capacity and paid no dividends to its sole proprietor.[41] The board, therefore, looked abroad for other markets.

Entry by Cape Explosives into the Australian market appeared to be well timed for both the company and its new customers. A combination of German and British companies formed into the High Explosives Trade Association (HETA) in 1907, dominated by Nobels, made it certain that

[39] RH, Rhodes House, MSS Afr. s. 128. Quinan papers.
[40] CPP, G. 84-1904; G. 54-1905; G. 54-1906.
[41] DBCM, *Annual Report* (1908), 33; (1909), 25; between 1903 and 1923 the Explosives Works paid only 2 dividends amounting to £80,000 on a total investment of £1.3 million; *Annual Report* (1936).

price rises would follow. With the Association supreme, mining companies in five states approached Cape Explosives in 1908 as 'a declaration of war on the HETA in general and on the Nobel Dynamite Trust in particular'.[42] The Kimberley board of De Beers dispatched Quinan to Australia to 'capture all the trade'. At the same time it was becoming clear that the Rand market would have to be shared more equitably with Nobel's Modderfontein factory and the factory run by Kynoch Ltd. in Natal. Acting on preliminary information from Australia, Cape Explosives offered the same terms as the Rand contract to its new clients on a production cost and percentage basis for 5 years and the optimistic assumption of an extra 80,000 cases for export sales every year.

As Cape Explosives' share of the Rand market declined, the Australian outlet was eagerly promoted. Up to 1914, expectations were consistently disappointed: Australia took no more than 3 or 4 per cent of total sales.[43] The reasons for this slow expansion lay in a vigorous campaign by the HETA manufacturers to compete with contract terms and appeal for tariff protection against dynamite produced by 'black labour'. There was also some objection by miners to 'fuming' in a product which used sodium nitrate. The biggest drawback was that South African explosives were not included in the preferential tariffs negotiated between the two dominions. A final factor was lack of regular shipping, and the purchase by Cape Explosives of the SS *South Africa* to provide transport incurred high running costs with little return cargo. In the end, the new outlet was simply not self-financing as intended, and had to be supported by covering transport costs under the total trading operations of the company.

Those operations were based on an annual production capacity of over 400,000 cases by 1913. But, in practice, the company sold much less, as South African demand was hit by Rand strikes. In Australia, however, the war weakened the Trust companies and increased the volume and percentage share of Cape Explosives dramatically to provide nearly all the Commonwealth's imports of explosives, 1920–2.[44] For the first time the company paid a dividend in 1917. But with the dissolution of the Trust, British firms were reconstructed into Nobel Industries Ltd., and began an intensive campaign from 1920 to win back the domestic market, reducing De Beers's share to the point where the mining company was no longer willing to support an unprofitable overseas venture and fight for business in a highly competitive market in South Africa.

---

[42] Peter Richardson, 'Nobels and the Australian Mining Industry, 1907–1925', *Business History*, 26/2 (1984), 156–92.
[43] *Dominions Royal Commission, Minutes of Evidence*, pt. II, Cd. 7707 (1914), 144; DBCM, *Annual Report* (1913); Richardson, table 2.   [44] Ibid.

One advantage of the investment, as Rhodes had intended, was a reduction in the price of a monopoly product from over 60s. per case to 45s. 6d. by 1911, where it remained until the inflationary years of the war. In Australia, too, there was a substantial drop in price, after the entry of Cape Explosives into the market. But De Beers could not escape very high internal freight charges (£12 a ton from the works to Johannesburg), which were lower for competitors.

Accounts of the net return from Cape Explosives are not available; nor is it easy to attribute annual dividends, interest, or 'rents' to particular holdings shown in the De Beers' balance sheets. Returns from investments in the 1890s were hardly more than £20,000 to £30,000 a year, with occasional windfalls from sale of shares. These sales were particularly useful in 1893 to cover a fall in the market for diamonds, and in 1896 to get rid of politically embarrassing holdings associated with Gold Fields of South Africa. After 1901, there were additional rents from former LSAE lands, and this source of revenue plus income from leased companies just about covered liabilities for these assets.[45] Diversification into other diamond mining companies in South West Africa and the Transvaal raised dividends to about £150,000 a year. This income included operations to finance and run the Fourteen Streams Railway Company, by agreement with Milner, during 1905–9, for a profit of £111,363, when capital was repaid handsomely and the line was taken over by the state. But it is hard to support Meyer's accusation that De Beers was in danger of becoming a 'general finance company', either from the scale of holdings or from dividends, compared with the value of fixed assets and returns from diamond sales. As Oats argued before his shareholders in 1914, the company's principal investment remained in diamond mines.

Taken as a whole, all investments including other mines, cold storage, dynamite, railways, coal, and land in Rhodesia and South Africa increased their book value 1890–1905, to £2.6 millions. They were written down considerably between 1907 and 1909, during the recession, and they were greatly augmented from the outset of the First World War by a joint venture with Barnatos (for the syndicate) in South West's diamond sales, by the acquisition of holdings in Premier (Transvaal) DMC, as well as by 'reserve investments for the stabiliment of the diamond trade' from 1917.[46] By the end of the war, investments in all forms stood at £8.5 million almost as much as tangible fixed assets. About a third could then be considered as ventures outside diamond mining, valued at £3.1 million in 1919, led by Cape Explosives, cold storage, farms, tramways,

---

[45] Ibid. (1910), 24.   [46] Ibid. (1917).

and collieries. The coal interests had never paid a dividend, but they were to become important later, as South African industry developed. Cape Explosives and the Cold Storage paid nothing either till after 1917. The company possessed 450,000 acres of land in the Union and 250,000 acres in Rhodesia, well-stocked, but realizing very little from occasional sales. Earnings of £342,600 on investments in 1919, excluding sale of shares, came principally from diamond mining. In many ways the worst investment had been in British consols, as initiated by Rhodes and approved by the board. Even before the war, it was admitted De Beers should have sold them earlier, and the company earned very little interest from this declining security. They still figured in the reserve at a nominal value in 1915, when they were converted into British War Loan stock. Thereafter, the general reserve fund was kept separate from the 'stabiliment' built up from profit balances and invested in diamond company and associated shares only. By the end of the war, both reserves stood at over £4 million.

In a sense, this division of the company's reserves reflected the two historical lines of policy in consecrating surplus to protection of the industry and to investment in securities offering a long-term yield, rather than development ventures derived from the period of Rhodes's chairmanship. After his death, the board played safe, avoiding speculations in South Africa.

But it was caught with the legacy of close association with the syndicate which Rhodes had been forced to accept, first on the syndicate's terms and then on his own. Eventually, this association which was strengthened by keeping so many of the directors in London and augmenting sales by profit-sharing proved costly. It attracted the attentions of the British Inland Revenue, as soon as Rhodes's contract of 1901 became financial news, in the wake of commutation of the life governors' interests.

TAXATION

The Inland Revenue commissioners took the view that De Beers was liable for taxes on profits made on resales through London. At the same time, their interpretation of the company's functions made it liable for British tax on operations connected with the sale of diamonds, irrespective of registration in a British Dominion. In reply, De Beers insisted they were a 'Colonial Company', admitting liability only on profits through syndicate sales and on tax on dividends drawn by shareholders in the United Kingdom.[47] Worse was to follow. For, at the Cape, political pressure

---

[47] *The Economist*, 27 Aug. 1898, 2 Sept. 1899; DBCM, *Annual Report* (1902), 24.

mounted for a diamond tax on a company regarded as a 'monopoly'; and in 1904 a Cape Colony company tax was introduced, costing De Beers some £140,000 a year.

Caught for the first time between rival demands from the imperial and the colonial state, De Beers set aside funds in a suspense account and contested the decisions of the British courts as far as the House of Lords. In the High Court, the judges took the view that under the syndicate contract of 1901 the company was resident in the United Kingdom for tax purposes, although its mining operations were elsewhere. In the Court of Appeal, De Beers' business was described as that of 'diamond merchants' carried on by the London directors. This misinterpretation was corrected by the Lords, but the appeal was dismissed with costs in 1906, leaving the company liable for £768,000 for the 6 years 1901–6 (reduced after argument to £500,000). But as long as they were so classified as a London business, they would have to pay tax on the whole of their profits 'just as if our five mines and works were situated in Cornwall'.[48]

In retaliation, there were threats to close the London office, stop the purchase of all British machinery, and to sell direct to America. It was particularly hard for Progressives to be squeezed at both ends of the imperial network, when the Cape had just agreed to a 3 per cent preference for British manufactures, and such miserly compensation had been paid for losses in the Boer War. The Cape Assembly passed a resolution, moved by Merriman, deprecating imperial taxes on colonial firms. Representations were made to the 1907 Imperial Conference. But colonial protests did not stop the Cape government legislating to increase its own tax on profits in excess of £50,000 annually. And in London, Asquith told the premiers and agents-general that colonial companies were free to change their articles to remove ambiguities about their seat of management and direction.

There was little else to do but accept 'Asquith's challenge'. The company's legal adviser, Bourchier Hawksley, trustee and friend of Rhodes, had the delicate task of explaining to a special general meeting how it was that the original articles of association (which did not mention the Cape) left such a wide initiative to the founder-directors. It was difficult to say why in 'a fluid Board' so many more were resident abroad than in South Africa, recording minutes which had fallen into the hands of the courts. But his conclusion was simple enough. If the Lord Chancellor was correct in his judgement that 'real control' was exercised from London, as the place of negotiations with the syndicate, then London board

---

[48] Ibid. (1906), 54.

meetings had to be ended and all doubts removed about the true seat of business. The amended articles preserved the grand intentions embodied by Rhodes and his fellows in the original, but careful changes ended the anomalies, reducing the London office to a share transfer office.[49]

The last of the British tax liability was paid off for 1908–9 in the midst of the first serious market recession the company had had to face since 1890. With no diamond sales from January till June 1908, the crisis was met by closing the De Beers and Dutoitspan mines and retrenching black and white labour, while waiting for the syndicate to take up new options. No dividends were declared on deferred shares. Even so, reduced expenditure and balances from previous years enabled the company to pay for diamonds produced and held back at cost of production, while meeting £400,000 in tax liabilities. The syndicate was expected to use its funds to uphold the price of higher-class goods until the market revived, in the face of German and Transvaal competition to sell cheaper varieties of stones.

Public declarations of confidence were matched by the private assessments of the Rothschilds writing to 'cousins' in the Paris bank. By 1908 it was known that sufficient resources had been built up through the reserve to work the mines left open and meet the standing charges on debentures and preference shares.[50] Rothschilds took the view that the company could borrow not only against their fund of British consols, but also against their holding of £750,000 debenture shares in the Cape Explosive Works with interest fully guaranteed under the contract with the Transvaal Chamber of Mines. These two 'securities' alone, it was explained to the Paris Rothschilds, amounted to £1.8 million and more than covered first charges at £1.3 million, and it was not expected the recession would last long.

This judgement by New Court proved accurate, but the management had been sufficiently frightened to make an effort to pay off old first mortgage debentures and Bultfontein 'obligations' some five years early in 1910, just as the new Union Treasury gave notice of a 10 per cent profits tax. A fairly consistent policy was then followed by the board under Francis Oats to increase liquid assets and securities to meet any crisis, and hold additional stocks of blue on the floors. Hence the mammoth buildup of two general and special reserves 'to keep the confidence of the Syndicate up, so that a time of depression would not

---

[49] DBCM, *Annual Report* (1907), and extraordinary general meeting, 32–7; for amendments see DBCA, Board 1/1/1, and meeting 14 Mar. 1908 for ratification.
[50] RAL, XI/130A/2 1908, Rothschilds (London), 4 Mar. 1908.

induce them to sell diamonds at a loss'.[51] The general reserve and the 'stabiliment' fund were, in effect, part of a policy of backing the selling organization financially in a crisis, as well as holding back on production and sales. As they were now 'to all intents and purposes a Colonial Company', total tax liability lay with the Union's profits tax, a 5 per cent income tax and a dividend tax of 7½ per cent under a consolidation act of 1917.

By then, too, the board had begun to change more frequently, as a quarter of the sixteen directors were required to retire every year from 1912. There was less resistance from the new generation to South African investments, though there was considerable disillusionment about many of the legacies of the 'Rhodes period', with the exception of investment in sources of diamonds. The new directors concentrated on the physical management of the most important source of diamonds in the world, in conjunction with the syndicate. Investments outside diamonds had not paid off in the short term. In South West Africa, they had backed a copper mining company and missed out on the diamond discoveries of 1908. And at the Cape the venture into dynamite did not pay for nearly 20 years. On the Rand, they had missed golden opportunities offered through Wernher, Beit and Co. who did not repeat the offer. The company turned to building up its reserve instead, as competition from new sources of supply outside the monopoly channel of the 1890s called for new tactics to counter the policies of rival companies and the South African state.

---

[51] DBCM, *Annual Report* (1911), 28; (1912), 32–5; and for a survey of all investments, DBCA, Board 3/1/1. De Beers gave an inflated figure of gross revenues paid to the government in evidence to the Dominions Royal Commission, 1914, at £776,000. In addition to normal company taxes and a profits tax, the company paid some £42,000 in licences, royalties on mine extensions on to Crown land, hire of convicts, registration of labour, plus £76,000 in railway rates, totalling £400,000 to £500,000 at that date, depending on diamond sales: *Minutes of Evidence*, 13.

6

Monopoly Challenged

Premier (Transvaal); German South West Africa

NEW sources of diamonds had always been recognized as a possibility. But neither De Beers nor the syndicate mustered their resources to take defensive action, when rumours of alluvial discoveries in the Transvaal reached the press late in 1902. At the centre of this news was the purchase by Thomas Major Cullinan's land and prospection syndicate of the farm of Elandsfontein near Pretoria from the impoverished Prinsloo family for a reported £52,000.[1] With evidence that part of the farm covered diamond deposits, the syndicate of financiers, surveyors, and company directors quickly floated the Premier (Transvaal) DMC with a capital of £80,000 held largely in vendor shares and set about proving their claims.

Cullinan's company took another 7 months to come up with undisputed evidence that it was in possession of the world's largest diamond pipe, concentrated under 73 acres of the farm—a mere fraction of the superficial area purchased. De Beers' only link with Premier's first board of directors was through the presence of F. A. English on the new company's London committee; no shares were acquired. There is no evidence that Cullinan offered the management of the mine to Wernher, Beit and Co., as is sometimes claimed; and none of the syndicate had a stake, leaving the field to S. Newmann and King, whose two partners acquired seats on the board and a monopoly of diamonds produced.

There is some truth, however, in the charge of complacency on the part of De Beers' management. But the consolidated company was in no position financially to launch into a competitive bid for freehold rights or vendor shares, before the mine came into production from May 1903.

---

[1] A higher price was given in the earliest company reports—£93,449, for both halves of the farm (Prinsloo's and Minaar's 'portions'): see H. P. Cartwright, *Diamonds and Clay* (Cape Town, 1977), 46–51. The members of the syndicate and founder-directors were financiers, directors of companies, a lawyer, and a surveyor. Of the 10 in South Africa, only Cullinan and A. H. Oppenheim kept their holdings and their seats on the board for more than 4 or 5 years, and 2 sold out almost at once.

For the first few months, there were genuine doubts about the depth of deposits and the likely yield. Both Wernher, Beit and Co. and De Beers were kept informed of the results of trial bores and scattered sampling of the surface of the mine area of the farm through engineers in the employ of H. Eckstein and Co.; and they read the first detailed geological report by Professor Molengraff in February 1903. More clandestine intelligence from 'secret agents' in March and a test on a sample of 100 lb. of concentrates from Premier suggested much lower yields than the one carat or more per load claimed by Culliman.[2] At least it was clear the mine was not 'salted'. Francis Oats still remained sceptical, even after a visit with Alfred Beit, but his directors accepted the evidence of the potential value of the new pipe, when Molengraff's report was confirmed by the engineer G. A. Troye.[3] The last doubts were ended by the discovery of a stone of about 25 carats in April 1903.

From within the syndicate, a group led by F. T. Gervers began to manœuvre to acquire shares in the company, as well as the right to handle Premier stones, running into solid opposition from Sigismond Neumann, who hoped to use his advantage to obtain entry into the combine from which he had long been excluded. The initial yield was maintained at 0.74 carats per load; and the first roughs were sold at about 30s. per carat which was equal to the average price of goods from Kimberley.[4] Whether the company would pay high dividends depended, however, on novel decisions about the ownership of precious stones.

STATE PARTICIPATION

Unlike the Cape, Transvaal governments had vested in themselves mining rights and the disposal of precious minerals on private as well as state lands. The allocation of selected and leased areas to the owner, in the case of gold mines, also applied to precious stones under a badly-drafted law of 1898 by which the owner could select an eighth of the mine area, before the state threw open the rest as a public diggings.[5] Cullinan's

[2] BRA, HE 263, Reyersbach to Wernher, Beit, 12 Jan., 9 Mar., 1903; S. J. Jennings to Eckstein and Co., 12 Jan. 1903; HE 7, J. M. Jones to De Beers, 10 Mar. 1903; Oats to Hirschhorn, 23 Feb. 1903.

[3] BRA, HE 230 59D, G. A. Troye, 6 July 1903, and submission of the 'Transvaal Diamond Mining Association'.

[4] BRA, HE 263, Reyersbach to De Beers, 25 May 1903.

[5] The Precious Stones Law no. 22 of 1898 was not published before it was passed by the Volksraad; see too Manfred Nathan, *The Gold Law of the Transvaal and the Orange Free State*, 5th edn. (Johannesburg, 1934), 20.

syndicate was quite happy, however, to operate under Kruger's legislation, intended for small alluvial discoveries. An eighth of their 3,460 acres was far more than their unprecedented 73 acres of diamond pipe which could be worked to the exclusion of other prospectors. They accepted, moreover, that the law required revision to provide for increased revenues from licences.[6]

But from early 1903, there were clear signs that the new state under reconstruction by Sir Alfred Milner could not allow the unexpected diamond bonanza to escape through the ragged mesh of the Transvaal's outmoded law. In order to face the huge cost of repatriation and resettlement in the war-torn colony, advances were made from other South African colonial treasuries, and a British guaranteed loan of £35 million was arranged at the time of Chamberlain's visit (December 1902 to January 1903).[7] Just at the moment when the British colonial secretary laid down that the mine-owners would have to pay for 'their' war, Cullinan's men uncovered a treasure trove to help meet the new burdens imposed on the state.

For, in co-operation with Alfred Beit and the mining houses, it was agreed by Chamberlain and Milner that the loan would be serviced mainly from railway rates and other duties, as well as an increased tax on gold profits. A revision of the gold law was undertaken by a select committee of the Legislative Council in 1903 to change the scale of dues from leased mining lands. But as late as the customs conference at Bloemfontein in March 1903, official doubts persisted about the estimate of railway revenues. With the strong possibility of a budget deficit of up to £450,000 in the Transvaal's fiscal year, a government share in diamond sales looked doubly attractive as a source of ready funds and relief for the gold mining houses faced with rising costs, labour shortages, and a fixed price for their mineral. If gold production could not be taxed too hard, someone else would have to pay.

---

[6] Premier (Transvaal) DMC, *Directors' Report and Statement of Accounts* (1903), 6. 4 members of the syndicate sold their shares, when the draft ordinance was published, and the price rose from £26 to £32: BRA, HE 263. Published plans show an area of 3,515 claims (30 by 30 Cape feet), or 72.6 acres, within a slightly larger 'Mine Area'.

[7] COCP (African South), 681, Chamberlain to Milner, 19 and 20 Feb. 1902; *The Cambridge History of the British Empire*, vol. 8, *South Africa, Rhodesia and the High Commission Territories* (Cambridge, 1963), 637–40; Bod., Milner dep. 177 and dep. 168, Eckstein to Milner, 21 Jan. 1903. The mining groups also agreed to underwrite a further loan of £3 million (abandoned as too costly by 1907). The budget was not, in fact, in deficit for 1902/3: cf. A. Mawby, 'Capital, Government and Politics in the Transvaal: A Revision and a Reversion', *Historical Journal*, 17/2 (1974), 399. But Mawby is substantially correct in the debate that no concessions were made to the gold mining industry so far as revenue was concerned; see too D. J. N. Denoon, *A Grand Illusion* (London, 1973); and more generally, T. R. H. Davenport, *South Africa: A Modern History*, 3rd edn. (Basingstoke 1987), 225–7.

Behind this policy of using the diamond field to avoid undesirable imposts on gold, Percy Fitzpatrick intrigued in his multiple roles as president of the Chamber of Mines, businessman, member of the nominated Legislative Council, and confidant of Milner and his officials. While he exaggerated his part in drafting new legislation to revise the Precious Stones Law, he certainly aimed at extracting as much as possible from Premier to pay for the 'ten millions of war debt', and never changed his opinion that the eventual terms of the relationship between the state and the diamond mine were too generous to the company.[8] Less obviously, it also suited Wernher, Beit and Co. and De Beers to see a rival in which they had no investment taxed.

A more discreet but direct influence on the legal status of the new company was exercised by the attorney-general, Sir Richard Solomon, who was given a conducted tour by the mine manager in May 1903 and was influenced by the forecasts of William McHardy for very high yields. Writing immediately to Milner, he enthusiastically calculated that some £18 million in diamonds was at hand in the surface claims to provide a windfall:

I went out yesterday to see the Premier Mine and am very much impressed. It is a tremendously big proposition (to use the language of a company promoter). I had a long talk with the manager whom I know well. He said as far as he can judge there are about 3,500 to 4,000 claims in the mine which makes it 2½ times bigger than the biggest mine yet discovered (Jagersfontein). I saw the blue ground myself taken out from different depths as far as 750 feet below the surface. It is soft as any Kimberley blue I saw. The yield so far has been between 1½ carats to 2 carats a load [sic], but of course tests have only been made from about six or seven spots. The manager says it will take 10 years working hard to exhaust the yellow ground which like mines in Kimberley is about 80 feet thick. I made a calculation which is . . . that if there are 4,000 [claims] in the mine there should be 18 million loads of yellow ground & if the yield is only 1 carat to a load and diamonds come down to £1 a carat that means £18,000,000 in the yellow alone. The manager tells me he can work the yellow ground when he has the full machinery for 1/- a load. You will see therefore what the profits will be.

After the yellow is exhausted, there is the blue ground which past experience shows is inexhaustible. The blue has yet to be worked, but also judging from experience in Kimberley the yield of the blue should not be different from that in the yellow. The state ought to have a nice nest egg in this mine and we deal with our share on business lines and not sentimental ones.[9]

---

[8] For Fitzpatrick's version, see his *South African Memories* (London, 1932), chs. 6, 7.

[9] Bod., Milner dep. 181, Solomon to Milner, 10 May 1903 (Confidential); 31 May 1903. Solomon was legal adviser and then attorney-general for the Transvaal, 1901–7.

(12a)

12a. Solomon Barnato (Solly) Joel, 1911.
12b. Ludwig Breitmeyer.
12c. Sir Julius Wernher

(12b)

ILL. 12.

(12c)

Like Fitzpatrick, Solomon was prepared at first to allow to the owner 25 per cent of surface claims on the farm, in return for working the mine. But the focus in the new legislation was on the proclaimed portion, or 'Mine Area', containing the mineral wealth, and not on the area of the farm, as in the case of gold prospection. And when Solomon circulated his draft ordinance to review the 1898 law, he unsentimentally allowed only 30 per cent of profits from production to the owner, and the remainder to the state. When the terms of the draft ordinance appeared in a *Supplementary Gazette*, they were more generous, allocating the product of four-tenths of the mine's area to the owner, and the remainder to the state.[10]

The reasons for the change are not clear (possibly Milner was less grasping than his law officer). But with the right of prior selection gone, there was less advantage to the company from a forced partnership with the state from which the public was excluded. Fitzpatrick still thought the terms too generous and opposed the ordinance all the way through the Legislative Council and in the select committee appointed to hear evidence on the case.

Two principles were at stake: legal and exclusive ownership of a share of the mine, as allowed by the state; and consequential state participation in net profits, without risk. In the select committee Cullinan gave no reasons for his preference for the old system of claim selection and an eighth ownership of the whole farm, except a wish to prove the pipe from boreholes and leave the unpayable portions to the state to throw open to the public or not. As for profits, he wanted six-tenths, leaving four to the state as compensation for no licences. Other witnesses connected with H. Eckstein and Co. and the gold mines supported Fitzpatrick's case for a more limited share of returns from production to the owner—between an eighth and a quarter—in return for complete control over workings and no extra imposts. Only one witness stressed control of output in an uncertain market rather than division of the profits. The Rand Chamber of Mines kept silent, as the principle of state participation applied only to precious stones. But Fitzpatrick, as president of the chamber, had plenty to say behind the scenes to Milner in order to extract as much as possible from diamonds rather than gold:

The more I think over the Diamond Law the more indefensible does the present proposal seem. The witnesses before the select committee have failed hopelessly to make out any case & the only thing that stands out clearly enough is that they are utterly unreasonable—insatiable. The cant of it all.

---

[10] *Transvaal Gazette*, 22 May 1903.

Cullinan (Chairman of the Premier Co.) gave figures which showed a profit to be earned by the installations now on order (outside cost of which is £100,000), of £4,600,000 *per annum* and over 55 Million sterling down to 500 [feet] level—after absurdly contracting the pipe on his diagram, in order to frighten us out of offering him ⅛ selected [claims]. My figures given in the Leg. Council were [borne out?] by him exactly—that is he gives the same data but does not make the enormous deductions for safety that I made—hence he shows about 25 to 30 Mill. profit in the first 50 ft. instead of 8½ as Wernher, Reyersbach, Jennings & I have all made it out separately.

I mean to stick for my figures of 25% undivided as a *liberal* share to owners & mean to ask if they intend treating the owners of precious minerals as well as they treat owners of precious stones even if I have to vote alone. I hate to have to do this and seem to impute foolishness or neglect or bias. Cullinan's figures are absurd even if correct because a *sale* of 5 Mill. annually is impossible & will not be for many years to come but I learn from Wernher that a sale of 1 Mill. is possible. Now my object in writing is to suggest that Govt. should seriously consider the evidence of the Select Comte. &, if they feel it warranted, make up their minds to accept the ¼ for the owners *before* all this is publicly discussed and [not] *after* when it will look like yielding to pressure & because of the publication of facts which they must have known [sic].

Premier were £40 today in spite of all our warnings to the owners in Comte. that they may only get ¼. That means 3¼ millions for their claims! . . .

Reyersbach has just encl. a letter from the delectable Oats which teems with abuse of me for being so 'unfriendly to us' (De Beers) & curtly refusing all information. So you see I am lost to grace in all eyes.[11]

When the draft ordinance became law in the Legislative Council, the minority view of the committee favouring four-tenths ownership of 'net product' by the company was accepted. Litigation was begun and then dropped, because a long legal wrangle would have prevented the sale of diamonds. Without representation on the Premier board, the Transvaal government and its reconstructed mining department sat back to take its share of the proceeds.

---

[11] Bod., Milner dep. 216, Fitzpatrick to Milner, 10 July 1903; dep. 304, 301, Legislative Council, *Votes and Proceedings* (1903) and for the Select Committee report. Premier fits awkwardly into the Denoon–Mawby debate on government relations with the mining companies. The interpretation here that Premier was offered by Fitzpatrick and the Chamber of Mines as a sacrifice to avoid unwelcome taxes on gold is supported too by the fact that Milner seriously considered selling off a tenth of the state's six-tenths interest in the mine in 1904 to raise more money for the Transvaal: dep. 323, Milner to Lyttleton, 28 Aug. 1904. But improved revenue enabled him to avoid this. The company continued to complain, and pressed, in vain, for a sliding scale of state shares from retained profits: Premier, *Directors' Report* (1910), 21; see too A. H. Duminy and W. R. Guest (eds.), *Fitzpatrick South African Politician: Selected Papers, 1888–1906* (Johannesburg, 1976), 387, for his opinion that Premier would 'pay for the ten millions of war debt, if we have to do it'.

Once firmly established in the market by increasing the volume of cheaper diamonds, Premier threatened to upset everybody's profits which had been sustained by the single-channel sales agreements between the syndicate and De Beers. Julius Wernher who visited the mine in December 1903 first appreciated the scale of the new challenge. His accurate guess that yields would drop was sobered by the knowledge that investment in machinery for open-cast production using direct treatment without weathering on floors would result in seven million new loads hauled and washed every year. The discovery of the Cullinan stone of just over 3,000 carats in June 1905, the largest uncut diamond in the world, promoted Premier's shares, but gave no joy to the merchants (Ills. 10, 11).[12]

The new men of Premier's board—H. J. King, John Jolly, and Adolphe Wagner—who joined the remaining members of the 1902 syndicate were in no mood to compromise. Neumann and King controlled sales and set up their own diamond office in London in the charge of W. Busch in 1907. Cullinan became something of a figurehead. Wagner who knew a great deal about the structure of the diamond market and owed his directorship to Neumann dominated the management at the Cullinan Building in Johannesburg, and had himself appointed 'commercial director' in 1907. McHardy, who as mine manager was a veteran from the days of the Kimberley mining board and Kimberley Central, dominated production techniques and handed them over to his son, much in the dynastic manner of Gardner Williams at De Beers. The London committee of Premier was graced by Lord Charles Montagu, guided by Sigismond Neumann, and inspired for over 30 years by the equally veteran Richard Hollins from his vast experience as miner, financier, farmer, and director of companies. Like other absentee directors, he used an 'alternate', G. W. Hollins, to carry through policy in South Africa. In 1907 and 1908, there was an influx of new men, as the old syndicate members capitalized on their premiums, leaving only Cullinan behind in the chairman's role. The intake included as managing-director Percival Ross Frames, former digger and lawyer, F. Von Hessert, who had worked for the French Company at Kimberley in the 1880s and for Rand companies, and the company director, A. A. Auret, who, like Hollins, was a member of the Chamber of Mines. Apart from Neumann, King, and Frames, the board was strong on mining and management experience and weak in knowledge of the diamond trade. Wagner set

---

[12] BRA, HE 263, Reyersbach to Wernher, Beit and Co., 30 Jan. 1905 (reporting the 'fine blue-white block' found which would be a 'white elephant' unless cut up).

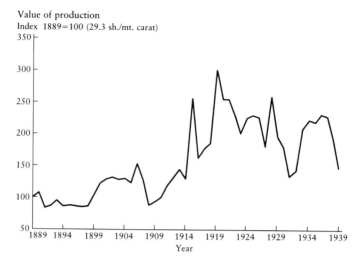

Value of production
Index 1889=100 (29.3 sh./mt. carat)

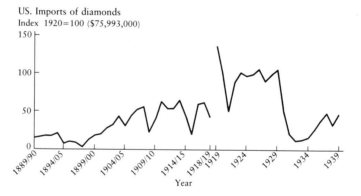

US. Imports of diamonds
Index 1920=100 ($75,993,000)

FIG. 7. South African mine and alluvial diamonds: valuation of production and US imports of diamonds, 1889–1939

out to provide this guidance by opposing any overtures from De Beers or the syndicate.[13]

The expanded board was encouraged to take this independent line, too, by the immediate success of sales through Neumann to Antwerp and Amsterdam 1903–5, when there were generally good prices for all classes of stones and a rising demand in the American market. In 1906, this

[13] Premier, *Directors' Reports* (1903), 25–7; (1905), 41.

pattern, which was part of a long-term trend since the mid-1890s, was broken. The early profitability ratios of Premier began to slide, as costs rose and the Transvaal government, after 2 tax-free years, claimed its due of 60 per cent of net profits (see Appendix A.3 and A.4).

The directors resisted any negotations with the syndicate as long as they could. From the first shareholders' meeting in 1904, there was a deep antagonism towards De Beers in Wagner's presentation of the annual reports, strongly marked by sarcasm and more legitimate resentment of the 'Premier Diamond Law' of 1903. There was, too, an undercurrent of political rivalry in 1905 between Cullinan as vice-president of the Transvaal Responsible Government Association (which was closer to Afrikaner leaders and Het Volk) and the Progressive Association led by Fitzpatrick and the mining magnate Sir George Farrar in the emerging constitutional struggle.[14]

Forced to reconsider their independent policy in 1907, Premier's board began negotiations with the syndicate and De Beers through a small committee chaired by Cullinan and co-ordinated by the Hon. H. C. Hull, lawyer and treasurer in Botha's first cabinet, following the victory of Het Volk and responsible government for the Transvaal in February. A quota agreement for sales to the syndicate and other buyers in a ratio of 30 to 70 per cent by value, between Premier and De Beers, was accepted.[15] The change of policy was defended by the directors (and particularly by Frames) as support for an 'effective monopoly' in the interest of keeping up prices. In fact, all deliveries ceased in January 1908, and the agreement was suspended at the onset of the short depression of 1907–8.

Premier weathered the crisis rather better than its rivals, as lower quality stones kept selling at falling prices, while higher-priced stock was held back by the syndicate. Neither Frames nor Wagner felt any compulsion to revert to the quota agreement, when prices recovered, after desperate efforts by a reconstructed syndicate to support continued purchases.[16]

There were also political lessons in this episode which had a lasting influence on those who were to administer future Union governments. When deliveries of diamonds from De Beers and New Jagersfontein ceased, explanations had to be furnished to the politicians of the Transvaal and the Orange River Colony by the syndicate and De Beers, emphasizing

---

[14] n. 11; and Anne E. Bennett, 'The West Ridgeway Committee: Its Role and Significance in Relation to Political Developments in the Transvaal, 1905–7', M.Phil. thesis (Oxford, 1984), 5–6.

[15] BRA, WB Inland, Wernher to Gervers, 26 Aug. 1907; Premier, *Directors' Report* (1907), 4.

[16] Newbury, 'The Origins' 18–19.

ILL. 13. Francis Oats and directors, 1912. *Front left to right:* G. W. Compton, C. E. Nind, Francis Oats (chairman), H. Mosenthal, Capt. T. G. Tyson. *Standing, left to right:* A. Viallate, David Harris, H. P. Rudd, F. Hirschhorn.

the interdependence of company profitability with employment and public revenue, and stressing the need for a common policy on production levels.[17] When Premier's venture into a quota system collapsed, Cullinan, Wagner, and Frames pressed their view on Hull and Smuts (as colonial secretary) that Premier was a special case requiring sufficient production to cover working expenses. This piece of special pleading was taken to heart as a reminder of the need for full employment at the mine and a safeguard for state revenue. It was repeated when Cullinan saw Smuts privately in March 1908 to argue in vain for a revision of the 1903 Precious Stones Law.

The broken agreement of 1907 confirmed the Premier directors' view that they had made a bad bargain with the overseas syndicate, incurring loss on a stock of diamonds they had deposited with the merchants in London, instead of selling them for what they would fetch in Belgium

[17] DBCA, 2/5/2 (Diamond Committee), May 1908; BRA, WB Inland, Wernher to Solomon, 10 Mar. 1908.

and Holland. So shareholders were told that Premier would act alone. De Beers was roundly blamed for 'over-production'; and Francis Oats was attacked personally by Wagner with threats to 'break' the Kimberley 'monopoly'.[18]

But how well founded was Premier to take an independent line in production and sales? Because of the relative ease of working open cast sites, the mine was able to raise its hauling and washing capacity very quickly within the first 5 years of operations to eight or nine million loads annually. This scale of production surpassed Kimberley and Wesselton in mechanical efficiency and avoided the extra costs of the floors. By 1909, Premier treated as much ground as all the De Beers mines.

The yield was also equal to De Beers at some two million carats a year. But the poor quality of the stones averaged about a third of Kimberley prices, especially when sold outside the syndicate. Behind the angry displays by Wagner at annual meetings lay a certain knowledge that Busch and his Continental buyers could only clear accumulated stocks for lower resales, compared with syndicate prices. Saddled with the necessity to pay three-fifths of net profits to the government, the company made no effort to reduce production or hold back stock, as De Beers or Jagersfontein did, by accumulating unprocessed clay on the floors or by passing on the cost of storing unsold diamonds to the London merchants. Once processed by Premier, diamonds were sent for immediate sale.

The company still had, it is true, the advantage of lower production costs at 3s. or 4s. per load, which was better than De Beers's cheapest workings at Wesselton.[19] Measured in terms of the cost per carat recovered, all charges were kept to about 8s.. until the 1908 recession. Thereafter, they rose, as recruiting costs for labour rose (Appendix A.3). General charges in the form of office expenses and directors' fees were much lower, however, than the older companies with diversified interests, and they declined relative to on-site mining costs which accounted for up to 90 per cent of annual expenses. Labour charges remained the major item, as the wage bill for skilled and unskilled men rose steeply, despite increased mechanization. When Premier joined the Witwatersrand Native Labour Association in 1909, there was an exceptionally steep rise in recruitment costs till 1913, in competition with the gold mines, high turnover, and high mortality rates. On the other hand, the unit cost of labour remained static, so far as African workers were concerned, at a daily rate of about

---

[18] Premier, *Directors' Report* (1908), 4.
[19] The statistics of production are not strictly comparable, because of the difference in operations between Premier and mines at deeper levels and with floors.

3s. (without food) and housing within the closed compound surrounding the mine area.

Consequently, the very large margin of gross profits which cushioned the adverse effects of falling prices narrowed between 1908 and the First World War. When production was resumed in 1916, the upward trend in costs from wartime inflation was contained by downward pressure on wages and a reduction of the labour force resulting from the use of compressor drills and a smaller capacity for hauling and washing. At the same time, participation in the wartime system of marketing diamonds through London and the syndicate enabled the Premier mine to benefit from improved contract prices.

There were, therefore, two distinct stages in the development of Premier mine, reflected in business performance and in the composition of its board. The first from 1903 till about 1912 was characterized by hostility to the single-channel structure evolved by the syndicate and De Beers; and the second was marked by changes in company ownership and a forced accommodation with 'monopoly' marketing, resulting from the wartime experience of both the company and the government.

As long as diamonds could be pushed on to the market through Busch and Neumanns in London during the period of rising American demand, Premier's high trading profit yielded high returns on the limited amount of capital employed to start the company. Large post-tax profits ensured dividend payments (Appendix A.4). Once it was clear that no responsible government in the Transvaal would change the 1903 law, the directors reconciled themselves to making what they could for themselves and their shareholders, leaving little in reserve. They changed the capital structure of the company at the beginning of 1905, before the balance of political power was known in the Transvaal, by splitting shares into two preference shares with a nominal value of 5s. and four deferred shares with a value of 2s. 6d. in order to bring in a larger number of smaller investors. The preference stock (non-voting) carried a dividend of 250 per cent, while holders of the deferred shares were entitled to what could be paid out of the rest of the retained profits. Over the next decade shares with a high premium were sold by four of the founder directors and members of Cullinan's original syndicate, and large numbers of Continental shareholders were attracted into the preference shares. With the exception of 4 years, dividends of about 13s. on a 2s. 6d. deferred share were paid till 1920. Altogether, Premier returned £4,120,000 to shareholders in that period of 18 years. Over the same period, the Transvaal and the Union governments took a cut, after the first 2 tax-free years, amounting to £5,229,500.

The expectations of Fitzpatrick and Milner that the open-cast mine would sustain a high level of taxation were therefore justified. Their successors clung to this view, and the only concession wrung from the Treasury in 1908 permitted the creation of a small reserve fund from the government's share of profits.[20] Politicians engaged in creating the new state gave little thought to the consequences for the market at large.

But in London, where the syndicate was restructured after the disasters of 1908, by admitting a larger participation by Barnatos and bringing in Wernher's Central Mining and Investment Corporation, a very different view was taken of the uncontrolled marketing of cheap stones. The syndicate had been severely shaken and was powerless to stop Busch lowering prices, complained Wernher, while some of its own members, such as Abrahams 'with only the ideas of grocers', were too terrified to put up money in a crisis.[21] More important, Breitmeyer, as Wernher's successor perceived (like Beit before him) that the diamond market had been dangerously reliant on cash purchases for resales when bankers refused credit. This, in turn, affected diamond company shares in 1908, casting 'a shadow over the whole of the South African market which has never been more discredited than it has at present'.[22]

A year later, the syndicate was in a much stronger position: a new contract with De Beers was in view, though it raised contentious issues about participation in the purchase of stock from 'outside mines' which Oats was eager to pursue. S. B. 'Solly' Joel, nephew of the famous Barney, was welcomed into the combine for his increased stake and his abandonment of subparticipants. But despite the prosperity of 1909 and 1910, neither the new syndicate nor De Beers could face buying up Premier diamonds, and it was feared the Transvaal company was beginning to hold back diamonds produced, as a reserve to drop on the market any time.

Unable to talk Premier into a new combination, the syndicate took steps to buy its way into the company's directorate instead. By 1911, Barnatos had acquired 106,050 deferred shares giving them a third interest in the voting stock of Premier. Two seats on the board went to J. Munro and G. Imroth, as representatives of Barnatos; and Joel as principal partner in the merchant house, joined the London committee of Premier alongside Neumann. At the same time, the evidence of the registers for the issue of share warrants to holders of preference stock suggests considerable activity in the transfer privately of bearer shares, particularly

[20] Act 31 of 1908.   [21] BRA, WB 31, Wernher to Hirschhorn, 12 June 1908.
[22] Ibid., Breitmeyer to Hirschhorn, 1 May 1908.

ILL. 14. Politicians and officials, Department of Mines

1 (*top left*) The Hon. F. S. Malan, Minister of Mines, 1912–1924

2 (*top right*) The Hon. F. W. Beyers, Minister of Mines, 1924–1929

3 (*above left*) The Hon. A. P. J. Fourie, Minister of Mines, 1929–1933

4 (*above right*) Sir Robert Kotze, Government Mining Engineer, 1910–1926

5 (*left*) H. Warington Smyth, Secretary of Mines, 1910–1927

by H. J. King (for Neumanns) and, more significantly, by Anton Dunkelsbuhler for the syndicate, paralleled by purchases of deferred shares by Barnatos with their voting rights. It was at this period, too, that the finance house of Barnatos consolidated its very large holdings in New Jagersfontein, where it owned 55 per cent of deferred and 65 per cent of preference shares by 1910.[23]

Barnatos' expansion and Joel's boardroom coup in Premier ended the career of Adolphe Wagner, who resigned at the end of 1912 in a storm of invective and self-justification, after alternates had been mustered to vote against his proposal to reduce the number of directors.[24] Jolly and Von Hessert went too, leaving the field clear for policy changes put through by the merchant-directors and their alternates, in alliance with Frames who perceived the shift in power, and with the concurrence of Neumann, King, and their alternate, Paul Dreyfus. In 1913, Joel was confirmed as a full director, and the shareholders were lectured on the merits of not forcing stock on to the market and 'the great desirability of a diamond combine'.[25]

THE DIAMOND REGIE

Whether such a combine could deal with the second major challenge to single channel sales from German South West Africa was more problematical. Both the syndicate and De Beers had sufficient contacts with German business and government to keep a close watch on this source of production from the first discoveries in April 1908 on land owned by the Deutsche Kolonial Gesellschaft. A secret report on the finds written by Hans Merensky for H. E. Eckstein and Co. in 1909 was considered to be so sensitive that it was kept from everybody on the De Beers board, except Oats and Friedrich Hirschhorn, and was forwarded promptly to

---

[23] RH, Central Mining and Investment Corporation, MSS Brit. Emp. s. 412, 'Premier (T) DMC Ltd. Register of Share Warrants to Bearer. Preference'. The 160,000 preference shares outstanding carried no voting rights; see too 'De Beers Consolidated Mines Ltd. Deferred Shares issued in Exchange for Premier Deferred Shares' [1921–3] for the pattern of holdings in Premier by the end of the war; and below, ch. 7. For Barnatos's control of New Jagersfontein see 'Exchange of Registered Deferred & Preference to Ordinary Shares: The New Jagersfontein Mining & Exploration Company Ltd. 1909'. After the Barnatos, there were 674 holders of deferred shares and 288 holders of preference shares (without voting rights) in the New Jagersfontein Company, led by F. H. Arnold, A. A. Hall, Otto Beit, G. J. S. and H. Mosenthal, JCI (the 'Corner House'), and A. and H. Abrahams. Among the smaller shareholders, French, German, Swiss, and Dutch registrations predominated, with few South African entries.
[24] Premier, *Directors' Report* (1912), 34–6.
[25] Ibid. (1913), 19.

Wernher.[26] But the London merchants were confident that 'Government interference and the high proposed taxation' would hold back South West's production, which was split among a large number of companies; and they were on sufficiently good terms with Bernhard Dernburg, banker and colonial secretary 1907–10, to be hopeful of restraining output, though nobody in the syndicate expected German diamonds to pass through their hands. The scale of operations which resulted in the sale of some 4.6 million carats worth £7 million 1908–13, took them, therefore, by surprise.

Indeed, the organization of the German fields was quite unlike anything in South Africa. Deposits were worked along the coast from 10 miles north of Luderitz Bay to the Pomona and Mamora Farm 60 miles to the south in a bare terrain of dunes, cliffs, and salt pans. Fifteen small companies held their concessions from the Kolonial Gesellschaft which funded the Deutsche Diamanten Gesellschaft to take over all other mining rights of the colonial company, including a monopoly area (*Sperrgebiet*) held by special agreement with the German Colonial Office.[27] There were few foreign investments in this sphere, apart from Kolmanskop Diamond Mines Ltd. and the German South West Diamond Company, both registered in Cape Town in 1909 and chaired by the politician, F. Ginsburg. A London-based Anglo-German Exploration Company held a few diamond claims in 1913. The major British interest lay in the Pomona Mine which paid a royalty of 8 per cent of diamonds found to De Pass, Spence and Co., as owner of prior mineral rights, and 1½ per cent to an even older Cape Town syndicate represented by Van der Horst. De Beers had only a small holding in one concession worked by the Kaukausib syndicate, though it had a considerably larger interest in the South West Africa Company of London and Berlin which had land and transport, but no diamonds.

Because of the scattered location of deposits, early estimates of the life of the fields put their proven reserves fairly low, leaving some of the richer gravels to a few consolidated companies such as the Diamanten Gesellschaft, Pomona, and Kolmanskop; and this estimate was accepted

[26] BRA, HE 163, Reyersbach to Hirschhorn, 7 Feb. 1909; Olga Lehmann, *Hans Merensky ein deutscher Pionier in Südafrika* (Göttingen, 1965); WB Inland 31, Breitmeyer to Hirschhorn, 21 Dec. 1908; Breitmeyer to Meyer, 11 Feb. 1909.

[27] CAD, MNW 258 MM 3490/14 for E. Oppenheimer and Alpheus Williams, *Diamond Deposits of German South West Africa* (Kimberley, 1914); *Memorandum on the Country Known as German South-West Africa Compiled from such Information as is Presently Available to the Government of the Union of South Africa* (Pretoria, 1915); for some of the legal background see H. R. Hahlo, 'The Great South-West African Diamond Case', *South African Law Journal*, 76 (1959), 151–86; also Demuth.

as late as 1913, when a team of De Beers representatives surveyed the territory. It was in the interest of the first miners, therefore, to work their concessions with a minimum of investment in infrastructure which was provided by the Kolonial Bergbau Gesellschaft and the government railways.

Special interest was taken by the colonial government in the marketing of South West diamonds, moreover, to ensure that the system of local consolidated taxation (royalties and export duty) encouraged maximum production according to the return on overseas sales. After a visit by Dernburg in August 1908, issue of licences was stopped, leaving the unworked Sperrgebiet to the Diamanten Gesellschaft. And in 1912 the consolidated tax on companies was levied at the rate of 66 per cent of diamond sales, less 70 per cent of the costs of production. The mechanism for handling this complex assessment of annual costs for each company was the control board, or Regie, set up in 1909 with a capital of £100,000 put up by German banks. Its primary function was to act as a selling agency financed by 5 per cent of turnover and interest on its capital. In 1913, the Regie's commission was divided with the government, which took powers to limit sales and fix a quota for each producer, according to the state of the market. The following year, the government bought half the Regie's capital from surplus revenue and allowed election of the board's eight directors to represent producers, merchants, and diamond cutting interests.

The revenue for this control came from the industry itself. The Regie avoided the London syndicate and sold the bulk of production through Antwerp and the houses of Coetermann and Kryn, in return for a percentage of rough stones for a German cutting industry. The Antwerp syndicate, moreover, successfully outbid most London tenders before 1913, when the price for South West stones rose steeply from DM 29 per carat to DM 45, producing a spectacular leap in South West Africa's revenues to over £1 million.

The full significance of this organization only dawned gradually on the syndicate and De Beers. From 1908, there were leisurely visits to Berlin by Hirschhorn and Breitmeyer to see officials at the German Colonial Office which they found 'overrun with Diamond Merchants and cutters from all quarters'. Wernher provided letters of introduction for Colonial Secretary Dernburg's tour of South Africa prior to his inspection of South West in 1908.[28] In return, they received little but promises of

---

[28] BRA, WB 31, Wernher to Hirschhorn, 16 May 1908. For Dernburg's tour see Hartmut Pogge von Strandmann (ed.), *Walther Rathenau Industrialist, Banker, Intellectual, and Politician: Notes and Diaries 1907–1922* (Oxford, 1985), 60–78.

co-operation. By 1909, when Francis Oats had also been to South West and to Berlin and raised Merensky's earlier estimates of the deposits, Wernher was more worried by the 'dodgy ways' of the Regie's representatives who sold as fast as they could and boasted to Breitmeyer that the colony possessed stores of diamonds 'like apples under a shaken tree'. Wernher judged that the syndicate did not yet feel the 'full weight' of this new source on the market, and he was impressed by the quality of South West parcels that found their way to London, confiding to Hirschhorn that 'in a way South-West Africa is really a greater competitor than Premier'.[29]

But there was little the syndicate could do, once the Antwerp houses secured a firm contract from the Regie, until the German producers forced a competitive tender in 1913 to raise prices. The London syndicate was only too willing to seize this opportunity to buy up South West stocks on an open market. Breitmeyer sought the support of De Beers to help finance the 'enormous expenditure' the tender entailed and contacted the new colonial secretary, Wilhelm Solf, in Berlin, for firm commitment to international regulation of the trade.

At Kimberley the De Beers diamond committee deliberated on this proposal as a major extension of company policy in April 1913. Francis Oats agreed to a joint tender with the syndicate as in line with purchases made of smaller mines (Voorspoed and Koffyfontein) to stop their production. Possession of South West diamonds would prevent them undercutting De Beers prices. Hirschhorn reported on Breitmeyer's negotiations with Solf in Berlin, giving the impression that they would be given only one chance to break the Antwerp monopoly by joining with the syndicate to fund purchases. Other directors and members of the committee such as H. P. Rudd and C. E. Nind were more hesitant; and Achille Viallate who spoke for directors in London criticized the venture and emphasized with great prescience its consequences for the company:

it would only be the first move and we would be obliged to go on to the next. During a certain period the production is going to increase and to keep up prices we should be obliged to lock up a part of the diamonds. Shareholders know that De Beers have no longer a monopoly of production. We say there are some mines which are looked upon as poor for the time being but which in other hands would produce diamonds and therefore it is better to use part of De Beers to buy those mines and keep control, but outside the mines there is a great deal of production of alluvial which is put into the market and which production is increasing and

---

[29] BRA, WB 32, Breitmeyer to Hirschhorn, 16 Apr. 1909; Wernher to Hirschhorn, 6 Aug. 1909.

to follow out the policy we should have to buy that production also and it is a question whether we should run that risk for the future.

He thought not, and favoured a more general agreement between producers, including Premier and Jagersfontein.[30] And yet, after further meetings in May, both the diamond committee and the full board of De Beers agreed to take a half share in a tender for the purchase of South West diamonds, though they did not succeed in capturing the whole supply which was divided with Antwerp at the high prices prevailing in 1913. To confirm their judgement the company and the syndicate sent their own investigators to South West Africa to examine at source the extent of the German threat to market stability.

The inspection party arrived early in 1914, consisting of Ernest Oppenheimer, Alpheus Williams, Achille Viallate, and Herman Hirsche, and made the first thorough examination of conditions of production and prospects for co-operation.[31] Their report concluded that the limited time period for the concessions enjoyed by companies made it unlikely they would willingly restrain their output to anything less than the one million carats set by the government for 1914. Hopes of discovering a diamond pipe had not been abandoned (indeed, they were encouraged by the 33 and 35 carat stones which turned up on the Diamanten Gesellschaft's claims in the Luderitz fields). Despite the near unpayability of a number of the smaller deposits, the four largest companies had lower operating costs and paid less to Ovambo and Cape workers than the South African companies. Many would be worked out within 5 years. But in the meantime 'limitation of sales and consequent higher prices would be in the best interests of all the companies concerned'.[32]

But how was such a limitation to be brought about while the market was so buoyant? While De Beers and the syndicate used their financial resources to meet Solf's conditions for competitive tenders, in return for generous quotas imposed on South West companies, other initiatives for an agreement with the Germans came from an unexpected quarter from within South Africa. Because of a forecast of falling yields from Premier mine, and therefore less revenue, Smuts in his capacity as minister of finance met with company directors in December 1913 to approve a plan which originated with J. C. Sheridan, a commissioner of the Inland Revenue, to bring South West Mines into a producers' cartel.[33] The

---

[30] DBCA, 2/5/2 (Diamond Committee), 7 Apr. 1913. Present were: Oats, Viallate, D. J. Haarhoff, H. P. Rudd, C. E. Nind, Alpheus Williams, and F. Hirschhorn for the syndicate.
[31] CAD, MNW 258, Oppenheimer and Williams, *Diamond Deposits*.   [32] Ibid. 57.
[33] CAD, TES 860 F 5/73, J. C. Sheridan, memorandum, 22 Dec. 1913; Smuts to Baron von Humboldt, 22 Dec. 1913; von Humboldt to Smuts 28 Jan. 1914. Cf. Frames to Fourie,

German Foreign Office approved the initiative relayed through their consul-general at the Cape, but insisted the negotiations be conducted in London, where a quota system could be debated with the London syndicate. Frames, as managing director of Premier, urged Smuts to agree, because of the poor performance of his company. Like the directors of De Beers he had come round to the view that the market could be influenced by signs of co-operation to reduce over-production and would improve for Premier 'at the mere announcement of a conference among producers'. His fellow directors, Imroth and Cullinan, requested permission to pass on the good news to their annual meeting of Premier shareholders, but were restrained by Smuts until the details had been settled. Frames also fretted for publicity, as news of the competitive tenders leaked out (through De Beers). He repeated to Smuts a warning that local competition from low-grade alluvial mining in the Transvaal could further reduce Premier's profit margins. It was important to counter rumours of Premier's recent record 'as this would place us at a very great disadvantage in securing the allotment in the diamond trade to which I think we are entitled' at the forthcoming conference.[34]

Thus, as the war approached there was a surprising willingness to co-operate in one sector of the mineral market. In South Africa the establishment of a Department of Mines contributed to the co-ordination of policies agreed more tentatively by the companies, because of the attitudes of officials to the whole question of cartelization in the diamond trade and their growing admiration for what they understood of German management of South West's share of that trade. The new department, moreover, under Smuts in 1910 and F. S. Malan from 1912, inherited the organization of the Transvaal, rather than the Cape. The department's secretary of mines, Herbert Warington Smyth, and the government mining engineer R. N. Kotze, had learned their business under Milner's administration and on the gold fields in the highly-charged political atmosphere of the Union's birth, and brought with them the numerous inspectors, surveyors, registrars, and geologists that went with a bureaucratic machine that knew its importance to the state. The enlarged inspectorate applied its expertise to a wide range of subjects beyond matters of safety, machinery, claims, and the record of employment and production. Its annual published reports were terse in comment and full

1 Dec. 1929 (claiming the initiative for this plan, and the eventual agreement): (unnumbered series), MM 182/61.

[34] CAD, TES 860 F 5/73, Frames to Smuts, 13 and 25 Mar. 1914. For the impression left on Smuts, who approved the plan from the inland revenue officer see Smuts to J. W. S. Langerman (High Commission, London), 5 May 1914.

in statistics; its departmental links with the Treasury and Department of Native Labour were more revealing in the unpublished memoranda and correspondence on the economic and social importance of an industry which had a turbulent political history until the 1920s.

The department, in any case, was not a friend of the diamond companies. From 1911, the inspector of mines was highly critical of the association of syndicate merchants with the boards of Koffyfontein and Jagersfontein in the Free State, and began to formulate suggestions for an 'independent' evaluation of diamonds through a government department to keep out major buyers such as Bonas and Co. and Barnato Bros. from sales by companies in which they were major shareholders.[35] The argument was applied to Premier with even more force from 1912, after the boardroom coup which brought in Solly Joel's directors. To some extent this pressure for control was countered from within the Treasury, where the commissioner for inland revenue argued that taxes on profits were more important than state participation in the details of the trade. It was agreed, however, by Sheridan that, in time, the Union government 'will be obliged to follow the example of the German Government and take control over the sale of South African diamonds'.[36]

There was also concern about the revival and spread of alluvial diamond mining in the Union, though for reasons which were different from the fears of the major producers. For the most part, this section of the industry remained concentrated in the traditional river diggings of the Vaal on private estates and government land. Spasmodic production supported prospection and mining by about 1,000 whites and nearly 300 Indians, coloureds, and Cape Africans, employing 7,000 to 8,000 black workers by 1912. This racial mixture of claim holders was not unusual for the northern Cape, but the toleration allowed under Cape provincial laws was not extended to the Free State on the claims at Zoutpansdrift, or among the 2,000 to 3,000 white miners in the Klerksdorp district. Returns were still small for the majority of these miners who averaged £10 a month, after payment of stores and wages. A few professionals and companies made more from a total production which accounted for only 4 per cent by weight of the Union's diamond output, but over 10 per cent by value. As prices for diamonds rose before 1914, more men were attracted into prospection for alluvial stones fetching over £5 per carat, compared with £2 for mine stones.

---

[35] CAD, TES 829 F 5/17, inspector of mines, report, Mar. 1911.
[36] Ibid., Sheridan to Secretary for Finance, 29 Apr. 1911.

On the whole, the mines department viewed the alluvial sector with disfavour, especially its individualistic and highly independent organization in the Cape:

The country obtains no material benefit from the alluvial fields. A good stamp of white man, who in many cases deteriorates morally, earns, on average, little more than the wage of an unskilled labourer. He absorbs a large amount of efficient coloured labour, which could be more beneficially employed.

Many of the diggers have wives and families living on the fields, and it is a frequent occurrence for the digger, after a spell of ill luck or possibly bad judgement, to be forced to leave his family to try to obtain work elsewhere. The status of penniless whites in close proximity to opulent coloured people is not pleasant to contemplate. This condition of affairs must be of frequent occurrence, as almost one third of the diggers on Government ground are Indians, coloured people or natives.[37]

But a production of just over £1 million a year could not be ignored, and there was no sign the department wanted to curtail alluvial output for the benefit of larger producers, however much it disliked the social consequences of the industry's spread into new diggings. There was little possibility, in any case, of raising revenue from the diggers whose licences and other fees amounted to less than 2 per cent of alluvial export values. Official attention concentrated on the big companies and the possible effects of German production on Premier.

From 1910, when consolidated statistics were available, it became obvious that about half of the government's revenue from the diamond industry came from its share of Premier's profits, while the rest was ordinary company taxation. While the industry represented about ten per cent of total mining capital in the Union, it paid much higher dividends at 33.4 per cent of nominal share values, compared with 11.7 per cent for gold shares, and much lower returns on investment in coal and other minerals. By 1913, diamonds provided the Union with over a third of all its mining taxation and contributed 8 per cent to ordinary revenue (Appendix A.5).

Hence the willingness of Smuts and Malan to accept Sheridan's proposal for an international agreement by a conference in 1914. When the date was set for July, the boards of De Beers, Premier, Jagersfontein, and Koffyfontein met in Johannesburg for the first time as a Union producers' delegation, though they did not agree on a joint strategy. Once in London, their representatives joined with A. Meyer Gerhard for the Regie and four members of the syndicate, Mosenthal, Breitmeyer, Reyersbach, and

---

[37] E. Langly, Department of Mines, *Annual Report* (1912), 177.

Anthony Oppenheimer, to hammer out terms for international quotas. Neither the Foreign Office nor the British Board of Trade was kept informed, and the status of the agreement reached was a commercial contract.[38] The agreement which was signed on 31 July 1914 adopted the limitation of a common 'pool' set at £12.5 million as the amount of total sales by the signatories in 1913, though a lower ceiling was set for the first year. Shares of total sales through the syndicate were fixed (with minor annual adjustments) at 48 per cent for De Beers, 19 per cent for Premier, 11 per cent for New Jagersfontein, and 21 per cent for the Regie, which would continue to handle all South West's output. For the details, the conference adopted the procedures evolved in contracts between the syndicate and De Beers: standard assortments and basis prices from a fixed date, a fixed percentage of profits for the selling agency from the resales (without profit sharing with the producers). There was also mention of a 'board of control' in the manner of the Regie, with two members nominated by each producer and regulation of disputes by 'commissioners' appointed by the Union and German governments (see Table 6.1).

As the war broke out a few days after the conference rose, the agreement was never in force. But its terms were of more than academic interest, because of the scale of quotas adopted and the general acceptance of the syndicate's methods of doing business as a model for the producers' cartel in the Union. It was, in fact, an enormous step forward in international regulation by contract in a trade which had been over-producing rapidly. The principal lesson of the period from 1903 had been recognized, when the syndicate and De Beers found they could influence the scale of resale prices for gemstones, but could not control the larger amounts of cheaper stones finding their way into cutting and industrial production shortly before the war.

For cutting had also expanded to employ 22,000 workers in Amsterdam and Antwerp, 800 in Germany, 400 in Switzerland, and smaller numbers in London and Paris. Even New York as the capital of the retail market for cut stones had some 300 diamond cutters. Stocks on hand at the beginning of the war were not as high as in the worst period of depression and were estimated at about £1.5 million in gemstones, shared between the London syndicate, the Regie, and the Antwerp houses.[39] In addition

---

[38] CAD, MNW 488, minutes and final agreement. The Union was represented by J. C. Sheridan; PRO, FO 368/1178, Gladstone to Harcourt, 7 May 1914, enclosing a minute from the secretary of finance, J. R. Leisk on 'forming a combination of diamond producers in South Africa'.

[39] CAD, MNW 4432 MM 2445/18. Antwerp held an estimated £500,000, Berlin £750,000, and London £222,495. Hirschhorn, memorandum, 1916; Demuth, 107–9.

TABLE 6.1. *London conference pooling and quota agreement, 31 July 1914*

	Pool (£)			Quotas (%)		
	1st year	2nd year	3rd year	1st year	2nd year	3rd year
De Beers	5,335,000	6,031,250	6,000,000	48½	48¼	48
Regie	2,310,000	2,687,500	2,750,000	21	21½	22
Premier	2,145,000	2,406,250	2,375,000	19½	19¼	19
New Jagersfontein	1,210,000	1,375,000	1,375,000	11	11	11
TOTAL	11,000,000	12,500,000	12,500,000			

Source: CAD, MNW 488.

there were some £3 million in small goods which were held back unsold (and possibly unsaleable) by the merchants in the two main syndicates to avoid dragging down prices for cuttable goods. In all, half of the annual world sales of rough diamonds was kept in the merchants' vaults.

Very little of this was revealed to the shareholders of the companies concerned, and only the German and Union governments were direct participants and in possession of some of the information on the structure of the trade. De Beers belatedly sent a copy of its privately-published report on South West to the Department of Mines late in 1914, but would not allow more than a small portion to be used in a government paper on the territory. Premier directors said nothing of the 1914 agreement at their annual meeting. Only Francis Oats dared to voice the hope that it might some day be renewed, when 'the Union Government will take the place of the German Government'. With the invasion of South West Africa already under way, this sentiment was warmly applauded.[40]

[40] DBCM, *Annual Report* (1914), 39.

7

Diamonds in Wartime

◆

THE immediate impact of the war was to suspend contracts with the syndicate and other buyers. Premier stopped production in August 1914, dismissing 850 white and 14,000 black workers, after Antwerp merchants failed to maintain prices. For the next 7 or 8 months, the international diamond trade was in a state of collapse, as banks suspended credit to the cutters, though some production continued in the alluvial mines. At Koffyfontein and De Beers, urgent requests from the Department of Mines to keep on white workers were met by temporary funding for relief projects around company estates, by provision of credit in the retail stores and by some charity from provincial administrations. The Department of Mines gave praise for the 'liberality' of De Beers, but took to task 'the financiers who may have made money by market manipulation in mining stocks'.[1]

In German South West Africa, a plan formulated at the time of the Agadir incident in 1911 was put into effect. Production continued till the end of September, but all diamonds were handed over to officials, rather than to the Deutsche Bank, as the representative of the Regie. They were kept at Windhoek until the Germans evacuated their colonial capital, when 75,000 carats were buried in a tin box 30 miles from Grootfontein, on the line of a possible escape route, by the authority of the acting-governor, Dr. Seitz.[2]

While the Germans hoarded and the companies retrenched, the South African government entered the war as part of the British Empire and with divided views on how far the recently-created Defence Force could be made to operate in enemy territory. Contrary to some interpretations, there is little evidence of 'mounting antagonism' between the Union and

---

[1] Department of Mines, *Annual Report* (1913), 101–2.
[2] COCP, *Africa South*, 1064 (1918), 'Reports on the Administration of the Protectorate of South West Africa for the periods (1) 9th July, 1915, to 31st March, 1916, (2) 1916', 23; Walker, *The Cambridge History of the British Empire*, ch. 27; Gail-Maryse Cockram, *South West African Mandate* (Cape Town, 1976), 13–25.

its neighbour, though consular reports to Pretoria had made a detailed assessment of German forces, which consisted of some 9,000 regular troops and reservists.[3] Against these, superior numbers of English and Afrikaner volunteers could be raised. The frontier was open to invasion, and there was sufficient naval support at the Cape to mount attacks from the sea. On the day war was declared, Botha's government loyally offered to release British troops in the country by deploying the Defence Force. The British government and a joint naval and military committee of the Imperial General Staff invited the South Africans to go further and attack the German territory to neutralize its wireless stations. Botha and Smuts successfully carried a majority with them in the Union parliament, after 5 days of debate, and the troopships sailed on 14 September for Luderitzbucht and Swakopmund.

But after the capture of the two coastal ports, divisions within the Union hardened. By October the country was under martial law, and a full-scale invasion of South West by land was suspended during the rebellion by 11,500 Afrikaners, mostly from the Free State, who followed senior officers, including C. R. Beyers, commandant-general of the Citizen Force, in opposing South African commitment to the war. This costly diversion, which was suppressed by other Afrikaners, kept Botha's troops busy till December 1914. Then he was free to launch his campaign along the railway line from Swakopmund, while General Smuts's columns worked their way inland from Luderitz and the border along the southern railway line to Gibeon. The war stayed close to the communications network, bypassing the diamond fields on the coast. Windhoek fell in May 1915 and the northern mining town of Otavi in July, when the remaining German forces consisting of 204 officers and 3,000 other ranks surrendered. The terms were generous enough; reservists returned to their jobs and their farms; the professional soldiery and colonial officials were interned in the Union. The only serious damage was to diamond mine stores, condensing plant, and rolling stock at Luderitz, which was made good within 2 months and to the Khan copper mine at Arandis which was soon producing concentrates normally.

From the outset of the occupation, the civil administrator, E. H. L. Gorges, who was personally responsible to Louis Botha, was anxious to restore the economy of the captured territory in order to employ the

---

[3] COCP, *Africa South*, 1064 (1918), 18; W. K. Hancock, *Smuts: The Sanguine Years, 1870–1919* (Cambridge, 1962), ch. 18; for other evidence from the Imperial General Staff reports on the course of the campaign see Colin Newbury, 'Spoils of War: Sub-imperial Collaboration in South West Africa and New Guinea, 1914–1920', *Journal of Imperial and Commonwealth History*, 16/3 (1988), 86–106.

resettled civilian population and reduce dependence on rationing. The Union government was eager to make up the financial deficit of £2 million revealed in March 1915, and to justify mounting military expenditure in Africa which entailed heavier domestic taxation and a massive public debt.[4]

There were good grounds for thinking the prize of war might at least pay its way. Normally the exports of South West Africa, consisting mainly of diamonds and copper, had maintained the favourable balance of payments for goods imported from Germany and elsewhere, though they had in no way met the vast expenditure on military campaigns. The local banks had accumulated sums amounting to DM 14 million, some of which had helped to finance the short war by a forced loan to the government Land Bank. Arrangements were made for merchants to obtain credit through branches of the Standard Bank and the National Bank of South Africa, and the Deutsche Afrika Bank obtained remittances of £300,000 through New York to pay for trade in imports from the Union. The South African banks were also willing from September 1915 to make advances to the mining companies, on the security of diamonds and copper ores. They began with the Pomona Company, whose head office in Berlin applied for an overdraft and permission to sell production in the United States.[5] The Ministry of Finance sanctioned this extraordinary arrangement for both Pomona and the Diamanten Gesellschaft, providing that production was limited to 10,000 carats a month. But the outlet to America was closed. All diamonds had to be deposited with the National Bank prior to marketing. Other advances were made to the German companies from Berlin through the Netherlands Bank of South Africa in December 1915, and copper ores from the Otavi mine were sold to the American Smelting and Refining Company of New York for as long as their contract lasted.

Gorges's administration had already issued a proclamation in July to regulate the possession of cut and uncut stones, and prevent casual prospection and purchase by members of the Defence Force. By then, the Department of Mines was in possession of a full analysis of local mining legislation made by ex-consul E. Muller; and the secretary of the department, Warington Smyth, visited the companies in August to check

---

[4] From the end of October 1915 the offices of military governor and chief civil secretary were combined, when Gorges (a former minister of the interior) was appointed by Botha. For the cost of the rebellion and the war see Walker, *The Cambridge History of the British Empire*, 751–9.

[5] CAD, TES 866 F5/951, United States Consul, Zurich, 9 Sept. 1915; National Bank of South Africa to Finance, 18 Sept. 1915.

up on the extent and location of their wartime production of diamonds which had not been accounted for. The attention of the ex-governor Seitz was drawn to this omission under the terms of the surrender:

After some correspondence and personal interviews, at which he exhibited a considerable amount of acrimony, he consented to give orders for their handing over, and an agreement was entered into between him and the Military Governor that the diamonds should be retained in safe custody by this Administration until the close of the war. The quantity received was about 15,000 grammes, or approximately 75,000 carats, and included the 'Ariams' diamond, a stone of 8 grammes, or 40 carats, and estimated as being worth about £5,000.[6]

After this small windfall amounting to less than a month's production, the Union and the South West administration moved cautiously between the policies of encouraging full employment and fathoming the complex system of German taxation. On the one hand, officials and politicians could hardly promote the welfare of German workmen in ex-enemy territory while mines remained closed at home. And on the other, they were encouraged to believe from Muller's preliminary analysis that they had inherited a higher level of taxation and fuller powers to control the sale of diamonds. Somehow, they were assured by the inspector of mines, German employment could be justified by taxes paid to the occupying state.[7]

In October 1915, therefore, nine diamond companies were allowed to reopen, if they could find funding from the National Bank. Men from the Kimberley diamond detective department moved in to keep a check on production, register finds, and prevent smuggling. But only Pomona mined diamonds at the end of 1915 and a few others began again in 1916. The provisions of the German taxation system were not applied, because they rested on a knowledge of returns from sales through the Regie; and until diamonds were sold, no export duties or company taxes were paid. The companies lived from month to month on advances from the bank against stones held by the administration. With credit short, only 13,408 carats were produced in the last 3 months of 1915; and in 1916, under higher quotas allowed by the administration, there was a production of 144,920 carats, using only white labour and equal to about a month's pre-war output. Even so, they could not be sold.

---

[6] COCP, *Africa South*, 1064 (1918), 23.
[7] CAD, TES 866 F5 951, Muller to Mines, 7 July 1915; Langley (inspector of mines), memorandum [1915].

SYNDICATE CONTROL

In the first place, access to the market for an international commodity was blocked by British controls aimed at denying raw materials to the enemy. The War Trade Advisory Committee (expanded later into the War Trade Department) was set up early in 1915 to carry out this difficult task. An interdepartmental conference approved a suggestion from the Board of Trade for a small diamond committee in July 1915, run by Alfred Mosely, a former Cape dealer, whose warnings to the Board about traffic in industrial diamonds through London to Holland were taken seriously. Mosely nominated two leading merchants, V. A. Litkie and Ludwig Breitmeyer, to serve with him on the committee with full powers to certify the import and export of rough stones.[8]

This channel gave effective control to the London diamond syndicate which decided the classes of stones most likely to be of industrial use and, therefore, to be kept out of circulation to neutral countries. All other stones exported to Holland for cutting passed through a similar committee of Dutch merchants and were monitored by the British consul in Amsterdam. Cut stones, in turn, were forwarded only through London to the United States. Lesser grades of stones and bort, such as the output from Premier mine—'useful in drawing wire and meeting other war requirements'— were not to be sold through Amsterdam at all, but were left to the six or seven specialized dealers and tool manufacturers who handled them in London.[9] On the advice of the War Trade Committee, the Colonial Office was informed that the export of South West diamonds for sale was unthinkable, as long as stocks of German diamonds held by the syndicate and amounting to about £500,000 were frozen by agreement with the British government. A telegram from the colonial secretary, Bonar Law, to the governor-general set limits to South Africa's freedom to market stones:

Ministers will be aware that stringent steps have been taken in this country and throughout the Empire to prevent the importation of diamonds of enemy origin and all diamonds entering or leaving this country are subject to expert examination. Any diamonds of enemy origin being imported are seized or refused admission and none are allowed to be exported without satisfactory evidence of origin. If large stocks of South West African diamonds were placed in the market and sent to Holland to be cut it would become impossible to discriminate

---

[8] CO, BT 11/9 C. 18875, Mosely to Board of Trade, 4 and 8 June 1915. Alfred Mosely (1855–1917) had been a diamond miner and dealer and was a large shareholder in De Beers. See Newbury, 'Spoils of War', n. 19.

[9] CAD, MM 1037, Schreiner to Finance, 2 Nov. 1915.

against stones of enemy origin. In order to obviate this difficulty Breitmeyer and Company and Diamond Syndicate who held stocks of German South West African rough diamonds about £500,000 in value made proposal last June which was accepted by His Majesty's Government that these should not be placed on market until the end of the war. It would be difficult to hold above Firms to their promise if considerable quantities of such diamonds placed on market and I would be glad, therefore, if your Ministers would consider whether some satisfactory arrangement could be made with above Firms in order to avoid this difficulty.[10]

Added point was given to this polite command when it was learned that some of the Regie's pre-war stocks had been smuggled out from Germany through Scandinavia to the United States. More embarrassingly, the South Africans were requested to put an end to other clandestine exports to London through the Post Office by members of the Defence Force stationed at Luderitzbucht.[11]

Secondly, there were sound commercial reasons for the syndicate to discourage sales outside its own channels. By extending the ban on exports of South West African stones to Holland, the committee reinforced the pledge of the syndicate to 'lock up' stocks which had become a threat to the price stability of cuttable varieties of gem stones. This ban included competition from Premier and poorer varieties from the Kimberley mines. A memorandum by Breitmeyer's agent, F. Hirschhorn, concluded that the closure of the South West mines had been a blessing which curtailed a dangerous competition between the syndicate and De Beers on the one hand, and Antwerp merchants on the other, in purchasing inferior grades. As Hirschhorn admitted in his note to the Department of Mines, the loss of South West production had

created quite a good market for the small diamonds *remaining in the open Market*; but it must be self-evident that this Market is for the same two reasons to a large extent artificial and requires the most careful handling. If the Union Government sell the stock already accumulated and a production of 30,000 carats a month to a third party, we would naturally have to be released by the Imperial Government from our engagement not to sell South West African diamonds during the War. The effect on small diamonds would be disastrous and might even reflect on big.[12]

[10] CAD, TES 866 F5/951, Bonar Law to Buxton [telegraph], 19 Feb. 1916.

[11] CAD, TES 867 F5/98, Prime Minister's Office 'Secret', minute no. 319; Easton (CID) to Detective Department, Kimberley, 8 Mar. 1915. One enterprising private had been found with 102 stones (58 carats) on his person.

[12] CAD, MNW 432, Hirschhorn, 'Confidential', [June 1916].

Finally, a sour note from the minister of justice, J. de V. Roos, questioned whether the Union had any legal authority to dispose of the assets of an occupied territory of the German empire.[13]

These constraints on the government's freedom of action were discussed with F. S. Malan and departmental officials by Alfred Mosely when he toured South Africa in May and June 1916. He advised that sales might be allowed through the United Kingdom, as a 'bulk purchase' of a strategic commodity, and not as periodic tenders, providing his committee acted as 'agent' for the Union. Desperate for taxes to ease the costs of a territory where his government had spent some £800,000 against a revenue of only £80,000, Malan provided a legal framework for official control in the Diamond Export Bill of June 1916, as stocks accumulated at the Cape branch of the National Bank. Fully aware of this situation, the London syndicate made a bid in June 1916 for 50,000 carats of South West diamonds at an agreed valuation in co-operation with the government's valuer, and a further 30,000 carats per month.[14] Because information on diamond traffic was passed on by the British censor to the Board of Trade and the diamond committee, Mosely was able to advise that the Antwerp syndicate would tender for stocks and discouraged acceptance of bids from this competition.[15]

On his return to England, Mosely was sent by the War Trade Department to Holland to arrange for the cutting of South West stones through trustworthy firms 'should it be decided to permit their export to Holland (under supervision) for that purpose'.[16] But lobbying by Breitmeyer through the South African High Commissioner in London and by Ernest Oppenheimer (on behalf of Dunkelsbuhler and Co.) through Malan encountered an unwillingness to do business with the syndicate if some other way could be found.

Once more the Colonial Office, through the governor-general, laid down the ground rules which governed the sales outlet for the rest of the war: all sales were to be handled through Mosely and the London diamond syndicate for reliable cutters in Amsterdam from whom the cut and polished stones would be returned for sale in North and South America 'by approved brokers'. A few sample parcels reached Mosely at his offices in the Union Bank Buildings, unsorted and uncleaned, in

[13] CAD, TES 866 F5/951, Roos to Mines, 22 Mar. 1916.
[14] CAD, MNW 432, syndicate to Hirschhorn, 10 June 1916; MM 2445/18, Mosely to Buxton, 7 July 1916; Mosely to CO, 1 Sept. 1916.
[15] Ibid., Mosely to Malan, 7 July 1916.
[16] Ibid., Foreign Trade Department to CO, 21 Aug. 1916.

October and November 1916. A syndicate tender for these was refused by Malan.[17]

The South African government became increasingly frustrated by the delay and the bargaining. It was argued in the Department of Mines that South West Africa was, in any case, entitled to a share of total Union output on the basis of the defunct quota agreement of 1914. There was great resentment at Mosely's suggestion that, if revenue was required, South West mines should be closed and Premier production increased as 'better for trade', though the department accepted his point that rough diamonds could not be sold directly to the United States, where there was only a small cutting industry and importers would not tender in competition with the syndicate.[18]

There was, too, mounting public pressure for some economic reward from the capture of German territory, when German seizure of foreign credit balances in Belgian banks was reported in February 1917. The *Cape Times* backed the popular idea of working the mines 'to the fullest advantage' and extracting the full measure of taxes allowed under German administration.[19]

A second proposal by the syndicate to Malan early in 1917, therefore, stood a better chance. It was made this time through Solly Joel, financier, chairman of Johannesburg Consolidated Investments, and the dominant shareholder in Premier mine, who was much better known to officials and politicians than the more distant and aloof Ludwig Breitmeyer. And when it was made, Mosely was in the United States, and the terms were not referred to the London diamond committee or the War Trade Department. Moreover, by the end of 1916, the London syndicate of merchants—Breitmeyers, Barnato Bros., Dunkelsbuhler, Bernheim, and Dreyfus—had revived and renewed their contract with De Beers on the model of 1910. To protect the price levels of this flow of goods, a plan for joint financing of purchases of South West African goods was also revived by Sir David Harris and Joel, in their dual capacity as syndicate members and De Beers directors, to meet the high cost of financial advances to the companies and wartime insurance.[20]

The new offer to purchase was approved by R. N. Kotze, the government mining engineer, who liked Joel's suggestion that negotiations were better conducted locally than in London. But he pressed for a ceiling of

[17] Ibid., Bonar Law to Buxton, 6 Sept. 1916; MNW 433 MM 2445/18, Mosely to Malan, 19 Oct., 8 Dec. 1916.
[18] Ibid., Mines to Mosely, 17 Jan. 1917; Mosely to Malan, 19 Feb. 1917.
[19] 'Protectorate Diamonds', *The Cape Times*, 3 Feb. 1917.
[20] DBCA, Board 2/5/3 (Diamond Committee), 24 Aug. 1916.

50,000 carats a month (close to 21 per cent of South African output) and rejected the idea of a 5-year contract. Kotze also insisted on profit-sharing. For the first time, the department was drawn into the complex details of a diamond deal and emerged after 2 months with a better understanding of what was involved. On 17 March 1917 the Union government signed an agreement with the syndicate representatives who offered to take an initial stock of 146,800 carats from South West followed by 6-monthly options on a production of 30,000 carats a month, at a basis price of 46s. 6d. As in the De Beers contract, there was a mechanism for periodic price adjustments and profit-sharing, after allowing 10 per cent of resales to the merchants. For good measure, the syndicate insisted on taking the captured 'Seitz' diamonds, in addition to the first bulk shipments which were to be sorted for the companies in South Africa and reassorted in London by a valuator approved by the government.[21]

On this basis, some 491,752 carats, including the sample parcels, were sold on a rising purchase price until February 1918 and were shipped to London for the South West companies. But for the government, there were several causes for dissatisfaction. Through their own failure to understand the German taxation system early enough and to make it work by provisional assessment of dues, the Protectorate administration got very little in the first years of the occupation. Revenues for 1915 and 1916 were not paid till the financial year 1918/19; and the handsome return of £201,019 for 1917 did not reach the administration's chest till 1919/20. The task of the administrator, who had to assess tax from the record of company profits after resales, was not helped by the refusal of the syndicate to adjust accounts to synchronize with his fiscal year.

Secondly, because of the method of preliminary evaluation by Leopold Herz on behalf of the companies at Luderitzbucht, and then in London by Willie Busch, who had handled Premier sales, there were complaints from the producers that syndicate prices were out of line with the initial assortments. Busch sided with the syndicate, and his inspection of the syndicate's books was supported by the South African Treasury, which found that the formula for adjusting the purchase price according to past sales of the goods had been honestly applied. The problem was an old one. On a rising market, producers itched for more frequent price changes to reflect resale prices, while in a poor market, they were glad to delay adjustment downwards. The Department of mines sided with the Protectorate, and requested a cut in the initial percentage allowed

---

[21] CAD, MNW 433 MM 2445/18, Kotze to Smyth, 27 Jan. 1917 (and note by S. B. Joel); MNW 429 MM 2352/18. The contract was signed by Malan, Joel, and Hirschhorn.

to the syndicate and a complete transfer of all sorting and valuation to South Africa, where the syndicate would take delivery. The government reserved the right, moreover, to hold back the balance of production in excess of monthly deliveries, for possible sale elsewhere. As a final thrust, the department refused to hand over the 'Seitz' diamonds.[22]

For the syndicate, Fritz Hirschhorn argued that profit-sharing had been conceded very reluctantly by Joel and himself, and refused to change the initial percentage, because the government did not share in any possible losses. He refused to consider taking delivery in South Africa, on the grounds that the original basis for assortments lay in the trial parcels sent to Mosely. If assortments and prices for different varieties were to be fixed by a local valuator (as they were for De Beers stones), then a new contract was called for. He could have 'no knowledge of Mr. Leopold Herz's valuations and how they are comparable with the basis on which the purchase is made by the Syndicate. It is obviously impossible to make any comparison unless the assortment were identical with that of the parcel of about 31,000 carats upon which the purchase was made.'[23] After this exchange, there were further fruitless meetings with Malan, Gorges, and Dr Krause, representing the producers, when Hirschhorn refused to give way.

Gradually, the Department of Mines acquired knowledge and was irritated by other points of difference arising from insurance costs for South West producers, the De Pass royalties on Pomona sales, and, not least, the probity of Busch, after rumours of a 'leakage' of some £150,000 of diamonds to outside buyers and accusations of an affair with 'the landlady's daughter'.[24] Nothing was proved, but a new valuator was found for Premier stock when Busch's contract ended. Officials fretted at the delayed rise in valuation which suggested, though they could not prove it, that large profits were being made from the 10 per cent of resales and half the net balance which went to the London merchants. After a review of 2 years' sales in the flourishing wartime diamond trade, the inspector of mines, E. C. Langley, considered the cost of marketing services too high. His remedy was to follow the German example of the Regie and control the trade through some form of official board 'in the Union'.[25]

At the same time, departmental experience of marketing of Premier diamonds strengthened the growing desire for tighter national management

---

[22] CAD, MNW 429, Smyth to Hirschhorn, 7 Feb. 1918.
[23] Ibid., Hirschhorn to Smyth, 26 Feb. 1918; Minutes and notes, 22 Mar. 1918.
[24] CAD, MNW 542 MM 2341/18.
[25] CAD, MNW 475 MM 2110/19, Langley to Mines, 14 Feb. 1919.

of mineral resources. Ever since 1914, the temporary closure of the mine and the rapid change in share ownership in the company had been regarded as a manœuvre by De Beers and New Jagersfontein to end the threat of a cheaper source of production, 'as it is believed to be in the interests of the Controlling Houses to sacrifice the Premier Mine for the sake of De Beers'.[26] As operations did not resume at Premier until 1916, officials in the Treasury and Mines Department were driven to reconsider the government's relationship with a company to which it contributed no capital, took 60 per cent of profits, and had no board representation. They did little more than set up an advisory committee to authorize the use of funds provided under Act 31 of 1908 to meet emergencies. Kotze expanded on the problem, as he saw it in 1915:

The difficulty arises from the same basic fact that faced Rhodes and others until the necessity for amalgamation dawned on them, namely, that diamonds are a luxury and that their economic production depends on a limited and regulated output. The State as such has a strong interest in seeing the industry established on as sound a basis as possible, but is hampered by the fact that its share of profits in the various diamond concerns is a varying one. If the more profitable mines of De Beers were alone worked, the maximum profit would be secure, but the ten per cent tax on profits in the resulting extra profit of that concern would not counterbalance the loss of sixty per cent of the profits by the closing down of Premier.

The only way out of this dilemma, in Kotze's view, was, perhaps, for the government to take a financial interest in De Beers, so that stoppage of Premier would not matter and would be compensated for by increased production: 'this gain being presumably accompanied by a corresponding advantage to shareholders, the interests of government and shareholders would coincide, and reliance could be placed on this coincidence, for the protection of the Government's interest'.

Proceeding boldly to his novel conclusion, the mining engineer pointed the government down the path pioneered by Rhodes: 'Such a result could however only be obtained by an amalgamation of diamond interests, i.e. by the absorption of the Premier by De Beers, on the condition that the Government's share of profit in the Premier is transferred in some equitable manner to a share in the amalgamated concern.'[27]

Fascinated by his scheme, Kotze went on to produce a table showing that the government could usefully take 15 per cent of the profits of such

---

[26] CAD, MM 34/14, T. Trevor (inspector of mines) to Malan, 11 Aug. 1914; TES 863 F5/90, minutes and memoranda by Sheridan, Kotze, and the mining surveyor, A. C. Sutherland, 1915.

[27] CAD, TES 863 F5/90, Kotze, 8 Mar. 1915.

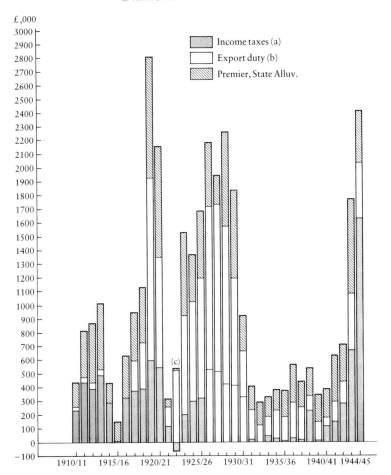

FIG. 8. Diamond mining revenues, 1910–1945

an 'amalgamated' company, instead of the current 10 per cent and 60 per cent from the separate concerns, and earn the same revenue as before (£600,000). If Premier were closed and De Beers output increased, the revenue would drop to £566,000.

His main point, however, was not to sanction closure of Premier, but to counter the temptation of De Beers' management to reduce the production of an unprofitable mine. To do this the government would have to force through a giant reconstruction of the industry and participate in profits to secure revenue at about the same level as before. Allowing his imagination full rein, Kotze dwelt on the possibility of 'amalgamating all the principal diamond interests in South Africa, including De Beers, Premier, Jagersfontein, Koffyfontein and perhaps, if German South-West Africa is absorbed in the Union, the larger producers in that country'. The time to act was now, while the mines were out of action, and the 1914 conference had 'clearly established the necessity of regulating and allocating the relative shares of production'. Here, then, was a scheme to rival the dreams and achievements of the 1880s. The state would be the new 'amalgamator'.

But when production did revive slowly at the end of 1915, the government was faced with a very different Premier board on which Barnato Bros. and JCI were solidly in command. In the Inland Revenue, J. C. Sheridan wrote an alarmed minute deploring the change from 'partnership' with the government to control by a lobby of powerful shareholders connected with the diamond syndicate, the Corner House, and De Beers. The clear risk was that production would be managed so as to sacrifice Premier.[28]

There was no immediate sign that this would happen. When S. B. Joel addressed the shareholders in 1916, outlining the policy that had been evolved by the syndicate, he went out of his way to include Premier in the strategies of regulating production so as to raise the price of all gemstones. Temporary closures had given a breathing-space in which the wartime syndicate had captured the major outlet through London for all the South African mines. He grandly enlarged on his role: 'I was enabled through the large interests I held in the principal mines, to exercise a control of the sales and to regulate judiciously the feeding of the market, that showed signs of expanding with the increasing wealth of the United States and other countries resulting from the War.'[29] Solly's 'large interests' were not in dispute: he owned half Jagersfontein, a third of Premier, and had a slightly larger holding in De Beers than the Rothschilds. But he did not 'control' syndicate members or tenders in London. He was also in error in claiming he had brought about the aims of the 1914 conference. No quotas had yet been applied, and the Union government did not see 'unexpected hundreds of thousands pouring into the coffers of the State'. In fact, state revenues from diamonds declined disastrously between 1914 and 1916 (see Fig. 8). If Kotze's visions left the diamond magnates out of account, Joel's explanations underestimated the involvement of the mining and financial bureaucracy in the industry.

---

[28] CAD, TES 863 F5/90, Sheridan, 'The Premier Mine', 22 Feb. 1915.
[29] Premier, *Directors' Report* (1916), 18–20.

Believing that Premier would be run down, the Department of Mines and the Inland Revenue were eager enough to come to terms with the syndicate through Joel's board in the first of a new series of contracts in 1916. These set limits to the amount of ground hauled and washed at well below Premier's capacity, in return for a rising valuation and improved prices over the following 3 years, by using the same formula as the De Beers and South West sales contracts. Although not a signatory to the agreements which included profit-sharing after an initial 5 per cent to Barnato Bros. (for the syndicate), government officials could only approve and accept the auditor's reports which detailed the methods of arriving at replacements and valuation, but disguised the profit on resales made by Barnatos. Requests for a complete set of accounts were refused.[30] From its own calculations, the Inland Revenue estimated that the Barnato syndicate made £1,328,722 on the first 2 years' operations, compared with a trading profit of about £900,000 for Premier.

Government departments, therefore, thought they had lost ground in their formulation of policies to be applied by F. S. Malan or the minister of finance, H. Burton. Kotze's ambitious plans for 'amalgamation' to defeat the syndicate on its own terms and to establish a South African cutting industry had to be shelved when the costs involved were considered. Indeed, much more that had been dreamed up in the department to accomplish full nationalization of all mines—coal, gold, and diamonds—went overboard, when scrutinized by a state mining commission in 1916 which envisaged possible compensation of £50 million to private owners.[31]

Unable to gather in taxes quickly enough through the German system in South West Africa, the government threatened, instead, a discriminatory diamond export duty on the value of De Beers production for sale. Intercepted cables passed on by the British censor informed the Union government that the companies and the merchants hoped for a dramatic improvement in 1917, when the United States joined in the war; and so a new export duty was levied at 5 per cent on the declared values of diamonds from all mines, except alluvial diggings. This distinction was based on a political judgement that the small amount exported from alluvial claims would not compensate 'for the disturbance that will be created in the minds of all the interested parties'.

---

[30] CAD, TES 857 F5/60, Inland Revenue to Premier, 5 Nov. 1917.
[31] State Mining Commission 1916–17 UG 6.–'17. Senate SC 5-1913 (Diamond Cutting Industry), 1913.

The incentive to continue their operations is not so much the actual yield as the remote possibility of a rich find. The gambling instinct is a great inducement. The bulk of these people can appropriately be described as falling within the category of Poor Whites and if we insist upon the exaction of a duty on alluvial stones and the alluvial industry suffers in consequence the Government will have to face the charge that they are unmindful of the interests of these Poor Whites.[32]

This tenderness was unanswerable for the moment, though the Department of Mines found Barkly West diggers willing to pay the duty as a 'war tax'. Diggers in the Free State or the Transvaal were adamantly opposed; and all were exempted, when the bill became law.

The wartime monopoly of sales through the United Kingdom, then, worked to the advantage of the syndicate, and government departments had to accept the domination of the market by Breitmeyer and Barnatos. As they monitored the steady percentage increase in monthly prices, officials perceived by 1918 an 'entirely new situation arising from the stronger position attained by the Diamond Control'.[33] Kotze agreed with the judgement of his mining inspectors and forwarded to Malan a recommendation, based on an erroneous presentation of the companies' 'relative profit', that the government could claim an even larger share through taxes. An additional justification was the argument that the companies were spending less of their retained profit in South Africa by 1917–18, and, therefore, 'the general benefit to the country must be diminished. It appears that in return for facilitating single control, the Government might reasonably take a larger share of the profit.'[34] By 1919, this assumption that somehow single-channel selling had been the work of the South African government, rather than a combination of war measures and the opportunism of Mosely's committee of merchants, was used to support a case for government construction of a 'Co-operative Selling Company' to divert the channel away from the syndicate and end the need for high commissions on sales.

Again, the idea was not new. De Beers' directors had pondered a combination of producers for marketing purposes from about 1910 in the Kimberley diamond committee. But Kotze had no conception of the finances involved. It was easier to turn to the diamond export duty again

---

[32] CAD, TES 869 F5/101, De Beers to Botha, 7 Apr. 1916; Brink to Burton, 28 Apr. 1916; Locke (Treasury secretary) to Burton, 11 May 1917.

[33] CAD, TES 857 F5/60, Frood to Kotze, 18 Sept. 1918.

[34] Ibid. Kotze to Smyth, 9 Oct. 1918. Kotze mixed net and gross profits for the companies. In fact, the rate of annual profit had not increased for De Beers, Premier, and New Jagersfontein in the war years: Kotze to Smyth, 9 Oct. 1918.

to extract greater revenue by raising it to 10 per cent in 1919. On the recommendation of the commissioner of the Inland Revenue, the political protection of the diggers was dropped and the measure applied to alluvial workings as well as mines. Inland Revenue officials, too, restrained the government from meddling continuously with the contracts arranged for Premier and South West Africa. Both the managing director of Premier and the administrator E. H. Gorges pressed Malan for more frequent changes in the purchase valuation, in line with net realized prices in London. The Inland Revenue, on the other hand, was well pleased with the rise of 80 per cent in prices paid to Premier, and was content to receive just over £400,000 by 1918 in divided profit from the Transvaal mine and a total of £240,000 from a share of profits on resales 1917–18. The Inland Revenue was convinced that such results could not have been obtained, if such a low grade mine had sold outside the syndicate. As for South West Africa, it was up to administrators there to manage the system they had taken over, without disrupting syndicate contracts with Union mines.[35]

But within the Department of Mines other key officials thought like Kotze. H. Warington Smyth, who had reconstructed the department under Milner from 1901, and remained as secretary under the Union government till 1927, was hostile to the syndicate. He recognized that the trade was 'in their hands at the moment, and naturally so, owing to the historical development of the situation, but opportunity should be taken to effect a change at the first favourable opportunity'.[36] The disadvantages he perceived in 'Syndicate control' were loss of revenue, influence over domestic output, constant haggling over prices, and the 'Existence of a powerful financial group, outside the Union, who only consider their own interest, which is opposed to that of the Union and partly also to those of the shareholders of the producers'. For Smyth, as for Kotze, the time had come to assert the government's right to manage.

It is hard to say how far F. S. Malan was influenced by this view. The minister had to keep in sight not only the interests of Premier and the government, but the question of the future of German mines in South West Africa which coincided with other decisions on syndicate agreements

---

[35] CAD, TES 863 F5/90, Locke to Inland Revenue, 30 Jan. 1919; MNW 542 MM 2898/16, Frames to Hirschhorn, 29 Sept. 1919.

[36] CAD, TES 871 F5/101 [1919]. Smyth began his career as secretary to the Department of Mines in Siam in 1891 and as director general of the Siam geological survey, receiving the Order of the White Elephant (3rd Class) for these services, as well as the more prestigious Murchison award from the Royal Geographical Society for his publications. He was a member of the Transvaal Legislative Council and the Executive Council in 1906 before transferring to the Department of Mines (and Industries).

with producers which were about to expire at the end of 1919. There is some evidence that Malan favoured the idea of a new selling organization. He was aware, too, that the London High Commission had recently made a full investigation of charges of 'monopoly' brought against the syndicate by London diamond distributors who resented refusal of sights by former German nationals (as most of the leading principals were) and whose complaints had been upheld by the Board of Trade. But, more immediately, interdepartmental minutes of his conversations with Gorges and Smyth in August 1919 recorded a decision to limit executive action to reviving the 1914 quota agreement as a basis for a conference of Union producers to strike a new deal with the syndicate.[37]

As for the wider issue of the German territory, it was well established before the signing of the Versailles Treaty in June 1919 that Botha and Smuts would press for the retention of South West Africa, however much Smuts was opposed to the policy of a 'vengeful peace' and large indemnities.[38] After Smuts's return to South Africa in July 1919, it was possible to envisage the extension of Union tax and mining laws to the territory which was to be treated as an integral part of the Union. Policies were announced in September 1919 to set up a new civil administration with extended legislative and executive powers, at the same time as the Union Parliament accepted the terms of the peace Treaty and the Mandate Bill. Customs, harbours, and railways were assimilated into departments of the Union; and mining operations had been closely supervised by the Department of Mines and by the Treasury for 5 years. In August 1919, South West Africa was automatically included in the programme for quota agreements among producers, at a series of conferences under the chairmanship of the minister of mines.

When the representatives of the producers met in September and November 1919, they accepted the 1914 division of percentage shares with little acrimony. On a value of some £12 to £13 million in diamonds which the syndicate was expected to purchase annually through its contracts with each producer, quotas were adopted and applied for a period of 5 years to allow De Beers 51 per cent, Premier 18 per cent, New Jagersfontein 10 per cent, and South West 21 per cent. Alluvial producers were not invited to the conferences. Acceptance by the larger number of South West producers and the administrator of an allocation on a territorial basis, rather than by company quotas, as in the Union, was influenced by Fritz Hirschhorn's optimistic forecast of very high profits

---

[37] CAD, MNW 488 MM 2331/119, minutes.
[38] Hancock, ch. 19, esp. pp. 429, 498.

on resales. If the rising market of the war period continued, small companies would do well; but if it contracted, the division of South West's territorial quota among them would be contentious and a source of trouble. Equally important, it was accepted there would be no separate selling outside the syndicate, and that, as far as possible, contracts would be styled on uniform principles for pricing, replacement of stocks sold, and profit-sharing. It was also agreed that if one producer failed to meet the annual quota, the shortfall might be supplied by another company (or by the territory's producers, in the case of South West Africa).[39]

More controversially, Malan tried to interest the delegates in Kotze's plan for a separate selling organization and got a very lukewarm response. De Beers had carefully considered this option, when the company took a half share in financing the purchase of South West diamonds by the syndicate. This early example of integration on the part of a producer into the marketing combine inspired some directors to think of forming their own purchasing company. But the plan was quashed by London directors as 'financially unsound, apart from Income Tax danger'.[40] Moreover, Malan's requests, as chairman of the conference, for information from Hirschhorn on such sensitive topics as deliveries in South Africa, methods of allocation to European buyers, and the syndicate's profits, got no response at all. Before the syndicate made an offer to the producers, as a body, however, it was agreed that a common stand should be made on price adjustment at 3-monthly intervals and on the length of contracts. But Kotze's suggestions for a 'Board of Control'—watered down to an 'Advisory Board'—held no appeal for the companies. On the insistence of De Beers a 5-year period for contracts was accepted, quarterly settlement of accounts with price adjustments, and a low margin of 5 per cent for the syndicate before profit-sharing.

Hirschhorn conferred with his London principals and relayed the syndicate's offer to the producers as a whole through Malan on 14 October 1919. The merchants would purchase £3 million of diamonds every 3 months as quarterly options with profit-sharing after 5 per cent, but with separate methods for arriving at price adjustment for each producer and separate pricing for inferior, or 'common' goods. The producers flatly rejected this proposition on the grounds that the discount margin in the

[39] See CAD, MNW 488 MM 2331/119, for minutes of the conferences. In all, there were 4 contracts between producers and the syndicate, 1 producers' agreement on quotas and 1 contract signed by the administrator on South West stocks of diamonds. The contracts for De Beers and New Jagersfontein were not presented in open session. The terms and application of these contracts are discussed below, ch. 8.

[40] DBCA, Board 2/5/3 (Diamond committee), 1917 and 4 Nov. 1919.

pricing formula was too high at 10 per cent, and because the syndicate was bound for such a short option period, compared with restriction of the producers' outside sales over 5 years. This impasse generated a heated discussion about other methods of sale, but they all had to be abandoned because of punishing tax liabilities incurred in the United Kingdom. More usefully, De Beers explained how the pricing formula with a high discount for the syndicate helped to reduce the quantity of diamonds produced for a falling market, as well as adjusting the price upwards as a reward for steady demand in the past. The leading company did not explain, however, that the formula might not benefit all producers of very different qualities of stones.

After more argument, the syndicate accepted most of the producers' terms on 5 November. These entailed a discount of only 5 per cent, and quarterly adjustments of prices, but an optional termination of the contracts by either side after 12 months. A deal was struck between the syndicate and the administrator for the South West producers to clear a delivery of extra stock at the end of 1919. Finally, the Union government agreed to surrender the 'Seitz' diamonds for an outright payment of £235,040. A committee of the producers set about formulating the separate contracts.

This remarkable harmony of interests in the producers' cartel was influenced by high prices at the end of the war. Politicians and officials had little reason to interfere at this stage with a system which gave to South Africa a monopoly of the world's diamonds. The general satisfaction with levels of profits and taxes also served to hasten negotiations for the consolidation of companies in South West Africa, where government approved of the private purchase of German assets.

CONSOLIDATED DIAMOND MINES AND THE MANDATE

The exclusion of the South West companies from confiscation and from seizure of assets by the Union's custodian of enemy property was consistent with the vain effort to make the territory pay for the cost of its capture, and with the determination of Botha, Smuts, and Department of Mines officials to see the companies pass into South African hands. South West, therefore, was not included in the custodian's valuation of assets in Union control in 1917, though he did collect the share dividends paid by the companies and by British companies in South Africa to resident German nationals and Germans elsewhere. The purchase of 'enemy' shares, moreover, which had been prohibited in wartime was first relaxed in the

United Kingdom, and one of the first companies to take advantage of this was Consolidated Mines Selection, which sold shares acquired from the Public Trustee to its own shareholders in January 1919.

As is known, Consolidated Mines was formed by Dunkelsbuhler and Co. to open up Far East Rand, and led to the formation of Anglo American in 1917 which brought fresh capital for participatory rights in Consolidated's gold mining leases. Prominent in the direction and management of both organizations were the Oppenheimers and the engineer W. L. Honnold, who was a link with J. P. Morgan and Company and Herbert Hoover. Ernest Oppenheimer was only 37 when American capital was enlisted for the huge investment required for Dunkelsbuhler's gold and coal interests. His biographers have stressed his long-term ambition to return to the diamond trade and its organization, which was his first apprenticeship, when he arrived in London in the 1890s. But it is still not clear how this was accomplished.[41]

Ambition was not enough by itself. Oppenheimer had been schooled at Kimberley from 1902 in the intricate negotiation of contracts arranged through the De Beers diamond committee, and in the politics and rivalry surrounding the attempt to arrange joint quotas with Premier. He learned something of South West Africa by participating in and writing up the De Beers survey in 1914. The source of his financial knowledge, however, lay in his subsequent experience of the construction of Consolidated Mines Selection and the Rand Selection Corporation from 1915, while based in London. Although he attended the Versailles Conference as an observer, and knew the opinions of Smuts on the future of the territory, the idea of outright purchase of German companies would seem to have originated with his Anglo American partner and ex-politician, Henry Hull, and the Cape business man Sir David Graaff, who put together the initial 'trust' to raise money and approach the German owners of the South West diamond companies. Their precise movements are not very clearly demonstrated. But all three, together with Dr E. Lubbert, W. Bredow, and A. Stauch from the South West mines, negotiated with representatives at The Hague in early September 1919, before formal acceptance of the terms of the Peace Treaty by the South African Parliament, and without reference to the custodian of enemy property.

The first notice of the success of the Hull/Graaff coup reached the financial press on 6 September, when it was announced that the South

---

[41] Edward Jessup, *Ernest Oppenheimer: A Study in Power* (London, 1979); Anthony Hocking, *Oppenheimer and Son* (Johannesburg, 1973), 87–9; Innes, 90–1; Gregory, *Ernest Oppenheimer*, 86–7. For some light on Honnold and his role in Consolidated Mines Selection, Hoover Library, Stanford, Cal. see W. L. Honnold, 'South Africa in World War' [1942].

West Diamond Company Ltd., registered at the Cape, had acquired the rights of the Luderitzbuchter Bergbau Gesellschaft to 10 square miles of the diamond fields.[42] The company was well financed at £250,000 in paid-up capital. On 1 November a few discrete lines in the press stated that Anglo and 'financial groups' had control of all the principal German companies for a nominal price of £3.5 million with the approval of the government. The 'financial groups', led by a London committee of directors, had been very busy, in fact, arranging funding through J. P. Morgan and Company. The news of their success reached Ernest Oppenheimer in South Africa on 24 October, in time to be relayed to Malan at the end of the month at the Pretoria diamond producers' conference. The exchange of notes with the Department of Mines was later released to the public.[43] In the middle of November there was news of a hitch over purchase of titles of the Kolonial Gesellschaft which brought back Messrs. Bredow, Lubbert, and Stauch with Hull to South Africa to sort out the problem and fix the selling price of shares to be paid to German vendors. The evidence released by the South African government in the form of a parliamentary paper confirms the prior purchase of the German companies before the formation of Consolidated Diamond Mines of South West Africa Limited [CDM] which was not registered till 1920, but is vague on the negotiations. Oppenheimer's formal announcement to Malan, 31 October 1919, merely lists nine companies purchased and amalgamated under Anglo's London committee. As a safeguard the government was asked for assurances that titles would be recognized, though the land registers were still closed; and permission was asked to make a cash payment to German owners overseas. A letter from the administrator, Gorges, confirmed the companies' titles, although the concession to the Kolonial Gesellschaft in the Luderitzbucht area was under investigation. On his own authority, Gorges presumed to declare that all other company titles which rested on the original concession were sound. More cautiously, the Department of Mines through a junior official approved the takeover and promised that conditions would not be less favourable than under the Germans.

[42] *The African World*, 6 Sept. 1919.
[43] CAD, MNW 488 MM 2741/19, Honnold to Oppenheimer, 24 Oct. 1919; Oppenheimer to Malan, 31 Oct. 1919; Malan to Oppenheimer, 3 Nov. 1919; and for some of the correspondence, Union PP, A. 1–'20, *Correspondence Relating to the Transfer of Certain Interests and Concessions in the South West African Protectorate to the South West Africa Consolidated Diamond Company, Limited*. Oppenheimer, Hull, and Honnold were on the board of Anglo. The first board of CDM consisted of Hull, Graaff, W. Bredow, C. L. Dalziel, Dr E. Lubbert, A. Stauch, A. W. Tait, and C. Weiss. The London committee which handled the financing and the purchases consisted of J. A. Agnew, W. L. Honnold, F. W. Green, and Louis Oppenheimer.

Thus, when the formal agreement, dated 23 November 1919, for the sale of the rights of eleven German companies was signed, they were already held by the Hull/Graaff Trust for a nominal sum to be paid in shares and cash by CDM. The real sum paid to the German vendors was much less at £2.8 million, because of the devaluation of the mark. The delay in verification of the titles of the Kolonial Gesellschaft entailed a second agreement with the purchasers, 24 November 1919, transferring the obligation to pay royalties to De Pass from the Pomona Company (as defined in 1912) to the new company. The South West Finance Corporation was set up separately from Consolidated diamond Mines with an identical directorate in April 1920 to administer these rights. It was not a cheap takeover. But with the good news from the producers' conference in October and November the shares of CDM gained a considerable premium.[44]

Although there is some evidence that De Beers' Kimberley directors might have tried to head off the move by Hull, it is clear that there was no resentment of the formation of the new company, when representatives at the conference heard of the amalgamation in October. Consolidation of the fragmented interests in South West Africa could only assist the formation of the cartel to do business with the syndicate. P. Ross Frames as a director of both De Beers and Premier was appointed co-ordinator between all the companies, and had no doubt that CDM would join in a common front against over-production and excessive taxation. De Beers had just decided, in any case, that joint purchase of South West diamonds with the syndicate during the war could not continue without risk of British taxes on profits from London marketing operations.[45]

But what was the position of the government and the Department of Mines on the transfer of assets by private sale? Some of the evidence which was not released in the parliamentary paper points to hasty approval of the transfer, before the terms of the mandate were known and debated, and before the method of handling ex-enemy assets had been fully decided. For the purpose of setting up the CDM, the assets of the German diamond companies were regarded as transferred from 1 October 1919, while capital was still being arranged. A hurried proclamation (no. 59 of 1919) brought the territory under Union mining laws and cancelled German company concessions held from the Kolonial Gesellschaft, following a report from a 'Minerals Concession Commission' in September which confirmed

---

[44] Union PP, A. 1–'20; and see MNW 890, J. H. Munnik, 'South West African Diamonds', 16 Mar. 1927, for an analysis of the agreements of 23 and 24 Nov. with the vendors.
[45] DBCA, Board 2/5/3, 1919; cf. Hocking, 87–9.

mineral grants made under early treaties. The way was then clear to transfer titles on 24 and 25 November, with the government's blessing, to the new company (which had yet to be formally registered). The essential position, as pointed out by Gorges in his letter of 3 November to Malan, was that although 'power is given in the Peace Treaty to eliminate German interests by expropriation and the transfer of proceeds to the Allied Reparation Commission . . . the Union Government have decided not to avail themselves of these powers in respect of property in South-West Africa'.[46]

The government encountered considerable criticism from the South African shareholders of the Pomona Company, who complained that they had been paid off at the rate of £25 for £5 shares currently worth £100, at the end of 1919, when the diamond market was exceptionally good. They objected to Hull and his friends in the Purchasers' Trust making a high premium out of a cheap option reserved for the company's founder-directors on 250,000 CDM shares. And they raised the delicate question of whether Hull, Graaff, and Oppenheimer had been 'trading with the enemy'.[47]

Malan dismissed this charge as a 'pure technicality'; but Smuts took a personal interest in the case of the Pomona shareholders at the end of 1919, when it threatened to become politically embarrassing. In the end, the government was saved from the threat of legal action by Administrator Gorges and his officials who pointed out that negotiations to take over Pomona had been completed before the spectacular rise in diamond shares, and that Pomona shareholders had been doing very well, as their lawyers agreed to take CDM shares instead of cash. As for shares in Pomona still in the names of German companies and nationals legally domiciled in South Africa, these were eventually released unsequestrated, along with the rest of the shareholders' scrip, to CDM.

Despite this haggling, Malan was able to include the 'South-West Deal' in his announcement of the general outcome of the conference of producers to a banquet of the South African Institution of Engineers on 22 November 1919. Outlining the terms of the general agreement on quotas, he took full credit for negotiations with the syndicate and for the control of South West diamonds by a company registered in the Union and to be worked with a government share of profits ('Applause').[48] A few private 'outside'

---

[46] CAD, MNW 488 MM 2741/19, Gorges to Malan, 3 Nov. 1919.

[47] Union PP, A. 1–'20; Hull argued that the vendor companies had changed their domicile to South Africa: Hull to Malan, 29 Dec. 1919. But this did not happen in all cases and only after Sept. when the original deal was struck at The Hague.

[48] *Sunday Times (Cape Town)*, 23 Nov. 1919.

producers in South West still remained unincorporated, and had to be allowed a small quota as part of the eventual agreement between the administrator and the syndicate in 1920. But both Oppenheimer and Malan were content to have settled the most contentious areas of ownership and control by separating the private purchase of German assets from the wider question of South Africa's policy on reparations and German assets seized in the Union.

Moreover, the Department of Mines found it essential to co-operate with Oppenheimer's new company to ensure valuation and sale of South West's production in South Africa, and to end the tedious and acrimonious method of channelling shipments to the syndicate through a London office. Busch was sacked; and on Oppenheimer's personal recommendation, the diamond valuator for De Beers, Arend Brink, a man of great skill and experience, and forthright opinions, a staunch supporter of the South African Party, was appointed by Malan to the post of government valuator at Cape Town. On a salary of £3,000, Brink became, in effect, adviser to the government on all aspects of the market, switching his loyalties, as the post required, away from the companies to the civil servants and politicians of the day. For the moment, however, he had to operate from offices loaned by CDM, as he began to handle South West diamonds on the basis of the sample parcels returned from London.

Other government departments were less accommodating with CDM. The Treasury without consulting the company, arranged for sales to be paid for in London as usual, which drew a strong protest from Hull that CDM was being treated 'as if it were enemy'. He insisted that the company become a signatory to proposed agreements between the producers and the syndicate, if it was to be bound by them; and he demanded the proceeds of all sales of production from 1 October 1919. He threatened to incorporate the company outside the Union, if the Department of Mines imposed the Union's new 10 per cent export duty on top of the existing 66 per cent tax (less 70 per cent of costs) which had originally consolidated a German export duty with other royalties.[49]

This stand brought to a head the internal debate on the Union's policy of treating South West Africa as a separate diamond-producing territory, but assimilating its taxes and regulations under the authority of the Treasury and the Department of Mines. Sir Robert Kotze had no doubt that the whole industry in the Protectorate could be run by a local

---

[49] CAD, MNW 492 MM 2986/19, Brink to Malan, 6 Dec. 1919. Arend Brink had been a dealer at Kimberley before joining De Beers. As 'Chief Valuator to the Union Government' he moved to the Cape in May 1920; Oppenheimer to Kotze, 11 Dec. 1919; Hull to Graaff, 23 Feb. 1920.

'Diamond Control Board', or state company, separate from the local Chamber of Mines. CDM objected to this plan, and the extreme solution of a government board was ruled out by Malan and other ministers in the Cabinet, on the grounds that it would assume authority for labour recruiting, and farmers in the Union might press for similar institutions. The Department of Mines then considered the idea of using Premier's relation with the government as a model for taxation. Sheridan in the Inland Revenue was asked to outline a supervisory body for sorting, valuation, and allocation of the territory's quota between CDM and the local 'outside producers'—in short revive the Regie as a quasi-official and consultative body, 'the pivot on which the whole German system worked'.[50] For the rest, Sheridan recommended state participation in a consolidated tax as before.

This proposal was scathingly dismissed by Arend Brink as 'crude and ineffective', because it fell short of the need for 'a responsible body . . . charged with full authority to carry out all the functions of the Regie as it existed prior to the Great War'. CDM obviously would have the preponderant voice on such a body. As Brink pointed out, the Inter-Producers' Agreement was purely a voluntary arrangement; and if it was terminated, it might become necessary for a revived Regie to undertake sales of Protectorate diamonds. Brink recommended a mixed board of control of at least two producers and three officials.[51] A conference of officials, company directors, and politicians met in November 1920 to settle the debate. In the end, a board of advisors was decided on, bound by commercial contracts negotiated through the administrator for the Protectorate and consisting of three producers and two officials. This was well short of the old Regie, but it was also clear that CDM would not be allowed to dispose of diamonds freely, without reference to the administrator and the wider cartel of producers. Furthermore, Malan insisted on applying the additional export duty for revenue, effectively raising Protectorate diamond taxation to a higher rate than in the Union. The Department of Mines then set about calculating the government's share of the price paid for Kolonial Gesellschaft rights and titles in which the German administration had participated. Documentation on this point had been obtained from Berlin through the British Foreign Office. The participation was less than had been thought, but when Kotze had done the valuation, the

[50] CAD, MNW 513 MM 1501/20, Sheridan to Hofmeyr, 30 July 1920.
[51] Ibid., Brink to Mines, 25 Oct. 1920; *South West Africa Government Gazette*, 26 Mar., 9 Dec. 1921.

Protectorate government took £400,000 in taxation on the first year's operations.[52] (See also Appendix A. 6).

By 1920, then, for the first time in the history of diamond mining practically all the known diamond-producing areas in the world were held or controlled by British and Allied subjects. This had come about by retaining a prize of war and treating it very differently from assets seized in the Union. In April 1920 a memorandum by the custodian had laid down the courses of action open to the government, making it clear that assets would not be handed over to the Reparations Commission. After restoration of property to domiciled Germans and settlement of debts and claims, the balance of £9 million was to be invested for 30 years, in return for government stock as a kind of forced loan. On the whole, as the custodian recognized, Germans in South Africa received 'far more favourable treatment than Germans in any other part of the Allied world'.[53] There were repeated reassurances they would not be sequestrated, which contrasted with the gloomy predictions put to the German vendors of the companies in South West Africa encouraging them to sell to the Hull/Graaff Trust in 1919. Stranger still was the admission by W. H. Fowle in May 1920, when the payment of accumulated dividends for Pomona shareholders was still delayed, that 'the Custodian of the Union has no jurisdiction over enemy property rights and interests in the South West Africa Protectorate'.[54] It was left to private speculators with the backing of American capital to carry out the purchase and consolidation which the Botha-Smuts government wished to see effected before taking a firm position on South Africa's treatment of ex-enemy subjects and property.

It is usually forgotten, however, that the marketing arrangements for South West's captured mines fell into the hands of the London syndicate as a result of the wartime policies of the British government. South Africa was not free to dispose of a strategic commodity outside the imperial network; and that network centred on the London merchants who cornered supplies and dominated the distribution of rough gem stones and industrial diamonds. To the chagrin of the Department of Mines, though not the Union's Ministry of Finance, Premier was also drawn

---

[52] CO 551/128 for the receipt from the German Foreign Office of records on the *Halbscheid Gesellschaft* (which did not function) and the *Diamanten Pacht Gesellschaft* from which the government had a royalty, and the articles of association of the Regie. The company was in immediate dispute with the administration for 1 quarter of the first year's taxes.

[53] CO 551/126, W. H. Fowle, 'Memorandum on the Disposal of Enemy Property', 29 Apr. 1920; Newbury, 'Spoils of War'.

[54] CAD, MNW 488 MM 2741/19, custodian to mines, 5 May 1920; Cloete to Smuts, 24 Sept. 1920.

into the single-channel for sales from 1916, partly as a result of the embargo on exports to Holland or the United States and also as a result of the change of share ownership which brought De Beers and Barnatos directors on to the board.

The take over coincided conveniently, too, with the revival of the 1914 quota system in a new set of agreements among producers and with the diamond syndicate. The government, through the Department of Mines and its minister, supervised rather than determined the course of those negotiations. The status of the Protectorate, moreover, where the exercise of the mandate was first vested in the governor-general and delegated to the administrator from 1919, precluded overt substitution of Union departments for territorial departments. Customs collected in the Union were assigned to the territory. There was no change in diamond taxation laws. The writ of the government mining engineer or the commissioner of the Inland Revenue did not run there, after 1919, and the functions of controlling and representing South West Africa's mining interests were concentrated in the legal personality of the administrator, who attended conferences of producers and signed contracts, assisted by an advisory board. In the last count, he took his orders from the Prime Minister. But he worked for the producers in the complex game of adjustment of quotas and marketing arrangements for the consolidated companies.

This legal spokesman also collected taxes, and the administration was not obliged, as the Germans had been, to contribute towards working costs. Having secured their prize and floated CDM, the directors were faced with an authority which was ambiguously installed as protector and receiver. The new administrator, G. R. Hofmeyr (a former Clerk of the House of Assembly), who was appointed by Smuts in August 1920, gave every indication he would fill this dual role, while leaving evaluation of the Protectorate's production to Brink at the Cape in the novel contractual system which operated for a decade.

PART III

Intervention and Accommodation
1920–1945

◆

8

'A wedge into the syndicate'

◆

THE sense of agreement and success among competing interests generated by the interproducers' conference lasted long enough to produce the basic outlines of the new cartel. The final draft of the document signed by the mining companies and the administrator of South West Africa, and approved by the minister of mines in February 1920 embraced the principle of sales through a single channel by quotas which would limit the total output of the Union and its Protectorate. Producers could not sell more than their share of the £3 million in diamonds which the syndicate offered to purchase during the first quarter of 1920 on the terms of their separate contracts. Equally important, they accepted a common method of determining future purchases through a formula, or replacement mechanism. The quantity of diamonds to be delivered in subsequent periods of 3 months was to be determined by the value of syndicate sales in the previous 3 months: 'the amount of such sales to be calculated on the net realised prices', less 5 per cent to cover administration and the cost of any duties or insurance. Only the syndicate could raise the quarterly total of quotas, from its knowledge of past movements in the diamond market and its judgement of future prospects. Each of the producers was, of course, furnished with reports on the performance of their goods, the prices obtained for all syndicate sales, amounts unsold, and the working of the replacement clauses. Harold T. Barber, a former Inland Revenue official, was appointed by the conference and the government to inspect the syndicate's accounts and provide this information, but not the details of resales to dealers in Europe. In the case of South West Africa, the administrator exercised the powers of the old Regie to determine the contribution of the CDM and lesser producers to the territory's quota of 21 per cent with the assistance of a Diamond Advisory Board of officials and company representatives. If any of the Union or Protectorate producers failed to supply their deliveries, the remainder were bound to make up the shortfall in proportion to their quotas. Founded on the euphoria of rising prices during the war, the cartel did not expect any of its members to fail.[1]

Malan and his officials now had a direct stake in the successful working of the system which appeared to ensure revenue from Premier and funds for the Mandate administration. Their knowledge of the ways in which the industry worked at the level of marketing, as well as production, had expanded considerably through the contracts negotiated with Barnato Bros. and Breitmeyer's wartime syndicate. But they did not see the separate contracts with profit-sharing made with De Beers and New Jagersfontein, and which were to contribute 51 per cent and 10 per cent quotas, compared with 21 per cent and 18 per cent from CDM and Premier. In practice, these confidential agreements did not differ greatly from the pre-war models negotiated by De Beers, and were taken up with regulating the wide variety of qualities and classes from the companies' producing mines. But so long as these agreements remained confidential, Malan, Warington Smyth, and their inspectors were uneasy about the power of the syndicate to enforce terms on the producers. Sooner or later a contest of commercial and political wills was bound to occur.

CARTEL CONTRACTS

It occurred first in South West Africa where the administrator, E. H. L. Gorges, resented the exclusion of a number of local, unamalgamated 'outside' producers from the territory's quota. Were these four or five minor companies and syndicates to be allowed any share of sales by the Advisory Board dominated by CDM? CDM's liability to Union income tax which the courts had yet to decide was used to persuade H. C. Hull and his board to come to terms. An attempt to raise South West's agreed quota was opposed, however, by Cullinan and Frames on behalf of Premier. Hull was obliged, therefore, to allow the outsiders to take advantage of high prices, by arguing for a special purchase of their diamonds by the syndicate up to £200,000 annually in a supplementary contract approved by the conference and signed by the administrator in April 1920. Any excess would be subtracted from CDM's 21 per cent, so the Advisory Board was made responsible for keeping these independent operators in order.[2]

---

[1] CAD, MNW 541, 'Memoranda of Agreement', 27 Jan. 1920; and all supplementary agreements.

[2] Ibid., MM 2095/20, minutes of meetings, Mar. and Apr. 1920; CDM, *Annual Report* (1920). The outside producers in South West were: South West Protectorate Diamonds Ltd. (Lewis and Marks); Meob Protectorate Diamonds Ltd.; the C. A. Lagessen, Meob Diamond Syndicate; Schuster, Goenbrecht and Blank; Namaqua Diamonds (formerly Kolmanskop); CAD, MNW 786 MM 1744/25.

This solution was accepted with bad grace; and Hull as chairman of CDM cast doubts on the wisdom of conceding to the syndicate a monopoly channel for 5 years, hinting that his company would reserve its right to find alternative outlets:

I need not enlarge on this aspect beyond saying that the unsettled conditions which the war has produced or that new large discoveries of diamonds in South Africa and elsewhere, or that a crisis in the demand for diamonds would inevitably involve joint and concerted action by the parties to the present combine. Therefore it seems to me unwise to lay down a hard and fast period for the duration of the combine. I would rather lay down the principle that, provided the conditions and circumstances of diamond production in the Union and in the Protectorate remain substantially as they exist at present, all the Producers pledge themselves to stand by the combine.[3]

This qualified support for the cartel alarmed Frames as intermediary between the producers and the syndicate. The syndicate, he knew, would not be pressured into changing the current agreement or leaving open-ended the duration of its terms, and the period of 5 years would have to apply to all. For a while he threatened to withhold the Union producers' consent to the outside quota for South West.

Inside the Department of Mines, Malan, Smyth, and Kotze took the cue from Hull and inclined towards Administrator Gorges's contention that any 'excess' production from South West might be sold outside the syndicate. This attitude was also supported from within the Justice Department, where an official minuted that the government should 'stick out' for better terms for the territory from both the syndicate and the Union companies: 'After all they are more anxious for these transactions to go through than we are. I do not suppose the Syndicate want to sell our diamonds otherwise than through [them]. In other words Frames and Hirschhorn are bluffing and we will 'call' them.'[4] But they were not bluffing. And the syndicate required that the administrator be held responsible in law for the terms of the territory's commercial contracts. The deadlock threatened the main interproducers' agreement of February 1920, while Gorges argued for the right to sell more diamonds. The leverage exerted by the delay was not quite sufficient, however, to break the united front of the Union companies, and the Department of Mines began to fear for the integrity of the structure so recently created. After more acrimonious exchanges between Smyth and Frames, the administrator

---

[3] Ibid., Hull to Gorges, 26 Apr. 1920; Hull to Frames, 30 Apr. 1920; Frames to Mines, 16 July 1920.
[4] Ibid., E. L. Matthews, Department of Justice, minute, 22 July 1920.

was persuaded to sign all agreements and accept the total limitation on sales implied by the monopoly outlet.

The outcome reinforced the departmental view that the syndicate held most of the cards in determining quota levels, based on the price and replacement formula, while remaining free to take extra purchases outside the conference cartel. Indeed, the Kimberley diamond committee of De Beers informed Frames officially about such purchases, mainly from Union alluvial producers. The New Jagersfontein Mining and Exploration board, which was also aware of this defensive buying to keep up prices, argued that it was to the advantage of the Union companies to prevent their sales being undercut on the European market 'at prices probably below those which the Syndicate could afford to sell'.[5]

But when the news filtered through to the South West administration that the syndicate was in the market for other 'outside' goods, the Luderitz Chamber of Mines wanted it stopped. The Department of Mines saw in this purchase of stock from the river diggers (some £3 million was forecast for 1920) confirmation of the power of 'monopoly'. The inspector of mines E. Langley warned that it was possible for the syndicate:

to flood or starve the trade in accordance with its interests. For example it might purchase largely and then withhold the big producers' consignments until such time as its outside goods had been disposed of. The trade cannot wait and moreover large dealers are not prepared to forfeit their position on the syndicate's lists by refusing the price offered. The Syndicate is moreover able to flood the market at any time in case of serious competition by other buyers.

Such an alarmist opinion of the unlikely way in which major investors in the Union companies might ruin their sales in order to favour the diggers, suggested to Langley a remedy which the department took very seriously: 'The only solution appears to be by Government control through the constitution of a body similar to that of the Regie which would benefit the State and all producers at the expense of London speculators.' Langley did not push this idea very far and intended such a control to apply, at first, to alluvial diamond production in the Union, in order to market the goods at a profit and for the benefit of the diggers. Later he grandly concluded his report with the suggestion that state marketing might be applied 'to the whole diamond industry in South Africa, whereby the Government, the big and small producers, as well as the State in general,

---

[5] CAD, MNW 541, W. H. Solomon to Frames, 11 Aug. 1920; Frames to Gorges, 13 Aug. 1920; Langley to Mines, 31 Aug. 1920; DBCA, Board 2/5/3 (Diamond Committee), 22 July 1920.

would be beneficially affected without any monetary assistance from the Government'.[6]

While the departmental minutes revealed considerable interest in this proposition, the case for greater state intervention had to be shelved while the syndicate and the Union producers faced market recession towards the end of 1920 and early 1921. At Premier mine, all labour was 'repatriated' and most of the whites were made redundant. The Trading Fund set up by the government in 1908 was drawn on to provide revenue for essential maintenance. De Beers cushioned retrenchments for whites with *ex gratia* payments, but the company's ample cash reserves of £1.6 million were almost reduced to nothing by the end of 1922. Other mines were forced to close. All blamed the sale of 'Bolshevik' diamonds, thrown on to a market already reduced by a decrease in purchasing power in Europe and America.

The syndicate reacted by reducing the total of quotas in the quarterly adjustments from £3 million to £2,573,000. In June 1921 the producers agreed to relieve the combine of the obligation to hold stocks by reducing their replacements still further, when sales fell below £1,250,000 in any quarter. From the pinnacle of record sales in 1920, the industry fell into a trough of uncertainty. Far from being able to 'flood or starve the trade', the syndicate had the greatest difficulty purchasing quotas. The first major test of the structure of the cartel left it largely intact, but changed the assumption that all members would be treated equally by means of the quota system.

The general mechanism for handling the production of the four producers followed the pre-war practices evolved for De Beers. After preliminary sorting by the companies, diamonds were either stored in the Union banks or sent to be registered for export through the Diamond Detective Department offices of the South African Police at Kimberley and Johannesburg. Stones from South West Africa were passed for sorting to the government diamond valuator, Arend Brink, who had set up his office in May 1920 in Cape Town, and then followed a similar route overseas. In London, the syndicate divided up stocks from different mines for reassortment, with some mixing of similar classes and priced the assortments for dealers' sights at resales (see Table 8.1).

The pricing system for the goods of each company, which had evolved its own specialist vocabulary since the 1890s, rested, by 1920, on the basis valuation determined through the price formula and related to the average carat values for varieties of stones in the 'standard' parcels supplied

---

[6] Ibid., Langley to Mines, 31 Aug. 1920.

TABLE 8.1. *Methods of sale and valuation: company to syndicate*[1]

1 *Quantities:*
hauling
washing → preliminary sorting and valuation → Diamond Detective Department, Customs, shipment → London: reassortment, syndicate stock → dealers manufacturers

company stock → Union banks and Government Valuator[2]

2 *Values:*

1 by basis valuation:

negotiation, assorted and unassorted lots; contract, standard parcels of sample production.

2 by formula from:

net realized prices (NRP) on previous period of sales.
Pre-1916 NRP = gross sales less realization expenses.[3]
Post-1916 NRP = London landed cost, or gross sales plus stock on hand less realization expenses less stock on hand. Syndicate commission (5% or 10%) deducted from NRP, before new basis valuation calculated.

3 purchase price paid by syndicate to company:
pre-1916 based on difference between NRP and estimated future net realized prices to give 'total average carat price' for periodic deliveries; post-1916 this difference termed a percentage on old basis valuation.[4] This gave a new provisional minimum price with additional payments from profit sharing, if applicable.

[1] The terminology and the general pattern are deduced from De Beers and Premier contracts, 1901 to 1925, and the reports of H. T. Barber. There are variants in the outside contracts from 1925 and in the contracts for South West Africa. See too CAD, TES F5/90, Lock, report, 22 Feb. 1922.

[2] For South West Africa diamonds.

[3] Brokerage, shipping, insurance, duties, commission.

[4] The standard formula evolved by 1919 was $\dfrac{e+g-f-a}{b+c+d} \times h \times \dfrac{95}{100} = x$ (new average carat value for the standard parcel for ensuing sales period.)

in which: e = gross re-sales in previous sales period;

g = stock on hand at net realized prices at end of sales period;

f = realization expenses;

a = stock on hand at net realized prices at beginning of sales period;

b = total value of diamonds delivered at purchase price;

c = duty paid on b;

d = insurance, postage, registration on b;

h = average carat value for standard parcel for preceding sales period.

If the items a, b, c, were not present (as at the end of 1921), the provisional minimum price could not be calculated. Although basis valuation was fixed on the standard parcel, value could be changed by changes in quality within the delivery of subsequent assortments and was adjusted by the formula according to the performance of these qualities at resale. See also CAD, TES F5/90, Lock, report, 22 Feb. 1922.

by the mines. If the composition of deliveries changed, the total value of a delivery (and its average price) could also change, though the accounts suggest changes arising from average quality were not great in the 1920s, except for De Beers mines. The addition (or subtraction) of a 'premium' determined by the difference between past and current basis valuations yielded the provisional minimum price for new deliveries. In the case of South West Africa, for example, the post-war agreement with the syndicate fixed the standard basis of assortment on a parcel of 8,006 carats; and each lot in the parcel was valued separately to determine the new average value per carat for each quarter. In theory, if the net value of sales in the previous quarter's deliveries yielded a high surplus over the purchase price for that quota, then carat prices could be raised as the basis for a new purchase price. If there was little surplus, or if the syndicate was left holding a large stock of South West goods, the formula lowered carat values for the new period. A poor-yielding mine like Premier might not be able to make up its quota in quantities sufficient to offset falling values, and its replacement delivery could be shared among more successful mines.

When all companies ran into falling prices early in 1921, replacements dropped for the last quarter of the year. From the syndicate's point of view, the high hopes of 1919 were dashed by 2 bad years, when resales plummeted, followed by a recovery in 1922 and a high percentage of resales until 1924 (see Table 8.2). It became apparent that not all stocks from each producer were selling equally well on the market. Furthermore the price adjustment formula, which should have served to take this variation into account and redistribute quotas could not be applied in all its rigour without shutting down the poorest mines in the CDM group and in the Transvaal for a period longer than the recession, thus confirming the suspicions of government that the weak would be sacrificed for the strong in order to protect the interests of De Beers and New Jagersfontein.

The reasons for not enforcing the consequences of the price formula on the weaker producers by cutting down their deliveries lay with the tough stand of the new administrator of South West Africa, G. R. Hofmeyr, on the need for revenue, and the threat of government controls made to the producers' conference in June 1921. For the first time, the syndicate recognized that the government might not be able to accept continued quota reductions for political and financial reasons. The four main producers were obliged, therefore, to accept a general reduction in replacement deliveries for the rest of the year, until stocks in London were reduced to £3.5 million, irrespective of resales for De Beers and New Jagersfontein. Thus, the burden of the depression was thrown on to the producers as a whole, who were allowed no more than £186,000 in

TABLE 8.2. *Syndicate purchases and resales from Union producers, 1920–1930*

Year	Loss or gain on total purchases (£)	Loss (%)	Gain (%)
1920	− 1,154,681	− 12.0	
1921	− 1,102,469	− 68.0	
1922	+ 2,159,956		+ 70.0
1923	+ 637,439		+ 8.8
1924	+ 3,686,427		+ 68.9
1925	− 1,126,308	− 13.8	
1926	+ 1,240,085		+ 14.8
1927	− 85,929	− 1.2	
1928	+ 880,957		+ 14.7
1929	− 297,824	− 4.5	
1930	− 1,702,912	− 53.0	

Source: CAD, MNW 183/31, H. T. Barber, reports, 1929, 1930, Annexures.

deliveries for the quarter ending December 1921. In compensation the syndicate offered to take £3 million from January 1922 as a total replacement for quotas sold.

But there was a split between CDM and the administrator on one side, and other producers, with accusations of collusion between De Beers and the syndicate at the conference in June 1922, because De Beers had made advance deliveries regarded by the South West Advisory Board as a breach of the interproducers' agreement.[7] In reply, Frames attacked Hull and the CDM for administrative favouritism which had preserved the 'extra' quota for local outside producers.

The position of Premier, however, was more perilous than the rest, because the mine fell short on its quota deliveries late in 1921 and early in 1922, when volume could not make up for falling prices. Having failed to deliver, the company lacked the basic elements in the replacement formula concerning previous purchase price, duty, and insurance paid. A Treasury report complained that the syndicate agreement had been a 'disaster' for the Transvaal mine, which the government might be obliged to support once again from trading and emergency funds. The general reason for this predicament lay in the terms of the contract and 'the continued stagnation of the diamond trade which has resulted in a large accumulation of diamond stocks in the hands of the Diamond Syndicate in London, thereby affecting the formula for determining, or fixing the

[7] DBC, Board 2/5/3 (Diamond Committee), 16 June, 3 Oct., 4 Nov. 1922.

provisional minimum price to be paid to the Company'.[8] In the past, as Barber's reports showed, Premier had done very well and had raised its provisional price to 200 per cent over the basis set in 1915. By the first quarter of 1922 the new provisional price had slumped to only 25.17 per cent above the basis price. The average gross profit of the Premier company 1920–3 was hardly sufficient to keep the mine running.

Reluctance on the part of other producers to tamper with the pricing formula, which would have required renegotiations of all contracts, led to the suspension of the formula altogether from the end of 1922 till the end of 1925. There was a general acceptance of the syndicate's ceiling on the volume of deliveries at £7 million for the year, spread equally over each quarter. But the basis valuation and provisional prices were arranged with each company by periodic negotiation. This still left the syndicate holding increasingly large stocks of low-grade goods. Extra funding was required by the five merchant houses led by Barnatos and Breitmeyers, and the Anglo American Corporation was admitted to the syndicate in 1924 with an 8 per cent contribution to the stake, leaving the technical control of stocks to the experienced wholesalers. At the same time, the annual delivery from South African producers was cut further to a maximum of £6.4 million, and replacement of net sales was reduced to 75 per cent of past deliveries for all mines. Worse still for the successful producers, existing contracts were liquidated in 1924 by the reconstructed syndicate; and profit-sharing ended, 'as the Producers will have no interest in the realisation of the diamonds by the Syndicate, the latter bearing the entire risk'.[9]

Because of the change which allowed the syndicate more flexibility in the prices it paid by negotiation, the year was a very good one for the merchants with a large gross profit (see Table 8.2). It was also a good year for De Beers; and the question which still worried the government was whether the major producer was favoured at the expense of less profitable companies.

The evidence is complex in the audited accounts of resales which the syndicate was required to submit to the Department of Mines and the Inland Revenue for the CDM group and Premier, compared with similar accounts supplied to De Beers.[10] From Barber's reports on these accounts it seems clear that the way in which the sales contracts worked made some producers more valuable to the wholesalers than others, but there was

---

[8] CAD, TES 863, Lock to Inland Revenue, 27 Feb. 1922.
[9] DBCA, Board 4/4/1, Hirschhorn to DBC, 5 Jan. 1924.
[10] CAD, MNW 543, 482, 541; DBCA, Syndicate, 6/3/1, Barber reports, 1926.

TABLE 8.3. De Beers sales to Syndicate, 1920–1930

Year	Deliveries ('000) mt. cts.	+ Premium on or – basis valn. (%)	Provisional minimum price (£'000)	Price per mt. ct. (s.)	Index (1920 =100)
1920	725.0	+ 90.37	4,933.5	136.07	100
1921	141.6	+ 68.73	688.2	97.20	71
1922	472.3	– 18.47	1,474.8	62.46	46
1923	1,056.7	+ 2.18	3,681.9	69.69	51
1924	775.4	– 2.57	2,565.4	66.19	49
1925	1,065.9	[a]	3,913.5	73.43	54
1926	1,118.7	+ 1.73	4,540.3	81.17	60
1927	1,070.8	– 8.13	3,920.2	73.20	54
1928	929.6	– 14.17	2,593.5	63.50	47
1929	720.1	– 11.94	3,252.9	90.38	66
1930[b]	297.2	– 17.30	1,363.8	91.70	67

[a] Between the last quarter of 1922 and the end of 1925 the formula for changing basis valuation was suspended, and the half-yearly provisional minimum price was reached by negotiation: DBCA, Board 6/3/1, Barber to De Beers, 12 August 1926.
[b] For January to June 1930. The syndicate was relieved of the obligation to purchase quotas for the last half of the year, but undertook to buy a total minimum value from the four conference producers, De Beers, New Jagersfontein, Premier, and CDM, during 1931 under the 1931–4 agreements: MNW 183/31, H. T. Barber, report, 31 Dec. 1930, Annexure E.

Sources: CAD, MNW 183/31, H. T. Barber, reports; DBCA, Board 5/3/1.

every incentive for the syndicate to maintain its monopoly of supply by offering quotas to all producers. Firstly, De Beers' resales, as a percentage of conference goods, were consistently higher than the 51 per cent quota of annual deliveries, rising to 68.3 per cent in 1926. As resales values for Premier, New Jagersfontein, and South West outside mines deteriorated, there were shortfalls in the periodic deliveries for all these sources, and De Beers and CDM took up these deliveries. Secondly, De Beers was able to boost the value of its own deliveries by including small quantities of selected, high-grade stones, particularly in 1923 and 1925–7 (see Table 8.3), thus earning higher prices on resales. For this reason the index of De Beers sales to the syndicate, while substantially below its 1920 level, remained fairly steady throughout the 1920s, and even displayed a tendency to improve, before the rapid downturn in 1929. The company could not entirely escape replacement penalties for lack of sales in volume 1927–9, and there was a notable decline in the 'premium' to be added or subtracted according to the pricing formula. But its sales performance was a rock of stability in a sea of fluctuations.

For the syndicate, there was the advantage that the quality goods of the major producer grossed very high profits on resale. The net resale profits, after deduction of standard charges, still left a handsome return on the turnover of De Beers diamonds; and it could be argued that this source, plus some alluvial sales, enabled the syndicate to sustain net losses on other goods and the overall cost of holding unsold stock, until the general collapse in 1930, when all deliveries had to be suspended in the second half of the year.

In turn, manipulation of the qualities of its goods enabled De Beers to keep up its basis valuation at 90 per cent of net resales. Harold Barber, therefore, in his reports to the company took a remarkably sanguine view of the fall in prices after 1920, because of the greater quantities disposed of by De Beers, following improvements in production technology at the Kimberley mines, although poorer stocks accumulated in the hands of the syndicate. Mixing all De Beers diamonds from Wesselton, Bultfontein, and Dutoitspan also helped, he thought, because the average quality was still high enough to sustain the basis valuation and replacement levels of the company and accounted for its fairly quick recovery from the 1920–1 recession:

The average quality of the goods delivered during 1925/26 was considerably higher than during the preceding two years and so practically all the goods delivered during each of those periods were assorted in the period of delivery

TABLE 8.4. Gross resale prices for De Beers diamonds, 1920–1930

Year	Price per mt. ct. (s.)	Index (1920 = 100)	Syndicate gross profit (s.)	Percentage on resales (%)
1920	171.92	100	35.85	26.3
1921	121.75	71	24.55	25.3
1922	116.75	68	54.29	86.9
1923	94.75	55	25.06	35.9
1924	124.42	72	58.23	87.9
1925	117.25	68	43.80	59.7
1926	113.30	66	52.10	64.2
1927	128.00	75	54.80	74.9
1928	112.30	65	48.90	76.9
1929	78.20	46	– 12.10	– 18.0
1930 (Jan.–June)	103.17	60	11.40	12.5

Source: CAD, MNW 183/31, H. T. Barber, reports, 1929, 1930, Annexures.

[indicating a quick turnover in London] and this is the main reason for the increased average gross selling-prices per carat realised from re-sales.[11] (Table 8.4)

Barber also revealed that during the short period of 'negotiated' prices 1922–5), the De Beers basis valuations were not allowed to fall to the same extent as those of other producers, in order to inspire 'confidence' in a company that was the market leader and produced remarkably little 'rubbish' or 'sand' useful only for industrial purposes. For the syndicate was also taking 'common goods' of low quality from other sources in Angola and the Congo at about 5s. per metric carat. This was more than the market thought industrial bort was worth. But, as Barber explained, 'the Syndicate cannot lower the price of Common Goods without also lowering the price of the next higher quality, and this would lead in turn to a lowering of the price of the second higher quality and so on up the scale of qualities'. In other words, the syndicate was obliged to pay more than it wished to keep control of low-grade diamonds; and, in compensation, it pushed the sales of deliveries from its best customer. Consequently, Premier had been heavily penalized by the syndicate, because of unsold goods 1920–1, when the average gross profits on the Transvaal company's resales were hardly more than 7 per cent and insufficient to cover the syndicate's realization costs. From 1921 Premier's deliveries were constantly below its quota of 18 per cent.

THE COMPANIES

The general effect of this differential treatment of its client producers by the syndicate, in order to sustain prices, was a major factor influencing company performance during the 1920s. The Premier (Transvaal) company was most likely to fare badly in any system of quota control which penalized low-grade production. The company never again exceeded the gross trading profits of its pre-war years, though it did not fare too badly in the mid-1920s. The reason was that general charges and mining costs were kept remarkably steady by running down old plant in the direct treatment system without investment in new machinery. Labour was recruited through the company's participation in the Witwatersrand Native Labour Association for about 60 per cent of requirements, and was increased or laid off according to production targets, reaching a maximum

---

[11] DBCA, Syndicate, 6/3/1, H. T. Barber, report, 12 Aug. 1926.

daily average of about 5,000 Africans and 480 whites. Daily rates for labour were held down to just over 3s. for men who were compounded and bought their own supplies. The wages bill in the aggregate represented about 40 per cent of working costs, rising quite steeply, whenever production was stepped up (Appendix A.4).

In this way, Premier management was able to operate a very flexible system on a remarkably small original capital investment. The company paid out £900,000 in dividends on deferred shares in the 1920s for 5 years and £1.8 million in preference share dividends. A third of the deferred shares, representing half the nominal capital of the company, were acquired by De Beers in 1922, in addition to the 33 per cent interest bought from Barnatos in 1917. Eventually almost all the deferred shares came into the possession of De Beers, and nearly all the preference shares in the late 1930s.

But over the same period, £3.8 million went to the government for its participation in profits. Government funds through the trading and emergency vote were frequently drawn on to make up for the lack of working capital. Consequently, the index for the return on capital employed is distorted, whenever the company's liabilities exceeded its assets, as in 1923 and 1924, and by the unusually small amounts of working capital, 1925–9, when government funds made up shortfalls. In other words, Premier was deviously subsidized, at the same time as heavy taxes and dividends were drawn from retained profits on sales. While it operated, it became a milch cow for both the government and its major shareholder, De Beers.

Although Thomas Cullinan remained as chairman till his retirement in 1923, the company was run by P. Ross Frames and five directors who came to represent the syndicate and De Beers by 1924. In their annual message to shareholders they took a pride in a record of production for no new capital expenditure.[12] By 1925, it was company policy to curb output in the face of competition from similar cheap grades sold to the syndicate outside the Union. As the government was not represented on the board, there was no public debate on the issue. Frames's reasoning was quite sound, however, from the viewpoint of the syndicate and the Union group as a whole:

The more diamonds we have to produce to fill our quota, the more inferior qualities will be put upon the market, which means that we shall be the innocent cause of further reducing the market value of common goods. This is a vicious

[12] Premier, *Directors' Reports* (1920–30), esp. 1924, 1925.

circle; but we cannot overcome the difficulty whilst there is a limited demand for rubbish and inferior qualities.[13]

The company would not be allowed to go to the wall, but it would not be allowed to drag down the price of superior qualities of cuttable stones. It was simply allowed to run down, as spare parts for machinery failed to arrive and its quota went unfilled.

By contrast, New Jagersfontein Mining and Exploration had always been under the control of Barnatos and produced the fine quality stones which De Beers and the syndicate were anxious to defend on the market. The company's quota was not always filled in the 1920s, though it was never penalized in terms of basis price. This remained consistently high at 80 per cent over the 1920 index of 100 during the last half of the decade, while De Beers and the South West group declined. Consequently, the company paid a steady average of 25 per cent on its deferred shares for a total of £1.8 million.

The structure and finances of CDM reflected the special position of the company in the Mandate, where it was expected to support much of the cost of administration through the taxation system inherited from the German period. As in the early days of De Beers over half of Consolidated's capital of £4.5 million consisted of 8 per cent mortgage debentures, which required a high level of trading profits to meet redemption charges and pay a dividend. Trading profits were extremely variable in the 1920s; the debt to equity ratio remained at between 50 and 70 per cent; and CDM showed very poor post-tax returns on capital employed (Appendix A.7). No dividends were paid during the first 5 years, followed by 6 years of payments at 10 to 12 per cent amounting to £2.5 million. This sum equalled taxes paid to government 1920–30, amounting to 47.6 per cent of gross profits—the highest tax level of any producer in the South African group. With some justification, Hull and Graaff complained they were worse off than the German companies had been.

They were also saddled with mounting mining costs. Techniques at company plants were at first relatively simple, consisting of excavation of the trenches and marine terraces containing alluvial deposits, followed by sieving, jigging, and magnetic separation to remove the diamonds from sand and gravels. The small labour force of 285 whites and 2,500 Ovambo and Cape Coloureds was used flexibly, and dispensed with during the 1921 depression. As the labour force was built up again to meet quotas,

---

[13] Premier, *Directors' Reports* (1925), p. 15.

Ovambo had to be recruited through the South West administration, and this became increasingly difficult because of the unpopularity of the harsh conditions at the mine sites. By 1923, over half of the labour force of 5,000 consisted of 'outside' recruits from northern Botswana, who suffered a high mortality rate after arriving with scurvy or tuberculosis.

A decision was taken to cut down on hand labour by investment in new screening plant at Kolmanskop and new concentration plant at Elizabeth Bay. Retained profits were squeezed, just at the period when the company was required to accept a quota well below its productive capacity. Increasingly, the board as well as the administration resented this limitation. The extra allowance for local 'outside' producers raised deliveries for the territory to 23 or 24 per cent of conference sales. But there was considerable force in the argument that the most highly-taxed producer could not expand in volume to utilize the extensive reserves which were known to exist in South West by the mid-1920s. In the Union, the quotas applied to companies. In the Mandate, the quota applied to a whole territory.

This was not an argument which appealed to De Beers as the company emerged from the war period with sales at their highest peak at 256 per cent over 1890 values, having done well on sales of South West diamonds on joint account with the syndicate. After the death of Francis Oats, direction was led by Sir David Harris on behalf of the syndicate. Harris continued the 'stabiliment' fund from wartime profits and investments which stood at £2.4 million by 1921 and was maintained at this level through the 1920s. His successor as chairman, P. Ross Frames quickly fell in with syndicate policies, and explained the origins and use of this fund as the stake taken by De Beers in other diamond companies, paid for out of profits. By 1925 those companies included Premier, New Jagersfontein, and smaller mines, such as Koffyfontein, which were kept out of production. Indeed, Frames took the idea of expanded holdings further and revived plans for a buying and selling company based on De Beers. The 1921 recession ended this dream with severe retrenchments, no dividends for three years, and near exhaustion of the cash reserves before trade recovered in 1923.

Nevertheless, the production and profitability ratios of De Beers in the 1920s indicated both the general soundness of the company's finances and the ways in which the stock of deliveries to the syndicate were sold off in preference to other stocks to keep the company that way. The index of diamonds recovered and sales on the diamond account displayed very little increase over pre-war output, and administrative expenses rose considerably. But the major item of direct mining costs was kept low,

TABLE 8.5. *South African diamond mines: annual index of real wages, 1911–1946*

Year	Real Wages (1936 = 100)		Earnings gap ratio [(2) as % of (1)]	Current cash wages (£): annual averages (all mines)	
	Whites (1)	Blacks (2)		Whites (1)	Blacks (2)
1911	98	111	15.1	265.6	40.1
1912	95	108	14.9	267.3	39.9
1913	96	109	14.9	272.4	40.7
1914	93	108	15.4	261.8	40.2
1915	103	65	8.2	306.3	25.2
1916	99	83	11.2	309.6	34.6
1917	93	83	11.8	319.3	37.7
1918	91	77	11.2	332.6	37.2
1919	82	74	12.0	331.9	39.7
1920	82	75	10.5	411.7	43.3
1921	84	70	11.0	384.8	42.4
1922	74	91	16.3	280.0	45.6
1923	88	88	13.2	325.5	42.8
1924	90	87	12.8	336.9	43.2
1925	90	91	13.3	337.1	44.7
1926	93	92	13.1	341.5	44.8
1927	92	88	12.6	340.6	42.9
1928	93	87	12.3	344.8	42.3
1929	94	87	12.3	345.5	42.4
1930	97	88	12.1	347.4	42.1

1931	84	88	13.9	290.7	40.3
1932	75	78	13.8	247.6	34.1
1933	74	86	15.3	237.9	36.5
1934	83	87	14.0	270.6	37.8
1935	98	94	12.7	319.0	40.5
1936	100	100	13.3	326.0	43.2
1937	97	100	13.6	324.2	44.1
1938	95	98	13.7	326.9	44.7
1939	97	99	13.5	336.0	45.5
1940	92	100	13.7	335.1	46.0
1941	89	108	17.1	314.9	53.9
1942	96	123	18.5	333.9	61.9
1943	96	138	19.2	362.9	69.8
1944	100	100	14.5	363.8	52.7
1945	114	133	17.6	400.0	70.5
1946	111	138	16.5	453.7	74.9

Sources: Department of Mines, *Annual Reports 1912–1947*; *Official Year Book of the Union of South Africa (1940, 1950)* [retail price index base 1910 adjusted] . Alluvial diggings excluded.

even allowing for the inflation of prices. The explanation lay partly in investment in direct treatment plant from 1923 for Wesselton and Dutoitspan. The expense of the floors was ended, but without any great reduction of the total labour force which remained at about 1,500 whites and 6,600 blacks from 1923 to 1929.

More significantly, labour charges, which had risen steeply during the war, displayed a downward trend 1920–30, even discounting redundancies in 1920–1. Allowing for inflation and recession, real wages for both blacks and whites were fairly static during the 1920s at Union diamond mines and decreased further in the 1930s (see Table 8.5). Earnings did not recover to pre-war levels until the Second World War. Similarly, the level of current cash wages for black and white workers, in terms of annual average payments, remained completely flat. The earnings gap ratio between black and white wages, moreover, settled at a steady 12 to 13 per cent.[14]

The claims made by De Beers directors for savings in the production process, therefore, must not be seen simply in terms of increased mechanization, but as a reduction in working costs by downward pressure on wages and flexibility of employment levels. Whites were compensated to some extent by redundancy pay, but there was no compensation for dismissals among the migrant labour force.

As a result of increased mechanization, there was some improvement in efficiency, from the consistent pre-war levels of 2 to 3 loads per man/day to 4.7 loads in the late 1920s. On the other hand, the new plant which had a capacity of 1,000 loads an hour was not employed to the full, compared with the great tonnages shifted and processed before 1914. On the whole, it was disciplined production and success in marketing high-grade goods through the syndicate which help explain De Beers's profitability ratios. Pre-tax profit on capital employed was the highest in the company's history in 1919 and 1920; and even the post-tax profits on all capital, including investments, stood at a healthy 14 per cent from 1923 till 1930 (Appendix A.2).

The company also began to trim down many of the non-mining investments which had accumulated since the days of Rhodes. When Frames reviewed the results of 'diversification' in 1923, he admitted to large losses on farming and cold storage, and little return, as yet, from underwriting Cape Explosives. The Alexandersfontein Hotel and its private electric railway began to show a small return from 1924, but the

---

[14] Compared with gold mining, current earnings were lower for whites in the diamond mines, but higher for black workers. Real earnings fell more sharply in 1921 and 1931.

manufacturers of dynamite and fertilizers at Somerset West could not compete with imported explosives and superphosphates.[15] After 1924 this situation improved with the formation of African and Explosive Industries Ltd. which bought out Kynochs and was owned equally by Nobels and De Beers. Cold storage interests were sold off, but Rhodes Fruit Farms were kept for sentimental reasons. The consequence of increased investment of some £3 million in other mining companies and the restructuring of the explosives venture was a steady revenue of over £500,000 annually from 1925 till the end of the decade.

A less welcome consequence for the company was its increased importance for taxes to the state, at some £300,000 to £400,000 annually, after recovery in 1923, amounting to about 4 to 5 per cent on all capital employed, but as high as 37 per cent of pre-tax profits. This factor explains some of the hostility voiced against the government at meetings of shareholders. Sir David Harris took particular exception to misstatements by Sir Robert Kotze which implied that dividends were higher than taxes (they were not). The company also took exception to an article by S. P. Joubert, published with the approval of the Department of Mines, which accused De Beers and the syndicate of organizing purchases from companies and syndicates in the alluvial fields to the exclusion of the diggers: this was branded by Harris as 'the outcome of a mind saturated with prejudice'.[16]

THE POLITICS OF CONTROL

These were the opening salvoes in a series of exchanges between the company and the department in which the former was blamed for collusion with the syndicate and the latter was charged with reflecting 'the eccentricities, weakness, and masterfulness of politicians' at a period of growing outside competition to the South African producers' conference.[17]

Underneath the polemic, the chairmen of De Beers and Anglo American made very different assessments of the danger of competition from uncontrolled outside sources and worked in different ways to meet this threat. Neither Frames nor Oppenheimer feared the level or quality of alluvial production from the Gold Coast, where Selection Trust leased

[15] DBCM, *Annual Report* (1923), 30–2.
[16] Ibid. (1921), 32; see, S. P. Joubert, 'Alluvial Diamond-Diggers in South Africa', *South African Journal of Industries* (Sept. 1921), 702–12.
[17] DBCM, *Annual Report* (1923), 32.

concessions in the Akwatia region and formed the Consolidated African Selection Trust to exploit them in October 1924. Production from all Gold Coast companies by 1925 was still under 100,000 carats a year, and the bulk of this was industrial material.[18] There was more to worry about in British Guiana, where production by small syndicates and alluvial diggers climbed to over 200,000 carats in 1923 during the Kurupung rush, sold on the open market. But the principal challenge came from Angola and the Congo diamond fields, producing since 1913 and expanding rapidly in the early 1920s.

Anglo American sent an engineer, F. A. Unger, to report on the Central African companies in 1923. The Congo group was dominated by the Société Forestière et Minière (Forminière) established by the Belgian state and the Société du Beceka incorporated in 1919. Three lesser concerns held concessions, but were managed by Forminière. The colonial government had a half-share in all the companies and the remainder of the capital was held by Belgian banking houses and an American financial group led by T. F. Ryan and Daniel Guggenheim and associates. The Angola Diamond Company (Diamang) had been incorporated in London in 1917 with the participation of Forminière and the Angola government. From 1924, Barnato Bros. had a 20 per cent holding which it later sold, as dividend payments were very small before 1926, because of the 35 per cent share of profits and monetary advances paid to the government.

Unger warned that Forminière's group system would soon produce over 400,000 carats a year of low-grade industrial material under £1 per carat: 'This is a point to be considered when it is remembered that the object which Barnato Bros. and the Anglo American Corporation had in view in doing the Angola deal was limitation of output.'[19] With co-ordinated operating methods and the cost efficiency of each plant totally under Belgian control, there was no reason why this production should not be expanded to offer for sale the best grades at 12 or 13 diamonds per carat for industrial purposes. The reserves were 'enormous' and output could easily be doubled. At the date of Unger's survey labour averaged 9,000 workers for all Forminière mines, paid at 25 f. (Belgian) a month (6s. 3d.), including rations. Such low wages (by South African standards) would have to rise, and there was a plan to reduce hand labour and increase the use of steam and electricity. These 'field' costs were about a third of total costs per carat produced, which, in turn, were about a

[18] Greenhalgh, 39, 232–4.
[19] CAD, MNW 691 MM 3510/23, F. A. Unger, report, 10 Aug. 1923. For Belgian investment in Diamang see Gervase Clarence-Smith, *The Third Portuguese Empire, 1825–1975: A Study in Economic Imperialism* (Manchester, 1985), 129–30.

ILL. 15. On the starting line for a 'rush': Vaalboschputte, Lichtenburg (1926?)

quarter of the final sales price to Antwerp buyers. Not surprisingly, Forminière made a profit of 15 million f. (Belgian) million a year on a capital of 32 million f., but handed over half of this to the colonial government. By contrast, costs in Angola at over £2 per carat ruled out serious competition for the present; and talks between Ernest Oppenheimer and the Portuguese high commissioner at Loanda in July 1923 ensured that there would be co-operation on employment of foreigners and, possibly, on marketing arrangements through the syndicate.

It is important to recognize, therefore, that although Anglo had some influence with the principal outside producers by 1924, there were no firm contracts channelling or limiting production, except in Angola. A different strategy was employed by De Beers which was manœuvring for co-operation at an international level, when Frames, acting for the Union cartel, arrived in London in April 1924 to discuss marketing, in the light of the 1921 recession, with the colonial secretary, J. H. Thomas, the Belgian ambassador, and the Portuguese representative for Angola.[20]

But no official diplomacy could be undertaken while the Union was in the throes of the elections in June 1924 which brought J. B. M. Hertzog's Nationalists to power and F. W. Beyers to the Department of Mines. Frames reported on his mission to the new minister in August, advising the government to co-operate and take up suggestions for an international conference with J. H. Thomas, who visited the Union in September along with E. H. Marsh from the Colonial Office.

[20] CAD, MNW 716 MM 1343/24.

At the same time, Oppenheimer submitted a succinct memorandum on world diamond supplies. He predicted that alluvial production in the Union would add £2 million in diamonds to the conference producers' £7 or £8 million. Outside the Union, Angola, the Congo, and British Guiana were expected to offer another £2 million for sale. This might be contained, he suggested, by Anglo and Barnato Bros., which had a holding in the Angola concessions; and he reported 'friendly arrangements' between the London syndicate and the importers of Congo diamonds in Antwerp. But there was no influence exercised in the Guiana alluvial field. In short, the Union still supplied 83 per cent by value of the world's diamonds, and this was expected to continue, unless new discoveries were made. Oppenheimer opposed the idea of any international conference which could

only be justified if the Union could secure a larger proportion of the total trade than 83 per cent. I believe a Conference by showing the Producers outside the Union that we are alarmed will lead to the contrary result. It is bad policy to try and meet the contingency of fresh discoveries outside the Union before they arise.[21]

By emphasizing the predominance of the Union's position, Oppenheimer effectively undermined the tenuous construction built up by Frames which aimed at an international quota system, before current contracts with the syndicate ran out at the end of the year. Time was needed for a new round of agreements, 'or to establish an independent association for the disposal of the diamonds produced by both De Beers and Premier companies'.[22] But Beyers was too new in office to make this kind of decision and turned to his permanent officials for guidance. They were more impressed by Oppenheimer's argument; and it was Warington Smyth who dealt with J. H. Thomas and agreed to nothing. The idea of an international conference was dropped.

For in the Union itself there was no agreement on what to do next. When producers met in conference in September and November 1924, they made no advance on the terms to be negotiated with the syndicate for the next contract period, mainly because they could not decide how to apply the old price and replacement formula with profit-sharing on a basis suitable for the poorer mines. At most, the syndicate was prepared to offer £3,750,000 in purchases from conference producers for the first 6 months of 1925, on 1924 prices, provided that deliveries from South

---

[21] CAD, MNW 716 MM 1343/24. Oppenheimer, 'Notes on the World's Diamond Production', 25 Aug. 1924.

[22] Ibid., Frames to Smyth, 24 Sept. 1924; and interview with Beyers, 3 Oct. 1924.

West's outside firms were reduced to no more than £70,000, instead of £100,000 for the first half-year.

During the impasse, Warington Smyth used what he knew of the commercial history of the contracts since 1920 to attack the syndicate, whose policy was 'to grab more than its fair share of surplus profits, and with the plea of new discoveries of low grade stones in the Belgian Congo, to depress prices to the Premier Mine'. Smyth blamed the periodic price adjustments for 'periodic six-monthly crises' when 'all the cards are in the hands of the syndicate'. Responsibility for accepting the syndicate's terms lay with the directors of companies who with the exception of Frames he considered to be largely the creation of the merchant shareholders. The only way out was to set up a government 'Diamond Agency' run from Cape Town to take the control of the market away from Kimberley. The 'Agency' would then sell directly to overseas buyers. Indeed, surmised Smyth,

the mere threat of legislation of this kind will probably bring the Syndicate to its senses and make them very ready to meet the producers by providing long period contracts based on reasonable initial prices and share of profit . . . There has been in the past a general reluctance or fear of entering into competition with the Syndicate in the very technical subject of diamond selling. The probability is, however, that with the aid of men like Ross Frames (as the General Manager), Brink (as Chief Diamond Valuator) and other men who would rapidly seek employment with the Government, the Government Agency would soon build up a staff thoroughly able to meet the Syndicate on its own ground, in fact I believe the Syndicate would collapse and half its members would rush over to the Government in their anxiety to be in with the spoils.[23]

This was a bureaucrat's answer to a commercial problem, and one he knew would find a sympathetic reception within the new government. Smyth (probably a supporter of the Nationalists) was aware that a political move in the direction of state control would find widespread popular consent among many English, as well as Afrikaner, voters. The new Ministry had a vocal constituency among unemployed whites in the Transvaal. As an English-speaking voter for Hertzog and one of President Kruger's 'Rooineks' expressed the case, diamonds were the remedy for the 'poor white problem'. With government subsidies to the alluvial mining camps and profit-sharing for white workers, the government could engage

first class Diamond Cutters at present here in the country, and sell the 'output' cut and polished, and thus obtain far higher prices, and at the same time open

[23] CAD, MNW 786 MM 1744/25, [Smyth], 'Re Diamond Position', 4 Dec. 1924. I attribute this to Smyth on the evidence of his initials.

up a valuable 'Diamond Cutting Government Monopoly'. Which is a great and crying necessity in this country. No person engaged in any capacity on the Diggings to be allowed connection in any way with the purchase or sale of any precious stones, under a Penalty of Ten Years Hard Labour. No natives, coloureds, or asiatics to be allowed on or in close proximity to such a Digging.[24]

Guided by these and other interventionist opinions, the new minister of mines, Beyers, made his own notes on the 'intricate' state of the diamond industry under syndicate domination and set his officials to drafting a diamond control bill.[25]

Meanwhile the producers and the syndicate struggled to reach agreement on new contracts on 22 December 1924, when the syndicate made its final offer on the same lines as before, but with an increase for South West outside firms. Beyers would not accept that these extra purchases would have to be accompanied by a reduction of the general quota of the four main producers by 3 per cent. And he would not hear of a syndicate proposal to insert in the new contracts a cancellation clause, to be effected if 'adverse legislation' was passed by the government. Having failed to reach an agreement, Beyers set a deadline for 12 January 1925, and threatened use of 'emergency powers' to arrange separate sales for South West Africa outside the syndicate.

Reactions to this ultimatum reflected the diversity of commercial and political interests in the debate. The administrator of South West Africa urged state control; Frames still hankered after an international conference as a basis for settling domestic differences; Arend Brink, whose technical advice to the department allowed him to comment on most of the correspondence, was inclined to accept the syndicate's terms, even the cancellation clause, in order to keep the producers together 'pending legislation'.[26] Lesser figures on the fringes of the play now sensed that the whole single-channel system was on the verge of breaking down and that quite new parts could be written.

The first of these was H. Gutwirth, broker for G. Gutwirth and Sons of Antwerp, who made an offer to purchase South West's outside production through the agency of Brink. Brink favoured this separate deal as a competitive example to persuade the syndicate to raise the 1925 purchase offer for the Union and the Protectorate to £4 million. As the deadline set by the government approached, Frames rushed to Cape Town

---

[24] CAD, MNW 744 MM 2699/24, A. B. Stewart to Beyers, 2 Dec. 1924.
[25] CAD, MNW 784 MM 2788/24, personal notes by Beyers, 1925, on negotiations with the syndicate and on the Diamond Control Bill.
[26] CAD, MNW 786 MM 1744/25, Brink to Mines, 3 Jan. 1925.

to confer with Sir David Graaff on a concerted policy with CDM and called on Beyers on 8 January, the eve of the producers' meeting, to warn him that producer co-operation was breaking down. But he did not learn of Brink's secret contract, which was to be used to push the syndicate hard.[27] At the meeting on 9 January, provisional quotas were agreed with 3 per cent for the South West outsiders. But Beyers was still not satisfied. Behind the scenes in Kimberley, the diamond committee, through Frames, began to negotiate with the syndicate for a separate contract with De Beers and Premier, thus abandoning CDM and New Jagersfontein in the hope this would be acceptable to Beyers and salvage the major producer. By 17 January Brink had taken his clandestine negotiations to the point where he had a draft contract between the administrator of South West Africa and Gutwirth and Sons which he thought brought in a useful third party from among the Antwerp merchants 'and also drives a wedge into the Syndicate'.[28]

Inside the Department of Mines, it was felt that all this double dealing was getting out of hand. Brink's initiative for an independent buyer for South West's outside producers was acceptable only if it did not detract from South West's quota. As Beyers minuted, 'we shall be doing well if we close with the Syndicate and if we accept the other offer', in the belief that the market would not be 'overstocked', because De Beers would have to keep to its old quota.

The manœuvre was threatened, however, when CDM and Oppenheimer (then in London) got wind of the Gutwirth offer. To keep this interloper out, Oppenheimer fell back on an 'undertaking' given by the government in February 1920, at the formation of CDM, that ex-German assets not amalgamated by the company would not be used in competition. The point was made strongly to Beyers on 16 January; and it was reinforced by CDM's board, which took the argument a stage further by claiming that in return for Anglo's financial backing in 1920, as approved by the Union government, CDM would be free to make its own agreements outside the syndicate, if no contract for 1925 was concluded.[29]

Arend Brink denied there had ever been such an 'undertaking' approved by government (and no written evidence has been cited in the archives), though CDM felt certain enough to threaten 'remedies at law', if any South West stock was disposed of by the administrator in an arrangement with

---

[27] Ibid., Brink to Mines, 8 Jan. 1925.
[28] Ibid., Brink to Mines, 17 Jan. 1925.
[29] Ibid., Brink to Mines, 17 Jan. 1925. The provisional agreement between Administrator Hofmeyr and Gutwirths states a purchase of up to £2,100,000 (beyond South West's production), which is an error for £200,100.

Gutwirths. But already Anglo had acted on 15 January and made a counter-proposal to purchase the full 21 per cent of South West Africa's quota.

The offer came as a bombshell to other producers and the syndicate. It can be understood, however, as a defensive action against the Brink–Gutwirth proposition to cut some of the Protectorate's production out from the single channel, and possibly enlarge this bridgehead at a later date with the connivance of Administrator Hofmeyr. And it was an opportunistic move to set up a new selling organization by using Anglo and CDM. A long cable from Oppenheimer to Beyers on 15 January justified the coup further by claiming that Anglo had limited purchase agreements with Angola, the Congo, and West Africa:

All these benefits to South African diamonds [sic] mining industry will be lost if South West diamonds now sold to Antwerp . . . and have assurance from company [CDM] that in case break with Syndicate diamonds would be offered to us. I appeal to Government in interests diamond trade generally uphold this engagement—it is not reasonable to present Anglo American with ultimatum that we should get reasonable time [to] negotiate permanent contract if four producers definitely break with Syndicate which if possible should still be avoided.[30]

Some of this was bluff. Negotiations for agreements with the Congo and 'West Africa' were tenuous, to say the least, at this stage; and Brink was quick to point out that any such contracts brought little direct benefit to Union producers and were primarily 'in the interests of the purchasers' [Anglo]. He advised that the undertaking given to the Oppenheimers by the founders of CDM not to allow small producers to break away was 'invalid', and did not bind the administration to anything. The notion that sales through Antwerp would end Anglo's profitable participation in the syndicate or its own arrangement with CDM he dismissed as 'ridiculous'.

But this was to miss the point behind the syndicate's dilemma. The merchants had not managed to keep the single channel going because of their reluctance to give special terms to South West and because of their anxiety about government legislation. In the vacuum, Oppenheimer stepped in, and the full outline of his proposal was relayed to Beyers by Brink on 17 January. For 1925, Anglo offered to buy the 21 per cent South West quota at 24 per cent above 1924 prices for the first 6 months and with application of the usual price formula for the rest of the year. The sellers were offered a generous 60 per cent of profits, after the first

[30] CAD, MNW 786 MM 1744/25, Oppenheimer to Beyers, 15 and 16 Jan. 1925.

7½ to Anglo. Any other deals for the territory were excluded; and the offer was 'not to be disclosed for the present in consequence of Oppenheimer's present obligations to the syndicate'. Brink advised the minister to approve.[31]

The last point was one of some delicacy (and has been passed over in some sources). These terms were proposed while Oppenheimer's two participants in the new syndicate, Anglo and Dunkelsbuhlers, were still members of the old one under Breitmeyers. It is not surprising that they were immediately expelled on 21 January 1924. The breach was made worse, after the expulsion, by another 'confidential' offer from Anglo to De Beers and Premier on behalf of Anglo and Dunkelsbuhler and Co. It is hard to see why this news would not leak out; and 2 days later Louis Oppenheimer cabled Brink to tell Beyers that the offer from the breakaway syndicate had been disclosed through the De Beers board, as a way of getting better terms from the rump of Breitmeyer's syndicate with Barnatos and JCI. 'Frames is acting very correctly, but his hands may be forced. Am sure Minister's word would have the effect that we get fair play and Producers get best terms.'[32]

The split meant that there were two sets of proposals and two syndicates seeking the approval of the government through Brink. Oppenheimer's offer to South West (in effect to his own company and the outsiders) was sanctioned by Brink, Beyers, and Hofmeyr at once on 17 January; and Beyers urged Brink, as principal negotiator, not to accept anything less for Premier 'as the Government is materially interested in profit from Premier'. Louis Oppenheimer continued to lobby Frames from London, insisting that the Anglo syndicate had the advantage of outside agreements elsewhere in Africa. But Frames continued to act 'very correctly' and concluded a contract for Premier and De Beers on 26 January with Breitmeyer and Barnatos's group, very largely because the terms were good for the favourite firm and because Sir Ernest had broken one of the syndicate's unwritten laws. He even summoned up enough courage to revive the idea of a buying and selling company based on De Beers and discussed this with Brink and Beyers at the Cape in February. But the minister could not be persuaded to allow Premier or South West

[31] Ibid., Brink to Beyers, 17 Jan. 1925. Compare the version by Louis Oppenheimer cited in Gregory, *Ernest Oppenheimer*, 156–7. The government did not have an offer for all South West diamonds; the 'memorandum of protest' to save face omits to state that Oppenheimer's offer was only made to CDM. It is clear, however, that syndicate insistence on protection against adverse legislation was the main point of difference between Anglo, Dunkelsbuhlers (Louis Oppenheimer), and the rest of the syndicate.
[32] Ibid., Louis Oppenheimer to Brink, 24 Jan. 1925; DBCA, 2/5/3, Louis Oppenheimer to Frames, 24 Jan. 1925.

producers to participate in such a scheme as shareholders. As a parting gift, the minister handed Frames a draft copy of the bill for government control of diamonds which he had just sent to Oppenheimer.

Before the bill came before the Assembly in April, both syndicates made their purchases, one from CDM and the other from the three remaining producers. An exchange of letters between Frames and Oppenheimer to limit volume to under £4 million for half the year got nowhere, and both sides jockeyed for sales for the second half of the year. Breitmeyer's merchants still insisted, however, on no control of the size of quotas by a government minister. It was still unlikely, however, that any minister would approve a contract which allowed the merchants to terminate purchases in the 'event of any legislation affecting Diamonds or financially prejudicing the Buyer's interests', especially in the case of Premier. Anglo did not insist on any such safeguard in its contract with CDM; and, as a bonus, Oppenheimer agreed to take over sales for the local outside producers from the Gutwirth agreement which was allowed to expire at the end of 1925 (after some angry correspondence between Brink and his clients). In commercial terms, there was not much to choose between the two syndicates, as quotas and the old replacement formulas were to remain the same. Politically, however, Oppenheimer's group made no intractable conditions which the government could not accept.

When the Diamond Control Bill was debated, Beyers took time to explain at length the government's position. The legislation was intended as an enabling act with powers held in reserve, rather than an onslaught by the Pact on De Beers or other companies in the Union (however much their directors supported the South African Party). The syndicate was the main target, making 'millions of profits' in good years, but weak in the 1921 crisis when it was most needed. Because negotiations broke down in 1924, explained Beyers, companies felt free to look for new offers (though no mention was made of the Gutwirth intervention). The temptation to make political capital out of Oppenheimer's role was irresistible; and with some skill the minister was able to lay the responsibility for the breach with the syndicate at Anglo's door, taking up Brink's phraseology from his notes on departmental correspondence:

I am glad to be able to tell the House that a wedge has been driven into the syndicate, and that no less a person than an hon. member sitting on the opposite side of the House who is connected with the Anglo-American Corporation—in which, I understand, American capital is interested to a material extent—was materially a participant in driving this wedge into the Syndicate. Now the whole object of this Bill is not to carry out everything that is stated in it, but to have a sword of Damocles hanging over combinations and combines like the syndicate.[33]

Beyers took full credit for using government powers to secure a new deal for South West's outside producers on a 5-year basis at a level of £224,000 in annual purchases. He brushed aside the threat of competition from the Congo, Angola, or Guiana, on the grounds that South Africa had all the 'big diamonds of the world', conveniently ignoring the general effects of common goods production on price levels.

Later in the debate, Beyers toned down his reference to Oppenheimer's coup. He confessed that the government had 'forced the position, and the hon. member, representing the financial interests that he does, was compelled by the force of circumstances, to make an offer for the 21 per cent. of South West diamonds'. He also hinted (erroneously) that Oppenheimer had left the syndicate before this offer was made.[34]

A certain amount of correspondence lay behind this grudging attempt at an apology for causing political embarrassment to a man who was a political opponent but a government ally against the old syndicate. For the record, written exchanges about what had taken place in January 1925 were deposited in a formal memorandum by Oppenehimer and a measured reply by Brink. Both versions were short on dates and omitted much from the chronology. But the essence of Oppenheimer's story was that he had been approached by Brink to save CDM's sales. An identical offer by Anglo to De Beers and Premier had resulted in improved terms from the old syndicate and he could claim (by forgetting his expulsion from the syndicate) that the competition had been beneficial for the producers. For his part, Brink denied (correctly) that he had approached Oppenheimer and conveniently left out the reason for CDM concern over sales to Antwerp. Otherwise, he supported the bland conclusion that offers to De Beers and Premier had been improved by this manœuvring.[35]

With honour satisfied by these departmental affidavits, the parliamentary debate could continue into July. At the centre of the government's control scheme was a diamond control board, like the German Regie, with powers to confiscate and sell, if producers could not find a channel agreeable to officials. It was recognized that such a board might require capital funding, and provision was made for joint financing

---

[33] *Assembly Debates*, 2 Mar. 1925; and CAD, MNW 748 MM 2788/24 for Beyers's notes.

[34] Ibid., 9 Mar. 1925.

[35] CAD, MNW 786, Oppenheimer, 'Memorandum', 27 Mar. 1925; Brink, 'Comments on Memorandum Furnished by Sir Ernest Oppenheimer', 28 Mar. 1925. See Gregory, *Ernest Oppenheimer*, 158–9 for Oppenheimer's submission. Brink's comments are not mentioned.

by government and producers with a reserve for purchasing stock in a slump. As a member pointed out, the board would also have to make advances if the board went into business. The alluvial diggings were excluded for 'political considerations', and their £2 million production fell outside the board's powers.

The Opposition's attack on the bill was weak and unconvincing. The government was able to argue that the South African Party in office had seen the necessity for controls. The Transvaal legislation was a useful precedent from a period when Patrick Duncan had been 'the Trotsky of Lord Milner's kindergarten'. The Diamond Cutting Act of 1919 and the German system retained in South West Africa drew departments of state into the business of production and marketing. Some expert criticism from Sir David Harris on the lack of expertise among officials was deflected by Beyers, who alluded to Oppenheimer's support for restructuring the syndicate. Finally, Hertzog stressed the inevitable outcome for an industry which had difficulty in presenting a united front: the business of diamonds was too important by 1925 to be left to businessmen, 'because the diamond industry and the State cannot be separated'. The same arguments were repeated in the Senate by Beyers who emphasized that powers need not be applied, if the buyers and sellers ran their own affairs without disrupting trade and revenue. To some senators it all sounded like 'socialism'; to others, it looked like a way of getting higher prices from competing merchant groups, and all clauses were passed and the act was promulgated at the end of July 1925.[36]

The government now had an instrument which it could use to determine quantities produced, set minimum prices, and call for returns of production. All sales agreements required ministerial approval. A 'Diamond Control Board' might be established to buy and sell, issue advances, and fund monopoly sales through its own officials.

Very little of these Draconian powers was ever brought to bear on the industry:[37] but the threat was there, unless the merchants and companies set their house in order. The signs were, by the time the act was in force, that the house was coming under new management. The argument between the rival syndicates was really over the maximum purchases they felt it was prudent to offer to the producers, not about the principle of a single channel for sales. Breitmeyer was prepared to go as high as £4.2 million for the first half of 1925, if Anglo could be brought back into

---

[36] *Assembly Debates*, 12 and 16 Mar. 1925; *Senate Debates*, 14 July 1925; Act No. 39, 1925.

[37] It would seem that no regulations had been issued under the act as late as 1946: CAD, MNW 784 MM 1691/25, Diamond Corporation to Mines, 4 Feb. 1946 and minutes.

the fold. Oppenheimer favoured a lower volume of £4 million with an increased allowance for South West's outsiders; and this was the offer which found favour with the administration in the Mandate. Barnatos and S. B. Joel sensed who was likely to win and defected to the Anglo combine. When the old syndicate was about to collapse in July, Anglo, Barnatos, 'and friends' made a counter offer of a 5-year contract to De Beers and Premier. The terms were less generous for the last half of 1925, when Union producers were to be limited to a total sale of £2,750,000. Oppenheimer was willing to make this up with larger sales of up to £4 million in 1926 in order to improve the interests of the shareholders and to 'assure the revenue from diamonds which the Minister of Finance is budgeting for'. This time he got an assurance from De Beers that his offer would not be disclosed to any director with a personal interest in the diamond trade.[38]

Frames and his board now had to choose carefully. Brink reminded the company that all contracts required ministerial approval under the new act; and to New Jagersfontein he went further, warning that inter-producer agreements 'must be considered and approved by the Executive Council'. Faced with this sanction, the Kimberley diamond committee (without its syndicate representatives) decided to come to terms with the 'Joel/Oppenheimer' syndicate, in order to avoid a board of control. They drew some comfort from Oppenheimer's assurance (not relayed to the Department of Mines) that shortfalls in deliveries could be made up by successful companies, as in the past. The final details were worked out in August 1925 and agreed to 'reluctantly' by London directors, because they perceived that Oppenheimer had no real control over outside sales from the Congo or Angola.[39] As Frames explained later to his board, the final factor tipping the decision in favour of the new combine had been the refusal of the Union government to allow South West producers to join any new selling company in opposition to Anglo; and the weight of Rothschilds came down on the side of the merchant group which could command most of the Union sales.

Oppenheimer rounded off his triumph by his election to the De Beers board, 21 July 1926. He had been present at diamond committee meetings on behalf of Anglo throughout August to work out the details of the new contract. He had improved his standing with the Department of Mines

[38] CAD, MNW 786, Oppenheimer to De Beers, 15 July 1925; Oppenheimer to Beyers, 18 July 1925.

[39] DBCA, Board 4/4/1; diamond committee, 24 July, 6 Aug., and Sept. 1925, esp. 289–90; CAD, MNW 786 MM 1744/25. Morgan Grenfell and Co. were included ('friends') as participants in purchases of Angola and Congo industrial goods.

by sending in correspondence between CDM and De Beers on quota disagreements which he claimed would be detrimental to South West Africa. At the end of August, he was able to announce that the new syndicate of Anglo, Dunkelsbuhlers, and Barnatos had concluded quota contracts with all the Union producers and had extended the South West CDM and outside agreements of 14 May 1925 to synchronize with the rest which would end in December 1930. The territory's terms, moreover, were improved to allow profit-sharing at 65 per cent, after an initial 6 per cent on resales by the syndicate. More doubtfully, much was still made of the syndicate's 'influence' with other outside producers, in order 'to stabilise as far as possible the diamond position throughout the World by effecting sales through one channel'.[40]

His position was further improved in the eyes of the government by the intemperate attacks of Sir David Harris on the Control Act. Inside the Department of Mines, Brink took particular exception to Harris's references to civil servants, and primed Beyers for a reply in the Assembly on the 'evil effects' of the old syndicate.[41]

Accordingly, when all the new agreements with Premier, De Beers, New Jagersfontein, and South West went to the department in November 1925, there was no real doubt about approval. A conference of producers held at the Cape was less a debate than a confirmation of quota levels already decided informally by Brink, Frames, and Hull, by which the old percentages were maintained with an extra 3 per cent to the South West outsiders up to £200,000. In press releases the government took the credit 'for the breakup of the reconstituted original selling syndicate [sic]', and the impression was given that Beyers had insisted on the general deal with Oppenheimer's group.[42] The source of these claims lay in memoranda prepared within the Department of Mines for the minister by Warington Smyth. The old syndicate, according to these briefs, was ended by government action; and the government prided itself on the price adjustment formula, improved terms, and the allowance of larger deliveries for the South West outsiders. The Union, therefore, could hope to retain £6 million of an estimated £12 million in world sales, including Union alluvials.

These were large claims. The more usual interpretation of the breakup of the syndicate has been to regard the episode as an astute piece of organization by Sir Ernest Oppenheimer to save the industry from

---

[40] Anglo to Hofmeyr, 14 Aug. 1925.

[41] CAD, MNW 784, Brink, 'Notes for the Minister'; *The Cape Times*, 25 Aug. 1925.

[42] Ibid. [Brink], 'Improvement in Diamond Position as Result of Government Action' (for press release), 27 Nov. 1925; Smyth to Beyers, 27 July 1925.

self-destruction and from government control.[43] Neither explanation gives sufficient weight to the intrigues of Arend Brink in undermining the single-channel system by offering an entry into South West Africa to Antwerp, or to the collusion between Beyers and Oppenheimer by the time of the second reading of the Diamond Control Bill. The work of Frames, as co-ordinator, moreover, was important for all the Union producers until the final decision by De Beers to accept the new syndicate's terms. His ideas for an international conference and the much-discussed 'buying and selling' company, as ways out of the deadlock, came to nothing for the moment, but they were to be revived again in other forms. Amid the self-congratulation, moreover, the government paid no attention to the greater threat in the Union, which came not from the struggle between buyers and sellers in the syndicate and the cartel, but from those still left outside the system by the Control Bill, which did not apply to the alluvial diggings.

[43] Gregory, *Ernest Oppenheimer*, 120–2, 125–63; Hocking, ch. 5.

9

Alluvial Mining

◆

BECAUSE of the spectacular yield of the kimberlite mines in the Union, alluvial mining in the shallow deposits of ancient river beds remained a secondary system until after the First World War. Until the discovery of other kimberlite outcrops in Africa in more recent times, the great pipes of the northern Cape, the Free State, and the Transvaal dominated production of gem stones and near gems in terms of quantity, though not in terms of value. The proportions changed rapidly, as alluvial terraces and diamondiferous gravels were uncovered in the 1920s, making the Union and South West Africa's variety of production more typical of the widespread exploitation of alluvial diggings elsewhere in the world.[1]

The river diggings had never died out, after the pioneer phase of the late 1860s. But they were neglected, and remained concentrated between the Vaal and the Hartz River and Bloemhof in the Transvaal for nearly 40 years, until rising prices encouraged prospection northwards into the Lichtenburg and Ventersdorp districts along a belt of alluvial gravels about 90 miles in length and 2 miles wide. This was diggers' country where deposits lay in small 'runs' and irregular hollows and potholes, and were fairly easily worked at shallow depths. From 1926 much richer alluvial fields in marine gravels were discovered along the coast of Namaqualand from the mouth of the Orange River, particularly at Kleinzee and Alexander Bay.

POVERTY TRAP

As the bulk of new discoveries lay outside the Cape, the Union government took the opportunity in 1919 to repeal the outdated Transvaal ordinance of 1903, and laid down new conditions for the proclamation of diggings

---

[1] For alluvial diggings elsewhere see Greenhalgh, 16–17; CO 111/663, for reports on the development of the Mazaruni and Puruni fields in British Guiana in the 1920s.

on state or private land. Owners' and discoverers' rights were recognized by allocation of a proportion of claims, if owners chose to apply to a mining commissioner to have their farms changed into a mining camp. Authority to control a rush was divided between diggers' committees and the commissioners, but, in general, all that was necessary was to be in possession of a digger's certificate in order to occupy by ballot, or by a controlled steeplechase, a pegged claim of 45 feet by 45 feet.[2]

The 1919 Precious Stones Act left much that was unclear on the responsibilities for administration between the commissioners and the owners of farms. The reform could not be extended in its entirety to the Cape, because there were private lands where the Crown had no vested rights to dispose of minerals. Owners, moreover, could employ their own labour to prospect and work claims, and these men did not require certification. The system of permitting open occupation of diggings by a rush from a startline sounded fair enough for the athletic, and rushes of up to 7,000 or 8,000 people took place in the early 1920s. It was not unknown for diggers to employ fast runners, though vehicles and horses were not allowed. Balloting favoured seasoned and experienced diggers, who pre-selected their sites and paid for a survey in advance of the draw (Ill. 15).

But experience showed that claims on private farms were not entirely open to the diggers. Prospection by the owner could be extended long enough to 'pick the eyes' out of claims, before the rush. Subdivision of farms enabled owners to lease prospection rights to syndicates and private companies before the diggings were proclaimed. In the majority of cases, noted a mining inspector, 'claims were pegged by business people, professional men, Civil Servants, bank clerks etc., and companies and syndicates were also formed for the purpose of acquiring and working large areas of ground'. This surprising assertion about the proportions of entrepreneurial capital and diggers' labour was supported by an early study of the diggers in 1921 which classified them into professionals permanently engaged in mining, 'fortune-hunters' from the salaried and property-owning class (including many farmers), and the rest— some 43 per cent of the sample surveyed—who were drawn from the ranks of the unemployed.[3] The reason was probably the loophole in the 1919 legislation which permitted multiple ownership in the form of 'discoverers' claims, and, secondly, the rapid and extensive working of gravel runs by syndicates employing gangs at wages the diggers could not afford.

---

[2] Act no. 15, 1919 Precious Stones (Alluvial) which repealed Ordinance no. 66 (1903).
[3] CAD, MNW 981 MM 1430/29, McNeight, memorandum, 19 Mar. 1929; Joubert.

All employees: annual averages
Diggings:
Index 1912=100 (17,885)

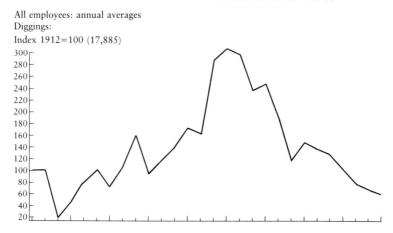

Mines
Index: (1912=100 (43,358)

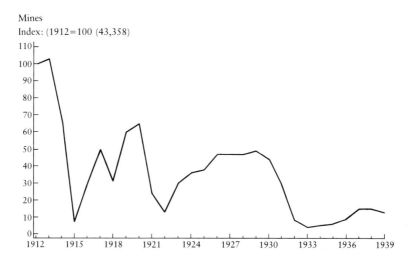

FIG. 9. Union of South Africa: labour employed in diamond mines and alluvial diggings, 1912–1939

One of the difficulties in the way of coming to a firm conclusion about the inputs of capital and labour into alluvial production was the speed of prospection in the early 1920s which took the Department of Mines by surprise. As late as 1923 the government did not have a complete list of all diggings or 'diamondiferous' farms open to prospection. Indeed, the department relied on De Beers to prepare a survey map.[4] This revealed in 1924 that there were 309 alluvial diggings concentrated in the Transvaal and the Cape, some going back to the 1870s, and others worked out and abandoned. The working population at these diggings, therefore, was for most part nomadic, shifting to new sites as rushes took place and labour was in demand. But the bulk of sites occupied for more than 6 months were worked by multiple partnerships and syndicates. At the height of the alluvial revival in 1927, there were perhaps 50,000 whites and 90,000 Africans at the diggings.[5] They clustered on 158 farms and portions of farms in the four mining districts of Barkly West, Klerksdorp, Lichtenburg, and Pretoria. The nucleus of the whites, however, was made up of professionals and syndicates with access to commercial capital, accounting for perhaps a third of the alluvial mining force, while the rest were urban and rural flotsam and jetsam, mostly unemployed. It was from that nucleus that the bulk of production derived, leaving very little for casual prospectors.

Consequently, the sectional interests represented in the administration and politics of the alluvial expansion of the 1920s were far narrower than the ostensible populism of politicians' appeals on behalf of 'the diggers' as a self-employed entrepreneurial group. The extent of that group was largely fictitious and kept before the public by press descriptions of the very real poverty and deprivation in evidence at the diggings. It was precisely because the success rate was so limited and the standard of living was so low for the majority that alluvial production was difficult to control. The lucky strike doubled as a system of outdoor relief which had to run its course.

The oldest, and in many ways the narrowest, interest group was based on the Hartz-Vaal river diggings, established in deep alluvial claims and with a tradition of local government that went back to the 1870s. A Vaal River Diggers Union was formed in 1920 to press for a number of reforms arising from the special conditions of the river sites. River diggers often employed large numbers of workers to dam streams and pump out water with capital subscribed by mercantile investors, in return for a number of claims and their production. Diggers were willing enough to continue this version of mining 'on shares', but, with the rise in the price of alluvial stones, they wanted a restriction on the number of claims used as security

---

[4] CAD, MNW 689 MM 8451/23, Inspector of Claims to Mines, 15 Mar. 1924.
[5] CAD, NTS 2203 326/380, 'Committee of Investigation into the Conditions on the Alluvial Diggings', 1937.

for a return on investment. Similarly, although they had the power to refuse certificates to new diggers, they now wanted to extend this power to owners' claims on the bordering river farms, especially if such owners handled the sale of diamonds found on their property. They resented, too, their dependence on owners' trading stores and access to water supplies.

Little interest was taken in the plight of the river diggers by the Department of Mines which put its faith in the new Board for the Control of Alluvial Diamond Interests set up in June 1920 in the Cape, under the terms of the 1919 act, with representation from the diggers' committees and owners of private estates, and chaired by the head of the Diamond Detective Department. Consequently, the older committees continued to meet separately from this instrument of government, and passed their traditional resolutions on enforcement of control over IDB, the reservation of alluvial fields to white diggers, and fierce opposition to the 10 per cent export duty. The Alluvial Board of eleven elected members, under Colonel Thomas Middleton Davidson, extended representation to the Transvaal in 1921 and received a subsidy of a few thousand pounds from the Department of Mines and an office in Kimberley. Its first programme echoed many of the usual grievances and added new suggestions such as control over trading licences at the diggings, closer administration of the pass laws, the fingerprinting of labourers, and limits on the brewing of native beer.[6] Its only achievement was the system of balloting for claims.

By 1924, the annual conference of diggers' committees at Kimberley was important enough to become an occasion for visits by parliamentarians, officials, and provincial dignitaries, as the Board acquired political influence, but little administrative responsibility. A whole series of mining inspectors and under-secretaries from the department reported on their deliberations and took counsel from their petitions. They did not have things all their own way, as clients of departmental patronage. Some committees were disbanded in 1928, because of 'irregularities' (bribery) in the issue of diggers' certificates. And although they had ways of making their voices heard through the Alluvial Board, the committees had very few statutory powers. The Board was reformed under 1927 legislation and headed by a mining commissioner and two representatives from the Transvaal mining districts and nominated members from the Cape committees, continuing as a pressure group dedicated to the proclamation of new diggings and exclusive management of claims.

[6] CAD, MNW 543 MM 3223/203; MNW 689 MM 2262/21.

But given the weakness of provincial local government in the rural areas and the 'hierarchical nature of the authority structure in South Africa' which had emerged under the Union, departmental officials, the magistracy, and the police bore the major responsibility for the alluvial fields as an administrative and social phenomenon.[7] Continuous petitions from below only underlined the absence of effective authority based on popular representation. The Public Service Commissioner's Reports for the late 1920s indicate that allocations to the districts from provincial and Union revenues actually decreased, as local income taxes were levied on the mining community. These allocations, in any case, fell far short of the funds required to service the mining camps with elementary sanitation, hospitals, schools, and roads, probably for the reason that such communities were considered to be transient locations deserving of charity, rather than a devolution of financial and judicial powers to local boards.

In this vacuum, the Diamond Detective Department, with a total establishment of fifty-five detectives, constables, a senior inspector, and numerous 'traps', moved in to register finds and control sales. From 1926, the department was called on to check the returns of over 40,000 diggers, alluvial companies, and a hundred licensed buyers. The accuracy of these returns depended on the commissioner of the Inland Revenue's assessment of tax on diggers selling over £300 worth of diamonds a year. By 1927, they were dealing with 5,000 or 6,000 registrations and sales a month containing the essential 'information relative to finds for income tax purposes'.[8] Gradually, in conjunction with the magistrates' courts and the mining and native labour commissioners, the detective branch of the South African Police took over the provincial commissioner's authority in this specialized area of supervision and enforcement of the Precious Stones Acts.

Apart from the diggers, two other pressure groups demanded the services of these officials and appealed to the politicians. One formed itself into the Transvaal Diamond Buyers' Association in the mid-1920s to monitor the entry of brokers into the highly competitive market of the alluvial fields. The association was particularly anxious to end the system of advances or credit to diggers, by which buyers obtained a lien on production. More immediately, they were influential in denying licences to non-whites. The head of the Detective Department, Major Brink,

---

[7] Anthony de Crespigny and Robert Schrire (eds.), *The Government and Politics of South Africa* (Cape Town, 1978), 82–4.

[8] CAD, MNW 875 MM 816/27, Diamond Detective Department, Report for 1926; 852 MM 2884/26.

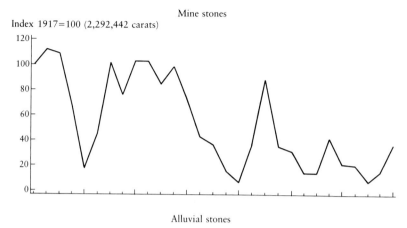

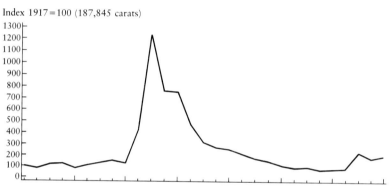

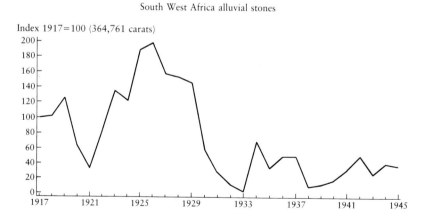

FIG. 10. Union of South Africa: quantities of mine and alluvial diamonds sold, 1917-1945

Mine stones

Index 1917=100 (44.75 sh/mt. carat)

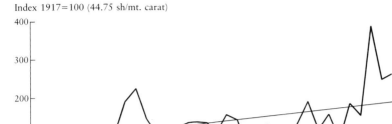

Alluvial Stones

Index 1917=100 (110.92 sh/mt. carat)

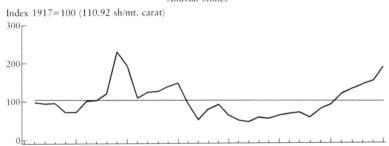

South West Africa alluvial stones

Index 1917=100 (45.9 sh/mt. carat)

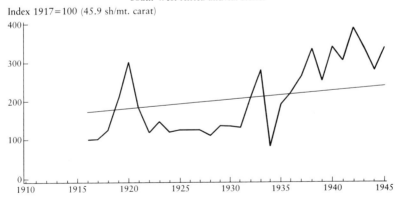

FIG. 11. Purchase prices of mine and alluvial diamonds, 1911–1945

supported them by arranging his own tests for would-be dealers and refusing to sanction licences for those without competence or knowledge of grading and valuation of stones. They also intervened to prevent the entry of Indians into the trade, even where they possessed such knowledge and were sponsored by the Bombay Indian Merchants' Chamber. Legally, the Diamond Trade Ordinance made no distinction on this point. But the Detective Department set itself to judge the issue for the Department of Mines and successfully upheld the buyers' objections on the grounds that it was 'contrary to public policy' to have Indians or coloureds dealing in stones.[9]

Carrying more weight with politicians, the Western Transvaal Landowners' Association was also formed in the early 1920s with Max Fleischack as chairman to protect their rights under the 1919 act. They exercised these rights by reserving homestead and agricultural land, as well as claims on proclaimed diggings; and many made an additional living by selling water and stores to the diggers. They looked with envy on the Cape practice of reserving mineral rights to owners on those farms still under old Free State titles; and they made the point that mining and excavatation by mass occupation left land unfit for farming. Denied representation on the Alluvial Board, they threatened to reduce the number of farms proclaimed by refusing prospection.

The administration and politics of the alluvial fields, however, took on the appearance of a social emergency, rather than a reasoned debate between competing interests. The reasons for this lay in the spectacular yields, quantities sold, and free-market structure which the Transvaal and Cape alluvial diggings had in common with British Guiana and the Gold Coast in their opening phases of prospection and development. Compared with mine stones, Union alluvials began to improve from a very low basis of annual sales before 1917, as the price index for goods from the diamond pipes and from South Africa moved up sharply during the First World War (see Figs. 10, 11; appendix A.8). An additional attraction for prospectors were the low overheads and the much higher prices per carat enjoyed by Union alluvials, compared with the mines. The general average of stones produced and sold was at first of higher quality, because of the share of river diamonds, and because the growing number of Transvaal diggers concentrated on selling grades of over a quarter of a carat, ignoring chips and smaller remnants, or lacking the technical means to recover diamonds suitable only for industrial bort. When the Lichtenburg diggings were opened up from 1926, the

[9] CAD, MNW 897 MM 2282/27, Detective Department to Mines, 9 Nov. 1927.

predominant quality of finds declined to under half a carat. Earlier selection of the most payable sites meant that much bort was wasted, before the largest syndicates and companies moved into the Lichtenburg area. But the selection made sense for those whose capital outlay included little more than sieves, washing tables, picks, and shovels. The indexes of production and sales also suggest that little was held back from sale by the diggers whose margins were tight and whose need for ready cash encouraged greater activity, when prices fell. Sales of alluvials were less influenced by the recessions of 1920–1 and the early 1930s, as producers struggled to maintain past income levels, while the mines cut back.

As a result of this feverish rush to the diggings, peak production was concentrated in a few years of the late 1920s, when both the quantity and the total value of alluvial diamonds drew level with the mines. Alluvials exceeded mine stones by weight from 1932 to 1935, in the depths of the depression, and again in 1941–3, when mines in the Union were closed down. Moreover, over the whole period from 1917 to 1945, alluvial mining in the Union was relatively uncontrolled, compared with the mines. The annual average of quantities sold from mine production was three times the average for alluvial diggings (excluding South West Africa). But proportionate to these averages, alluvials displayed much greater annual variation, as diggers and the government sold all they could, compared with steadier quotas sold through the syndicate and the Diamond Corporation.[10]

There were differences, too, in the behaviour of prices for alluvial and mine stones. From a much higher base, annual prices for alluvial stones followed a rising trend till 1924, and then began to slide at a faster rate than mine stones, as production increased at the diggings. Alluvial prices began to recover gradually from about 1932, against a continued decrease in production and widespread buying for the Diamond Corporation. Real prices for alluvials declined 1911–45. The general effect of the recession had been to narrow the price differential between the two sources of diamonds in the Union, and this continued into the 1940s (when for a few years mine stones overtook alluvials in average carat values). Again, over the whole period between the two wars, variation from the annual average price was much greater for alluvial stones than mine stones,

---

[10] The mean of sales of mine stones by weight 1917–45 was 1,238,332 mt. cts. and the standard deviation 829,283 cts. (coefficient of variation = 66.9). For alluvials, the mean was 469,549 mt. cts. and the standard deviation 491,281 (coefficient of variation = 104.6). The current price mean for mine stones was 58.2*s.* and the standard deviation 29.1*s.* 1911–45 (coefficient of variation = 50), while the mean for alluvial prices was 108.5*s.* and the standard deviation 48.9*s.* (coefficient of variation = 45), identical to South West prices.

TABLE 9.1. *State and private alluvial diamond sales, 1926–1933*

Years	Total sales	Kerksdorp, Lichtenburg		Namaqualand	
	mt. cts ('000)	mt. cts ('000)	%	mt. cts ('000)	%
1926	3,983.8	3,047.9	76.5	375.2	9.4
1927	6,198.3	5,212.2	84.0	375.0	6.0
1928	5,957.2	2,811.4	47.1	2,571.7	43.1
1929	6,864.8	2,583.1	37.6	3,762.8	54.8
1930	2,861.1	1,463.2	51.1	1,166.7	40.7
1931	1,505.5	775.3	51.4	509.0	33.8
1932	1,148.9	372.3	32.4	490.4	42.6
1933	1,411.0	493.4	34.9	252.4	17.8

Source: Department of Mines, *Annual Reports of the Government Mining Engineer* (1926–33).

suggesting greater volatility on the open market during and after the alluvial rush of the late 1920s, and, probably, a decline in quality as the better gravel runs were worked out.

There is a need for caution, however, in this broad interpretation of the presence or absence of market 'controls' on producers in the two modes of production. First, there was the impact of state and other alluvial diggings in Namaqualand. While some of this output was held back, state alluvials of very high value (nearly £20 per carat in 1929!) constituted about a third of all alluvial sales in the Union 1929–33, and were as high as 50 per cent of sales in 1930. Thereafter, the government accepted the need for restriction, and the volume and total value of alluvial sales fell, while the average carat price rose. Undoubtedly, prior to the Namaqualand discoveries, Transvaal alluvial sales from Klerksdorp constituted by far the highest values. From 1928, the contribution of Klerksdorp and Lichtenburg districts to Union alluvial sales was shared with Namaqualand at a combined total of 80 to 90 per cent of values until 1931. In terms of market 'indiscipline' the state had been as big a culprit as the diggers at the height of the alluvial boom (see Table 9.1).

Secondly, alluvial mining in South West Africa should be taken into the account. On the whole, sales of South West stock came under the same quota restrictions as other conference producers. Average sales were about half the volume of Union alluvials in the period from 1920 to the Second World War. The South West index followed Union mines fairly closely, and variation from the average annual sales by quantity was closer to Union mines than Union alluvials. The average price for South West stones at 91.7s./ct., 1916–45, was closer to other alluvial prices, but variation from the average current price followed the pattern for mine stones, reflecting the same syndicate and corporation control over production levels and sales.[11] (Figs. 10, 11).

As the crisis of the late 1920s deepened, blame was heaped on the 'uncontrolled' diggings by the companies and (more privately) by officials for the predicament of 'over-production'. The problem really lay in production for immediate sale, so far as the diggers were concerned, and in the desire of the state to profit from its extraordinarily valuable diamonds from Alexander Bay, to offset falling diamond revenues from other sources. The companies and the state were better able to hold back production; and, in time, officials accepted the wisdom and the cost of this strategy. But the majority of the diggers did not, and sold whenever they could.

For conditions at the diggings precluded a concerted withdrawal from the market in the wider interests of selling less and raising prices for future sales. If there was any unanimity at all among the wide variety of entrepreneurs in the alluvial fields, it was centred on cutting costs through more efficient control of labour (including losses by IDB) and on the proclamation of further diggings, in order to increase the volume of sales from new, higher-yielding claims. In his early survey of the diggings, Joubert distinguished carefully between the cost structure of the river alluvials and the camps on the veld. The fifteen 'old fields' along the Vaal were settled communities run like small companies 'living in decent houses with schools for the children and competitive stores for supplies'.[12] Work on shares with blacks and coloureds in the Cape diggings probably increased, as costs rose, and was commented on by Joubert. On the other hand, local diggers' committees actively discouraged common law associations with African women, as much as they tolerated both the presence and organization of the coloureds. There were also a few Asians at the Cape diggings, no more than a couple of dozen.

Control of labour on the Cape claims turned on the question of certification and mobility. Black labourers did not need certification and their movements, wage levels, and bonuses for finds were open to competitive bidding between claim workers at the level of syndicates and partnerships. The number of petitions demanding an end to the cost of

---

[11] For CDM see ch. 10. In fig. 11, the wide fluctuations in the index of South West prices in the 1930s arise from sale of small quantities of highly-valued stones.
[12] Joubert, 700; Department of Mines, *Annual Report* (1923), 19.

such bidding in the early 1920s is a good indication that employers did not have a servile labour force.

The labour inspector and the protector of natives in Griqualand West, moreover, resented assertions of administrative control by the Alluvial Board. They dismissed any parallels with the old Kimberley Protection Board (funded from company contributions to stamp out IDB). They pointed out that various pass systems had been tried at Barkly West, ending with a simplified method of charging sixpence per pass for a labourer from nearby locations. There had always been demands by diggers for police powers, recovery of 'deserters', and standard wages. But they stood out against the exercise of such functions by the new Board, and recommended instead increased recruitment by labour contractors in the Transkei to remedy labour shortage caused by the influx of diggers to new claims on Cape farms.[13] The Department of Labour, therefore, set itself against the Alluvial Board and tolerated more casual practices which avoided registration fees in favour of occasional visits to the police station by a digger 'to purchase as many 6*d.* passes as he has labourers each month'. Hospital fees required under an 1874 ordinance were not collected at all. Indifferent enforcement of the pass regulations allowed workers to come and go in Barkly West more freely than in the Labour Districts of the Transvaal. Above all, the director of labour resisted handing over labour supervision to the police, because 'the real crux of the matter is that diggers want absolute and complete control of the natives with a minimum of trouble and expense to themselves'.[14]

Compared with the compound system at the mines, diggers judged the pass system to be 'useless' as a means of lowering costs. There was trouble on the diggings, therefore, with strikes of labourers at Klipdam and Windsorton in 1921 over wages. Bechuanaland workers complained that weekly earnings had been reduced to 8*s.* with food for a 12-hour shift. Local diggers also refused a request from the Department of Mines to grant certificates to enable Africans and coloureds to obtain licences.[15]

The gradual hardening of demands for labour controls was most evident in the new diggings, such as Brakfontein, which was the largest camp in the Cape in 1923, and in the Transvaal. There, the Alluvial Board

---

[13] CAD, NTS 2044 58/280, Barrett to Director of Native Labour, 6 Nov. 1919.

[14] CAD, NTS 2053, Native Labour to Native Affairs, 28 Oct. 1921. Barkly West was made a Labour District in 1912, but some of the diggings did not fall under this regulation where 1874 registration regulations still obtained. Labour drawn from the Native Areas of Kuruman and Taungs had to carry registration passes but not travelling passes.

[15] Ibid., Chief E. Mattaba and others to Malan, 14 June 1921; Smyth to Native Affairs, 1 July 1921.

came down heavily against shareworking with Africans. While the Lower River Diggers Committee was satisfied that their recommendations on licences for coloureds could be trusted, the Board wanted such licences limited in application to the province where they were issued, out of respect for Transvaal legislation restricting certification to 'European males'.[16] The minister of mines, Malan, promised to give favourable consideration to these distinctions in revision of the 1919 act.

This was begun by the 1923 Select Committee on the Precious Stones Bill which met under Malan's chairmanship. No final draft was produced at this stage, but the Alluvial Board representatives advanced their case for a legislative attack on farm proprietors' rights and an end to licences to coloureds and old Free State titles in the Cape. It did not accomplish more because the diggers were divided among themselves on how far the Board or the committees could be entrusted with the task of assessing taxes or issuing certificates. But, by 1924, it was established that Cape African and coloured diggers could not migrate to the new alluvial fields.

Before the diggers' pressure group could enlist state support for further revision of the 1919 act, they were overtaken by the more general crisis arising within the alluvial market from increased production. Earlier records of returns to diggers identified the Cape river sites as the richest area until 1920. The highest price on any alluvial site was paid at Herbert in December 1919 for stones worth 377s. 9d. per carat. For the period 1915–19, returns averaged £7 a month for all diggers and labourers, and £45 a month for whites employing labour or working alone, in all three provinces with alluvial diggings. But the Transvaal sites were making returns well under the average for the Union, because very large numbers were making next to nothing. In 1920 only a third of the Transvaal diggers reported finds of diamonds; and out of these lucky 1,748 operators (including syndicates), 20 per cent did not cover their expenses. Joubert concluded that only 35 per cent of the diggers made enough to live on; and his survey supported the observations of the mining inspectors that 'the alluvial diggers are a manufactory of poor whites'.[17]

To take the Transvaal was to take the worst case; and Joubert did not separate out small companies and partnerships. Better statistics were collected by the Alluvial Board from 1924. These showed that the average monthly return for Cape diggers and their labourers was £8. 18s. But for whites, as employers, the return was £36. 14s. per month, which

---

[16] SC 9A–'23, *Second Report of the Select Committee on the Transvaal Precious and Base Metals Act Further Amendment Bill*, 22.

[17] Joubert, 709 (citing T. G. Trevor, Department of Mines *Annual Report* (1917)).

suggests a considerable decline in earnings since 1919. For the first time too, the report showed that some 12 per cent of employers and shareworkers consisted of 224 coloureds and 87 'natives' as licensed diggers. The report went out of its way to explain that coloured diggers produced a higher proportion of better stones by weight and value; and it pointed to the very low average earnings of the black diggers—£3 per month—despite the fact that their finds were in the higher ranges of carat weights. Significantly, these higher weights fetched much lower values on sale to buyers than the average value for similar stones sold by whites and coloureds.[18]

The Board did not go on to draw the obvious conclusion that returns for blacks were so low because buyers discriminated in their valuations between these and other diggers. This inference would also account for the much higher production by whites of 'small and inferior stones' which were accepted by the buyers, but paid nothing at all if offered by blacks and coloureds. The material was used instead to support the argument that all diggers suffered at the hands of the buyers, because they did not know the current prices of diamonds sold overseas.

On the eve of the production crisis, therefore, the Board examined alternative schemes for 'co-operative' marketing of alluvial diamonds. They took the advice of Arend Brink, the government valuator, who proposed 'Co-operative Selling' at fixed prices set by officials like himself, either to the syndicate or to independent buyers on contracts with penalties for outside trading.[19] The Board preferred more 'voluntary' channels, fearing that compulsory pooling of marketable alluvials would only benefit the largest purchasers and not the diggers who would have to accept valuators' prices. It was revealed by the discussions that there were some sixty licensed buyers in the Union acting for ten exporters. The exporter received 7 per cent on his purchases for overseas principals, and from this he had to pay the salaries or commissions of his buyers and all expenses, except the export duty, borne by the buyers. It was explained by G. Scott Ronaldson, a Kimberley diamond dealer and financier who did not favour Brink's scheme, that if gross profit on the local sale of £1 million in diamonds was around £70,000, some £40,000 went to the buyers, after expenses of 30 per cent. He was able to show that alluvial stones had increased their price advantage over mine stones since 1913; and he warned that true co-operative principles entailed shareholding in the enterprise

---

[18] 'Alluvial Output', *DFA*, 7 May 1924.
[19] CAD, TES 886 F5/172, S. Lord, 'Report of the Sub-Committee on Systems of Disposal of Alluvial Diamonds', 22 Sept. 1922.

by the diggers which meant risk of loss, as well as promise of profits. He suspected (and the Board agreed) that Brink's scheme was

an effort on the part of some interested parties to secure control over the diggings in some such way as the production from the mines and South West Africa is at present controlled. You may be sure once the Scheme is in operation, every effort will be made to restrict the River output as it suits the Government and the big producers to limit alluvials and encourage increased production from the mines and the South West where they are both largely interested.[20]

Coming from a man who was about to pioneer prospection in Namaqualand and go into partnership later with Chester Beatty's Selection Trust, this was fairly sound advice about manœuvres originating with De Beers and Anglo American to buy into the alluvial fields. But it did not help the diggers to secure 'fairer' prices, meaning prices closer to those obtaining on resales overseas. For this to happen, argued S. Lord who represented the Cape on the Board, some way had to be found of checking that the price declared on brokers' notes, as the basis for the export duty, bore a fixed relationship to the prices paid to diggers. Writing to the minister of finance, Lord was sceptical of the modest mark-up of 7 per cent suggested by Ronaldson; and he had no faith in monthly declarations of finds to the Detective Department or even in notes sworn before a justice of the peace.[21] He observed that prices declared in the broker's note handed to the digger–seller were taken as basis valuation prior to export. These notes, he alleged, were open to falsification by collusion between the buyer and the seller for a low declared value and less export duty: 'An easier and safer means of defrauding the Government is hardly conceivable.'[22] He also confirmed the difference in prices paid to black and coloured diggers in the Cape for their larger stones:

The coloured producers realized 15/9 a carat less for their vastly superior stuff (separately classified) and 29/11 a carat less for their whole superior output— i.e. for all classes of stones combined—than the 'Whites' did for their inferior output (classified and unclassified). The native diggers received no less than 78/- a carat lower price for their superior (unclassified) quality stuff, than the 'Whites' did for their inferior.

[20] Ibid., 'Mr. Ronaldson's General Remarks'. Lord thought the figure of 7% return to merchant-exporters too low, but accepted it in his own analysis sent to the minister of finance, N. C. Havenga.

[21] Ibid., Lord to Havenga, 19 Dec. 1925. Even an old digger and dealer such as Lord did not know the Detective Department exercised this function.

[22] Ibid., Lord cited a case of the purchase of a stone declared at £450 and sold at £900.

Lord's main point was that in the open alluvial market prices paid to diggers were subject to wide fluctuations; and those paid to coloureds and blacks were flagrantly discriminatory. Apart from the injustice, the buyer's mark-up may not have reflected the 'basis' price, because of the temptation to undervalue prices on the broker's note. In the case of mine stones sold through the syndicate, duty was paid on the provisional minimum price which changed every 6 months; and duty was adjusted retrospectively, whenever this price was altered by the performance of sales abroad. No such inspection of exporters' books and regulation of the duty was made in the case of alluvial sales to determine who bore the cost of this tax.

Faced with this criticism, Treasury and the Inland Revenue were content to rely on the growing expertise of the Detective Department in Johannesburg and Kimberley to certify that the declared value of exported diamonds was, in fact, the market or selling price within the Union. Suspiciously-low declarations, it was claimed, were investigated. Some diggers, officials conceded, might be 'bamboozled by some of the nomadic buyers'. But they did not really answer Lord's charge that a buyer and a digger might 'bamboozle' the detectives and the government by under invoicing.[23] Any circulation of lists of prices (as the Board requested) was ruled out by the Department of Mines, because alluvial prices could not anticipate London prices. If these fell, officials argued, buyers would not keep to any 'list', and might not purchase at all.

PRECIOUS STONES

As the alluvial sources in the industry expanded after 1924 and more statistics became available on the monthly quantities and categories sold, the South African press took up the case of the diggers. The usual argument was that buyers deliberately defrauded the producers and that average output was not sufficient to cover wages and other expenses. The mining syndicates were accused of cornering the best farms and promoting others to be opened to the public, after they had been 'prospected' by speculators.[24] Clearly, a debate was opening up on the politics of the alluvial fields.

---

[23] CAD, TES 886 F5/172, Inland Revenue to minister of finance, 18 Jan. 1926.
[24] *The Star*, 24 July 1926; *Sunday Times* (Cape Town) 25 July 1926; see CAD, MNW 852 MM 2384/26 for departmental comments.

Nothing could stop the decline in returns, however, as more diamonds were produced than the buyers wished to purchase. By 1926, the farm Elandsputte, which had just been proclaimed, accounted for well over half of the Transvaal's alluvial production for the June period. Of the 6,681 diggers working there, 1,526 registered finds valued at £46,571, yielding £30. 10s. per month for the successful, out of which they had to pay wages for both white and black workers. For the unsuccessful, there was no way of paying wages at all.

Views were divided about the diggers who did not register finds. Major Brink, as head of the Detective Department, argued that the diggings such as Elandsputte yielded little caratage per claim, 'too insignificant to tempt buyers'. The Department of Mines did not believe this unlikely story and agreed with popular opinion that IDB was 'rampant' at the alluvial diggings, and that the size and value of stones were secondary considerations. Brink's argument, however, was really in defence of the trapping system. He did not think, after 24 years of experience, that IDB could be eliminated entirely. The situation encouraged smuggling because of the expansion in the number of buying centres—there were eighty in the Transvaal, half of them at Bloemhof—and Brink had even been called on to deal with diamonds filtered in from South West Africa on to the open market. His lists of these and other cases showed that the alluvial fields provided an excellent outlet for other sources, and that it was very difficult to provide evidence for a conviction, even where 'whole families' were suspected.[25]

Whatever the level of IDB (the Department of Mines estimated it at about £1 million a year in 1930), the statistics of social deprivation, rather than criminality, came to dominate the public debate on the diggings from 1926. Earlier warnings from the Alluvial Board and inspectors of labour that Provincial Councils could not fund the necessary amenities and that deprivation might force 'the gradual stoppage of public diamond diggings' to end indigency and 'the utter devastation of the soil' began to be taken seriously.[26] As a veteran of the diamond fields, S. Lord identified the gradual exhaustion of all alluvial claims as the major reason for the decline in earnings. The old Cape diggings at Barkly West were no exception to the general trend in falling alluvial prices from 1925. Lord indicated that narrowed margins had been compensated for, first, by reduction of African wages, and second, by selling out claims to syndicates and companies using machinery and

[25] CAD, MNW 876 MM 816/27, Report of the Diamond Detective Department, 1926.
[26] CAD, NTS 2203, A. C. Van der Horst, 4 Sept. 1924.

larger gangs to effect economies of scale and recover all the diamonds present in the gravels:

An adult native wage of 15/- a week used to be the normal rate on the diggings. Now [1936] the standard rate is 10/- gross or 8/6 net. Clearly, therefore, it is no longer possible to curtail expenditure and increase profits through wage reductions, since the rate has already reached its lowest economic level and any further encroachment on the native's meagre earnings could only have the effect of aggravating the general position on the diggings.[27]

Lord's later survey confirmed contemporary reports in the late 1920s and early 1930s which described the labourers of Barkly West as 'detribalised' and unable to augment wages by food production. Those who resided in urban locations and worked at the claims also had to pay rent, but most of the 9,000 males and females at the river diggings were in hovels. Conditions of credit imposed by storekeepers turned such workers into quasi-chattels for diggers who paid them in tickets valid only at one store. Work had been extended to 13 hours a day. There were occasional outbreaks of typhus. The inspector of labour recommended a minimum wage. Lord sought more general remedies in the financial structure of alluvial mining by relief from taxation and the establishment of state-subsidized industries and industrial schools.

But why had so little been done for important rural constituencies at Klerksdorp, Lichtenburg, or Barkly West, which were all safe Nationalist seats, held, in one case, by a cabinet minister? Despite abundant evidence of declining prices and general poverty, the mining commissioners and the department persisted in looking on the alluvial diggings not as a source of unemployment, but as a massive opportunity for outdoor relief and resisted all proposals to close them down.

It must be realised that the alluvial diggings are solving a tremendous question of unemployment, and far from being a burden to the State they are contributing vast sums to the Government coffers derived by 10% export on all diamonds. Further, they are bringing in a steady flow of new capital each week into the country from overseas which is duly circulated.[28]

But this ignored the changing sources of production on the diggings, which were passing into the hands of syndicates and companies in the areas of highest yield, leaving the human tide which had flowed in on the flood of earlier high returns stranded in the pools and backwaters of the lesser alluvial claims.

---

[27] CAD, NTS 2203, Lord, 'Economic and Social Conditions on the Old Diggings', 1936.
[28] CAD, MNW 918 MM 496/28, Mining Commissioner Mathews to Mines, 1 May 1928.

In any case, the evidence of the Diggers' Relief Committee, who met with the representative of five churches in 1928 to bring the poverty of the unemployed to the notice of the district magistrate, flatly contradicted the assertion that alluvial claims could support the population associated with them. But their suggested remedies—soup kitchens and the proclamation of more farms as diggings—encountered a lack of funds at the disposal of a magistracy and a reluctance to compound the problem by spreading it over a wider rural area.[29]

Later in 1928, official complacency received a jolt, when the practice of refusing to pay wages due led to the only serious labour crisis on the alluvial diggings. There was a strike by 35,000 workers in June 1928, beginning at Grasfontein and spreading elsewhere in the Lichtenburg district. The importance of this incident lay in the recognition by officials that the diggers had brought the strike on themselves by cutting wages below levels paid on the Rand, the coal mines, and the Natal plantations, or by defaulting altogether. The mining commissioner for the western Transvaal recommended a minimum of 16s. per week. The diggers' representatives blamed labour discontent on the fall in prices, the attractions of 'beer drinking, gambling and illicit traffic in diamonds', as well as the activities of the Industrial and Commercial Workers' Union (ICWU) which had stepped outside the urban centres to organize the strike.[30] They could not pay such a high wages bill. In the end, it was left to individual employers to revise their own rates, and the commissioner persuaded the labourers to return to work.

By 1928, the Alluvial Board and the politicians turned to political remedies to meet a situation which defeated the mechanisms of an open market, the resources of local government, and the charity of the churches. The advice coming from the Department of Mines to ministers had contained ample warning of the impending crisis. Sir Robert Kotze in 1924 and F. A. Nixon in 1926 urged some form of curtailment, and Kotze would have restricted all diggings to whites only.[31] Nixon argued against such a measure on the grounds that black labour was needed to remove the overburden for an early return to employers who could not afford to pay whites' wages. If the diggings were not to be closed down, what were the courses of action open?

---

[29] Ibid., Minutes, 10 Mar. 1928. The churches represented were: Dutch Reformed, Apostolic, Full Gospel, Church of England, and the Salvation Army.

[30] CAD, MNW 935, 'Meeting held at the South African Police station on Wednesday the 20th June 1928'.

[31] CAD, MNW 938 MM 2651/28, memoranda, 1928.

The richer claims might be leased to syndicates and companies, as suggested too by Kotze and Brink. But this would be very unpopular politically, Nixon recognized, because a concessions policy took away 'the poor man's chance and throws it into the hands of the financiers'. Failing that, state mining on selected claims with white labour was a possibility, but only in areas where the state owned lands. Private diggings, such as those run by Lewis and Marks through their Vaal River Estates and Development Company, under a Free State title, employed diggers as tributors. This solution, acknowledged Nixon, if applied elsewhere would only lead to the consolidation of large blocks of claims by owners and the exploitation of the digger 'for the benefit of the capitalist'. Finally, the government might tackle the question by restricting proclamation of new farms and the certification of diggers. This method would encounter opposition from landowners and would run counter to 40 years of traditional public 'rights' to claims.

Whichever way it turned, therefore, there were dilemmas of control and confiscation, regulation, and political cost for the government. The dilemmas were reflected in the long history and numerous drafts of the Precious Stones Act 1923–7. Smuts's government had taken advice from diggers' pressure groups and landowners in two select committees in 1923 and 1924 which revealed wide divisions between the diggers and the Alluvial Board on the one hand, and the farmer-proprietors and companies on the other. The Department of Mines shrank from advising the government to assume powers forcing withdrawal of private land from prospection, and remained antipathetic to the diggers, without wishing to deprive the state of their taxes. Unwilling to allow greater powers to the board to control prospection and risk closure of farms altogether, Malan and the South African Party shelved the much-revised bill and left it to the Pact government of 1924 to find a solution.[32]

A new version of the bill was laid before the House by the incoming minister of mines, F. W. Beyers, in 1925 and ran into continuous amendment and opposition from supporters of the Transvaal Landowners' Association. When it was reintroduced in 1927, the need to limit production was coupled with the need to reform prospection and sort out the conflicting rights of diggers and proprietors. The Diamond Control Act of 1925 had avoided the whole topic of alluvial mining; and the department and politicians strained to turn the new measure into both a control of output and a limitation of sales of claims to companies. Within the department, Warington Smyth also saw the bill as an opportunity

---

[32] CAD, MNW 522 MM 2162/02, Nixon to Smyth, 22 Feb. 1924.

to consolidate different alluvial regulations throughout the Union, on the model of the Transvaal, and administer to the social needs of the diggings by increasing the powers of central departments over health and sanitation.[33]

Whether all this could be contained in a single act was doubtful, and the Pact politicians had to steer carefully between offending landed interests in rural constituencies, outraging the diggers, and causing further damage in the diamond market by allowing prospection and production to continue unchecked. Furthermore, there would be trouble from Cape constituencies if old Free State titles were abolished, and resentment if they were not.[34]

As presented to the House, the 1927 Precious Stones Bill was a long and complex instrument with two main aims which were not entirely compatible. On the one hand, Beyers defended the measure, especially during the second reading in April, by copious populist references to preserving the diggings for 'the small man' and for 'natural persons' (meaning whites), as opposed to corporations. On the other hand, he clearly intended to stop the exhaustion of the diggings by companies, syndicates, and owners during the prospection stage. The bill, therefore, was to restrict alluvial output, so far as corporations and owners' claims were concerned, but was at first unclear whether restriction would apply to diggers in general.

The methods by which these aims were to be achieved were the abolition of the 'rush' in favour of a ballot, and reclassification of alluvial areas proclaimed as diggings. The bulk of these were reserved for diggers, but they lost the system of credit from storekeepers. Secondly, alluvial claims on Crown land might be sold or leased. Finally, state alluvial claims could be proclaimed in areas of new discoveries, taking this form of mining out of the market altogether. The restrictive clauses of the bill were aimed at corporations and diggings on private lands in the Cape. The number of persons employed by syndicates was limited; and prospection on Crown and private lands was also limited. This latter provision applied to those Cape lands where there had been no reservation of mineral rights to the Crown since the 1870s. Henceforth, if they were prospected, the state would take a share of the finds. But existing private diggings on the Vaal were left untouched. More generally, the practice of subdividing property under prospection to increase the number of owners' and discoverers' claims was abolished. As the member for the alluvial district of Christiana explained:

[33] Ibid., Smyth, memorandum, 23 Mar. 1927.
[34] Ibid., Nixon to Smyth, 30 Mar. 1927.

We find instances where a piece of land has been cut up into fifty small portions, and the companies have formed a company for every one of these fifty small portions, and for one of these small portions of land they have issued 500,000 shares of 5s. each, while the whole lot is, perhaps, not worth more than £100,000. What then happens is that the syndicate itself drives up the prices of the shares of the company—we know how it is done—and as soon as the shares are worth £1 the 500,000 are delivered to the public, and in a few weeks' time they are worth nothing, because the ground has, in the meantime, been exhausted.[35]

The sting in the legislation for the companies was that invalidation of subdivisions was to be made retrospective to a date which Beyers later accepted as April 1927 (under pressure from the Senate); total prohibition of company claims in areas reserved for diggers was also made retrospective to the same date.

Opposition in the Assembly was predictable, but not entirely effective. There were accusations of 'statutory robbery'. Sir David Harris rejected the whole idea of retrospective legislation and threatened a price war between the mining companies, restricted by quotas, and the diggers, who were not thus restricted. Sir Ernest Oppenheimer, on the other hand, found the bill 'long overdue' and ranged through the arguments in favour of restriction in a manner which was less than critical, except on the issue of retrospective limitation of company claims and the threat to old Free State titles in the Cape.

More important for the government were the reactions of Nationalist Members with seats in the alluvial mining constituencies. Some of these who had farm owners as well as diggers to answer to were hard put to support all clauses. W. B. De Villiers (Barkly) approved increased powers for the Alluvial Board, but opposed the retrospective action of the legislation on companies, restriction of credit, and any tampering with Free State titles. On the other hand, P. C. De Villiers (Klerksdorp) defended the diggers and urged increased access to claims. The Ventersdorp member, L. J. Boshoff, wanted owners' claims reduced, in favour of the prospector and the diggers. H. H. Moll (Christiana) performed the difficult feat of speaking for both landowners and diggers by supporting the general restrictions imposed on the syndicates and little else. Finally, the perceptive Nationalist member from Troyeville, M. Kentridge, defended the measure as consistent with policies implemented by Kruger and Milner who though 'not a socialist . . . did exactly what the present Minister is doing' by asserting state rights over precious stones.[36]

---

[35] *Assembly Debates* (Apr.–June 1927), 2811.
[36] Ibid. 2794–5.

But would it all help end the crisis in over-production? As the government laboured through the long clauses in the Assembly, a clause was added in April, late in the day, giving powers to limit output on the alluvial fields by the simple method of not proclaiming more diggings. Already there had been an outcry from Lichtenburg, when the mining commissioner curtailed trading at the diggings. A telegram from a local Party organizer to the Lichtenburg member (and cabinet minister), T. J. de V. Roos, objected to the section which allowed lease or sale of alluvial areas on Crown land to companies and sounded a warning:

Party is now in control of the country through the support of the labouring classes who are now astonished to learn that Government intends protecting syndicates and capitalists and to use their supporters as pawns. Unless clause 74 of the proposed law is removed there is a real danger of general disturbance. Thousands of women and children and diggers are strongly of opinion that you should very carefully consider this matter before clause 74 is passed.[37]

The Senate, however, accepted such Crown land sales to companies and added a few more concessions of its own. Beyers went to the Press to announce the government's refusal to accept all the Senate amendments and threatened to force through the measure at a joint sitting of both Houses. Less cautiously, he stated that the main object of the bill was not 'and never was to limit production'.[38] He was to regret this, when he courageously visited Bakers in the heart of the Transvaal alluvial diggings, 14 July 1927, to explain the bill in detail to 'an extraordinarily large meeting' at the buyers' offices. Limitation of output was now admitted to be 'the most important clause in the Bill'. He made heavy weather, therefore, of the reported opening of state alluvial diggings at Alexander Bay, rashly promising them to 'poor people'. (At this, the roof of a buyer's office collapsed under the weight of enthusiastic diggers.) But the possible restriction of diggers' output was passed over quickly with an assurance that the Nationalist government would not take such a step, though a future government might have to.[39]

The Precious Stones Act was in force from November 1927. It consolidated many of the powers vested in the state to exercise rights over diamonds on Crown and private lands, though it did not revoke past concessions and claim purchases prior to April 1927. More authority was given to the mining commissioners, rather than the Alluvial Board, to supervise prospection and decide on proclamation. Subdivision by

[37] CAD, MNW 522 MM 2162/20, A. J. Gouws, 14 May 1927.
[38] *Die Bürger*, 1 July 1927.   [39] *The Star*, 14 July 1927.

owners was not permitted, until a farm was proclaimed, thus preventing speculation in claims. More immediately, all prospection was stopped throughout the Union for a year from mid-1927, in order to avoid making any proclamations if discoveries were made.

There were complaints about restriction of credit to diggers, but the Department of Mines ruled that this only applied to diamond dealers holding an interest in claims. It became established that coloured diggers would be less likely to receive certificates in any province, especially if they worked claims on shares, after a ruling by the new government mining engineer, Dr H. Pirow, who blamed them for 'the enormous congregation of white and coloured people on the diggings far above their capacity, and it was essential that a stop should be put to this evil'.[40]

The diggers' Alluvial Board would have agreed with this assertion, but it was only a shadow of its former self, as its powers passed to the Alluvial Diamond Board consisting of a mining commissioner and only two representatives. The new body was soon at loggerheads with the department on the matter of old Free State titles which it wished to investigate and on the appointment of the chairmen of diggers' committees as justices of the peace. It went over the heads of officials to the minister; and it published its proceedings in the Press. Above all, it clashed with the Department of Mines and the government over the closure of Namaqualand diggings to the public. And in this campaign, it was supported by the Congress of the National Party, in August 1928, which blamed Namaqualand production for the fall in the price of alluvial stones over the previous year.[41]

The government had kept very quiet about the development of Namaqualand; and it was even more reticent in the run-up to the 1929 elections, when the minister of justice, and member for Lichtenburg, Tielman Roos, was criticized by his constituents for not speaking out in the debate on the 1927 act and taking a more vigorous stand on proclamation of diggings. He resigned on other issues and was replaced by A. J. Swanepoel, a Nationalist with impeccable qualifications—war veteran, farmer, diamond buyer, and member of the Dutch Reformed Church. It was some comfort, however, that Hertzog's new ministry retained seats in all the key alluvial districts of the Transvaal and the Cape.

But discoveries along the bleak Namaqualand coast to the north and south of Port Nolloth illustrated the ways in which politics was sacrificed to the need for revenue and co-operation with private companies. The

[40] CAD, MNW 988, Pirow to J. S. Mzoyi, 9 Jan. 1928.
[41] CAD, MNW 1113 MM 25/32. The Congress detected a fall of 45%.

pioneers in this prospection—Hans Merensky and his companions Wagner and Becker—dealt personally with Beyers to obtain official recognition of discoverers' rights in 1926 for claims at Alexander Bay, bordering the south bank of the Orange River.[42] Other discoveries in 1925 and 1926 on farms centred on Kleinzee south of Port Nolloth were worked by a syndicate formed by two Kimberley businessmen, G. S. Robinson and J. Van Praagh, in partnership with the London merchant J. Jolis. Engineers from Chester Beatty's Consolidated African Selection Trust [CAST] inspected and reported favourably on the claims, and the West African enterprise purchased a half interest in the syndicate. A small part of this holding was sold to Anglo American immediately, probably as a result of agreement between Beatty and Oppenheimer on sales of Gold Coast diamonds through the syndicate.[43] In July 1927, the Ronaldson syndicate sold out to Anglo and Barnato Bros., and in January 1928 the joint interests of Beatty and Oppenheimer in the large patchwork of farms around Kleinzee were formed into Cape Coast Exploration, which was effectively run by Anglo, and registered in Johannesburg with Oppenheimer as chairman. By 1929, the company had added to the properties under prospection, and controlled a total of fifty-six farms covering 750 square miles of the coast south of Port Nolloth. A similar strategy was used by Anglo to control output from the rich Merensky claims by the formation of the Hans Merensky Association as a partnership between the discoverer, Oppenheimer, Sir Julius Jeppe, and Gustav Becker on 31 December 1927, which contracted to sell all diamonds through Oppenheimer's syndicate on the basis of a standard parcel and for standard assortments in one of the most complex of all the selling agreements.

Once the news of the Namaqualand finds spread, the Department of Mines was inundated with requests from unemployed diggers for prospection rights in areas not controlled by the companies.[44] These centred on the Crown lands bordering the Merensky claims at the Orange River, and government mining inspectors surveyed the area, keeping their results within the department, until the passage of the 1927 act enabled the state to set up its own enterprise on claims that promised to be as rich as those developed by Merensky. Some 5,000 acres were proclaimed as a State Alluvial Digging, from 17 March 1928, under section 75 of the act, and a second area also on the south bank of the river was

[42] CAD, MNW 811 MM 2796/26.
[43] See below, ch. 10; C. A. Kidd, 'CAST in Namaqualand' (London, 1983). I owe knowledge of this reference to Dr Peter Greenhalgh; see too A. J. Wilson, *The Life and Times of Sir Alfred Chester Beatty* (London, 1985), 155–6.
[44] CAD, MNW 888 MM 1527/27.

proclaimed in 1929. The diggings were run by a committee of management under the government mining engineer. Its first chairman, J. D. Marquard, began production in May 1928 with a small white labour force 'borrowed, as a temporary measure' from the Hans Merensky Association. After hand sorting, diamonds were flown out from Alexander Bay to Cape Town on a service provided by the South African Air Force and charged to the Department of Mines.[45]

The government now had a useful stake in a more valuable sector of the alluvial industry in the Union, which went a long way towards compensating for falling revenue from Premier mine. Moreover, under the 1925 act, it possessed powers to limit the sales of rival enterprises. This it chose to do in 1928 by restricting sales of Cape Coast Exploration goods from Kleinzee to £6,000 a month, and by requiring that all production of Merensky Association diamonds be deposited, along with the State Alluvial goods, at the valuator's office in Cape Town for release to the syndicate as the government thought fit.

Effectively, therefore, Cape Coast was limited to sales of £72,000 a year; and Merensky diamonds were frozen, while the government was free to sell either through the syndicate or through independent channels in London. One of the conditions for a limited sale of Merensky stock in 1928 was that the syndicate should take 100,000 carats of State Alluvial production as well. Further requests for release of diamonds were turned down on the advice of Arend Brink, on the grounds that earlier lots had outclassed government stones and were sold quickly, while Alexander Bay alluvials were not.[46] By September 1929, only 120,000 carats of Merensky diamonds had been released and production stopped altogether, leaving 340,484 carats in the hands of the government valuator, A. W. Powell. After release of a further 40,000 carats, these were sealed up till 1936.

The situation at the Union alluvial diggings by the end of the 1920s, therefore, was complicated by the political expediency of the government's legislation which limited development by companies in favour of the diggers, but stopped proclamation of new diggings for much of 1927 and 1928, while its own State Alluvial Diggings were expanded in Namaqualand. The entry of the state into active production in competition with other Namaqualand producers undermined the efforts of the syndicate, through Anglo and Barnato Bros. to limit sales and bring all

[45] Department of Mines, *Annual Reports*, (1928, 1929).

[46] CAD, MNW (unnumbered) MM 182/60, minutes of meeting between Oppenheimer and Beyers, 30 Nov. 1928.

the Union into a quota system based on monopoly contracts. To some extent Oppenheimer and Barnato Bros., in conjunction with Lewis and Marks and three other alluvial companies, were able to manage the richest sources of production in the Transvaal, such as Lichtenburg, by purchase of farms through the High Level Gravel Syndicate (HLG), formed specifically for this purpose.[47] And for a time, early in 1927, Oppenheimer appeared optimistic that this source of outside sales by the diggers to the independent buyers could be contained.

The terms of the Precious Stones Act made it unlikely that this strategy of pre-emption could continue, and the government was not prepared to lease farms to monopoly companies. There was no sign during the debates on the bill that Oppenheimer foresaw government policy in Namaqualand, but his appreciation of the need for limitation of new diggings clashed with his desire to continue strategic acquisitions by syndicates led by HLG. Hence arose some of the ambiguities in his contributions to the debate in April 1927: he welcomed greater government control of the diggers, but not retrospective restrictions on the companies, at least not as far back as the date of the formation of HLG. The only possible way out, as he indicated, was for the diamond syndicate to buy alluvials through the open market in the Union. He claimed that £1 million of river alluvials had been accumulated in this way by the end of 1926, and that at least half of general alluvial production had been purchased by the syndicate in 1927.[48]

Inside the Department of Mines, the legacy of hostility towards the syndicate was still sufficiently strong, as long as Warington Smyth was secretary, to preclude any co-operation in marketing. Smyth thought that world consumption was keeping pace with increased production in 1927, which he put at about £14 million. The syndicate was well able to hold back a £1 million from resales. Outside production (by which he meant non-Union) amounted, he thought, to £2.5 million, or only 18 per cent of the diamond trade, and was no threat to South African diamond revenues.[49] In any case, departmental suspicions were fed by the researches of J. H. Munnik, ex-miner and Nationalist member for Vredefort, into CDM's acquisition of South West companies in 1919, and the flotation of United Diamond Fields of British Guiana by Joel Barnato and Harris, which promised in its prospectus to increase production abroad. Far from steadying world production for the benefit of all

[47] Gregory, *Ernest Oppenheimer*, 176–8, 216–17.
[48] *Assembly Debates* (1927), 2703, 2718, 2725–6.
[49] CAD, MNW 890 MM 503/27, Smyth, memorandum, 5 Apr. 1927.

producers, argued Munnik, the outsiders 'controlled by Sir Ernest Oppenheimer' were regarded as competitors of the Union, where the syndicate was engaged in 'a pleasant little parlour game' to restrict alluvial mining for its own purposes.[50] The riposte of the government, therefore, was to open up its own monopoly at Alexander Bay.

Furthermore, the Department of Mines and its ministers, Beyers and Fourie, took the view that the whole of the Namaqualand claims were exceptional, because of the small amounts of exceedingly rich runs of gravel. A 'digging community' was 'out of the question', argued the mining inspector, because of the precarious water supply, isolation, and risk of starvation on difficult terrain. Equally important, if the area had been thrown open, the market would have been flooded with very high quality stones; prices would have fallen quickly; and the western Transvaal would have been 'depleted . . . of its digging population with resultant loss to the commercial and farming communities'.[51]

More to the point was the windfall revenue from the proceeds of State Alluvial diamonds under the Financial Adjustments Act of 1928 which paid a portion of net earnings into the ordinary revenue account, and the remaining 85 per cent into the loan account of the Union's consolidated revenue. The unpublished results of this state venture from October 1928 to March 1930 showed that the government made a huge profit by sales through the syndicate and its own selling office in London. For the expenditure of only £421,466, there was a net profit of £4.9 million.[52]

Suspecting that untold riches were being withheld, the new Alluvial Diamond Board pressed in vain for public access. Others resented the policy of limiting employment to 'Namaqualanders', and took the means of redistribution into their own hands. Kleinzee was raided in 1929 by a gang of fifty masked men who broke open the company safe but missed the bulk of Cape Coast's production which had been flown out. More enterprising people organized an abortive 'rush' from Port Nolloth to the state diggings which came to nothing and was blown up into a story of a 'raid' by 5,000 Namaqualanders.[53] At the same time it came to light that there had been considerable 'leakage' from the government sites. Diamonds were found buried along the fence; and production was stopped for a few months in 1929 while watchtowers and searchlights were

---

[50] CAD, MNW 890 MM 1687/27, Munnik to Beyers, 17 Mar. 1927; *Cape Times*, 30 Nov. 1926. For United Diamonds see Colony of British Guiana, *Reports on Administration* (Georgetown, 1928), 243.

[51] CAD, MNW 981 MM 1430/29, McNeight, 19 Mar. 1929.

[52] CAD, MNW 953 MM 1500/301, and MM 1138/29 for accounts.

[53] *The Star*, 13 and 18 May 1929; CAD, MNW 988 MM 1816/29.

installed. For the first time, too, in the history of South African diamond mining an X-ray machine was installed to check 150 white workers. By the end of the year the State Alluvials surpassed anything attempted by the mining companies, with 'heavy police patrols, aeroplanes, floodlights and searchlights' to stop IDB in a total population of 240 whites and 2 blacks.[54]

While the alluvial boom lasted, then, the government took over 40 per cent of sales of this source of diamonds in the Union and 20 to 30 per cent of total Union sales of mine and alluvial stones between 1928 and 1932. It is also noticeable that those who managed government alluvials shared the diggers' preference for selling all caratage produced and holding nothing back in reserve. Although it is clear from government statistics that a percentage of alluvial production was not sold from 1928 onwards, the privilege of holding stocks from this source was left to Cape Coast and the Merensky Association and, of course, to the syndicate which purchased Union alluvials, but could not resell anything like the same volume (see Table 9.1).

Alluvial mining continued through the 1930s with sales reduced to about half of the Union's total sales and revived quickly during the Second World War. When it did, it was dominated by sales from Namaqualand, as the sources in Klerksdorp, Lichtenburg, or Barkly West, and lesser sites yielded less to the companies and the diggers. Like the West African alluvial 'winners' and the British Guiana 'porknockers', the small independent claimholders on the veld were vulnerable in an open market and suffered from considerable inefficiency, when they encountered declining yields and inferior material.

For much of the period they were the scene of intermittent relief works, rather than industrial investment. Schools with soup kitchens (for whites) were funded by the Transvaal provincial administration from 1930. Some alternative employment for a few hundred was found on the roads and in forestry. But disease was rife, and the adverse publicity and articles on the plight of the rural poor entered the consciousness of a generation at the onset of the wider depression of the 1930s. The extent of the alluvial contribution to this social disaster was measured in a report by a committee for the Ministry of Labour and Social Welfare in 1936. There were still 11,000 whites and 40,000 blacks in the six alluvial mining districts, but only 13 per cent of the diggers worked at a profit. The proportion of 'very poor' was well above the Carnegie Commission's percentage for the

---

[54] *The Rand Daily Mail*, 11 Sept. 1929. Detection operated on the principle that diamonds fluoresce under X-rays.

state as a whole in the mid-1930s. Some 60 per cent of Europeans and most of the blacks fell into this category. Despite low wages, the committee felt that conditions for African labourers were marginally better than farm workers. This sanguine view was not supported by the Lichtenburg native commissioner who observed that large numbers of Tswana, Xhosa, Zulu, Baralong, and Griqua had decamped from the locations, which he had condemned as unfit for habitation with high mortality from disease. The general recommendation of both the committee and the commissioner was to close the diggings altogether as poverty traps yielding too few precious stones to pay for the dreams of too many.[55]

[55] CAD, NTS 2203/236280, esp. report for 8 Feb. 1937.

10

Crisis and Reconstruction

◆

BECAUSE of the expansion of alluvial mining both inside and outside
the Union in the late 1920s, the appearance of stability and order under
the Diamond Control Act and the new syndicate formed by Ernest
Oppenheimer in 1925 was more superficial than real. The syndicate
consisting of Anglo American, Dunkelsbuhlers, Barnatos, and JCI was
financially strong and was a major investor in the producing companies.
Participation was broadened a little by allowing a sale of 6 per cent of
funding to Morgan Grenfell and Company, approved by the acting-
minister of mines in March 1926, in order to spread the risk involved
in an increased purchase of industrial diamonds. Otherwise, contracts
remained much the same, except that the basis valuation for conference
producers was adjusted every 6 months, instead of quarterly, and profit-
sharing was in abeyance. Judging from the gross resales of the new
syndicate, there was little profit to share. In only 2 years between 1926
and 1930 was there a net surplus from resales on the total purchases of
conference goods (see Table 8.2).

But if the syndicate could not sell all diamonds at a profit, it could
handle the flood from the alluvial producers in South Africa and abroad,
and favour the better-priced stones of De Beers. For part of Oppenheimer's
claim to supersede the old syndicate rested on his promise of a good
working relationship with these outsiders in West and Central Africa.
For reasons explained in Chapter 8, the claim should be accepted
cautiously for the period before 1926. At most, Barnato Bros., Dunkelsbuhlers, and Anglo had a financial interest in Angola's Diamang by 1923,
though it is not clear whether any sales contract existed at that date.[1]
Some sales were made for African Selection Trust [AST] by 1924,
in conjunction with an independent Antwerp syndicate; and Otto
Oppenheimer made agreements for sales of AST gem stones in 1925,
without obtaining any kind of monopoly. There were 'contacts' with

[1] Compare Gregory, *Ernest Oppenheimer*, 129–32; and Greenhalgh, 230–3.

British Guiana producers the same year, but again no firm control of a highly-fragmented local market.

Only in 1926 was a monopoly agreement signed with Chester Beatty's West African group by Barnatos and Dunkelsbuhlers, on behalf of the syndicate, for annual purchase of fixed quantities of Gold Coast stock at 240,000 carats rising to 270,000 carats over 5 years in equal monthly parcels. The price was still open to annual negotiation between Beatty and Otto Oppenheimer, starting at 23s. 2d. per carat, as fixed by the Crown evaluator for Gold Coast stones, with a discount of 13.7 per cent (or 3s. 2d.) on the initial price.[2] The syndicate buyers also had a right to any excess annual production up to a fixed limit. Penalties in the event of non-delivery arising from strikes or 'native risings' were excluded. It was conditional, however, that the agreement could be terminated if contracts with South African producers were suspended, so as to avoid the charge of favouring an outside supplier. On the whole, the terms were remarkably favourable to the syndicate in the length of the monopoly and the size of the discount. Despite contacts with Angola and Oppenheimer's seat on the board of Diamang, the first agreements with the Companhia de Diamantes de Angola in 1926 were for sample parcels. In 1927, a contract similar to that with Beatty was signed for annual purchase of a minimum of £400,000 in diamonds, limited to a maximum of £800,000 for a period of 5 years with prices fixed by negotiation. Agreements with the Congo companies Forminière and Beceka in 1927 also ran for 5 years, but stipulated a preference for certain types of cuttable stones under a limit of £750,000 annually, and there were limits to the amount of bort and industrial goods.

In all, these agreements entitled the syndicate to purchase up to £2 million a year from these outside sources. Less certainly, Oppenheimer and Barnato moved into British Guiana in 1926 with the formation of United Diamonds Limited, but it was not until 1928 that this company secured the claims of five minor syndicates and was able to exercise an influence on the level of production in the colony.[3] For the rest, both the syndicate and the South African government kept a watch on other possible sources such as the first reported finds in Tanganyika in 1926, which were, as yet, of low yield and worked inefficiently.[4]

The syndicate concluded, therefore, it could contain the outside threat of over-production; but it was less than certain that Union alluvials or

---

[2] DBCA, syndicate 6/2/1, Agreement, 15 June 1926.
[3] CO 111/663; Colony of British Guiana, *Reports on Administration* (Georgetown, 1928), 132.
[4] CAD, MNW 842, Van Eyssen, reports, 1926 and minutes.

later government production could be managed in the same way. Much depended on the financial success of the leading producer in the Union, which was used as a basis for gradual integration into the selling organization.

The way for merchant domination of De Beers was cleared by the resignation of Frames in 1926. Oppenheimer was elected to the vacant seat on the board, but no new chairman was appointed for another 4 years. The deputy-chairman, Lord Bessborough, was a distant figurehead in London, and meetings at Kimberley were usually chaired by Sir David Harris. The important diamond committee was run by Stow, Compton, Pickering, and Hirschhorn. It met less frequently in the late 1920s, as the selling policies of the company were meshed with the buying preferences of the new syndicate. Possibly it was not necessary for Oppenheimer to assert himself to claim chairmanship immediately. More likely such a move would have been opposed by the unforgiving Breitmeyer, who remained as a director till March, 1930.

In the intervening years the annual reports by Harold Barber on syndicate sales indicate that there was a deliberate strategy to build up the corporate strength of De Beers and limit, as far as possible, South African and outside alluvial production by agreed quotas (see Tables 8.3 and 8.4). In the case of De Beers there was a decline in the provisional minimum price paid by the syndicate through the decade of the 1920s, but the effect of this was not really severe before 1928, and prices even recovered slightly in the crisis period of 1929 and early 1930. Similarly, the index of gross resale prices for De Beers diamonds held up fairly well, after descending from the very high level reached in 1920. The percentage of gross profit for the syndicate on sales of these stones was also high until 1929. This performance, it has been argued in Chapter 8, compensated for the poor returns on sales from other mines, or indeed no sales at all. For, in 6 years out of the 11, 1920–31, resales could not keep pace with purchases of conference diamonds at agreed quotas (Table 10.1). But in every year except 1928 and the last half of 1930, De Beers was able to add to its initial quota, under the inter-producers' agreement, by small amounts allocated usually from Premier or South West's CDM, where there were shortfalls on resales.[5]

An understanding of the way in which the syndicate favoured a high-quality production from the leading producer helps to explain the reasonable business performance of De Beers in trading profits and

---

[5] DBCA, syndicate 6/3/1, H. T. Barber, reports; CAD, TES 863 F 5/90, H. T. Barber, reports.

TABLE 10.1. *Sales to the syndicate by conference producers, 1920–1931*

Year	De Beers £	%	Premier £	%	New Jagersfontein £	%	South West: CDM and 'Outside' £	%	Total sales £	%	Gross resales £	Koffy-fontein[a] £	Cape Coast Exploration £
1920	4,507,848	50.06	1,914,645	21.26	982,212	10.9	1,599,849	17.76	9,004,554	100	7,849,873	105,856	
1921	715,179	44.2	266,876	16.6	140,140	8.67	492,513	30.5	1,616,708	100	514,239	35,064	
1922	1,474,667	47.98	522,183	16.99	285,249	9.3	791,211	25.7	3,073,310	100	5,233,266	41,183	
1923	3,722,367	51.47	1,281,206	17.7	570,613	7.89	1,656,700	22.9	7,231,486	100	7,868,925	297,824	
1924	2,666,336	49.88	945,770	17.69	507,978	9.5	1,224,441	22.9	5,344,525	100	9,020,952	211,175	
1925	4,145,770	50.74	1,382,442	16.9	679,834	8.32	1,961,408	24.0	8,169,854	100	7,043,546	313,825	
1926	4,233,926	50.6	1,428,887	17.08	649,304	7.76	2,050,688	24.5	8,362,805	100	9,566,890	267,504	
1927	4,046,149	58.7	708,209	10.27	515,670	7.48	1,620,862	23.5	6,890,890	100	6,804,961	259,262	(211,755)[b]
1928	2,953,408	49.35	1,045,741	17.4	595,858	9.94	1,389,864	23.2	5,983,871	100	6,864,846	184,103	36,188[c]
1929	3,382,379	50.7	983,650	14.76	678,084	10.17	1,617,698	24.28	6,661,811	100	6,363,987	221,439	108,678
1930	1,740,904	54.19	525,468	16.3	305,883	9.52	640,253	19.93	3,212,508	100	1,509,596	168,631	87,116
1931	738,211	52.8	238,004	17.0	121,516	8.69	300,000[d]	21.46	1,397,731	100	1,245,289	no sales	72,000

[a] Koffyfontein sales were treated as Union 'outside' sales, like alluvial production. It is not certain that the syndicate purchased all of this or all production from Cape Coast. All values are declared purchase prices and differ from estimated production values in Department of Mines *Annual Reports* where sales from different sources are not supplied. South West sales are taken from the administrator's reports for the Protectorate and do not distinguish between CDM and local 'outside' fixed supplements to the quota.

[b] Production of diamonds by vendors from 1 July 1927 to the formation of the company taken over by Cape Coast Exploration and sold in 1928.

[c] July to December.

[d] Estimate.

Sources: CAD, MNW 183/31; MNW 182/39, H. T. Barber, reports, 12 August 1926, 31 December 1930; DBCA 6/3/1, Barber, 7 September 1933.

post-tax profits. After the 1921/2 recession, trading profits climbed back to high levels, and the profit on capital employed reached unprecedented heights in 1926 and 1927, as mining costs were reduced (Appendix A.2). Labour charges, moreover, as the major part of direct mining costs, declined in real terms for both black and white workers in all the deep-level diamond mines in the Union between 1911 and the 1930s. It is also clear that the cost of black wages to the industry was decreased more by redundancies than wage cuts before 1931, when there were large lay-offs and the De Beers convict station was disbanded for good. The numbers of white to black workers indicate that the latter were more quickly dispensed with and hardly recovered to more than a one to three ratio in the 1930s. Both groups, of course, lost earnings in the recessions. They can hardly be said to have gained much from periods of prosperity, if the annual wages bill, as part of working costs, is compared with post-tax profits, in the case of De Beers. White earnings at current prices were slightly less than earnings for whites in the gold mines, while black wages were higher (reflecting smaller numbers taken on). To some extent, white workers were cushioned against the worst effects of the 1930s recession by the paternalism of the companies, by apprenticeship schemes, and by job mobility from Kimberley into the gold mines, where the labour force expanded on an improved gold price.

De Beers, then, managed to weather the crisis rather better than other mines, despite contraction of production. There were high returns on preference shares, and the company continued to build up ordinary reserves and keep intact the 'stabiliment' fund used as a reserve for the diamond trade at a level of about £2.5 million. By contrast, Premier mine, which was dominated by De Beers directors, was virtually shut down for much of the early 1930s. CDM had low profitability ratios, though it remained in production and paid heavy taxes to the South West administration. But the company had a very high debt ratio, which was reduced only by a rescue operation mounted by Anglo which bought £1 million of CDM's debt and increased its share capital to £4,480,000 in order to make new investment in plant.[6]

But even De Beers' sales could not support the syndicate sufficiently to preserve single-channel selling. Oppenheimer's claims to have organized a unified policy of controlling outside producers did not include all the Union diggers or government alluvials in Namaqualand. By 1929 the syndicate had purchased about £10.6 million of the £15 million in diamonds produced by the Transvaal, Cape, and Namaqualand diggings

---

[6] CDM, *Annual Report* (1919) and annual meeting, 29 May 1929.

over 5 years. But it could not sell all this stock; and with some justice Harris complained: 'The outside producers have been riding on the backs of the four big mining companies.'[7]

The government and the Department of Mines welcomed this turn of events, but drew a distinction between Union diggers and other African outsiders, whom it was less willing to see saved from the perils of over-production by syndicate intervention. A measured view of the outside agreements was provided by the inspector of mines in South West Africa who had a good grasp of the detail of the Congo, Angola, and the Gold Coast contracts of the late 1920s. L. G. Ray made the point that limitation by these producers was conditional on the maintenance of a fixed replacement level for the Union at or below the £8 million allotted to the conference by the syndicate in 1925.[8] And in the case of the Congo and Angola, basis prices were synchronized with Union prices for mine stones of cuttable quality. The threat from the outside lay not so much in gem stones as in the enormous potential for increased production of industrial goods from the Congo in competition with Premier's lower grades. This weapon would be used by colonial governments, if South Africa could not or would not restrict its own alluvial mining.

Temporary suspension of new alluvial proclamations was as far as the government was prepared to go in 1927. The politicians and the Department of Mines remained adamant on the sale of state alluvials outside the syndicate to London or to cutters in the Union, and refused to release more than small amounts of competing Merensky Association stock to the syndicate. But what was gained in this direction was lost in the case of Premier. By 1928, the syndicate regulated sales of inferior goods from this source in proportion to Congo deliveries, and the change in the sales contract for Premier confirmed the departmental view that the Transvaal mine would be sacrificed to alluvial production elsewhere.[9]

The syndicate was able to do this, because the 1926 agreements with Union producers allowed it a 10 per cent margin (compared with 5 per cent in 1920) which was applied to Union common goods. As Barber noted:

It is a very fortunate circumstance for the Conference Producers that the very large quantities of diamonds stated to exist on the properties of non-Conference Producers are diamonds of low qualities and not of the best qualities, but it appears to me that this fact is based purely on chance and in view of the increasing

---

[7] DBCM, *Report* (1929), 29.
[8] CAD, TES 953, L. G. Ray, report, 16 Feb. 1927.
[9] Ibid., TES F/261, Oppenheimer to Premier Mine, 2 Oct. 1928.

means of transport leading to a more intensive exploration of the remote part of the world this position may at any time be wholly changed.[10]

By 1930, Barber was less worried about new discoveries than the syndicate policy of carrying huge stocks of these goods in addition to the £6.6 million held for conference producers (the highest for the whole of the recession), because the prices of common goods would pull down the price of gem stones if released on to the market.

The Department of Mines was impervious to any of this argument. When Smyth retired as secretary in 1927, he handed over to L. P. Van Zyl Ham a departmental brief which was still committed to the pursuit of state control through a 'board'. This commitment was shared by Dr H. Pirow who had replaced Sir Robert Kotze as government mining engineer at the end of 1926. For these officials, as for A. P. J. Fourie, who replaced Beyers as minister in 1929, the problems of falling revenue, sales to local cutting firms, and supervision of the producers' agreement were best handled by a version of the Diamond Control Board provided for under the 1925 Act. The need for expert advice had become acute, because Brink was now regarded as 'in the hands of the Diamond Syndicate'. Agreements were about to run out by 1930, but the new terms were less of a worry to Pirow than the thought that the government might lose revenue from sales in competition with outside producers. Pirow appointed himself to a Diamond Control Advisory Committee, together with M. Sutherland who had been chairman of the Diamond Cutters Licensing Board, J. de Villiers Roos, Dr H. M. De Kock, and P. Ross Frames, who was unemployed after his resignation from De Beers. The committee lasted for little more than a year, but acted as a buffer between Oppenheimer's syndicate and the government during the difficult negotiations undertaken to save the industry in the opening phase of the crisis of 1930.

The government's immediate appreciation of the serious decline in the diamond market at the end of 1929 was blunted by the need to refer to Pirow's board and by an over-optimistic interpretation of information on the level of demand in New York. The change of minister in August 1929, when Beyers was replaced by Fourie in a strengthened Nationalist administration, did not help, though N. C. Havenga, as minister of finance, took a close interest in mining revenue during the depression.

One of the first actions of the Advisory Committee was to post De Kock to the United States, where he reported that stocks were 'below normal',

---

[10] DBCA, syndicate 6/3/1, Barber, 12 Aug. 1926.

because large amounts of diamonds were believed to be held up in Europe, pending a change in the American tariff to free entry for roughs and 10 per cent on cut stones.[11] The opinion of local cutting firms, dealers, retailers, editors of trade journals, and the Federal Reserve Bank, which was heavily involved in financing the diamond trade, was that since August 1929 tariff policy dominated buyers' orders, as importers awaited cheaper goods. Prices held up very well on the eve of the crisis. The Reserve Bank reports forwarded by De Kock showed that the monthly index for 1929 went below the average for the previous year only in the last 2 months, and the drop was not significantly lower than the average for the previous 4 years. The new government valuator at the Cape, A. W. Powell, who like Brink had access to more pessimistic information from the London merchants, could not persuade the Department of Mines secretary that a fall in the demand for European cut and uncut goods, arising from the tariff factor, was likely to continue, despite the level of prices. Not even the news of the Wall Street Crash shook the department, which advised diggers through the press that the effects would be 'temporary'.[12] Reluctant to believe that anything unusual was happening and with a firm faith in the correctness of its 'control' mechanism, the government was unwilling to concede to Oppenheimer's syndicate co-operation necessary to stave off the worst effects on producers.

THE DIAMOND CORPORATION

The crisis towards the end of 1929 at first slowed down and then stopped sales of syndicate roughs, because the selling organization could not clear large stocks contracted for since 1926. The task of the organization now included a series of agreements with outside producers, as well as the Union conference and purchases on the open market for Union alluvials. The extent of the damage done to the syndicate's credit with the industry was assessed by Harold Barber in August 1930 by taking a long view of operations in the 1920s. From his sources of information, which comprised the books and vouchers of the syndicate for all its client sellers and the oral testimony of brokers and buyers, Barber was strongly in favour of the mechanism of single-channel selling which had evolved over 40 years, during which period prices had risen by 200 or 300 per cent.

[11] CAD (unnumbered), MM 182/50; 182/62, Dr M. H. de Kock to Fourie, reports, 1929, 1930. The committee is sometimes termed a 'board' in departmental exchanges.
[12] CAD, MNW 1003 MM 2789/29, Powell to Ham, 10 Oct. 1929; *The Star*, 9 Dec. 1929.

It was not in the interests of the merchants to accept reduced prices for a quick turnover of capital, because the artificial value of diamonds would depreciate: 'as a consequence of this they would lose their appeal and this in turn would lead to a complete collapse of the Diamond market'.[13] Without such confidence inspired by a large and well-financed organization, small buyers would hesitate to lay out £10,000 to £50,000 in cash for purchase of roughs for manufacture. In good times, with resales through the syndicate at the rate of £12 to £15 million a year, the merchants could tolerate £1 or £2 million through independent channels: but in a depression, with trade contracted to between £4 and £6 million, marketing uncontrolled goods represented a very large proportion of the total trade 'and has the effect of taking the control of what trade there is out of the Syndicate's hands just at the time when it is most important for the good of the trade as a whole that they should maintain control of it'. Prices reduced by indiscriminate selling took years to build up, judging by the disposal of Lichtenburg production for 1927. Barber blamed this sale plus other outside sales for 'the present standard of reduced prices and the sale of the world's output for 1927, and 1929 for an aggregate sum of approximately thirty-seven million pounds instead of forty three millions'. The price fall was still operative and would continue in conjunction with the financial depression. 'This means that it would have been better for the Diamond industry as a whole including the Lichtenburg diggers if the whole output of the latter could have been purchased for higher prices and flung into the sea or effectually destroyed.'[14] That was not how the problem of over-supply and poor prices was viewed from Ventersdorp or the rural slums of Lichtenburg. Barber did not ignore the diggers' plight in this situation, but he omitted any reference in a technical report to the political implications of such a sacrifice. In any case, his evidence pointed to undercutting of syndicate prices on the Continent by 15 to 20 per cent by South African alluvial stones; and this supply was now supplemented to a smaller extent by cut goods from the Union 'at constantly decreasing prices'. The value of resales of conference goods in the first half of 1930 was only half of the value of resales of all goods to dealers and manufacturers, and the syndicate attributed this low percentage to the high quality of goods sold by the Union government to South African cutters from its Namaqualand stocks.

[13] CAD, TES 5/270/2 (ii), Barber, report, 7 Aug. 1930. Barber, report, 7 Aug. 1930. Barber's analysis confirms the position in New York. He found prices in the Union were 13% below 'pre-Lichtenburg' [1927] prices, but recovering in 1929.
[14] Ibid.

Barber's analysis of sales for the government and the producers may have reflected, of course, his intimate relationship with the syndicate participants. But the consequence of holding back stocks of conference and outside goods on a falling market strained the finances of the organization to the point where some restructuring was unavoidable by the time the American Depression aggravated the situation. Harris hinted at the formation of a new buying company in which producers would participate in December 1929 at the De Beers general meeting.

The syndicate was to be rescued in stages by transferring half of all stocks of South African alluvials, state goods, and other outside goods to a Diamond Corporation, written down to a value of £4.9 million. For the stocks handed over, the syndicate received £1,250,000 subscribed in cash by conference producers and shares in the corporation up to a value of £1,250,000 which the producers were eventually to take over from the syndicate. Thus, in Dicorp's articles which accompanied its registration in the Union, 18 February 1930, with a capital of £2.5 million, the old syndicate principals—Anglo, Barnato Bros., Johannesburg Consolidated, and Dunkelsbuhlers—retained half of the capital and offered participation to the producers in a minimum subscription of 25 per cent of shares allotted (£1.25 million). In the event, CDM and Premier had no funds to meet this offer, and De Beers and New Jagersfontein subscribed 90 per cent and 10 per cent of the new capital.

The directors of Dicorp were F. H. Hirschhorn, R. F. Philipson-Stow, Oppenheimer, Harris, S. B. Joel, J. B. Joel, Louis Oppenheimer, and Walter Dunkels, described as representing the five Union mining companies and Anglo, JCI, Barnatos, and Dunkelsbuhlers. Altogether, they stood for a vertical integration between producer and merchant, who shared the burden of sustaining the market between the biggest diamond mining houses, and the single-channel seller. But the financial weakness of most of the producers precluded any grand co-operative 'buying and selling company' in which all would invest to save themselves. The reserves and borrowing powers of CDM, Premier, and New Jagersfontein depended in 1930 on the renewal of further contracts, quota agreements among themselves, and the approval of the Union government for this strategy.

Towards the end of 1929, when it was realized by those about to float the corporation that some companies would not be able to participate, Oppenheimer made a generous offer from the diamond syndicate of payment for advance deliveries over and above the normal replacement of some £3 million of conference producers' goods for the first half of 1930. There was to be a good deal of misunderstanding and recrimination about the precise terms, sent round before new contracts had been discussed and accepted. The offer read:

Owing to the stagnation in the Diamond Market caused by the debacle on the New York Stock Exchange, the replacement figure for the January–June 1930 period will be adversely affected to a serious extent. In order to assist Producers during this difficult period, I am prepared to take from them, in the quotas fixed in the existing Inter-Producers' Agreement, an advance delivery of £1,000,000, half to be paid for during the six months ending on the 31st instant, and the remaining half during the six months ending 30th June 1930.[15]

It was made clear in the circular letter that this advance would rank as part of the replacement for the last half of 1930, if no new agreements were worked out by then. If they were, the advance would be an additional fixed purchase over and above later quotas.

The offer was welcomed by the Department of Finance and the Inland Revenue. But it was treated with the greatest suspicion by the Diamond Control Advisory Committee under Frames. Various hidden motives were surmised, ranging from a speculation on a price rise later in 1930 to an outright bribe in order to influence the outcome of new negotiations on contracts. It was unlikely, anyway, that the Premier company would be able to deliver anything like its share of the £1 million on time, or at a later date. The syndicate members were still the largest shareholders in Premier:

It is almost certain that the Premier will fall short on its contribution to this advance delivery and consequently such shortfall will probably be made up by the De Beers Company and the Consolidated Diamond Mines of South West Africa, it being questionable whether the Jagersfontein Company will be able to deliver its own contribution. The De Beers Company will, therefore, be entitled to deliver £127,500 of the Premier Company's shortfall and the Consolidated Diamonds remaining £52,500.[16]

This ability to take advantage of replacement substitution, it was suggested, would enable De Beers to sell, in all, an extra £637,000 from its stock of £3 million in diamonds in time to show in the annual accounts in June 1930 for the profit of the company and the confidence of the trade.

It was not a bad guess, based on Frames's knowledge of how the company had worked in conjunction with the syndicate earlier, when De Beers continued to sell at a high level through the 1920s. On the other hand, neither the Advisory Committee nor Treasury officials could see

[15] CAD, TES 5/132, Oppenheimer to Premier Mine, 27 Dec. 1929.
[16] Ibid., Diamond Control Advisory Committee, 27 Feb. 1930.

any reason for disapproval of Oppenheimer's offer by Fourie. Indeed, the Treasury pressed for acceptance on the grounds that anything was better than retrenchment and loss of taxes. Accordingly, Van Zyl Ham replied for the Department of Mines to De Beers and other mining companies that Fourie consented to the advance delivery and payment, provided it was regarded as an outright and extra sale, irrespective of new sales agreements, and that it should be conducted 'quite independent of the Premier Company's position'.[17]

Oppenheimer immediately withdrew the offer on 18 March, and a stiffly-worded letter arrived at the Department of Mines from De Beers threatening closures in the absence of additional income. On behalf of the producers the company also protested at any delay in official approval of the new sales contracts agreed with the syndicate in February at a conference in Cape Town. That meeting had taken place in the knowledge that the volume of conference trade had been no more than £3,090,000 for the last half of 1929, and no more than £2,121,600 was allowed on the replacement formulas for the first half of 1930. It had also been laid down that the proportion by value of conference to outside purchases would be roughly at five to three, as in 1929. The advance delivery would have raised this share considerably for the South African mines. Syndicate stocks at the end of 1929 stood at £4.2 million for the four South African companies and £7.9 million for outside goods including the Merensky Association (£2.7 million), government state alluvials (£1.3 million) and other producers from South West, West Africa, and the Congo (£3.9 million). The syndicate (and the new corporation) were prepared, by the advance delivery, to take £3.2 million for early 1930, as against only £1.2 million in diamonds from Union alluvial mines and outside producers. In effect, the syndicate offered to cut back proportionately on both outsiders and Union producers, but gave the Union mines a 'bonus' through the advance.[18]

Apart from the fact that such a 'bonus' probably went against the understanding on overall quotas between the Union and outsiders in the Angola and Congo agreements with the syndicate, it left the government as an extra participant in a conference to which it did not subscribe. The offer also favoured Premier's low-quality goods against Congo alluvials. The Treasury saw this point; but the Department of Mines did not, fixing instead on the narrow fact that Premier would not be working to full

---

[17] CAD, TES 5/132, Van Zyl Ham to De Beers, 15 Mar. 1930.

[18] Syndicate sales of outside goods for the last half of 1929 were £1,768,000 (37% of total sales) compared with £2,644,000 for conference producers and £273,000 for the government; CAD (unnumbered), MM 182/32, Oppenheimer to Mines, 27 Jan. 1930.

capacity and would have to lay off labour and lose the government revenue.

To show they meant the threat of closures, the syndicate directors stopped work at Jagersfontein from April 1930. A High Court action to counter this was considered, but rejected in the Department of Mines; and a trial of strength between Fourie and Sir David Harris over allocation of the mine's quota ended in a confession of the government's inability to settle this in favour of alluvial diggers or CDM.[19]

When the offer to take an advance delivery from all mines was renewed in April, the department accepted, but it still attached conditions designed to make Premier a special case by keeping a maximum number of work shifts operating which the corporation refused. Approval of the new sales agreements was delayed again, when it became known that Premier would only get 8.9 per cent instead of 18 per cent of the Union producers' allocation. If there was insufficient income for this mine, the government would either have to agree to closure (with all the political consequences that entailed) or find a subsidy from Trading Funds, as had happened in the past. The Treasury opposed any policy leading to a permanent charge of this kind. When this was put to Fourie, he came to agree with Oppenheimer that the Diamond Corporation would take sufficient stock from Premier during 1931 to pay for working expenses, without insisting on a higher quota. In the Department of Mines, officials still suspected that directors of Premier aimed at keeping the mine working only in order to prove it unpayable and unworkable.[20]

For the full year 1930, the syndicate and the Diamond Corporation took £3.5 million from conference producers and £2.6 million from the outsiders, but stocks had been reduced very little. The first report of the corporation showed a gross profit of £94,606 and net profit of only £8,909. Stock in hand at the end of the year for the corporation's holdings of outside diamonds had increased to £9.2 million compared with £7.8 million for 1929 in Union alluvials and other African production, Marensky Association diamonds, and government diamonds. On 24 December capital was increased by creation of 2,500,000 new shares in order to take over all the syndicate's stocks and become the sole distributor. These stocks were revalued at £4.9 million and the corporation issued the equivalent sum in 5½ per cent debentures redeemable in 10 years. The situation, then, was that the corporation had paid for its transfer of diamonds from the syndicate in debentures and in shares which

---

[19] CAD, MNW 1025, New Jagersfontein to Mines, 24 Apr. 1930.
[20] Ibid., McNeight to Ham, 5 Dec. 1930.

producers agreed to purchase within 5 years.[21] The cash subscription by the producers at £2.5 million was mostly paid by De Beers. After this, the corporation was left with a working capital of £100,000, on which it had made a small profit at the end of the first year. Altogether, the corporation had taken over £12.2 million accumulated stocks by the end of 1930 revalued and written down well below their cost to the syndicate.[22]

In 1931, representatives of the producers, the syndicate, and the new corporation met in London, and it was agreed in contracts signed on 13 and 19 December that the merchants would take a minimum of £1.2 million for each half year up to a maximum of £4 million for the year. It was understood that producers lost their right to replacements on the scale of July–December 1930 purchases and sales.

The rules had been changed and the replacement mechanism suspended in favour of a fixed purchase to be shared by all. It was later argued by the Diamond Corporation that Fourie and his officials fully understood this change which was embodied in the new sales agreements for 1931–4 and approved by the Executive Council in December 1930.[23] It was also claimed that Fourie agreed not to make any demands for right of delivery from Premier under the old sales agreements at a conference with corporation representatives in December. In other words, the new minimum/maximum quota was a substitution for, not an addition to, the old delivery scales, so far as the conference producers' mines were concerned.

The Diamond Control Advisory Committee contested this view on the grounds that the new agreements were not properly in force until signed by the governor-general. Worse for the corporation, the minister's approval of the debenture trust deed, necessary as payment to the syndicate for taking over all stocks of diamonds, was also delayed. The administrator of South West Africa had not been party to this disputed agreement. The attorney-general found that the minister of mines could not release the syndicate from any obligation to sell for this official, who exercised the functions of the Regie. Anglo's CDM could not negotiate this release on its own. The effect of this judgement was to hold the syndicate to taking CDM's share of the extra offer of an advance delivery in 1930.

---

[21] CAD (unnumbered), MM 182/39, 'Report of the Directors', 16 June 1931. By the terms of the trust deed of the corporation, payments for debentures were spread: DBC 32½%; Barnatos 22½%; CDM 12½%; Anglo 12½%; Dunkelsbuhler 12½%; New Jagersfontein 5%; JCI 2½%. For the position regarding Merensky diamonds see ch. 9.

[22] CO, BT 11/2726, Bliss, App., p. xxx.

[23] CAD (unnumbered), MM 182/29, Diamond Corporation to Mines, 19 Feb. 1931.

Dicorp now issued an ultimatum threatening to regard the new agreements as invalid unless ratified before the end of April. There would be no advance payments, though an advance delivery from Premier would be accepted to keep the mine ticking over. Much was made of the decline of the European banks' confidence in the Union.[24] Rifts now appeared in the once solid front offered by the Department of Mines and the South West administration which complained that government alluvial production was favoured, while cut-backs had led to unemployment on CDM mines. The Department of Mines denied possessing a special reserved quota, other than an allowance for sales to South African cutters of £375,000 every 6 months. The administrator was told the agreements would be ratified.

The recriminations continued throughout April with accusations from Dicorp of departmental lies and argument as to whether the debenture trust deed came under Union or European commercial law. By May 1931, the depression overshadowed everything else. There was an angry conference on 5 May between Dicorp, De Beers, and departmental representatives at which Oppenheimer complained of 'nasty things' said about Anglo and himself, 'insults' from the Advisory 'Board' run by the ex-minister Beyers and Frames, ending with a threat to 'leave the industry'.[25] Less personally, he enlightened Fourie as to the condition of the European diamond market, undercut by cheaper South African stones (which he blamed for a fall in De Beers shares) and losses sustained by writing down stocks transferred to Dicorp.

Fourie professed himself to be 'absolutely astonished' at this outburst. But he conceded a number of important points: a separate selling agency for government polished stones and roughs would keep to 'London parity' in co-operation with Dicorp. He denied he had agreed to release the syndicate from the replacements based on sales for 1930, and made it clear that the more fundamental worry for the government was competition with other African outside diamonds even in the fixed proportion of purchases accepted by the Union conference. He consented to the new agreements of December, as far as producers in the Union were concerned. Most important for the Diamond Corporation, Fourie agreed to sanction the debenture deed for the date of issue— only 6 days away. But he would not agree to push the administrator to release the syndicate from its obligation to take extra deliveries for 1930, and Oppenheimer left the meeting unsatisfied on this point.

[24] Ibid., Diamond Corporation to Mines, telegram, 15 Apr. 1931.

[25] Ibid., 'Memoranda re Diamond Agreements', 5 May 1931. Also present at this scene were: Stow, Friel, Gratton, and (ironically) Kotze for the corporation and De Beers; Fourie, Pirow and McNeight for Mines.

Others were dissatisfied too. Barnatos threatened to withdraw from the corporation ('We are fed up', complained Joel); and further personal discussions were required between Oppenheimer, the administrator of South West Africa, and Fourie, in May, when all agreements were sent to the governor-general for signature. To prevent misunderstanding, a memorandum outlined the results of the battle. This accepted the new guaranteed minimum purchase of £2.4 million for 1931 and a method of spreading payments monthly by bills on the corporation. This facility for discounts was backed by Rothschilds who allowed payments by 90 days bills to producers instead of the usual cash settlements on sale. Premier was kept going by advance payments in return for reduced working; the minister sanctioned the cancellation of 1930 deliveries by South West Africa.[26] The administrator accepted the terms of this agreement. In return, Dicorp offered to 'do something' for South West, perhaps an extra £150,000 in diamond purchases.

Why did the minister give way? Fourie's procrastination and eventual consent to the terms offered by the Diamond Corporation covered an intense debate between his ministry and the Department of Finance on how to safeguard revenue from diamond mining, without sacrificing the weakest mine in the process. Was the government's stake in Premier worth the cost of damage to the new buying organization? From 1922, the Union government enjoyed very high revenue from the industry compared with gold mining, which is a reflection of the profitability of the leading producers and the tenacity of the Inland Revenue in extracting the export duty on all classes of stones sold through the records of the Diamond Detective Department. In addition to the dividend tax, income tax on companies, export duty, and a share of profits from Premier, the government drew an additional and spectacular profit from the sale of state alluvial diamonds from 1929. In all, diamond receipts accounted for 5 or 6 per cent of ordinary revenue and considerable credits were made over to the loan account (Appendix A. 5). There were 6 years in the 1920s when ordinary diamond revenue exceeded state revenues from gold mining. The Department of Finance and the auditor-general fully understood the plight of Premier.[27] And they were equally anxious to keep up the mining revenue of South West Africa, where CDM and the small outsiders contributed about half the ordinary revenue of the Mandate till 1927, after which there was a disastrous decline. But they were less

---

[26] CAD (unnumbered), MM 182/29, 'Memorandum', 18 May 1931, and the more circumspect press release, *The Cape Times*, 19 May 1931.

[27] *Reports of the Controller and Auditor-General* (Pretoria 1927/8), 1021.

intransigent in doing business with the corporation, in order to preserve whatever the export of diamonds could contribute.

Uncontrolled alluvial production was seen, therefore, as a threat to public revenues, because the diggers' export duty in no way compensated for the losses to the mining companies and the possible collapse of the diamond market. The inspector of mines in South West Africa had perceived that this threat was a matter 'which affects the Treasury more closely than any other department of State' and sent his reports on the deterioration of South West revenues directly to Havenga.[28] In the stalemate which followed the Oppenheimer offer in December 1929, the Department of Finance and the Inland Revenue were appalled at the obstinacy of their colleagues in the Department of Mines. For different reasons, Sir David Harris also intrigued with Havenga, threatening to close New Jagersfontein; the secretary of finance warned that the Treasury was unable to estimate revenue from diamond mining for the financial year 1930/1; and the minister of mines was told not to count on any funds to keep Premier going as had happened in the past. Frustrated by the delay in reaching a clear decision on the relationship between the Diamond Corporation and the government, the Inland Revenue protested at the 'almost wanton sacrifice of an assured revenue', and Premier's directors (all De Beers men) petitioned officials in Finance to persuade Havenga 'to check the mad career of the Mines Department whose minister and his advisers are doing their best to run the Premier Company on the rocks'.[29]

In the end, it was brought home to Fourie by Havenga and his officials that alluvial competition which could be checked under the 1927 act but not stopped, for political reasons, would mean the loss of Premier. By 1931, when Fourie agreed to the corporation's terms, much more was at stake. After talks with Dickenson, representing Dicorp, in July 1931, the commissioner of the Inland Revenue, A. F. Corbett, took the unusual step of recommending relief from the diamond export duty, in order to keep the corporation going. This could only be done, he argued, by assisting Dicorp to send abroad £2.7 million in those classes of stones which were still saleable in London, 'to keep the Market active and effect all the sales possible (for the future advantage of the producers by way of quota) . . . But they cannot export without payment of export duty and so serious is the financial position of the Corporation that they

---

[28] CAD, TES 953 F 5/251, L. G. Ray to Finance, 10 Mar. 1927.
[29] Ibid., TES F 5/312, Inland Revenue to Mines, 21 June 1930; Edington to Farrer, 29 Jan. 1931.

cannot find the funds to pay that duty.' The ailing corporation, in short, would be allowed to defer payment of £270,000 until diamonds were sold. The government would get its money eventually, or it would get no export duty at all: 'For if the Corporation cannot find the means of paying export duty, it will not export.'[30]

Such a step, however, was in conflict with the law under the 1917 act on diamond exports; and Corbett risked being held personally responsible for any registration of exports without payment. He would do it only with Executive Council direction and indemnifying legislation in the next Session of Parliament. Accordingly, an agreement was signed with Oppenheimer and A. C. Wilson for Dicorp which was further favoured by paying the duty eventually in sterling at a discount of 25 per cent against the South African pound (after Britain had left the gold standard). A Financial Adjustments Act in 1932 covered Corbett's action and was passed without much comment, unnoticed by the alluvial diggers and supporters of the government, and without revealing that it was the Diamond Corporation that was being assisted.[31]

Despite long statements by Oppenheimer at De Beers' general meetings and to the press on reorganization and government co-operation, the department regarded the whole business as a tactical defeat, rather than the beginnings of a reconciliation between state and private industry. Fourie remained unreconciled to the predominance of De Beers in the new structure. The fact that the Congo and Angola companies agreed to suspend deliveries from July 1931 did nothing to lessen the political damage to the Pact arising from retrenchments in the Union. As commodity prices for wool and maize worsened and South Africa remained on the gold standard, losing millions from the flight of capital overseas in anticipation of a change of financial policy, De Beers was regarded as vulnerable but large enough to destroy lesser mining communities built around Premier, New Jagersfontein, and Koffyfontein. The remedy, according to Van Zyl Ham, was to increase production from the State Alluvial Diggings, 'either by an increase of personnel or the employment of long-term convict labour, or even by allowing approved persons to start operations in Namaqualand on a scale that would provide employment to a sufficient extent to compensate for the unemployment' at the pipe mines.[32]

The most the department got, however, at a period of financial stringency, was an agreement with Dicorp to continue purchasing on the

---

[30] CAD, TES F 5/317, Corbett, 'The Diamond Industry and Export Duty', 15 July 1931.
[31] *Assembly Debates* (1932), 4953.
[32] CAD, MM 182/29, Van Zyl Ham to McNeight, 30 and 31 Dec. 1931.

alluvial fields on the same scale as in 1931, providing the government cut sales of its own stones to cutters to a level just sufficient to cover expenses at Alexander Bay. In such ways were the corporation and the state forced into a grudging compromise 'with the object of stabilising and maintaining prices' (as the agreement stated). Even this compromise ran into difficulties, because Dicorp also sold to South African cutters from CDM stock, and these stones were held to be more suitable than state alluvials. Fortunately, the local cutters' demand rose, and the state could not supply enough roughs without extension of the prospection area in Namaqualand and new investment; and both of those factors ran counter to budget restriction and restriction of new claims.[33]

THE COST OF CO-OPERATION

The cut-backs were severe. For 1932 and 1933, the index of production from Union diamond mines was lower than any period after amalgamation in the 1880s. Premier, Jagersfontein, and Dutoitspan were closed except for maintenance in 1931, followed by Wesselton, Bultfontein, and Cape Coast (Kleinzee) in 1932. CDM stopped work at Elizabeth Bay, but continued exploration and development at Oranjemund. Until 1934, the Union producers met any quotas arising from sales from their accumulated stocks. Quotas purchased under the 1931–4 agreements dwindled to a mere £1 million in 1932 with a devaluation of 5 per cent for payment in sterling. There were losses on resales of all producers' goods over this period, and losses on the £5.6 million conference stocks in London which were valued in sterling.[34]

Consequently, the net profit shown by Dicorp for 1932 was still low, at just under £300,000 and included revaluation of stock, following South Africa's departure from the gold standard. The corporation was really propped up by the producers during its first 4 years (and, therefore, by De Beers). This was done in a number of ways. The minimum purchase obligation was ignored by postponing deliveries. Payments from the corporation were deferred, more especially to De Beers, which was owed £1.4 million by the end of 1933. The members of the old syndicate accepted a delay in payment of interest on their debentures. And the outside producers in West and Central Africa accepted reductions in their

[33] Ibid., MM 182/44, McNeight to Pirow, 5 Sept. 1931; General Manager, State Alluvial Diggings to Mines, 22 Jan. 1932.

[34] Ibid., MM 182/31, Barber, reports for 1931 and 1932.

TABLE 10.2. *Diamond Corporation and Diamond Trading Company sales, 1933–1943*

Years	Total resales (£'000)	Union and South West Africa (£'000)	2 as % of 1
	1	2	
1933	3,396.7	1,918.0	56.4
1934	3,719.2	2,942.7	79.1
1935	6,325.0	3,482.8	55.8
1936	8,456.6	4,142.3	48.9
1937	9,151.2	4,869.1	53.2
1938	3,673.9	1,606.5	43.7
1939	5,864.7	2,124.2	36.2
1940	6,144.3	3,018.0	49.1
1941	7,414.4	3,793.0	51.1
1942	10,694.6	3,505.0	32.7
1943	20,400.1	5,644.0	27.6

Source: BT, 11/2726, Bliss report, Appendix xxxiv; CAD, MM 182/37; and for slightly different totals, MM 182/108. In 1931 the conference had 54% of total sales of £2,319,682. Complete data for 1932 are not available but on ten months' sales valued at £2,854,000, only 23 per cent of conference goods were sold. Only at the end of 1934 was there a significant cutback in African 'outside' sales.

minimum quotas. But they did not suffer reductions in sales in proportion to the ratio established informally with the Union; and the corporation turned over a greater volume of outside goods in the crisis years than it did for Union mines (except in 1934).

They got away with this because of the increased amount of state alluvials sold and which did not form part of this agreement. The Gold Coast, Congo, and Angola authorities could claim that the Union volume of sales had to be regarded as a territorial contribution to the world market, including South West Africa; and this allowed them about £2.4 million in sales to Dicorp in 1931 and 1932. But within the Union, only the conference producers were held by the government to be limited by the five to three ratio. Those which were penalized were Premier, which had hardly any quota at all, and South West Africa, which had a nominal quota of 25 per cent of Union conference sales under the 1930 and 1934 agreements, but an effective quota of only 7.5 per cent of all Union and outside sales.[35] So much had the position changed by 1934 that the conference producers had 56 per cent of quotas, on the basis of world sales, while the Central, West African, and British Guiana producers had 31 per cent, and the government, Cape Coast, and Koffyfontein 15 per cent.

The reasons for this change require a wider framework of reference than the new marketing structure within the Union and overseas in the 1930s. But the interlocking investments between Union producers and the corporation were fundamental to the survival of this structure, because of the acceptance of financial sacrifices by the major shareholders. A second factor was the financial strength of De Beers, not simply as a producer of diamonds, but as a holding company living off its earnings from within and outside the diamond industry. More generally, there was an important shift towards profitable sales of industrial diamonds by companies outside the Union, which had a bearing on the use of this material in the Union itself. Finally, the government as a producer and patron of the diamond cutting industry accepted a measure of discipline by its incorporation within the new selling organization.

The sacrifices made by Diamond Corporation shareholders owed a good deal to the leadership of Sir Ernest Oppenheimer, though restructuring in a 'buying and selling company' by combining the interests of producer and merchant was not entirely his invention: with the chairmanship of Oppenheimer came an application of the methods of group finance and technical organization learned from Anglo American and Rand mining groups. The Earl of Bessborough went to become governor-general of Canada and was replaced by the financially experienced Sir Frank Meyer. General Sir John Philip Du Cane (former governor of Malta and a veteran of the Anglo-Boer war) served on the London committee as an influential negotiator with departments in Whitehall and the increasingly important group of companies run by Chester Beatty. Hirschhorn resigned and was replaced by Sir Robert Kotze, the ex-government mining engineer, who served as the most knowledgeable and experienced director, with an entry to South African departments of state. As a further recognition of Anglo's financial support, three Anglo men—E. H. Farrer, L. A. Pollack, and S. S. Taylor—were added to the board. And with Anglo's backing, the board raised £2.5 million in debentures to complete its acquisitions in New Jagersfontein Mining and Exploration, CDM, and Cape Coast

---

[35] *Report of the Commission on the Economic and Financial Relations between the Union of South Africa and the Mandated Territory of South West Africa*, UG, No. 16 (Pretoria, 1935) 135–244.

TABLE 10.3. *De Beers Consolidated Mines: profitability and earnings from investments, 1930–1945*

Years	Return on capital employed, pre-tax		Net trading profit (£'000)	Investment earnings (£'000)
	£'000	%		
1930	2,294.6	18.2	1,893.3	534.0
1931	121.9	1.9	−475.7	738.2
1932 (6 months)	−11.0		−78.0	67.0
1933	409.9	2.9	−14.3	242.2
1934	1,063.2	7.0	522.9	540.3
1935	2,132.1	23.0	912.1	1,448.0[a]
1936	2,959.8	33.7	1,699.3	1,260.5[b]
1937	2,479.1	30.0	1,646.4	928.7
1938	618.6	5.2	−241.6	956.2[c]
1939	857.0	7.7	194.0	759.0
1940	1,333.3	10.5	927.0	537.3
1941	2,255.2	19.9	1,460.8	924.1
1942	3,500.4	21.1	2,304.2	1,325.2
1943	5,240.3	23.8	4,003.3	1,366.0
1944	4,887.5	16.7	3,496.7	1,391.0
1945	7,659.4	37.1	6,733.0	925.4

[a] Includes a scrip divided from African Explosives and Industries.
[b] First dividend announced from the Diamond Corporation.
[c] Including sale of AEI preference shares after reconstruction.

Source: DBCM, *Annual Reports* (1930–45). Profits on investments include sales of shares.

Exploration. From September 1931, after the resignation of Alpheus Williams, Oppenheimer's board appointed A. A. Coaton from the Rand as manager to organize a central group administration for the technical services of De Beers and its associated mines.[36] He was joined by Donald McHardy from Premier, which was an equally significant shift of experienced talent. During the cessation of production at Kimberley, the engineers overhauled the direct treatment plant and introduced new machinery at Dutoitspan, Bultfontein, and Wesselton, though no washing operations were resumed till 1935.

Diamonds made little money for De Beers during the slump. There were losses on the diamond account in net trading profit 1931–3, and no

[36] Moonyean Buys, *Archives of the General Manager 1888-ca 1949 and Department* (DBCM, 1981), 27.

substantial recovery by sale of old stocks until 1936 and 1937, followed by more losses in 1938 (see Table 10.3). Company investments and sales of shares were the major sources of income, as well as the substantial reserves built up in the 1920s, moved from London and kept in Union treasury bills and loans. Funds for the 'stabiliment' of the trade were kept separate and increased. By far the biggest earner for De Beers was its 50 per cent holding in African Explosive Industries, supplemented by a rise in diamond company investments when the market improved after 1936. The Diamond Corporation too began to pay a dividend from 1937, when sales for the year moved up to £9 million. There were considerable changes in the ways in which these holdings were shown in the annual balance sheets; but open accounts, unquoted securities, and stabiliment funds amounted to about £6.3 million in all, and earned 22.8 per cent over the decade.

From these earnings, De Beers was able to meet very large contingent liabilities and pay interest on a third of the shares issued by the Diamond Corporation, underwrite a loan for New Jagersfontein, and accept about £1.4 million in debts from affiliated mining companies. In 1932, in the depths of the depression, all current expenses were met from investments.

While De Beers served to anchor the producers financially, and discipline mine production in the Union, the Diamond Corporation was free to adjust its proportions of goods handled for South Africa and elsewhere. It became clear that a much greater profit was made on sales of outside goods compared with conference goods. In 1933, for example, gross profits on outside producer sales was £634,413, or 86 per cent of all sales, compared with a mere £66,023 from conference producers and £37,405 on the Union government account.[37] For the first time, Dicorp allowed the Department of Mines to see these outside contracts. They were substantially renegotiated in 1932 to reduce and spread out deliveries and payments in the case of Angola, Forminière, and Beceka, and to limit deliveries from CAST for payments to meet working expenses. But given the very high level of stocks held at the end of 1932—£15 million, of which over a third was from outsiders—the government was still worried by the way in which Dicorp accounts of sales reflected greater movement of outside diamonds, at the expense of conference goods. Fourie could not rid himself of the idea that somehow the diamond industry should offer a form of economic relief and social welfare for whites and a

---

[37] Gross profits on resales by the corporation for the worst years were (1932/1933) outsiders' goods: £639,837/£634,413; conference goods: £242,688/£66,023; government: £18,306/37,405. Total net profits for 1932 and 1933 on the trading account were: £440,896 and £529,002, or some 29% on sales.

contribution to relieve indigency among blacks.[38] Negotiations between Oppenheimer, Kotze, and the minister during Fourie's last months of office, produced an explanation for this imbalance which indicated a major shift in the market for diamonds during the depression:

It will be seen that the recent sales in London consist to a very large extent of common goods which form only a small proportion of the value of the production of the Conference Producers and of very small diamonds known in the trade as 'sand', the production of which is practically confined to West Africa and the Congo. The limited market that at present exists for the type of diamond that is chiefly produced by the Conference Producers is wholly taken up by the sales of the Union Government to local cutters, and to a lesser extent by the Union Alluvial production.[39]

The irony of this situation was sharpened by Fourie's suggestion that a remedy might be found in 'an International Diamond Conference' to secure a 'fair' share for the Union (when such suggestions had been rejected in the past). He was reminded that outside producers had, in fact, co-operated in cutting back on deliveries. Any increase in their sales came from stocks already accumulated. In fact, they had delivered less than they were entitled to. De Beers, in any case, now rejected the idea of a conference: public failure of a producers' cartel 'would be so harmful to the trade that the very calling of it constitutes a danger'.

To heal the wound Dicorp offered to continue taking a proportion of five-eighths, as replacement of total sales, from the conference companies, no matter what the ratio of resales was. The South West Africa administrator, it was tactfully suggested, should be urged to fall in line with this. He did; and in 1935 a government commission on the finances of the Mandate had to swallow the fact that loss of revenue was bound to continue, so long as the quota for the territory was arranged on a company basis, and not according to productive capacity or its heavy dependence on mining for exports.

A change of political climate was needed before a new phase of company and state co-operation began. The appointment of Patrick Duncan as minister of mines in the coalition and fusion between Nationalists and the South African Party, following the elections of May 1933, coincided with negotiations for the new set of producers' agreements. These were completed in March 1934 and included the formation of the Diamond Producers Association, which combined the company producers and the corporation with the Union Government in equal membership. Quotas

---

[38] CAD, (unnumbered), MM 182/46.
[39] Ibid., MM 182/31, De Beers to Mines, 27 Feb. 1933.

applied to all, including the corporation, which had a liability for sales under the contracts with outsiders.[40] The government was strongly represented, moreover, on the board of management by three members, including South West's administrator, compared with three representatives for the corporation and the other producrs. The Union trade commissioner also sat on the London committee of the association and gained access to the business of the Diamond Corporation, as far as it concerned the producers. There was no longer any need for an official 'control board'— advisory or otherwise—and none was reactivated under the terms of the 1925 act.

The basic reason for this mechanism was to handle the accumulation of stocks together with current obligations to take deliveries. By making the corporation itself subject to a quota, and disposing of its diamonds as a fixed proportion of the sales and stocks of other members, there was some hope of getting rid of past purchases without frightening the market. The share of resales for corporation goods was fixed at a minimum of 12½ per cent, increasing progressively as sales in a half-yearly period exceeded £1 million. Other quotas were allotted to producers in the usual replacement formulas. These were, of course, reduced slightly by the dual quota system which brought in the corporation stocks for disposal. But there was some compensation in the stipulation that the corporation could only sell outsiders' diamonds up to the value paid for such stock, and any profits on these transactions were made over to the corporation's basic stock in an equivalent value of diamonds. In other words, outsiders were not permitted to benefit from ever-larger replacements, if their goods sold well, in competition with Union goods.

Soon after the election of the new coalition government in May 1933, Smuts intervened personally, at the Colonial Office, outlining the advantages of Dicorp, and inviting the secretary of state to assume powers to limit sales from the Crown Colonies, notably the Gold Coast and Sierra Leone.[41] As a monopoly had just been granted to CAST for exploitation of Sierra Leone diamonds, the Colonial Office looked on single-channel selling with favour, but was sensitive to any kind of holding or influence from De Beers and South Africa over a convenient source of revenue in the West African colonies. Agreements with Dicorp, in any case, required the consent of local governors, and they were equally unlikely to welcome restraint on exports in a period of depression.

---

[40] Ibid., MM 182/37, Diamond Corporation reports and constitution.
[41] CO, 267/641, Smuts to Wilson, 2 Aug. 1933 and minutes: 'Memorandum' [July 1933]. The Gold Coast was not so competitive and 2.5 million carats from the colony were held in London unsold at this date.

For the moment, Chester Beatty, according to Colonial Office sources, intended to operate in harmony with the quota restrictions of the new corporation. CAST continued in this way till 1935, selling through Dicorp, but keeping the company and its subsidiary Sierra Leone Selection Trust (SLST) 'quite independent', so far as levels of production were concerned.[42] From 1936, the contract for sales of Sierra Leone roughs and industrial goods worked as a percentage of Dicorp's total sales with a minimum quota, when such sales fell below £4 million. This proved very advantageous to SLST in 1938, when the minimum of £653,300 for 'serie' goods (cuttable stones excluding bort) represented 17.6 per cent of Dicorp's sales through the Diamond Trading Company—well above most Union producers. A new sales contract concluded at the end of 1938 and approved by the Colonial Office gave SLST a quota of between 9 and 12 per cent with a similar guaranteed minimum. The Office was comforted by the knowledge that Chester Beatty would 'squeeze the last drop out of the Diamond Corporation', and saw no need to agree separately with the South African government or with the corporation which handled outside contracts.[43]

In terms of volume, therefore, the 'single channel' derived goods from two different regulated markets one of which depended on negotiation with the corporation and one of which comprised the Union producers in the Diamond Producers Association [DPA] which took over the corporation's agreements within the Union. The DPA was, however, different from the old 'conference', or cartel, of companies operating under the eye of the minister of mines. The South African state was a full member with a quota, on the same terms as CDM or the Premier mine in which it still had an interest. As part of the general accommodation with the corporation, the government had agreed to abandon a separate sales office and market state alluvials through the single channel with parity prices in South Africa and London. A quota was accepted for Namaqualand goods from Crown lands.

Moreover, from 1931 the idea of a 'conference' of autonomous producers was somewhat notional, as De Beers expanded its holdings. The major company not merely owned the mines, but also backed the corporation financially by taking up most of its debenture issue. These shares came back to De Beers at once during the restructuring in 1933 as a means of settling the corporation's debts for past deliveries of diamonds and in payment for new deliveries. Quotas were set at 56 per cent for De Beers,

---

[42] CO, 852/11/2, Mathias to Blood, 9 Sept. 1935.
[43] CO, 852/210/12, Ransom, Minute, 13 Feb. 1939; draft contract, 31 Dec. 1938.

CDM, Premier, and New Jagersfontein, as the 'conference' producers in 1934, with 31 per cent for Dicorp, to clear past stocks, and 10 per cent for the government. By 1943 the 'conference' (or De Beers) quota stood at 64.5 per cent, and the corporation was reduced to 20 per cent, while the government expanded its share to 15.5 per cent. The partnership was complete as far as marketing was concerned.

While Dicorp continued to handle stocks taken over from the syndicate and to act as negotiator with outside producers, the distributing functions of the organization in London were run by the Diamond Trading Company [DTC] registered in South Africa, 9 February 1934. Its £1 million capital was subscribed by Dicorp, which retained the shares in return for an initial working stock of diamonds. Additional capital issues of £2 million were taken up by Anglo, JCI, De Beers, and CDM in 1938 and 1942.

The function of the DTC was to sell to dealers from deliveries through Dicorp and the DPA which handled sources of outside and South African goods respectively. Old rules prevailed: diamonds were taken at a provisional minimum price (called purchase valuation), arrived at by agreement and then by a formula taking into account prices realized. An additional purchase price was paid to the association according to resales above or below valuation at purchase.[44] Dividends were paid to the five shareholding companies from 1937, and the DTC was reimbursed by 5 per cent on sales up to £1 million with an additional 1 per cent on sales up to a maximum of 10 per cent on £10 million and over. Sales volumes steadily increased from 1934, exceeding the £10 million mark in 1942 (Table 10.2).

After receiving permission from the government to redeem its original issue of debentures by a new issue of £6.5 million at 4 per cent (£1 million of which went to pay off De Beers), the corporation was allowed to take a contribution from the Union producers to meet annual interest and redemption charges, in proportion to their quotas, while deferring payment on other liabilities. This raised the interesting question how far Premier DMC with only a 4.8 per cent quota could be allowed to participate with funds from state sources. The Department of Finance took the view that there was no obstacle to a subscription of £53,000 for the issue of debentures and a half-yearly payment of £10,000, as a 60 per cent state share of Premier's contribution. The real burden would fall on shareholders

---

[44] In the new formula the additional purchase price = 65% of the resale price, less 55% of purchase valuation, when the realized amount was more than purchase valuation; or, 96% of the realized amount, less 86% of purchase valuation, when the realized amount was less than purchase valuation: CAD, MNW 1158 MM 182/37, Dicorp, report, 11 June 1934.

of the other producer companies—De Beers, CDM, and New Jagersfontein. In the end it was agreed Premier might contribute to the debenture subscription, but not to interest and redemption charges.[45]

To round off the financial restructuring of the industry, Anglo separated all its diamond interests under a holding company, Anglo American Investment Trust Ltd., incorporated in South Africa, 20 May 1936, with a capital of £2.5 million and £1.5 million debentures issued to the parent company as payment for these assets and as security to other companies. It was indicative of the changed political climate that Oppenheimer refused to give details to the Department of Mines, but outlined the purpose and holdings of the Trust in a private letter to Duncan. In effect, Anglo's diamond subsidiary held interests in De Beers, CAST, Beceka, CDM, and the Diamond Corporation, and more were acquired during the 1930s. Such a holding in the case of Cape Coast, explained Oppenheimer, 'assists the De Beers Company in maintaining control . . . *vis-à-vis* Chester Beatty'; and a holding of 20,000 ordinary shares in CAST entitled Sir Ernest's two brothers, Louis and Otto, to seats on the board. In time, he hoped, the Trust would acquire a controlling interest in CAST.[46] Co-operation on a world scale was to be reinforced by a measure of corporate ownership.

CUTTING AND INDUSTRIAL OUTLETS

There was a good deal more to restructuring, however, than rivalry between copper and diamond moguls. The creation of a new selling organization from 1930 had been in the main a defensive operation to preserve De Beers and the corporation intact until the market revived. When it did, the share of world sales falling to the Union and South West Africa declined, as the total sales through the Diamond Trading Company increased. This worried the government after 1933 less than it might have done because of the growing success of cutting in the Union and because substantial amounts were earned from state alluvial mining to compensate for the loss of revenue from Premier.

During the 1930s, Union producers and the government moved towards participation in the end use of diamonds. The very old industry of diamond cutting which drew on the trade in gemstones in traditional European centres was paralleled by the increasing number of outlets for industrial

---

[45] CAD, TES 985 F5 323, Corporation to Mines, 4 Dec. 1933; Inland Revenue to Finance, 27 Dec. 1933.
[46] CAD, MNW 1113 MM 25/1/44, Oppenheimer to Duncan, 11 June 1936.

stones. For a long time, the main use of industrial bort had been within the roughing and polishing processes of the cutting factories. Recovery from the depression of the early years of the decade by industrial countries gave a stimulus to the sale of 'common goods' for manufacturers of diamond tools, while the venture of the state into diamond mining provided a new source of supply for a domestic cutting industry.

Such a step had been debated within the Transvaal Department of Mines and in the Press at the formation of the Union. The arguments against local cutting, to be protected by an export duty on uncut stones, came mainly from the producers, who would have to bear the cost of the tariff within prices paid to the syndicate or other buyers. Even mutual antagonists such as Adolphe Wagner, director of Premier, and Arend Brink, valuator for De Beers, joined forces to condemn the proposition. Wagner stressed the skills required (he had worked in the diamond trade in Antwerp and Paris) at different stages of manufacture from cleavage to final cutting and polishing of a rough diamond. Even if such skills could be attracted by high wages and a local apprenticeship system, South African manufacturers would have to sell on credit to the merchant-financiers who carried the trade in gemstones. Wagner could not see why these credit facilities available in London and on the Continent would follow a distant trade to South Africa, where the mining companies could not finance such an industry. In any case, the risks of IDB would be multiplied by increasing the number of people handling cut and uncut stones.[47]

Brink, on the other hand, was in favour of the transfer of a £5 million industry to the source of supply, recognizing the stimulus that would be given to other investment. But there were practical objections. Costs in 1913 would be about double those in Europe, where they amounted to an added value of 36 per cent on the price of imported rough stones. A very large export duty would be required to keep South African stones competitive—perhaps as high as 40 per cent on the local price of roughs sold to the European centres through London and Antwerp. In a period of recession, dealers and manufacturers would be required to hold very large stocks—as much as £19 million in 1908—which exhausted the credit structure of the trade. No combination of producers and merchants in South Africa could carry such a burden. Domestic cutting was a 'seductive proposition, but in practice it is utterly impracticable'.[48]

[47] BRA, HE 230, A. Wagner, 'Notes' [1907]; DBCA, Reports 3/1/1, 'Report on the Prospects of a Diamond Cutting Industry in South Africa', Mar. 1913.
[48] Ibid.

Despite this rejection by interested experts, the proposal retained its seductive appeal for the politicians, encouraged by the news that the United States had built up a small cutting industry during the war. The export duty of 1917 was applied with protection as well as revenue in mind. A group led by G. A. Hay, member for Pretoria, tried to influence Botha to reserve part of Premier's output for a similar purpose. The decision was left to Warington Smyth, who toured the European cutting centres in 1919 and rejected the plan. But Smuts and Malan were sufficiently interested to take powers under the Diamond Cutting Act of 1919 to licence entrepreneurs and their workers to handle precious stones in the Union and to enable the government to direct the sale of suitable stock from local producers.

There were several false starts. Kimberley businessmen lobbied Malan in 1923 for approval of a factory to be put up by a Belgian manufacturer, Jacques Korbf. On the eve of the 1924 elections, doubts were raised by syndicate merchants about the probity of Korbf, and it was left to Hertzog and Beyers to renew official contacts with the Belgian and his partner, Joseph Rosenstrauch. A provisional agreement was negotiated and signed in September 1927 for a factory of forty polishing mills, complete with skilled workers and 100 local apprentices, in return for a subsidy of £30,000 and a supply of suitable stones guaranteed by the government.[49] There were a few mills in the Transvaal at that date run by three licensed cutters, producing no more than £70,000 worth of gems for sale in the Union from a supply of Premier roughs bought by the diamond syndicate. A factory run by J. W. Vermy purchased and cut stones from the alluvial diggers. But the Belgian industry was sufficiently worried by this new development and the news of the Rosenstrauch deal to stage a strike of 3,000 workmen against acceptance of South African roughs with the support of the Belgian Jewellers Association and the 'Diamantclub' of Antwerp. In the Union, the Assembly hesitated to sanction the agreement and called on a select committee to re-examine the arguments. Fresh evidence from Belgium threw doubts on Rosenstrauch's business ability, and the committee rejected the plan for subsidies. Among the star witnesses was Arend Brink (now retired from his government post), who had changed his mind since 1913. He now supported a local industry, on the grounds that the rising export price of Union roughs and the limited duty of 10 per cent gave sufficient advantage to a cheaper market in local stones.[50]

---

[49] SC 3B-'28, Public Accounts Committee, May 1928: Diamond Cutting Agreement, App.
[50] Ibid. 5.

Belgian opponents of cutting in the Union kept up their pressure for a boycott. In Johannesburg, the Diamond Control Advisory Committee issued denials in 1930 that a local industry would harm Antwerp. The high cost of wages and the cost of Namaqualand stones made it impossible to sell cut stones from Union factories 'at lower than stable prices' (though these were not specified). The small number of local skilled workers posed no threat to Belgium 'with its army of 25,000 cutters, its 4,000 manufacturers and brokers, manufacturing over 50,000 carats of rough goods per week'. The Belgian workers were assured that 'there are no black men learning diamond cutting in South Africa'.[51]

Nevertheless, the wage differentials between South Africa and Europe were sufficient to attract skilled men, paid between £40 and £85 a month, or five times the levels obtaining in Antwerp and Amsterdam.[52] By 1930, there were sixty to seventy skilled immigrant cutters who expanded the demand for associated journeymen and apprentices, and jealously preserved their craft union. They were absorbed quickly into competing ventures run by the merchants or favoured by the government.

Not to be outdone by government sponsorship, the syndicate and De Beers set up the Kimberley Diamond Cutting Factory in 1929, worked by the South African Diamond Cutting Organisation (SADCO). None of the Union factories were cheap enough in their costs, however, to cut small stones, and they began to bid for state alluvial stones which were supplied in large quantities to the expanding industry in 1931 and 1932. Because not all Namaqualand stones were suitable for cutting, an understanding was reached with the Diamond Corporation to supply the balance of Union cutters' requirements at a price which would not be less than comparable government material. By 1932, some 400 to 500 journeymen and apprentices were employed in the Union in cutting half a million pounds worth of stones supplied for the most part from Namaqualand. While those finishing state alluvial stones prospered, the De Beers venture in Kimberley went into liquidation, because of the high cost of material supplied by the Diamond Corporation. A second select committee recommended a commercial agreement along the lines of the Korbf–Rosenstrauch proposals to resume operations and train apprentices. Accordingly, the SADCO factory was leased to Korbf and Klein, who revived the Belgian stake in the local industry and took on many of its former employees. Terms of contracts were changed, however, under pressure from the cutters and other small entrepreneurs, to reduce the

[51] FO, 371/14893, Press release, 4 Mar. 1930.
[52] CAD, MNW 1113 MM 25/1/36.

level of apprentices' wages and end an obligation to employ them when there was no work.[53]

After that adjustment in Union labour regulations, most ventures continued to expand, favoured by the duty on exported roughs and by not paying a dealer's commission when making purchases from alluvial buying centres, though there were still occasional closures, as the new industry found its level within the South African and overseas market.

To assess the market and opposition from overseas interests, the secretary of mines, L. P. Van Zyl Ham, toured the European cutting centres in 1934. He found little resentment of measures to favour South African cutters and a desire for price stabilization in the face of production of rough stones from Angola and the Congo. He rejected suggestions for an international system of control over exports of any kind, and left it to the Diamond Corporation to take the strain. He was more worried by the political repercussions of factory closures in the Union, because Beyer's policy had been to build up domestic cutting, and his successor, Fourie, would be exposed to criticism for allowing ventures to fail: 'It seems to me that the policy of the National Party Government was to create employment for these people; they may now turn round and say that the Fusion Government is breaking down that policy.'[54]

But as a pro-Nationalist civil servant, Van Zyl Ham need not have worried. Hertzog's new minister of mines, Patrick Duncan, handled criticism of the cutting factories by keeping to the old political arguments about local employment without extensive subsidies, while looking to the Diamond Corporation for an entirely new source of employment and exports in the expanding market for industrial stones. His department was content to use the Namaqualand state alluvials as a means of supporting the Union cutters by providing selected varieties of large stones sold at less than the current market rate for similar corporation stones. The original purpose of the 1919 act had been to provide diggers with a market at their door. But as the alluvial lobby complained: 'Events have falsified that prediction. Instead of enhanced local demand and extra competition, the diggers have been shut out of this home market by the action of the Government in granting preferential treatment to the cutters.'[55] They were ignored by the Diamond Cutters Associaton; they received less publicity in the Press; and their standard of living was low in an industry in which a cutter's apprentice received as much in a day

[53] CAD, MNW 1113 MM 25/1/31. Dicorp began selling to local cutters in July 1931.

[54] Ibid., MNW 1158 MM 182/77, Ham to Nixon, (Personal and Confidential), 2 Oct. 1934.

[55] Ibid., MM 21/3/35, S. Lord, 'Diamond Cutting and Control', 6 May 1933.

as an average digger earned in a week. The final ignominy was the 10 per cent duty levied on alluvial sales, making diggings unpayable, 'swallowing up the whole of alluvial profits leaving no margin at all for subsistence . . . It is now known for certain that this taxation does fall on the producer.'[56]

Ironically, the diggers were joined in this complaint by Sir Ernest Oppenheimer, who was still trying to persuade the Department of Mines in 1936 that the 10 per cent export duty was more of a handicap to the export of rough stones than an advantage to cut gems. But the Department of Finance still regarded the dwindling duty as a useful source of revenue: so the Diamond Corporation turned its attention instead to organizing a dual price structure for cuttable stones and industrial goods, to avoid some of the penalty on sales of 'common goods' in association with gem roughs.

For the 1920s and 1930s were a period when increasing uses were found for the industrial diamond. World demand for this variety, and the methods evolved to sell and distribute industrial diamonds had a bearing on the construction of the industry and the ways in which the South African state sought to promote diamond sales in co-operation with the Diamond Corporation and its shareholders.

Estimates of the production and use of industrial diamonds from 1900 rest on the definition of certain grades of stones and diamond material as industrial material, usually termed common goods, rejections, rubbish, and bort. Crushing bort, carbonado, ballas, and diamonds smaller than 1.5 mm. which are not cut for gems have usually been classified as 'industrial', or even as 'bort' to cover any material not of gem quality.[57] The expanded industrial use of such material derived from the outstanding quality of the diamond—its hardness for penetration and abrasion, fine grinding tolerances in comparison with steel or carbide, and the accelerated industrialization of the western world from the mid-nineteenth century. Diamonds were at the sharp end of industrial technology in drilling, polishing, dressing grinding wheels, shaping tools, and drawing wires through die stones. For each of these purposes there were many classes and qualities of stones standardized by numbers per carat, shape, freedom from flaws, and sometimes by origins (as in the case of Congo and Sierra Leone drill stones). Crushing bort is usually classified by weight, though there were a number of different 'borts', some closer to cuttable stones and much higher in price than the Congo variety.

---

[56] Ibid.

[57] For definitions, Henry P. Chandler, *Industrial Diamonds a Materials Survey* (Washington DC, 1964), ch. 1. Carbonado is a black cryptocrystalline material from Brazil; ballas is a spherical growth of small diamond crystals, while bort is angular and without cleavage.

The application of industrial diamonds can be (imperfectly) measured by the number of new inventions and adaptations embodying their use and by the rate of their consumption in the United States. The evidence of United States diamond patents indicates a steady registration 1865–1909, at the rate of a score or so every ten years, followed by a rising number in the next three decades, to seventy-six new patents 1930–9.[58] Thomas Edison took out a patent for employment of diamonds in 'phongraphic styli' as early as 1914. Hardness testing became a new application in the 1920s, and core drills and cutters for alloys reflected developments in the metal trades and automotive and aircraft industries in the 1930s. There was even a patent for 'synthetic carbonado diamonds', but General Electrics' more successful production of artificial small stones did not begin until the 1950s.

Estimates of consumption of industrial diamonds as a share of total diamond production prepared by the US Bureau of Mines, suggest that the two world wars accounted for much of this demand. Overall production of gem and industrial diamonds by weight 1900–46 increased fivefold, and industrials increased as a percentage of this total (Appendix A.9). The amount consumed by industry, however, remained very low until 1914, when there was a shortfall met by increased supply at rising prices till 1925. Thereafter, production was surplus to consumption by industry until 1940, after which there was again a shortfall annually down to the 1950s, supplied from stockpiled bort and other common goods classified earlier as 'unsaleable'. The proportion of industrial goods rose to a plateau of about 82 per cent by weight from 1932, reflecting the curtailment of gemstone production in the Union and the contribution of the principal suppliers of bort and low-grade stones from the Belgian Congo, Gold Coast, and Premier mine. All sources supplied some bort; the leaders supplied over 70 per cent of local production in bort.

There had always been marketing problems arising from inclusion of large amounts of cheap common goods in the price structure for diamonds purchased in long-term contracts, ever since the 1890s. The syndicate had recognized the difficulty in sales contracts by attaching special clauses on percentages allowable in the overall weight and value of goods purchased. The entry of the Congo and lesser alluvial producers into the controlled market posed difficulties on a much larger scale, though the old principle that poor goods benefited from gemstone prices still applied. The question was how far the new producers would shake the price structure for Union producers.

---

[58] Henry P. Chandler, App. B.

At the onset of the depression, an attempt was made to cope with the influence of common goods by setting up a new company specializing in bort and uncuttable stones, International Diamonds Ltd., run by Otto Oppenheimer, H. S. Johnson-Hall, and J. Jolis, with a capital of £150,000. The company offered to purchase the surplus of Diamond Corporation industrial goods up to 1.5 million carats for the first half of 1932 at a price of 4s. per carat with further options on Congo, Angola, and Forminière goods. This deal constituted the largest single sale of diamonds in Harold Barber's experience of the trade, and it presented a special challenge to Premier.[59] The exclusive contract was not well received in the London trade, however, and Louis Oppenheimer was obliged to admit other specialists in industrial goods, such as L. M. Van Moppes and Sons, into the arrangement. But by 1933 International Diamonds was in liquidation, and stockpiling continued.

Recognizing that the industry had entered a new phase of competition with the outside producers which could not be entirely contained within the framework of contracts administered by the Diamond Corporation, the Union producers, led by De Beers, advocated a more aggressive sales policy to find ways of marketing the excess of industrial stones. The Diamond Producers Association asked Dicorp to fund the necessary research and sales campaign in the Union and elsewhere by setting aside a portion of the brokerage fees paid in London by distributors sorting and marketing industrial goods, including the Diamond Trading Company itself. This was a serious step entailing changes in the 'realization' expenses allowed by contract and, therefore, required the approval of the Union's Executive Council. The Trading Company accepted responsibility for carrying this project through, and Dicorp promised to send a respresentative, F. S. C. Rogers, to Johannesburg to expand outlets into the drilling industry:

He will carry samples of our assortment of drilling diamonds and also samples of the goods we have rejected from our assortment in order to establish definitely the limits to which we can sort in future. It is also proposed to supply certain qualities of diamonds to bona fide drillers at a nominal figure for experimental purposes. Such diamonds would only be sufficient to make up one bit in each quality, the object being to broaden the basis of industrial diamond sales and completely eliminate the Brazilian Carbon.[60]

The assault on the hated carbonados ran into two immediate problems. The London dealers who handled industrials would not agree to any cut

[59] CAD, MM 182/39, International Diamonds to Dicorp 26 Feb. 1931.
[60] CAD, MNW 1115 MM 25/97, L. A. Pollack, 'Industrial Diamonds', 21 May 1934, encl. in DTC to DPA, 22 May 1934; DPA to Mines, 28 May 1934.

in their brokerage fees. The corporation or the Diamond Producers Association would have to pay for the estimated £30,000 for a 5-year research programme. H. T. Dickenson of Dicorp was asked to prepare a survey of American industrial use of diamonds to persuade the Association members to pay up. Secondly, the travelling salesmen who brought in sample drill bits ran into a bureaucratic maze of regulations on importation and possession of precious stones in the Transvaal. Nothing could be done without an import certificate, a permit from a magistrate, and endless form-filling.[61] Suggestions from the Department of Mines for an 'extra-legal' solution to the frustrations of busy mining men by a simple signature from the head of the Diamond Detective Department were refused by the police and the magistracy as contrary to the 1903 ordinance. A way around the maze was found eventually by registering drills at the Detective Department, and allowing the officer in charge to assume the functions of a registrar (to cancel revenue stamps), before sending the driller on to the Chief Magistrate for certification.

The alleged advantage of carbonados over diamonds for use as cutting agents in the 'crowns' of drills, as a matter of convenience rather than price, was quickly destroyed. When Dickenson submitted his survey of the American market which took 75 per cent by value of the industrial diamond trade, he was able to demonstrate that bort and 'fine hards' were now recognized as equally suitable, and cheaper, in sets on a 'crown' drill for continuous operations. Compared with a crown set with carbonados costing about £400, a crown set with borts cost £15. The conservatism of miners could be overcome and the market expanded by 'stabilisation of prices, propaganda, demonstration and research work'. The same criterion of price stability applied to acceptance by the automobile industry of diamonds for truing grinding wheels, rather than using metallic substitutes. Dickenson concluded that the market for industrials could be expanded by 'at least £1,000,000 per annum' through the organization of a research and development section of the Diamond Trading Company. Increased sales would turn a 'partially frozen asset' into cash; a broader distribution and greater turnover would ensure steadier prices and detach industrials from the fluctuations of the gem market. Best of all, diamonds sold for industrial purposes required replacement.[62] Unlike gems, industrial stones were not 'for ever'.

The implications of this proposal were explored by the government valuator, P. Granger, who pointed out that the accounts for sales of

[61] CAD, MNW 1115 MM 25/97, Mines to Commissioner of Police, 6 July 1934.
[62] Ibid., Dickenson, 'Industrial Diamonds', 6 July 1934.

the two categories of goods would henceforth have to be separated in the contracts of all producers with the Diamond Corporation. Louis Oppenheimer, he hoped, would determine the dividing line between industrials and gems. The matter came to a head in 1935, when the Trading Company raised the price of all goods by 7½ per cent and began to keep separate records for these classes of stones.

As the Producers Association well knew, the contracts between Dicorp and the Angola and Belgian Congo companies contained clauses governed by the prices paid to the association as a whole. The Companhia de Diamantes de Angola, for example, had the right, in the event of higher prices being paid to De Beers and CDM, to benefit from the more favourable terms. Consequently, any fundamental change in the method of price-fixing by means of the provisional minimum and the additional purchase price, on a basis price set at June 1933, might mean renegotiaton of the most important outside agreements. The association (especially De Beers) thought it better that the price formulas should be left intact for the two classes of goods—cuttable and industrial—with separate records and separate deliveries with a definite line of demarcation. Then, if the members agreed, no other explanations were necessary for the Angola Company or Forminière:

They will be informed that in conformity with what is believed to be in the best interests of all Producers, Cuttable goods and Industrial goods are to be dealt with separately, and it will be explained to them that the Policy will be to raise the price of Cuttable goods as Market conditions warrant it, but to maintain a stable price for Industrial goods, by which means it is hoped to expand the market—particularly in the Boart qualities.[63]

The members of the association agreed and so did the minister of mines, Patrick Duncan. A whole new schedule of standard prices for industrial goods was laid out early in 1936, leaving basis prices for cuttable gem goods unchanged. There were, however, some increases in 'near-cuttable' varieties on the borderline, in case market demand required a switch from one category to another, but the price of bort was further reduced in the late 1930s.

So, to avoid a massive price negotiation, it was accepted that there would be no change to the prices for industrial goods in standard assortments delivered by members of the association to Dicorp. But goods delivered by the corporation itself (i.e. back stocks taken over from the

---

[63] Ibid., MNW 1158 MM 182/86, 'Prices', 19 Aug. 1935.

old syndicate) could be delivered at reduced prices for the purpose of encouraging a market for industrial stones in the Union.[64]

By 1936 in South Africa considerable progress had been made in this strategy of persuading surface drillers charting the Rand reefs to use industrials rather than carbonados. A technique of securing stones to the drill crown by a copper amalgam was developed by the Minerals Research Laboratory, University of Witwatersrand, specifically for this purpose. Because near-gem qualities were not stockpiled in the Union, they had to be imported from dealers abroad in London, New York, and Amsterdam at prices only slightly higher than the Trading Company's retail prices. They were usually found to be residue stocks of Brown Melee from Premier, Kimberley, or South West Africa, and from alluvial production. Thus, to keep the mining community and the drillers 'diamond-minded', the coals were returned to Newcastle through the agency of the Producers Association.

To handle this supply, a new company, Boart Products South Africa (Pty) Ltd., directed by Oppenheimer, J. Jolis, H. T. Dickenson, and G. Scott Ronaldson, was set up to collaborate with the Diamond Development Company in London and market at stable prices. The gold mining industry, it was expected, would turn to the diamond drill. Rock penetration had been speeded up; deflection in boreholes had been reduced; and large grade bort was found to be suitable for all deep capacity drills.

In other areas of industrial use, the corporation found that South African industry still had to be 'educated' in the use of diamond-tipped tools. The corporation's agents made some progress by persuading the South African Air Force at their Roberts Heights factory to equip with diamond-tipped lathe tools to turn engine bearings; and South African Railways adopted locally-manufactured refacing tools with diamond cutting edges. The South African Iron and Steel Works began to order abrasive wheels from Kimberley at this date, and the Union Steel Corporation turned to diamond dies in their works at Vereeniging.

A great deal of this transformation resulted from patient salesmanship by F. S. C. Rogers, whose three reports charted the progress of marketing industrials in the producers' own backyard.[65] After converting the drillers to new techniques, he had concentrated on South African Railways and changed their methods of refacing commutators and machining brass, and opened the way for more experimental work on the use of diamonds

[64] CAD, MNW 1158 MM 182/86 Dicorp to DPA, 19 Mar. 1936.

[65] CAD, MNW 1115 MM 25/97, esp. reports for 1 Feb. 1935 and 21 Mar. 1936. Institutions canvassed by Rogers included the South African Railways and Harbours, universities, technical colleges, municipal engineers, power stations, the motor trade, the Royal Navy, Simonstown, the South African Air Force, stone masons, glaziers, and cutters.

for machining ferrous metals. Gradually he educated the railway engineers away from importing foreign truing tools (which, in fact, contained South African brown and grey stones) in favour of wheels imported through the Diamond Trading Company. By the end of 1936, reported Rogers, 'through the general revival of industry the use of industrial diamonds has become substantially extended and now almost the entire range of the South African industrial production can be placed in different spheres of industry with comparative ease'.

The significance of this breakthrough should not be overestimated, in terms of its impact on the local diamond trade. Diamond Trading Company direct sales of industrial goods in South Africa hardly reached more than 5,000 carats a year in the late 1930s, and values of such sales were well below sales of stones to the manufacturers of gems. But a certain amount was also reimported in the form of industrial tools; and the local sales removed a considerable quantity of South African 'common goods' from the competition of overseas sales. Furthermore, as the industrial trade grew, the cost of financing research was taken out of the hands of the Producers Association by Boart Products which paid for marketing out of profits. There still remained the problem of finding outlets for crushable bort, and there was little sign that the technology of diamond-bonded abrasives or diamond-impregnated metals in any way reduced the accumulated stocks of this material held by producers and by the Diamond Corporation prior to the Second World War.

In a review of the trade for the Producers Association at the end of the decade in 1939, Sir Ernest Oppenheimer attributed the survival of the Diamond Corporation to the transfer of ownership from London merchants to South African producers and corporations. This transfer had enabled the producers to fund the Trading Company which had been under-capitalized with an extra £2 million, at a time when money was needed to handle the flow of industrial material on the London market for the United States and Europe. At the same time, outside contracts became less of a burden to the corporation, because from 1938 the obligation to sell minimum amounts for CAST and SLST was changed to a percentage of total producers' sales, as in the case of purchases from Angola and Forminière. There was a safeguard for SLST, if total sales fell below £4 million, but this did not have to be applied in the improving market of the late 1930s. Moreover, some of the burden of handling the industrial series and bort was shared with SLST which kept unsold stock in West Africa or in London. Similarly, the very large quantities of Beceka industrial goods were contained by stockpiling in the Congo. Most importantly, the South

African government no longer insisted on a strict interpretation of a five to three proportion of conference to outside sales, recognizing that regional contributions to the world market could not be managed in this rigid way. Having begun the decade at loggerheads over approval of contracts and the corporation's articles of association, the government was now judged to be 'extraordinarily reasonable'.[66]

[66] CAD, MNW 1117 MM 182/98, 'Review of the Diamond Trade', 2 Mar. 1939; CO, 852/210/12, Mathias to Crown Agents, 3 Feb. 1939 (for changes in the West African contracts).

11

Strategic Mineral

◆

THE importance of industrial diamonds during the period of rapid rearmament in the late 1930s was well recognized by British government departments. The Food (Defence Plans) Department and the Foreign Office studied ways of denying iron ore and other minerals, including precious stones, to Germany in the event of war.[1] The results of these investigations were passed to the Board of Trade, which began to consider controlling the diamond market through London well in advance of hostilities.

The Board made its preparations by closely analysing and following the precedents of the First World War, assisted by memoranda on the strengths and weaknesses of the committee set up by Mosely. The primary purpose of this early planning in March 1939 was to stop supplies of industrial goods reaching the enemy. With the help of charts supplied by the London trade, officials absorbed the lesson that all diamonds were potentially 'industrial', whether originating as a by-product of gem stones, cleavages, and chips, or wholly from sand and bort. By looking at the work of the 1917 committees, they came to understand the difficulty of separating 'war' material from luxury goods, sold in series. One of the two principal merchant-distributors of industrial goods in London, L. M. Van Moppes and Sons, provided information about single-channel selling, the proportions of cuttable and industrial stocks available, and the reasons why the Diamond Corporation dominated 97 per cent of world sales to the exclusion of only Tanganyika, Brazil, British Guiana, and about half of South Africa's alluvials. By the outbreak of war, the Board of Trade had a good idea of the balance of production from the world's diamond sources and the monopoly centred on the selling organization which handled bulk purchases, after preliminary sorting in South Africa, Lisbon, and Brussels, for the seven or eight merchants who specialized in the distribution of industrial series and

[1] FO, 371/21699 (1938).

diamond tools.[2] No approaches were made to the corporation in this planning stage. It later became evident that Dicorp thought that Van Moppes had revealed too much about the ways in which the industry worked in order to control as many of its outlets as possible.

Britain's own requirements for industrial diamond materials were relatively small, and similar to Germany's at about £140,000 to £150,000 annually. But it was believed the Germans had been stockpiling through a series of barter trade agreements with South Africa from 1936. The fifth agreement for 1938–9 included large quantities of industrial diamonds valued at £115,000, in return for mining machinery for South West Africa. The Foreign Office did not think it desirable to interfere officially with this private deal, but the Dominions Office exercised as much persuasion as possible with the South African Government to stop up this outlet before the outbreak of hostilities.[3]

The control of exports under legislation passed at the beginning of the war immediately suspended supply from London to Amsterdam, Antwerp, and elsewhere, until the mechanism for distributing industrial stocks had been organized through a licensing system similar to that of 1915. This included an embargo on direct exports from British dominions (allegedly as part of exchange control) and was officially accepted by South Africa. By contrast with the elementary structure of 1915, departmental responsibility was shared with the Ministry of Economic Warfare and with the Ministry of Supply, which supervised stocks of diamond dies and other tools. Quite soon the Ministry of Aircraft Production declared a special interest in sources of industrial diamonds; and the Ministry of Labour from 1942 was responsible for the supply of skilled cutters. The Foreign Office watched over the complex negotiations with foreign governments and dealers. One feature of control did not change. All departments had access to telegraphic and other communications passing between the companies and their clients in the form of intercepts collected through the Post Office.

The most immediate action of the Board of Trade was to set up a diamond export committee which met from October 1939 till June 1940, under the chairmanship of Sir Henry Fountain. The composition of this committee with purely advisory functions reflected the numerous interests involved. Du Cane represented De Beers, Louis Oppenheimer the Diamond Corporation, and his brother Otto Oppenheimer the Union producers.

[2] BT, 11/1029, 'Export of Industrial Diamonds during The Great War', 8 Mar. 1939.

[3] FO, 371/21699, External Affairs (Pretoria) to DO, 8 Dec. 1937 and encls; Export of Goods Prohibition no. 2 (1939); Aronheim, 175. See too Raymond Dumett, 'Africa's Strategic Minerals during the Second World War', *Journal of African History*, 26/3 (1985), 381–408.

Chester Beatty or his representatives stood for CAST, F. A. Mathias for its offshoot, SLST, and for the Ministry of Supply, L. M. Van Moppes for the industrial diamond merchants, and I. J. Rozelaar for the diamond section of the London Chamber of Commerce. W. B. Topp represented the Union through the High Commission. The Ministry of Economic Warfare added its own official, Maurice Bridgeman (a director of Anglo-Iranian Oil), and occasionally other representatives connected with the trade were called in. This body was supplemented immediately by a small subcommittee of experts—Van Moppes, Topp, Louis and Otto Oppenheimer, and Rozelaar—which met frequently to examine parcels for export and advise the Post Office and Customs. Eventually, this subcommittee became responsible, until the end of the war, for all decisions on what was 'industrial' in the export trade, though it was reduced to only three members by the departure of Van Moppes senior for the USA in June 1940 and by an accident which removed Louis Oppenheimer.[4]

Like their counterparts in 1915, the *diamantaires* and the civil servants concentrated on ways of denying industrial and near-industrial stock to Germany by setting up control committees in Belgium, Holland, and France and by curtailing exports to the United States and Switzerland, until assurances were given by merchants that resales would not divert stock through neutrals. The work of setting up the foreign committees was undertaken by Van Moppes, Rozelaar, and D. B. Doyle (of CAST). The Belgian control was quickly organized under Felicien Cattier. Substantial quantities of Belgian gem and industrial stocks had been transferred to the United Kingdom early in 1939. But the Belgian government was reluctant to allow Antwerp cutters to transfer to new cutting centres, and the export committee agreed to the release of £3.2 million of stocks sold to Antwerp and Amsterdam by the Trading Company for the first 3 months of 1940. It proved impossible to establish a satisfactory regional organization in France, because of divisions among diamond interests in the *Chambre syndicale* in Paris and lack of co-ordination with government departments. The French Ministry of Public Works took charge of the distribution of stocks which were monitored rather than controlled from London. Supply to Switzerland was resumed in November 1939 for firms on an approved 'white list' drawn up by the British Legation in Berne. Exports continued to Italy and Japan in early 1940 on the basis of pre-war levels of sales. There was no possibility, as yet, of controlling supply to Germany from Brazil and Venezuela, except by refusing insurance cover on diamond mails in transit through London.

---

[4] BT, 11/2673 for minutes and correspondence winding up the committee; Aronheim, 178.

The most difficult case concerned exports to the United States. In order to secure a commanding position in the New York market, a control scheme was devised by Van Moppes and Otto Oppenheimer at the end of 1939 for distribution under licence to approved American buyers. Approval was to be given by the UK consul-general with the advice of a small local committee of leading representatives of the diamond trade. Opinions were divided in London on the advisability of using the consulate-general as a control centre. Beatty pressed for this solution; the Economic Warfare representative sensed opposition from the US government. Dicorp's men in New York argued for restriction of supply to 'old established firms' who would sell to 'old established customers', but this was resisted by Du Cane for the Diamond Corporation, probably because the list of consignees gave equal importance to the Trading Company's competitors in this specialized field. Officially, the State Department did not approve of this operation of a cartel within American jurisdiction. Unofficially, it was agreed the consulate advisers would act as 'trade consultants' in vetting local buyers, and the licence controls would be exercised through the Board of Trade from London. Licensed consignors would only deliver to informally-approved American buyers.[5]

Officials of the US Department of Commerce and the Treasury were less preoccupied with the need for stopping up possible supply routes to Germany than with the dramatic rise in prices following the export committee's curtailment of deliveries in the last months of 1939. The effects of this rise were very uneven. Swiss importers complained in early 1940 that the cost of their bort was two or three times higher than supplies to British manufacturers. Large stocks were seized by the Germans, following the rapid invasion of the Low Countries in May 1940. Between November 1940 and March 1941, the Diamond Trading Company raised the price of cuttable roughs exported to America by 20 per cent.[6]

The success of the export committee was, therefore, questionable. They were overwhelmed by the speed of events from April 1940, when the regional control of allies and neutrals was barely working. On the eve of the invasion of Belgium and Holland, Van Moppes presented a gloomy report on the effectiveness of the 'protection committees', on the uncontrolled export of diamond dies and tools from France, on sales by dealers in New York speculating in the market for cuttable stones (which could be used industrially), and on the open market for goods from Brazil.

---

[5] BT, 11/2673, minutes 14 Nov., 5 Dec. 1939; FO 371/24238 for lists of British exporters and American consignees.

[6] BT, 11/2673, minutes, 16 Apr. 1940; Aronheim, 180.

South Africa had not yet complied with requests for a single channel:

Industrial diamonds are still being sent from South Africa to Holland, Belgium and the United States of America for sale on the market in each case. Possibly that portion of the South African production outside the control of the Diamond Producers Association could be dealt with in a similar way to that suggested for Brazilian production [by Dicorp purchases]. In the meantime no export permits should be granted by the South African Government for industrial diamonds to be sent to the European and United States markets.[7]

The committee recommended the desperate measure of suspending all exports of industrial goods and borderline stones from London, until co-operation could be obtained from neutral governments. An unofficial delegation consisting of Du Cane, Chester Beatty, Otto Oppenheimer, Doyle, and Topp visited the US Embassy to explain to commercial representatives just why no diamonds should be delivered—as a 'moral embargo' to stop supplies reaching the enemy. The Economic Warfare members of the committee were less enthusiastic about such a drastic step, fearing that the fragile co-operation between United States importers and the British consulate-general would break down. In any case, the delegation got a cool reception and was told that the US government would take no steps to stop re-exports of diamonds by surface mail or through the international airmail service.

From South Africa Sir Ernest Oppenheimer was called to London by the Board of Trade, and attended the meeting which reviewed this impasse to advise on a number of points. He agreed that buyers for the Diamond Corporation and the Trading Company might be sent out to compete for Brazilian stocks. Suspension of sales of industrial goods would, of course, create a shortage, and the prohibition of sales of borderline cuttables would lead to an enormous price rise for higher qualities to make up for the loss on lesser goods. Oppenheimer's principal concern was that such a rise might make gem roughs unsaleable.[8] He was also worried by the collapse of the Belgian and Dutch cutting industry, and wanted 'talks' on alternative centres in the United Kingdom and South Africa. At this date he made an offer on behalf of the Diamond Corporation to the Board of Trade to make 'all categories of industrial diamonds available at moderate prices—certainly cheaper than those now charged—on the understanding that the resulting benefit is passed on to

---

[7] Ibid., minutes, 16 Apr. 1940.
[8] Ibid., minutes, 15 May 1940. Cf. Hocking, which omits his wartime role. For Oppenheimer's version which exaggerates his part in setting up 'control machinery' in Belgium and Holland (arranged well before his visit) see FO, 371/44590.

the Government'.[9] The context of the offer made it clear that sales would be made direct to British and French industries, cutting out the merchant-distributors—and in particular, the two firms of L. M. Van Moppes and J. K. Smit who would be asked to keep to their specialist trade in diamond tools.

The Board of Trade and the Ministry of Economic Warfare, however, still sought a way of controlling exports to the United States, bearing in mind Van Moppes's warnings of 'unreliable Refugees' in New York, and the 'bad effect' on American public opinion and the Congress of any kind of British interference. In a series of interviews with Oppenheimer, Sir Arnold Overton, Second Secretary at the Board of Trade, was unwise enough to give approval to a plan to shift all of the Diamond Corporation's stocks to America, without making it clear that this move should not include industrial goods. Sir Ernest was alleged to have written that the transfer would only apply to cuttable roughs. But the idea that diamonds should be put on America's Strategic Commodity List, and that stocks in the United Kingdom would be flown to North America 'for safe keeping' was eagerly promoted by Oppenheimer immediately afterwards on a visit to the United States.[10] And in discussions with American officials in July he freely contracted to make a sale of £2.5 million of industrial diamonds, in return for the right to set up an agency in New York holding a further £2 million of 'revolving stock' for replacements. In effect, no other 'strategic' reserve would be required; and the Diamond Corporation would have a foothold in America, despite the Sherman anti-trust laws.

At the last meeting of the export committee on 4 June, it was clear that an interdepartmental committee of the Board of Trade, the Ministry of Economic Warfare, and the Ministry of Supply was about to take over most of the functions of the advisors, though the small subcommittee of experts continued to supervise exports. The use of the consulate-general was confirmed as a control mechanism, in co-operation with the DTC and American importers.[11] But quite suddenly, officials were alerted by Consul-General Haggard that a terrible blunder had been made, and Overton hastily informed Oppenheimer on 15 July that the United Kingdom would not approve a bulk sale to the Americans. As Oppenheimer later reflected: 'Circumstances over which we had no control prevented this

---

[9] BT, 11/1653, 'Supervision of the Diamond Industry', 25 Mar. 1941 (a departmental memorandum which cites his offer).

[10] DO, 35/1097 for correspondence with the New York consulate-general concerning Oppenheimer's visit, May–Aug. 1940.

[11] BT, 11/267. The departments completed a census of stocks in the United Kingdom at this date.

scheme from reaching fruition.'[12] The circumstances were the refusal of the Board of Trade and the Treasury to permit any transfer of Trading Company selling to New York or to encourage direct exports from South Africa which would decrease revenue and taxes levied in London and overall strategic control.

The continued centralization of the trade through London implicit in this arrangement was threatened, however, by agitation among the alluvial producers in South Africa to break the embargo and export directly to the United States, because of delays in payments for deliveries to London, and because they suspected their 'trade secrets' became the property of London committees dominated by competitors. Smuts's government complained through the High Commission that alluvial producers had been threatened with lower prices from the corporation. Moreover, the government faced a good deal of political sniping from Nationalist members in alluvial constituencies. In the Assembly there were angry accusations that officials had been 'killing the diggings' to protect the mines. Colonel C. F. Stallard, as minister of mines (and an old warrior of English origins), gallantly defended Dicorp for its control over a strategic mineral and lectured the House on the functions of the selling organization. But there was no denying that South Africa's share of world diamond production had slumped. De Beers was content to close mines, and lease Kimberley to the government to make munitions in the machine shops and turn the compounds into infantry barracks, while living off reserves of unsold stock. But that did not help the diggers.[13]

In order to market the goods of the independent producers and provide an additional outlet for De Beers, the Union government took the bold step of approving Oppenheimer's plan for a separate selling agency in New York: 'The Union Government consider it very desirable that the direct export of alluvial stones to the United States should now be permitted as the retention of the embargo is calculated to depress prices. Stones would be exported only to buyers in the United States approved by the Governments of both the United Kingdom and the Union.'[14] The Dominions Office answered at length, admitting that the Union's effective system of exchange control no longer required an embargo on direct exports. But, it was argued, permission to the alluvial producers might open the way for direct exports by De Beers which would mean 'that London was being cut out of the trade, with corresponding loss to

[12] FO, 371/44590, memorandum encl. in Oppenheimer to Chapple (Dicorp), 12 Feb. 1945.
[13] *Assembly Debates* (May 1940), 7142–5, 7165.
[14] FO, 371/24238, External Affairs to High Commission, 2 Sept. 1940; DO, 'Note', 27 Sept. 1940.

merchants' interests and United Kingdom income tax'. Other colonial diamond producers might follow and break with the Diamond Corporation. The danger of a price war could not be ruled out. Assurance was given that consignor's trade secrets were revealed only to Economic Warfare officials and not to members of the Board of Trade advisory committee. The Union government was urged to agree that any lifting of the embargo would lead 'to progressive exclusion of London in favour of New York' and a weakening of London's advantage, when a cutting industry was re-established in the Low Countries after the war.

A memorandum from Mathias (who framed much of the above reply) warned that the flight of capital and refugees from Belgium and Holland might well lead to a transfer of the cutting industry to America or South Africa. And he cited the criticism levelled at the minister of mines in South Africa from alluvial constituencies as evidence that there was resentment at the exercise of controls in favour of sales for goods from the Belgian Congo.[15]

Sir Ernest Oppenheimer, therefore, who had left New York for South Africa 'much disturbed' by the British governmental veto on his operations in the United States achieved very little by taking up the matter with Smuts. There were other grounds for mistrust by the end of the year. The British departments discovered, from their intercepts of telegrams to the Diamond Corporation, that Sir Ernest had deliberately slowed down and deferred diamond sales through the Trading Company, in order to spread the corporation's turnover into 1941 and avoid excess profits tax. F. A. Mathias who spoke somewhat ambiguously for both the Ministry of Supply and the Chester Beatty group queried: 'What would be the position if the manufacturers of Spitfires and Hurricanes and our bombers adopted a similar argument and desired to cease work when their tax standard for Excess Profits Tax had been reached.'[16] In mitigation, Van Moppes reported, however, that there was no shortage of industrial diamond material. But the episode left a bad impression among the civil servants who had confirmed the use of the New York consulate-general as a control mechanism and were working their way, via interdepartmental committees, towards a more effective supervision of the corporation and the dealers in London, in the face of mounting criticism of the way the single-channel system operated.

[15] BT, 11/1553, 'The Diamond Industry', 9 Jan. 1941.
[16] DO, 35/1097/WT316/1, 9, 15, Haggard to FO, 21 Aug. 1940; Mathias to Bull, 5 Nov. 1940, and copies of Oppenheimer-Chapple cables.

CONTROLLING THE STOCKPILE

For, despite Oppenheimer's promise of pre-war prices if the middle-men were cut out of contracts between the Corporation and Allied governments, prices continued to rise and special qualities of industrial diamonds were even in short supply in the aircraft industries of the United Kingdom and in the Canadian and American mining industries. At a series of meetings at the Board of Trade, Van Moppes, Otto Oppenheimer, and Smit, as the leading suppliers were confronted with the Canadians' complaints of unwanted and expensive material, sold in series through the dealers, irrespective of specific requests for diamonds suitable for drilling. The merchants rejected the Canadian specifications as 'too narrow' in a trade which used the same methods to sell its industrial goods as its gem roughs.[17] They were 'aghast', when officials threatened to import and distribute supplies directly from the Congo. At the same time, Van Moppes revealed privately that the DTC had made a great profit from raised prices of goods sold to the Ministry of Supply and hoped to do the same with orders from the Canadian government. Chester Beatty, sensing official hostility to the corporation, offered sales at cost price to the diamond die controller in Supply, if given permission to break his contract, but this was refused from within the Ministry of Economic Warfare, which preferred a trial of strength with Otto Oppenheimer to open warfare between West African and South African producers.

Mathias at the Ministry of Supply explained that higher prices were being asked by the Diamond Trading Company, which sold directly to distributors, in order to cover the cost of war risks insurance. He regarded Oppenheimer's offer to reduce bort from 4s. to 2s. 6d. per carat as 'worthless'.[18] But the evidence is that the threat of government intervention in the market did bring about a reduction of 20 per cent in bort and other industrial goods in sales by the Trading Company to the merchant-distributors in April 1941.

The problem of selling the qualities manufacturers desired was less easily solved. The evidence for the paradox of abundant general stocks of bort and shortages of suitable stones for drilling and cutting accumulated rapidly early in 1941, as Canadian mineral exploration for nickel and cobalt intensified and the munitions industries expanded. The Board of

---

[17] Ibid., Snelling, 'How to Profiteer', minutes, Jan., Feb. 1941.
[18] BT, 11/1553, Mathias, 'The Diamond Industry', 9 Jan. 1941; Shackle, memorandum, 9 Apr. 1941.

Trade, after reviewing the structure of the single channel for producers through the corporation and the DTC, recognized that roughs of all qualities were sold in series. After the demise of the cutting industry, smaller and inferior stones for gem cutting had become unsaleable, while the new centres in the United States and the United Kingdom concentrated on better quality stones. But the industrial merchants had been forced to buy these poor qualities along with industrial goods from the Diamond Trading Company: 'the result has been to compel the industrial diamond merchants to raise their prices—it is estimated by at least 40 per cent. and in some cases as much as 60 to 70 per cent above pre-war prices—to the users of industrial diamonds, to compensate for the unsaleable material left on their hands'.[19]

Because, therefore, the Diamond Corporation and the Trading Company would not carry the cost of holding unsaleable stock, originating mainly from Forminière, this cost was passed on to the merchants in the United Kingdom. More immediately, Otto Oppenheimer agreed to sort special parcels for the Canadians which were distributed through the Trading Company and J. K. Smit and Sons.

The whole position was reviewed laconically by the permanent under-secretary at the Dominions Office with evident distaste for an industry with 'such a dubious flavour'. Clutterbuck informed the British High Commission in Pretoria that in Britain the Diamond Trading Company had, at length, met the Canadian demand, 'after persuasion, cajolery and thinly-veiled threats'. Abroad, huge quantities of diamonds had accumulated in the Congo where Sir Ernest Oppenheimer feared 'an audacious enemy raid by air, perhaps by a single plane, might result in the capture of these stocks worth several millions of pounds'. This possibility worried the British government less than the thought that the whole story was a manœuvre by De Beers to centralize all stocks 'with the object of transferring control of the distribution end of the industry to South Africa from London, where it has been located for decades. If these efforts were successful, the consequences would be a serious loss of taxation, foreign exchange and wealth to the United Kingdom'. Finally, to settle the larger question of the contribution of the diamond industry to the war effort, he explained, a 'Diamond Control' was sought, to replace the defunct advisory committee and end the multiple responsibilities of so many departments. No decision had been taken: 'one cogent reason being that there does not appear to be any man sufficiently conversant

---

[19] BT, 11/1653, 'Supervision of the Diamond Industry. Revised Board of Trade Note', 25 Mar. 1941.

with the trade and at the same time sufficiently disinterested to be given the job of Controller'.[20]

In the meantime, the Trading Company was asked yet again to supply the right type of diamonds where they were most needed, at prices close to those obtaining before the war. In a bid to withstand the pressures exerted on the corporation, Louis Oppenheimer offered to extend sales to the United States by contract with government agencies, as in the case of Canada, cutting out local merchants in New York. This drew immediate objections from Van Moppes on the grounds that replacement stocks would have to be assured within the United Kingdom, where merchant-exporters would be undercut by direct sales at lower prices. The Board of Trade was nervous that such a manœuvre was the first step in getting round the American anti-trust laws which had so far kept the Trading Company out of direct sales in New York. Countermeasures (inspired by Beatty) for direct purchase for UK merchants from CAST were rejected, because this would weaken Economic Warfare's overall 'control' and, more pertinently, the Union government would object to an attack on the monopoly.

An intercepted letter from Oppenheimer to Dicorp set their minds at rest by emphasizing that the idea of a US agency for the Trading Company should be dropped, because Smuts's government would not permit direct exports to the United States for the moment. An intercepted cable made it clear that attention would be paid to adequate proportions of industrial goods for United Kingdom and United States users.[21]

This cleared the way for bulk sales to the US government. But negotiations with the US Treasury by the Trading Company in 1941 for direct sales of £600,000 of industrial diamonds encountered considerable resistance to the normal procedure of selling in series an assortment which was left to the merchants to dispose of to manufacturers. If the merchants were to be cut out of the deal (as the company wished), the American manufacturers demanded a selection of 93,000 carats of industrial diamonds based on their requirements. The problem was solved by the Board of Trade and the American commercial attaché, Don Bliss; and in the manner of the Canadian deal, the corporation was obliged to supply through its distributor the grades that the American government desired, without 'Congo junk'. The outcome was so unusual that it was recalled by Oppenheimer later as 'a procedure fundamentally

---

[20] BT, 11/1553, P. A. Clutterbuck to C. R. Price (Secret), 24 Apr. 1941.
[21] BT, 11/1566, Oppenheimer to Dicorp, 22 May 1941; Oppenheimer to Trading Company, 29 May 1941. It is not impossible that Oppenheimer was aware of Post Office intercepts by this date.

contrary to trade custom' in his justification of the corporation's wartime policies.[22]

The Diamond Trading Company did not like it; nor did the Ministry of Economic Warfare, which was worried by reports of separate supplies of cut and rough stones reaching Palestine from South Africa for sale in the United States and continued re-exports by the US Industrial Diamonds Corporation by clipper to Lisbon and Switzerland. Following an Anglo-Belgian trade and financial agreement in January 1941 to raise production in the Congo, Belgian co-operation became a cardinal principle for British control through London, to counter any American intervention in the supply of industrial goods. For much the same reason of paramountcy over centralized distribution, close attention was paid to a South African trade mission, which established air links with Leopoldville and enquired about bringing stocks of diamonds to the Union.[23]

The Congo authorities were equally suspicious of the purpose of the South African mission, discerning the hand of the Diamond Corporation. The need to end complete dependence on the route through Kimberley (which was normally used at this period for the corporation's deliveries of Congo and Angola diamonds) led to departmental approval of a plan put forward by D. B. Doyle of CAST to move stored quantities of West and Central African stocks directly to the United Kingdom, if the Treasury would meet the cost of up to £39,999 in war-risks insurance. This would secure a direct supply of cuttable and best industrial stones, and it would keep the unsaleable industrials off the market. Otherwise, he suggested the whole of the Congo stocks, including nearly three tons of unsaleable Forminière diamonds, should be transported through Rhodesia to the Union: 'and thus fall in with the plans of the Diamond Corporation who wish to remove the centre of the diamond industry to South Africa in order to avoid double taxation'.[24]

The argument to save revenue for a small investment in the insurance needed for shipping saleable African stocks was irresistible; and the Board of Trade backed the idea. The unsaleable goods were left in the Congo on the advice of the Joint Service chiefs that there was little risk of their capture. Henceforth, 1.5 million carats of Forminière and 7,000 carats of Angola and Dubanghi diamonds would be added to the 26 million carats of bort and unclassified goods already in the United Kingdom, at the cost of some £40,000 to the Exchequer.

[22] FO, 371/44590; 371/29078.

[23] FO, 371/26351 (visit of de Vleeschauwer to South Africa) and South African trade mission to Leopoldville.

[24] BT, 11/1597, Doyle to Board of Trade, 2 Oct. 1941.

Having exerted their influence to cut down on South Africa's independent exports to America and head off any transfers to Kimberley, the Board of Trade and the Ministry of Economic Warfare threw their weight into curtailing the growth of a cutting industry in Palestine. This spectacular development among the refugee community accounted for £1.4 million in exports to America, Canada, and Mexico by 1941 and was based largely on the import of South African roughs. It was suspected of encouraging a clandestine trade in cut stones through Syria and Turkey to Germany, 'where they are bought by high officials of the Nazi party' minuted an imaginative official in the Dominions Office. A second reason for clamping down was pressure from the Belgians, who regarded cutting in Palestine as 'an unnatural industry' and a threat to their eventual rehabilitation as the principal centre for diamond cutting. Mathias strongly supported this view, and the Palestine High Commissioner, Sir Harold MacMichael, was told to curb the imports reaching the 'Palestine Diamond Club'.[25]

Economic Warfare was then well placed to announce to the New York consulate-general in November 1941 that tighter controls would be exercised over the issue of licences to approved American buyers. 'Speculators' were weeded out of the lists. Americans could, of course, buy in Brazil, but bort from that source was four or five times the London price. American dealers, therefore, had to accept a measure of single-channel preference, as consignees of the ten distributors regularly awarded licences from 1941.[26]

Among the producers at the British end, there was a near revolt by Chester Beatty in February 1942, when CAST and SLST demanded a quota for their new contract with the Diamond Corporation equal to that given to Angola. The potential breach was patched up by organizing CAST sales through Otto Oppenheimer, for the Diamond Trading Company, and pretending that Beatty was not dealing with Sir Ernest. Doubtless, the situation was helped by the appointment of Sir Cecil Rodwell, former governor of British Guiana and Southern Rhodesia, in his sixty-eighth year, as supreme diamond controller in the Ministry of Supply, while still a director of several of Chester Beatty's companies. He was admirably supported by Mathias, as a director on the board of SLST, controller

---

[25] DO, 35/1098/WT316/51 and 54, Snelling, minute, 3 July 1942; CO to MacMichael, 17 Nov. 1942; Mathias to CO, 10 Sept. 1942.

[26] FO, 371/29078, MEW to Washington Embassy, 14 Nov. 1941. UK distributors at this date were: W. Busch, Ehrman and Co., Fink and Fink, L. M. Van Moppes (senior), S. L. Van Moppes, J. K. Smit and Sons, J. Jolis, R. and L. Goldmuntz, J. Fouldes and Co., E. A. and P. Tiefus, the Diamond Trading Company, Diamond Realisations, and the Diamond Development Company.

of gem diamonds, and general adviser to all ministries on diamond matters. It was emphasized for American consumption that the Diamond Corporation would fall under Rodwell's powers.[27]

However cosmetic, the appointment was welcomed in the United States where it coincided with new controls over diamond dies and tools for export, and measures to prevent hoarding and to supply inventories and records of sale for the US War Production Board. From the beginning of 1943 maximum prices were enforced at 1942 levels.

But the United States government required more than co-operation on sales and sought the establishment of a stockpile in North America. In November 1942, two American representatives held a series of meetings with Rodwell, Mathias, and A. F. Lee (Ministry of Supply) to decide how large such a stock would be and who would be its guardian. Kept informed of this development by Du Cane, Ernest Oppenheimer strongly opposed the plan, on the grounds that outside producers would contribute 'run of the mine' material and would, therefore, help build up a stock of gem stones, as well as industrial goods, outside the control of the Diamond Corporation. The probability of a North American stockpile was all the harder to bear, because the Union had just failed in a second request to export directly to the United States as an ally in the war. The request was refused on the same grounds as before (by Mathias) as potentially damaging to central distribution through London and a dangerous shift in the market towards New York.[28]

Oppenheimer was assured, therefore, that the United Kingdom kept to the principle of sales through a single channel, and the reserve was to be only for emergencies. The companies, moreover, were fully consulted, and Beatty, Boise, and Doyle (before his death in November 1942) were just as strongly in favour, sensing that a transfer of stock under the auspices of Canada, rather than the United States, would defeat any moves of the Diamond Corporation to revive Oppenheimer's strategy of direct entry into the American market.

By the end of the year, it had been agreed that a reserve of 11.5 million carats would be established in Canada on which the United States and the United Kingdom might draw if stocks fell below those existing in June 1942. Prices were fixed at levels reached at that date. Supplies for the reserve, when the agreement was initialled in January 1943, were to be drawn from Diamang, CAST, SLST, Forminière, and the Diamond

---

[27] Aronheim, 192.
[28] DO, 35/1097 and 1098, Oppenheimer to Du Cane, 19 Oct. 1942; L. G. Ray to DO, 14 Nov. 1941; DO (draft) to South Africa House, Dec. 1942.

Corporation in proportions which allowed Dicorp and the two British producers to provide 48 per cent of the industrial goods made up of drilling, dressing, and grinding material, and crushing bort. The consequential agreements between the Ministry of Supply and the companies were treated at first on a private basis, rather than as intergovernmental negotiations as in the case of Angola and the Congo. The Belgian government caused trouble, as a major shareholder in Forminière, and refused to co-operate in providing accurate information on stocks and production levels, fearing, among other reasons, that the United States would secure the bulk of the cutting industry. But with wartime demand reaching its peak, matters were concluded between Canada and the United States as the major consumers, and the United Kingdom as a minor consumer of industrial material and 'because London is the market for diamonds'.[29]

Although the US Office of Economic Warfare was satisfied with this expression of Allied co-operation, the curtailment of supplies for American dealers through the licensing system applied with the help of the consulate-general served to harden the opinions of some government officials that the British covertly supported the 'syndicate' (as the corporation was still sometimes called) in its restrictive practices. There was annoyance all round at the continued efforts of Van Moppes senior to conduct his own negotiations for sales in New York with American officials on behalf of suppliers independent of the Diamond Trading Company. American understanding and knowledge of the trade, moreover, were significantly advanced within the State Department through the excellent intelligence and research in the reports of Don Bliss in 1943 and 1944, when commercial attaché in London, and which explained in some detail the structure of the selling organization and the reasons why its policies still resulted in dissatisfaction for American manufacturers.

Basically, the selling organization was still applying methods evolved for the distribution of rough gem stones to the distribution of industrial diamonds. The two cases of Canadian sales and direct sales to the American government in 1941 called this practice in question. But the British tolerated 'trade practices' for the bulk of sales to dealers and manufacturers through London consignors, while the Americans had reservations about the reasons for these 'practices', which they regarded as restrictive.

These policy differences were much less important, however, than securing industrial qualities demanded by North American manufacturers

---

[29] FO, 371/35518, Ministry of Supply to FO, 18 Feb. 1943; draft agreement, signed 26 Mar. 1943, and printed text 'Industrial Diamonds'.

through a supply system which sold all types of goods in series, and left it to the merchants to make up the assortments for particular customers, as in the trade in gem roughs. The problems which had already been encountered in US Treasury purchases from the Diamond Trading Company in 1941 were explored in depth by S. W. Hofman for the War Production Board in talks with Sir Cecil Rodwell in 1943, which ended in a joint memorandum aimed at explaining and remedying the intrinsic clashes of interest in the system.[30]

While recognizing the great value of a single channel for distribution and the adequacy of supplies for total demand, the two sides of the trans-Atlantic control team saw acute shortages in specific categories used by the tool trade amounting to some 700,000 or 800,000 carats annually (or about a twelfth of total UK, US, and Russian consumption). All of this material was selected by the trade from the Trading Company's industrial series which contained a large proportion of goods which merchants could not dispose of for industrial purposes. This situation arose, in turn, from 'the custom of the trade' in which all material not classified as suitable for sale as cuttable was separated out as 'industrial'. The Trading Company's industrial series contained about thirty-two categories of diamonds 'sorted and sized according to a practice inherited from the gem trade' without any precise relation to industrial use. With some help from the merchants, industrial stones were reclassified according to their purpose; and this revealed that shortages would inevitably result within the deliveries of 1.2 million carats of the industrial series scheduled for 1943/4.

The remedy suggested was not goods news for the Diamond Trading Company. For, to make up the quantities of high grade industrial stones, sold at industrial prices, the company would have to draw on corporation reserves of cuttable stones and so-called 'speculative' categories on the borderline which were held back pending demand on the market for gem stones. The negotiators recognized that the company itself as a distributor in bulk could not sort out the preferred categories. American merchants, therefore, were left with the rising demand for quality and larger amounts of unsaleable material on their hands, while prevented by price ceilings from making much profit on what they could sell. The company denied that the quality of past categories had been deliberately changed to the merchants' disadvantage; but the merchants encountered quality changes arising from variations in the supply from different producers, as old stocks accumulated before the war were exhausted. Whatever the reason, profit

---

[30] FO, 371/35518 (secret), 'Industrial Diamond Problems', 4 Nov. 1943.

margins were adversely affected, 'since merchants value industrial diamonds on a basis different from that on which the Trading Company values them and this has created difficulties in the efficient distribution of supplies to users in America'.[31]

So henceforth the amount of unsaleable material in the industrial series was reduced from about 30 per cent to a limit of 15 per cent. Sales prices for large stones were to be related to the ceiling on American industrial stones—at about 170s. per carat, thus removing the influence of higher gem roughs on the industrial roughs. More contentiously, to end the mistrust, secrecy, and evident ignorance of industrial practices in the use of diamonds, joint consultations between the Trading Company, merchants, and diamond tool makers were recommended to exchange information. Above all, the company was urged to supply information in advance of the qualities and size categories offered to merchants in assortments, to avoid disappointment over unexpected variations, and other precautions were suggested by merging series and offering them at sufficient intervals to standardize material. The reserve and the new sales practices worked well enough. Both sides drew materials from Canada in 1944, more especially for drilling; and the Trading Company handled unprecedented quantities of industrial goods in 1943, valued at nearly £17 million, which ate into its own reserve created during the 1930s, and were replenished with stocks from the Congo.

DEFENDING CENTRAL SELLING

British government departments were not entirely reconciled to the location of such a large quantity of unsold stock in North America; and after F. A. Mathias had leaked a copy of the Bliss report to the Board of Trade in 1944, there were suspicions that the Americans were overdrawing on available stocks in an effort to circumvent the single-channel monopoly.[32] Both Rodwell and Mathias foresaw considerable post-war problems if the balance of power in the diamond trade was allowed to shift to the other side of the Atlantic.

The immediate focus of their strategy lay in preparations for a revival of the Belgian cutting industry to assist the government to attract refugee diamond workers from the United States. With 300 machines available in Antwerp at liberation and three-quarters of the world's supply of

---

[31] Ibid.
[32] BT, 11/2716, 'Production and Distribution of Industrial Diamonds', 12 Apr. 1944.

industrial roughs in the Congo, Rodwell and Mathias calculated that the Belgians would be able to rehabilitate part of their economy fairly quickly. For security and the British economy, supplies would still be channelled through London.

This becomes a predominant factor, not only on future strategic grounds, but also on account of revenue to the British Exchequer. The retention of London as the centre is essential in so far as it maintains the value of the diamond and provides the Exchequer with at least £1,500,000 per annum under peace-time conditions. It may be estimated that the direct revenue to the Exchequer in the last financial year was at least four or five millions sterling.[33]

By September 1944, the Belgians were eager to begin attracting refugee workers back; and it was agreed by Economic Warfare that supplies of roughs should be sufficient to meet the capacity of the restored industry in Antwerp. The first stocks were sent at the beginning of 1945, just at the time when the Ministry of Supply came under pressure from the US War Production Board to increase the dispatch of stocks of crushable bort from the Congo. A review of the transfer of such material to the United States revealed that that there had been a massive redistribution in the location of industrial diamonds from 1942. For then the Congo and the United Kingdom held the totality of world supplies at 34 million carats. After 1942, sales by Dicorp, the location of the strategic reserve and annual consumption of about 9.7 million carats in the United States had left a stock of 12.5 million carats in the United Kingdom and the Congo, by December, 1944, and 23 million carats stockpiled in North America. There were suspicions that America did not need this vast amount, and that it enabled American dealers to pick over the bort and hoard quantities of industrial stones.[34]

To counterbalance this trans-Atlantic preponderance, British departments fell in with Belgian rehabilitation of their industry. A meeting of the Board of Trade, in May 1945, laid down the main proposals for a deal to reduce competition to Belgian cutting, while they built up their labour force, and to keep the major market for Congo stones in the United Kingdom. In the wake of the Allied armies, representatives from Dicorp and a party of civil servants went to Brussels to renew contracts with Cattier and F. Van Bree, chairman of Union Minière, who had directed Congo companies during the occupation.

---

[33] FO, 371/41073, Rodwell, Mathias memorandum, 31 Aug. 1944.
[34] FO, 371/48995, Bliss to Ministry of Supply, 16 Jan. 1945 and minutes.

As the basis for these contracts, an agreement was reached with the Belgian Minister of Colonies and Antwerp diamond interests which gave both sides what they wanted. In return for an end to British import restrictions on cut stones and curtailment of cutting in 'other countries' (understood as Palestine), and a supply of Gold Coast industrial goods, the Belgians agreed to acknowledge London as the centre of the diamond trade and hand over all reassortment of Congo stones to the Diamond Corporation, and renew contracts between the Trading Company and Forminière. There was less accord about the future of a cutting industry in Germany, but it was acknowledged that Antwerp should develop a machine-tool trade specializing in the application of industrial diamonds.[35] In short, the proliferation of cutting centres brought about by the spread of the market for industrial stones was to be stopped by the return of Belgians from America to a revived Antwerp and the concentration of distribution in London.

Some of this rapid co-ordination may have been influenced (at least in the policies urged by the Ministry of Supply and the Board of Trade) by the evidence that the State Department and, perhaps, the Department of Commerce were preparing their own evaluation of the centralization of the diamond trade. The assistant attorney-general, Francis Biddell, filed a suit on 29 January 1945 in the US District Court of New York against nine British, Belgian, and Portuguese diamond companies, and their stockholders and agents, under the Sherman Anti-Trust Act. All the companies headed by De Beers were cited for 'conspiracy to restrain and monopolize commerce' in the United States by limiting supply, raising prices, and compelling purchases through the Diamond Trading Company in series which included unwanted goods for payment in advance, thus preventing stockpiling in the United States.[36]

Some of this was manifestly untrue: stockpiling had proceeded uninterrupted since 1943. But the threat was serious, and De Beers only just managed to get agreement from the court not to freeze the company's American assets. The South African government sought diplomatic intervention, but the Foreign Office informed the Dominions Office that any representations from interested governments would have to be made jointly with the United Kingdom; and for the moment the department did not see how to intervene in what was a restraint of trade case, begun along with a series of anti-trust actions against British 'monopolies'. The Ministry of Supply looked on these actions as periodic 'cartel-baiting' on

---

[35] FO, 371/38891 and 48995, reports by Lee and Mathias, June 1945.
[36] FO, 371/44590.

the part of the Americans. The reason for the action, it was alleged, lay with the failure of American merchants to get direct access to Congo supplies in 1944, plus 'fanaticism on the part of an Assistant Attorney General'.[37]

None of this satisfied the South Africans. Oppenheimer wrote a short memorandum for Smuts, sending a copy to the Diamond Corporation, in which he outlined a very partial history of the policy of the selling organization in wartime, confusing dates and missing some of the point behind American merchants' objections to the ways in which the Trading Company supplied goods. He did reveal, however, that actions were taken after the Hofman/Rodwell talks to 'degrade' gem roughs for industrial purposes at lower prices than for gem stones:

Immediate steps were taken . . . and arrangements made to enlarge the range of industrial diamonds by degrading certain of the lower categories of gem diamonds into the industrial category. This was done solely to meet the wishes of the United States Authorities and De Beers and all its associates agreed to this procedure. Further, in degrading these gem diamonds the Producers established prices in relation to the intrinsic worth of the degraded goods for industrial purposes no relation being had to their value as gems.

Crushing bort was lowered from 4s. to 2s. 6d. per carat and pre-war stocks were used up, while production increased in the Congo. This was to miss the point again concerning demands for selection of the most used categories of industrial stones, which the Diamond Trading Company had met only reluctantly. But Oppenheimer's most telling debating point concerning restraint of trade lay in his reply that selection of approved merchant buyers stemmed from the controls exercised in the United Kingdom and the United States in wartime, and from the South African government's approval of contracts entered into with companies inside South Africa. 'The allegation that the sale of Diamonds by the Diamond Trading Company is restricted to favoured customers is incorrect. The facts are that in conformity with official regulations in Britain and the United States diamonds may only be sold by the Diamond Trading Company under permit to buyers approved by the Authorities in both countries.'[38] It was also probably true, as he claimed, that the corporation's contract with Diamang had been influential in keeping sale of production through Lisbon from reaching the enemy.

---

[37] FO, 371/44590, Lee to DO, 19 Feb. 1945; US Law Reports, *Fifth Decennial Digest*, 1936-1946, vol. 32, sect. 24, De Beers Consolidated Mines vs. US.
[38] FO, 371/44590.

Oppenheimer's representations achieved very little. When the South African Legation in Washington lodged its own official protest, without waiting for any co-operation from the United Kingdom, it employed the argument that a stockpile had been agreed between governments in 1943, despite any alleged restraint of trade by diamond companies. The State Department replied (correctly) that the case had been brought on other grounds against 'private business practices'.[39]

Inside the British government, there was a certain amount of paralysis on an issue of American domestic jurisdiction, and the only semblance of protest came through the Foreign Office which sent a mild note to Washington, contesting the Justice Department's extraction of documents from the War Production Board showing that SLST, as one of the predatory monopoly companies, had done business in the United States. But as the case wore on and the belief grew that the companies would lose, there was closer consultation by De Beers on the probable effects on the diamond trade. It was thought likely that diamond imports into the United States would be stopped—from London at any rate— losing some £15 million a year in British overseas trade. The Ministry of Supply pursued the line laid down by Mathias— that diamonds were a special case—and wanted the usefulness of the cartel brought home to the Justice Department by a Board of Trade mission in Washington. The members of this mission reported that such arguments were likely to have no effect, and the Board of Trade let matters take their course. Personal approaches by Du Cane and Oppenheimer to Sir Alexander Cadogan at the Foreign Office resulted in personal notes deploring the action at law, but offering no diplomatic support.[40]

In the end, the case was dropped, not because of any diplomatic pressure, but because it could not be shown to the court's satisfaction that De Beers or any other diamond company had exercised a monopoly over sales within United States jurisdiction. The effect in London was to strengthen the hand of those who argued, as Mathias and the Board of Trade did, that the interests of the Diamond Corporation and De Beers coincided with those of the United Kingdom, so long as these South African companies conducted so much of their business to the benefit of the country's dollar earnings and financial services.

In South Africa, this thesis of a complementarity of imperial and multinational objectives was more acceptable than at any other time in

[39] FO, 371/44591, Union Legation to State Department, 13 Feb. 1945; DO to FO, 11 Oct. 1945.
[40] FO, 371/44591, for minutes and memoranda on departmental opinions.

the corporation's history. The De Beers group bore a heavy burden of taxation in the Union at the end of the war, and was very willing to transfer some of this burden to overseas subsidiaries. The South African government prolonged the special war levy on the diamond mining companies well beyond 1945, when relief was given to the rest of commerce and industry, on the grounds that De Beers had profited from the war at a late stage.[41] For 1945, the De Beers group paid out £5.9 million at the level of 36 per cent on profits, plus the usual 10 per cent export duty on diamonds. £3.6 million of this went to the Union and £1.8 to the British government and nearly half a million to South West Africa. If there had ever been a move to centralize the diamond market in South Africa (as the British once feared), the end of the war was not the time.

Furthermore, De Beers was a very different company from the pre-war corporation. Subsidiaries were now fully owned, and they were opened and closed as suited the strategies of production. Gem stones had not been required during the war period, though the market improved from 1943, and trading profits were very high, at about 80 per cent on a low volume of output and very low working costs, 1939–45. There was a rising profit on capital employed from 20 to 37 per cent, because of steady returns on investments, and a post-tax profit of £3 to £4 million after 1943. De Beers Industrial Corporation was floated in 1944 to take over holdings in African Explosives and (Chemical) Industries.

In the main, the war proved a profitable period because of the volume of industrial diamonds disposed of from pre-1939 stocks (at a cost which had been written down by the Diamond Corporation). For the first time it was admitted in the *Annual Report* for 1945 that the wartime experience of selling in such volume to more demanding customers required 'entirely different methods' from those applied to the sale of gem stones. The Diamond Trading Company went on handling gem roughs, but industrial diamonds were made the responsibility of new subsidiaries, Industrial Distributors Ltd. and Industrial Sales Ltd., created to coincide with the negotiation of a new series of 5-year contracts with the Congo, Angola, and West Africa. The Diamond Producers Association contracts now included Premier mine, which was revived after 8 years of inaction and pumped out to take advantage of the rise in industrial goods. The shareholders in Industrial Distributors included De Beers, Anglo, CDM, JCI, E. Oppenheimer and Son, Diamang, and Dicorp. To cope with the tax problem,

---

[41] DBCM, *Annual Report* (1947).

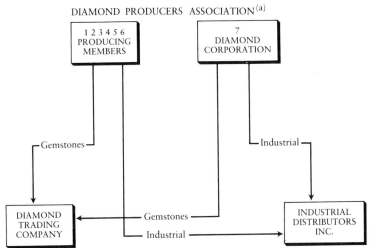

DIAMOND PRODUCERS ASSOCIATION[a]

FIG. 12. The Central Selling Organisation, 1946

two further subsidiaries, Diamond Products (Sales) and De Beers Industrial Diamonds (Ireland), were later added to the network.[42]

Prosperity in the diamond trade continued, moreover, after 1945, when the price ceiling on bort was lifted in the United States, and sales of gem stones expanded, as De Beers began to put about the idea that diamonds were an 'investment' and a hedge against inflation. Total sales of roughs for the year topped £24.5 million. In 1946, after the United Nations 'reserve' had been handed back to its owners among the companies or sold through the corporation, the United States legislated to establish a strategic stockpile of its own. Consequently, industrial diamond imports remained at their wartime level, after a slight fall in 1946–7, at over 10 million carats a year, and the price doubled to $3 and $4 per carat. In the phrase of Sydney H. Ball, trade journalist and member of the semi-official committee which advised the consulate-general in New York, the diamond trade was now 'a luxury-utilitarian industry'.[43]

---

[42] For the creation of the Diamond Purchasing and Trading Company (counterpart to the Diamond Trading Company, London) see Republic of South Africa, *Report of the Commission of Enquiry into the Diamond Industry of the Republic of South Africa and the Territory of South West Africa*, 1973, 23; and for transfer pricing to subsidiaries see P. W. Thirion, 'Commission of inquiry into alleged irregularities and misapplication of property in representative authorities and the central authority of South West Africa. Eighth interim report: Control by the state over prospecting and mining for, and disposing of, minerals in South West Africa' (TS, 1985), 111–123.

[43] *The African World* (London), 1 Jan. 1944; Henry P. Chandler, 96, 121.

The overall change in the diamond market was followed closely in the Board of Trade, after the disbandment of the Ministry of Economic Warfare. Indeed, the whole supervisory control system was reviewed in 1950 and the special value of centralization through Dicorp, the Trading Company, and Industrial Distributors, which passed 90 per cent of the world's diamonds through London, was re-emphasized.[44] The efficacy of such a system was very largely the product of the British government's continued co-operation with the enlarged multinational company after 1945. Vindication of the selling organization at official levels was not easy in a post-war Labour government, but it was strongly encouraged by the continued weakness of sterling and by the dogged advocacy of F. A. Mathias, who still haunted the ministries as special diamond adviser in the late 1940s.

The arguments for close co-operation with the corporation and special treatment of the diamond through a cartel of producers and a single channel for sales had been repeated by Mathias many times, and were summed up in a long and rambling memorandum which he served on officials in 1947.[45] Central control in London was justified, he claimed, because it had been so useful and profitable in war and had earned the nation at least £14 million, more than any other commodity (and a good deal more than net revenue from exports of whisky). Continued earnings depended on a recognition of South Africa's anxieties over the proliferation of pro-spection and output, especially in British colonies. Some form of collective 'regulation' had to be applied in conjunction with Oppenheimer and Beatty to restrict these sources by quotas and to limit manufacturing centres. If this was not done, Mathias argued, the policy of contracting for guaranteed minimum sales with outside producers—Angola, the Congo, Sierra Leone, and the Gold Coast—would place the selling organization in jeopardy, in the event of world demand falling below total deliveries. 'Disturbing factors' such as new concessions called for control. The case of Tanganyika was especially worrying to Mathias, because it had a potential production of £3 million a year and its concessionaire, John Williamson, was moving very reluctantly into a quota agreement with the Trading Company with prices set by negotiation, rather than the usual replacement formula.[46]

[44] BT, 64/752, 'Provisional Schemes for Wartime Controls Diamonds, Industrial and Gem, 1950'.

[45] FO, 371/62532, 'Diamonds', 14 Mar. 1947.

[46] For the combined effort of the Colonial Office and De Beers to bring Williamson Diamonds Ltd. into the fold see John Knight and Heather Stevenson, 'The Williamson Diamond Mine, De Beers and the Colonial Office: A Case-Study of the Quest for Control', *Journal of Modern African Studies*, 24/3 (1986), 423–45.

Mathias's colleagues were slightly embarrassed by this fervent outburst in favour of restrictive practices, though there was much they agreed with. The Foreign Office was for keeping a low profile, as the United States was not about to attack the cartel again. The Board of Trade made the point that the high price of gem stones served to balance the disposal of industrial goods at little above cost. It was hard to see what needed to be done, and Sir Sydney Caine called an interdepartmental meeting at the Colonial Office to see whether support for monopoly was justifiable. On the whole, officials thought it was. Diamonds could not be fitted into commodity agreements under the proposed International Trade Organisation charter for free movement of goods. The point of revenue from diamonds was well taken, especially as Britain was able to buy Belgian and Portuguese diamonds for sterling and sell them for dollars. On no account was the Diamond Corporation to be frightened away to South Africa. But no one could envisage a joint agreement with South Africa for control of concessions or anything more than *ad hoc* arrangements as new colonial fields expanded production. Prohibition of sales to new cutting centres, they thought, could not be justified, and the corporation was warned that it was vulnerable under any international trade agreements on this score.

All this was explained to Sir Ernest Oppenheimer, who visited Caine, to hear how much support he would get for further restriction of cutting in Palestine and control of Williamson's mine. For the cutting industry, Caine announced, open marketing would have to continue; but for colonial territories there were other levers to apply through the grant of licences: 'this, in effect, would mean that if diamonds were found in any considerable quantity the producer would presumably with the assistance of the Colonial Government concerned negotiate a sales quota with the Diamond Corporation.'[47] There were some territories where such a principle was difficult to apply, as on the Gold Coast, for political reasons. But it had been stated that the identity of interests between a metropolitan power and the multinational was at least as great as the longer and stormier relationship between the corporation and South Africa.

[47] FO, 371/62532, minutes, 'Diamond Policy', 20 June 1947; Caine to FO, 5 Aug. 1947.

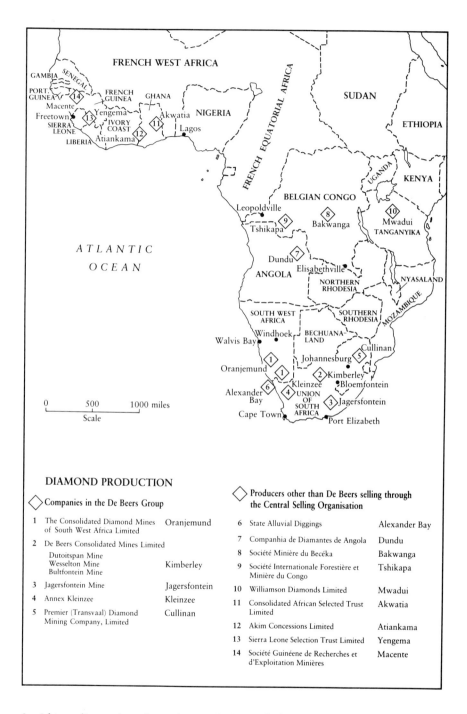

DIAMOND PRODUCTION

◇ **Companies in the De Beers Group**

1 The Consolidated Diamond Mines   Oranjemund
   of South West Africa Limited

2 De Beers Consolidated Mines Limited
   Dutoitspan Mine
   Wesselton Mine   Kimberley
   Bultfontein Mine

3 Jagersfontein Mine   Jagersfontein

4 Annex Kleinzee   Kleinzee

5 Premier (Transvaal) Diamond   Cullinan
   Mining Company, Limited

◇ **Producers other than De Beers selling through the Central Selling Organisation**

6   State Alluvial Diggings   Alexander Bay

7   Companhia de Diamantes de Angola   Dundu

8   Société Minière du Becéka   Bakwanga

9   Société Internationale Forestière et   Tshikapa
    Minière du Congo

10 Williamson Diamonds Limited   Mwadui

11 Consolidated African Selected Trust   Akwatia
    Limited

12 Akim Concessions Limited   Atiankama

13 Sierra Leone Selection Trust Limited   Yengema

14 Société Guinéenne de Recherches et   Macente
    d'Exploitation Minières

3. African diamond producers in association with the Central Selling Organisation

Conclusion

The minerals are ours being owners of the land.

Francis Oats to the Precious Stones and Minerals Commission, 1898.

The only way out of the domination of the Syndicate is for the Government to establish a Government Diamond Agency.

H. Warington Smyth, Secretary of Mines, 1924.

We continue to enjoy the good will of the Union Government.

Sir Ernest Openheimer, 1936.

AS indicated in the Introduction this study departs from the two more usual explanations for the growth and concentration of the diamond mining industry in South Africa sought in the iconography of the founders and the conflict between capital and labour. The entrepreneurs were important, but they worked in an unusual geological and political context. Conflicts there certainly were, and these resulted in the subordination of both white and black workers. But they were inherent in an industry which was vulnerable to fluctuating returns, a high turnover of migrant labour, and theft of its mineral product. They were aggravated by the rapid pace of technological change and company competition at Kimberley. But they were not unique to Kimberley's company investment and had their roots in the social and economic differentiation between black and white, wage labourer and claim owners, miners and landed proprietors, which stratified every alluvial rush in South Africa and elsewhere into winners and losers, employed and unemployed.

What distinguished Kimberley from the river diggings and later alluvial strikes was the phenomenon of early industrial monopoly and ownership of the means of production within a few dozen square miles by a small number of mining magnates. Hence the past and current fascination with a limited chronology, a single company, a few individuals on the supply side of a world-wide chain of mining, manufacturing, and distribution. There is much less material on the demand side to explain how merchant wholesalers and manufacturers coped with the increase in volume in the nineteenth century and a fall in prices aggravated by periodic trade cycles. Godehard Lenzen, in a pioneer work, attempted to grapple with this imbalance, but did not analyse the merchants' methods and contracts. Theodore Gregory recognized the gap too, but was diverted from revealing details of diamond marketing into a more generalized account of changes wrought by Sir Ernest Oppenheimer.

The result has been to place the weight of historical explanation for the organization of the industry on to control of production, following amalgamations at Kimberley in the 1880s, plus contractual agreements between South African producers and the London merchants to contain supply. Eventually, it is demonstrated that the producer cartel and the oligopsony represented by the London Diamond Syndicate merged their functions in the 1930s into the Central Selling Organisation controlled by De Beers. Outside South Africa, other producers were persuaded to join, in the interests of price stabilization.

The ghost at this long historical banquet of diamond riches in South Africa is the state, meaning the political executive and administration of Cape Colony and the republics which formed the Union, and contributed their legacy of laws and institutions. If the state has a role in mining by private entrepreneurs, it might be defined in general terms as legitimation of producers' concessions, in return for supervision and taxation. The concept in older imperial histories of a metropolitan or regional government favouring, or setting limits to, mercantile and industrial enclaves is familiar enough. There is a small but more recent literature on a new set of bargains arranged between successor states and large corporations, with occasional ventures into public ownership. The record is richest for the imperial phase of predatory concessions in Africa and elsewhere, and meagre for the post-colonial experience of dealings with the private sector, especially the multinational enterprise. In historical terms, South Africa was a 'new state', born out of an imperial war and a union of provinces and colonies which framed laws and created administrative institutions designed to deal with prospectors, diggers, and mining companies, in return for a share of their created wealth.

An important and historically neglected part of that legacy lay in the curtailment of Crown rights over precious stones mined on the farms of the northern Cape, which left the companies and De Beers with two private mines and two others under lease from a private estate. By the time of the incorporation of Griqualand West into Cape Colony in 1880, the diggers and the mine owners, through their control of local government, had laid down the framework for company hegemony over minerals, manpower, the town, and its market, with a minimum of legal or fiscal interference. Elsewhere, in the Transvaal, German South West Africa, and Central and West Africa, alluvial mining was a concession from the colonial state in return for rents and even participation in profits. Only the Gold Coast made such concessions from landed proprietors and in very different conditions of royalty payments to Akim Abuakwa chiefs. Nowhere else did the concessionary companies take over so much of the administration; nor did they escape for so long high levels of taxation for the benefit of the state.

This early weakness in state rights to dispose of precious stones and in administrative supervision explains the coercive and protective legislation framed by diggers and mine owners, who sought to regiment migrant labour and secure undisputed title in the mine areas in the early 1880s. Such legislation on claim tenure, the mine surround, the searching system, and the official survey of 1880 were the essential preface to joint-stock investment; and they were consolidated by the work of the 1882 commission and the legislation of 1882–3, which resulted in the Diamond Trade Act and the Mining Act. Once investment flowed into the corporate enclave, the purpose of such regulation of the 'interior economy' of the mines, epitomized in the compound system, lay less in the control of the labour market than in the control of the diamond market. The lasting legacy of that period of turbulence at Kimberley was not simply wage reduction or lengthy contracts, but the ability to measure output according to demand overseas. From this result, it is easy to argue that diamond mining in South Africa was shaped by the primacy of the entrepreneur in politics, at a municipal and state level. To do so is to see local industry only in terms of the production function.

For the second neglected topic in previous studies has been the concentration of diamond distribution in the hands of merchant principals and their agents. It was they, as much as the mine managers, who insisted on the reduction of an illicit trade in the 1880s, as they learned to cope with volume in production and promoted amalgamation between companies. As major shareholders or mayors of Kimberley, the diamond wholesalers transformed a speculative market in sales, by auctions at the Cape and London, into fixed-price sales in series to Continental dealers and manufacturers. They provided the necessary cash flow and arranged the debt financing which made mergers possible in a system of limited credit from local banks. The explanation given for company consolidation and the emergence of De Beers is both a technical and financial one, in which the backing of the wholesalers in their multiple roles of buyers, share brokers, and financiers was the essential component.

Company structure, therefore, reflected dual origins, in the administrative autonomy of the claimholders and the financial power of the major investors. Miners and merchants worked hand in hand. But they did not create any vertically integrated structure immediately: rather, the monopoly production enjoyed by De Beers for just over a decade in the 1890s was marketed under a series of contracts evolved by constant debate between the London and Kimberley sections of the board and the first diamond syndicates over who was to hold unsold stocks of diamonds, and how retained profits were to be used. Rhodes did not win that debate on the terms of the contracts, though he did prevail on the issue of profit-sharing towards the end of his life; and he diversified company investment into African ventures outside diamond mining. The company, however, was greater than the man; and the most important achievement of the 1890s lay not so much in the mechanics of production and labour control, which were relatively easy, but in the classification and resale of the bulk of the world's diamonds so as to restore wholesale prices and maintain the structure of credit built up by the Continental banks to service diamond manufacturing in Antwerp and Amsterdam. To that end, once profit-sharing with the producer was allowed, buffer stocks were held by the merchants' syndicate, as well as in kimberlite on the mine floors, making the wholesalers more vulnerable to market recession.

That vulnerability was soon demonstrated by new sources of supply from South West Africa and the Transvaal, and by the short crisis of 1908–9, which disrupted the steadily rising trend in wholesale prices after 1884. Because of its special relationship with Premier diamond mine, the Union government responded by encouraging the move towards cartelization among the leading producers, while treating the merchants' syndicate with all the suspicion reserved by new states for influential overseas combines which market their staple exports.

The primary reason, however, for this official concern was fiscal rather than any distrust of capitalist enterprise as such, or a hankering after nationalization in the department of mines. The major change between the long period of company autonomy and monopoly of production, and the subsequent growth of a production cartel lay in the example of taxation set by the British government, forcing De Beers to decamp legally from London in 1902, and in the even more forceful innovation of direct participation in Premier's profits by the Transvaal administration in 1903. Added point was given to the Union government's supervision of diamond mining by its frustration over British wartime regulation of the London market, which forced both Premier and South West companies into sales through the syndicate. Ministers and officials watched anxiously, too, while the syndicate flourished on rising prices and bought its way into Premier's board. On the other hand, the government approved the move on captured German companies which resulted in the formation of Consolidated Diamond Mines, in the hope that mineral revenue would help pay for the Mandate, and treated these assets separately from German assets seized in the Union. A diamond export duty was applied from 1916 with the aim of fostering a domestic cutting industry. Altogether, the First World War increased the role of the state at the British metropolitan end of the market and at the South African end, for both strategic and material reasons.

Thus, by the early 1920s, the state, through its Department of Mines, Treasury, and special adviser (the diamond valuator) was much better placed than Cape or Transvaal officials had been to act as patron of the South African producers' conference, and oversee the new series of contracts which regulated sales through the London syndicate. These contracts were a considerable advance on pre-war models in their attempt to regulate production and deliveries according to the sales of producers' goods. But not all members of the cartel benefited equally from single-channel selling, because of differences in quality, and the preponderance of De Beers and New Jagersfontein, which were favoured by the syndicate in order to build up financial reserves, while Premier's returns decreased and Consolidated Diamond Mines carried large debts and paid higher taxes for a relatively low territorial quota. Furthermore, competition from producers outside the cartel was not really contained by syndicate contracts prior to 1925.

How did changes in the country's executive influence government's relations with the industry? Considerable debate surrounds the historical importance of the advent of the Pact government in 1924.[1] But events on the Rand were not echoed at Kimberley; and the contribution of diamond mining to state revenues had a different profile from gold mining, because of contrasts in cost structures, profitability, and scale of the two industries. Militant unionism among whites was absent at Kimberley, if only because many of them were made redundant in the recession of 1920–1, and because they were cushioned by more favourable manning levels in relation to black and coloured employees, and by a measure of housing, insurance, and other benefits. Both industries shared, however, downward pressure on white as well as black wages in the 1920s and

---

[1] David Yudelman, *The Emergence of Modern South Africa*, 23, 42. If there must be a 'turning point', Yudelman's choice of 1933 is closer to the state and diamond industry's accommodation, though it did not solve the unemployment problem in alluvial mining.

1930s, and a colour bar which long preceded the legislation of the Pact politicians. So far as diamond mining was concerned, the change of government in 1924 accelerated a trend towards greater intervention, rather than marking a discontinuity; and it could be said to have exacerbated relations between the Department of Mines, the merchant directors, and their favoured companies—De Beers and New Jagersfontein. The clash between diamond capitalists and the Pact politicians centered on the crisis of over-production and not on the politics of 'Africanerisation' or job-protection at the work place. The tensions were real enough, however, and lasted from 1924 till about 1933, beginning with a breakdown in contractual monopoly and ending in accommodation between merchants, producers, and government during reconstruction.

Failure to reach agreement on contracts at the end of 1924 and the threat of separate sales to Antwerp gave Anglo American and Dunkelsbuhlers (inspired by Ernest Oppenheimer) an excuse to form a new syndicate; and the government took the opportunity to pass the Diamond Control Act of 1925. Oppenheimer's syndicate was favoured by the state for not opposing the new legislation; and the London merchants (and, therefore, the producing companies) moved to the new centre of gravity. Henceforth, the threat posed by the government's new powers was sufficient to maintain official supervision of the cartel. Oppenheimer, therefore, did not save the industry single-handed, but used the opportunity to stave off separate trading in South West Africa and contain the menace latent in the new legislation, reforming the syndicate around Anglo in the process, with the approval of the minister of mines, F. W. Beyers, and J. B. M. Hertzog.

The weakness of the new compact between companies, syndicate, and the state was that they ignored the revived production by small-scale entrepreneurs on private estates in the Union. As alluvial prospection expanded rapidly on improved wartime prices, the diggings became a social slum and a political minefield of conflicting interests. Farm owners, small capitalists, European and African claim owners, and labourers formed pressure groups and lobbied representatives from the alluvial constituencies. Local government agencies in the provinces were too poorly funded to cope and left much of the responsibility for registration and control to the Diamond Detective Department and a few mining inspectors. The Pact government failed to deal with this crisis. The long-delayed Precious Stones Act of 1927 restricted the alluvial companies, but abandoned the diggers by declaring a moratorium on proclamation of claims for a year, while the State Alluvial Diggings were opened in Namaqualand for exceptional state revenues, and rivals were curbed under the Control Act.

It took some time, therefore, for the government to react to the more general collapse of the diamond market in the early 1930s. Reconstruction in the shape of a new Diamond Corporation was paid for by the producers, led by De Beers, which relied heavily on its diversified investments, and was sanctioned with great reluctance by ministers of mines before 1933. The success of this operation has been justifiably attributed to Oppenheimer in the one detailed study made of the period. Like Rhodes, he was certainly at the centre of events during a period of rapid reconsolidation of producers' interests around the selling organization. But his was a very different order of talents. Rhodes was essentially a politician and sub-imperial strategist with a flair for utilizing the business and technical skills of his partners. Oppenheimer was a very gifted financier with much greater experience in corporate management and investment, and rather less ability in politics. His handling of debates in the Assembly and his confrontations with ministers behind the scenes were less of a political programme for the South African Party than a sustained search for compromise solutions between the Scylla of government control and the Charybdis of destructive competition in the diamond market. The compromise lay in holding back, after purchase, large quantities of Merensky, Cape Coast, and other alluvial stocks, at the request of government, in order to favour sales of valuable government state alluvials. This was followed by a complex adjustment of total purchases by the corporation in the 1930s which benefited the outside producers on contract more than the Union companies. The ratio of sales of Union goods, including government alluvials, on a basis of five to three with African outsiders, had to be abandoned. The government tolerated this balancing act, as long as alluvial sales from Namaqualand made up for loss of revenue from the decline of Premier. The final move in this accommodation was to bring the government itself into the cartel that was the Producers Association, after Patrick Duncan became minister of mines in the Smuts–Hertzog government of 1933.

In effect, the industry climbed out of the crisis of the 1930s because South African diamond production was used as the regulator for a measure of control by the Diamond Corporation over total diamond purchases inside and outside the Union. Mines were closed and purchases were held back from resale in the late 1930s, while outside minimum sales contracts and the rise of bulk industrial diamond sales favoured West and Central African producers. The result of this strategy can be appreciated by comparing the erratic price trends for South African mine and alluvial diamonds with other statistics for the value and direction of Union diamond exports between 1930 and 1946. For some years the activities of independent buyers in the alluvial market reduced the percentage of exports sent through London to under 75 per cent. In 1933, before government accepted the discipline of a quota, South African diamond exports to Holland and Belgium exceeded exports through the corporation; and it was not till the 1940s that the London channel recovered the total monopoly of resales which had been lost with the rise of separate alluvial sales from 1921.[2]

The main reason for this transition from departmental and ministerial antagonism towards De Beers and the syndicate to a concordat in 1933 with the restructured industry was the political change to a coalition government in the Smuts–Hertzog ministry, as well as changes of personnel in the Department of Mines. A less well-understood reason was that the Diamond Corporation worked to expand the use and sale of industrial diamond material, while the government pursued, unimpeded by the producers, its long-standing policy of developing a cutting industry in the Union. By promoting research and price stabilization for industrial diamonds, the corporation developed a new market for diamond tools in America, Europe, and South Africa. And by favouring the Union cutting factories the government found an outlet for its valuable alluvial stocks, taking them out of competition with producers. A sign of the times and the growing synthesis of state and corporation interests was the appointment to the board of De Beers in 1931 of Sir Robert Kotze, one-time partisan of closer official control, and of E. H. Farrer, former secretary to the Union Treasury and expert on company taxation.

There were social costs for falling into line with corporation policies. The sacrifices were periodically borne by the Cape and the Union's deep-level diamond mines to prevent over-production in the early 1890s, 1908–9, 1914–16, 1920–1; and the unemployment of the early 1930s (with longer-term closure for Premier) and the 1940s followed this pattern. Alluvial diggings were not subject to similar controls either in South Africa or Central and West Africa, with the exception of CDM in South West which fell under De Beers disciplines, though the social misery of reduced returns was, arguably, just as great.

Use of South Africa as the regulator of production was made easier for management by the operation of migrancy in the employment of

---

[2] British South Africa, *Annual Statements of the Trade and Shipping of the Union of South Africa and of Southern and Northern Rhodesia* (Cape Town, 1911–46). It should be noted, too, that Dicorp buyers of South African alluvial diamonds paid in the sterling equivalent of the old gold standard rates, to counter currency depreciation, when South Africa came off the gold standard. The corporation also sold at prices equivalent to valuation of diamonds on a gold basis, in purchasers' currencies, as agreed by the South African government: *The African World*, 7 June 1933, 384.

African workers and by the absence of militancy among the non-unionized white technical and supervisory grades. Because of the risk of violent price fluctuations, the mining and marketing of diamonds has been quite different from gold mining in the Union, and has resulted in a different labour history. Although there have been periods when state revenues from diamonds exceeded revenues from gold, diamond companies never achieved the centrality of gold groups in the financial structure of the Union or attracted such high levels of investment. Because low-grade ores were mined within a group system and at a declining real price until the early 1930s, there was a greater financial risk and greater conflict between capital and labour, and less flexibility in manning and production ratios. Continuity of labour supply has been a special feature of the Rand's organization with common recruitment paid for by companies. Labour supply has been intermittent, though elastic to demand, in diamond mining; and only Premier ever felt it necessary to participate in group recruitment. The response of the gold mining groups to the problems of low-grade ores has been to 'source' workers on a continuous strategy from outside and inside the Union, and spread costs through the industry. The response of the diamond companies to a decline in market demand has been to lay off workers in order to reduce quotas.[3]

There are other contrasts between gold and diamond labour in the use of closed compounds, the absence of rationing and provision of clothing, the piece work system, and the absence of monopoly agreements between diamond mines which helped to raise pay for recontracted workers to significantly higher averages compared with gold mines. Both sets of mines, however, showed little or no upward movement for black and white wages and salaries over the period from 1911 to 1945, measured against the retail price index (Fig. 13). And the gap between black and white wage levels which had widened at Kimberley before 1914 never really began to close until the 1960s. The industry, too, had its own version of an informal colour bar which became statutory in the Mines and Works Act of 1923. Black manning levels were never allowed to approach the one to eight ratio tolerated with difficulty on the Rand; and there were

---

[3] For 'sourcing' see David Yudelman and Alan Jeeves, 'New Labour Frontiers for Old: Black Migrants to the South African Gold Mines, 1920–85', *Journal of Southern African Studies*, 13/1 (1986), 101–24. In the case of diamond mines in South Africa, there may also have been some reduction of labour following increased mechanization in the 1920s, as well as a narrower field of recruitment from Lesotho and within the Union, as the mine labour force was further reduced by 43% 1930–50. There is some evidence of improved production and recovery rates for manpower employed over that period: Department of Mines, *Annual Reports* (1931–51), apps. More work is required to establish the precise differences and similarities between labour conditions in all sectors of the mining industry in South Africa.

(a) Real wages of black and coloured employees
    Index 1936=100=£43.2(base 1910)

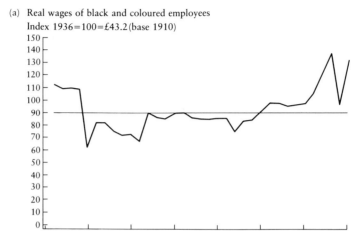

(b) Real wages (including allowances) of white employees
    Index 1936=100=£326 (base 1910)

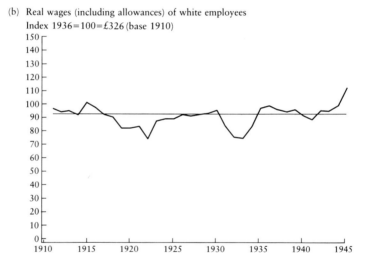

FIG. 13. South African diamond mines: annual average wages, 1911–1945: (a) real wages of black and coloured employees; (b) real wages (including allowances) of white employees.

periods in diamond mining when a one to three ratio of whites to blacks was quite usual. Defeated earlier by employers in their attempt to unionize in the early 1880s, Kimberley's white artisans and supervisors enjoyed a longer company patronage and kept out of the industrial warfare on the Rand.

It could be argued that the state aided and abetted in this discrimination; and at all stages the legislative and judicial framework of laws and the civil and criminal courts could be said to have worked to the mine owners' advantage for enforcement of registration and contracts of service, and the numerous laws against illicit diamond trading. It should be remembered, however, that internal policing and detection were in the beginning the responsibility of the mining companies, and remained so, even after the Diamond Detective Department of the South African Police refined its methods and took over supervision of export declarations at Kimberley and Johannesburg and on the alluvial diggings.

In other ways, administrative departments were much less efficient in enforcing the pass system from 1872, particularly when the Native Labour Regulation Act of 1911 extended the system of labour districts in the Transvaal to other provinces. Black and coloured claimholders continued to prospect in Cape Province; and the act did not apply the industrial colour bar to the alluvial diggings. In the end, agitation and pressure from the Board for the Control of Alluvial Diamond Interests, representing the alluvial diggers, succeeded where labour inspectors and the Native Affairs Department failed. The diggers drew support from the Urban Areas Act of 1923, which extended residential segregation to any industrial area, including Cape alluvial diggings. By 1926 the formalities of labour registration, approval of a contract of service, and a certificate of 'character' by a diggers' committee became standard features of alluvial mining recruitment, backed by penal sanctions.

But these were hollow victories, when alluvial mining degenerated into outdoor relief and general indigency. Both provincial and state authorities failed to provide an administrative structure to deal with alluvial mining, other than the magistracy and the South African Police. No other phenomenon of rapid industrial growth illustrated so well the essential weakness of the Union's local government outside the urban boroughs. In the end, therefore, the government had to swallow the bitter pill of white unemployment on the mines and white destitution on the diggings, while safeguarding its own sources of alluvial revenue, by sacrificing Premier to outside producers of low-grade industrial stones, and by joining the mine owners as a fully paid-up member which ran the state diggings at Alexander Bay with all the trappings of the closed compound.

In a sense, the state's legislative powers in the area of diamond mining were blunted instruments after 1927. So much of the parliamentary process leading to the Diamond Control Act and the Precious Stones Act was Nationalist rhetoric, in the face of the crisis in over-production and the changed position of South Africa as a producer in relation to other producers. As South Africa's share of the world market declined rapidly by weight, and less rapidly by value, the seat of the major marketing organization faced an unwillingness on the part of external colonial governments to make sacrifices. The British government supported CAST against De Beers, as part of Colonial Office commodity control programmes in the 1930s to favour oil, copper, zinc, tin, and diamonds. In turn, Chester Beatty's group agreed to restrict output and sales for the Gold Coast, in co-operation with the Diamond Corporation, but benefited considerably from the minimum sales contracts, by comparison with output in the Union. The same benefits applied to SLST, when it obtained an exclusive licence as a CAST subsidiary in 1932. The governments of Angola and the Belgian Congo were equally unwilling to forgo revenue, as competitors in industrial diamonds and gemstones. The Diamond Corporation could influence but not control such producers.

From 1939, moreover, the South African state lost influence over the Central Selling Organisation. As in the First World War, the British government, rather than South Africa, utilized the corporation and its Trading Company to exercise control over supply and distribution for strategic and economic ends. But because of the much greater importance of industrial diamonds, Canadian and American manufacturers objected to the quality of industrial stocks sold in series, and forced a reorganization of the London wholesale trade before bulk sales to the United States government were accepted in 1941. Stocks of Congo goods were transferred directly to London, rather than passing through South Africa. Independent cutting and sales of South African diamonds in Palestine were curtailed. A stockpile for North American and British manufacturers was established in Canada from 1942, despite South African objections. Under American pressure, corporation trade practices were refined and changed to provide the industrial grades most in demand under a price ceiling.

This policy of preserving London as the main channel and source of revenue from the wartime trade was confirmed by British and Diamond Corporation backing for the speedy rehabilitation of the Belgian cutting industry to counter the massive transfer of stocks to North America, and to attract refugee cutters back to Europe. In effect, British insistence on the continued location of central selling in London ended Oppenheimer's plan for moving the wholesale market to America, and reinforced the dominant position of the corporation in the industrial and gem markets from 1945.

What, then, was the nature of 'monopoly' over the historic period of concentration, cartelization, merchant combination, and vertical integration between producers and distributers? Clearly such an organization of a mining and commodity market did not simply spring phoenix-like from Kimberley as the result of amalgamations in the 1880s. Different explanations have been given which emphasize the peculiar nature of the commodity itself, sold as a luxury good and requiring careful adjustment of supply to demand, to avoid large fluctuations, as well as disposal of a heterogeneous product through a series of middlemen. Others have emphasized early relations between capital and labour, or the intuitive strategies of the leaders of business empires controlled by Oppenheimer or Chester Beatty, for whom cartelization and regional demarcation of interests were simply methods of preserving their corporations from mutual destruction.

The argument of this book is, first, that the influence of the demand side in the shape of the merchant-investors has been underestimated, particularly during the period when state powers were weak in the mining industry in Cape colony; and, secondly, that the role of the Union government and the British government has been underestimated in supervising and shaping the domestic and international structure of production and marketing as created around the South African companies and the syndicate until the crisis of the 1930s. The South African government then became a partner in the corporation which rationalized its functions to deal with production at home and overseas, and market gem and industrial goods through the London channel.

The first part of this conclusion can be better appreciated by reminding historians of the unusual circumstances of the diamond discoveries in South Africa on land that was already divided into farms and in the highly-concentrated endowment of five diamond pipes. The legalities of exploitation in these pipes mattered for joint-stock investment as much as the 'imperatives of the production process' in securing paid-up capital and a high proportion of unskilled labour.[4] But neither of these two factors on the supply side can be isolated from the 'imperatives' operating on the wholesalers in the chain of distribution that was constructed with remarkable facility between producers and manufacturers and the expanding retail trade in North America and Europe from the 1870s on. Diamonds are seen all too often as a preface to gold in South Africa, because of the ways in which migrant labour was utilized in both industries. But diamond wholesaling had a much more flexible price structure in the late nineteenth century. Indeed, it is a measure of the

---

[4] I borrow this phrase from the perceptive review article by Charles Perrings, 'The Production Process, Industrial Labour Strategies and Worker Responses in the Southern African Gold Mining Industry', *Journal of African History*, 18/1 (1977), 129–35.

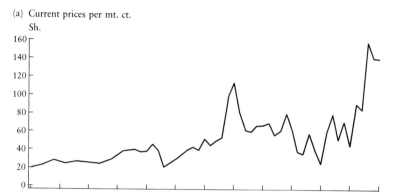

(a) Current prices per mt. ct.

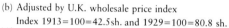

(b) Adjusted by U.K. wholesale price index

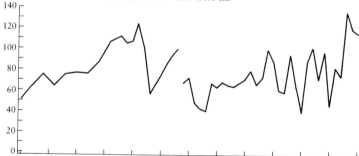

(c) Gold prices adjusted by S.A. wholesale prices

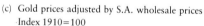

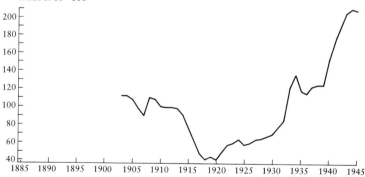

FIG. 14. South African mine and alluvial diamonds: prices declared, 1885–1945: (*a*) Current prices per metric carat; (*b*) Adjusted by UK wholesale price index; (*c*) Gold prices adjusted by SA wholesale price index

greater exploitation of diamond mining labour, particularly in the Rhodes period, that working costs were so rigid in relation to rising wholesale prices; and it is precisely because Rhodes sensed the widening differential between prices paid to his company and resale prices in London that he insisted on profit-sharing.

Thereafter (again, unlike gold mining), the contractual monopoly, rather than concentrated ownership, became the principal battleground for an increasing number of producers and the merchant combine. The diamond alluvial and mine stone wholesale index, adjusted for purchasing power, demonstrates just how successful the merchants were before and after the near-disaster of 1908–9 (Fig. 14). Until 1906, diamond prices adjusted against the United Kingdom wholesale price index, moved upwards much faster than the index in current prices. From 1910 until 1920, adjusted prices were not so spectacular, especially against wartime inflation. But diamonds performed far better than gold until the 1932 devaluation, in terms of their purchasing power, if prices for both commodities are corrected against the South African wholesale price index.[5] In the long term, moreover, between 1884 and 1945, the trend in adjusted wholesale prices for diamonds was clearly upwards, despite severe fluctuations in the 1930s.

Finally, comparisons are sometimes made with the pattern of monopoly growth discerned by Alfred Chandler for industries in the United States.[6] There are difficulties in the way of drawing easy parallels with corporations which not merely consolidated, but moved into the distribution of manufactures. The distribution of diamonds by wholesaling, manufacturing, and retailing was so widely dispersed that the extraction industry, in the period covered by this study, restricted itself to a measure of horizontal integration and eventual vertical integration with wholesalers. The mining companies did not move towards domination of the whole production and distribution chain.[7] De Beers did diversify, however, and investments in coal, dynamite, and industrial diamonds eventually paid off in ways that Rhodes would have approved. But Rhodes's predilection for investment in land did not pay off; and by 1940 the company

---

[5] I have preferred to use British wholesale prices as well as South African wholesale prices of imported commodities to establish a longer series (there is no South African price index for the 19th c.) See too Yudelman, 134–6; and cf. Frankel, *Investment and the Return to Equity Capital*, 90, table 2, which gives lower index values for gold than in Yudelman's table against both the South African wholesale and consumer price indexes.

[6] A. D. Chandler, *Strategy and Structure: Chapters in the History of the American Industrial Enterprise* (Cambridge, Mass., 1962), 383–96.

[7] Herman Levy, *Monopoly and Competition: A Study in English Industrial Organisation* (New York, 1977).

surrendered to Kimberley municipality half the land on which the town was built, while retaining as freehold land it rented. There was a similar surrender at Koffyfontein and Jagersfontein, and the long tradition of acquiring estates to cover rights to minerals and the mine surround ended.

Consequently, Chandler's four conditions for the development of historical monopolies require qualification in the case of South African diamond mining. Accumulation of resources was considerably foreshortened at Kimberley, compared with the American cases, and rested on monopoly titles to sources of supply. Secondly, rationalization by vertical integration was postponed, but a contractual monopoly with the leading company and later competitors was established by the wholesalers which served as the basis for the integration of the 1930s. Similarly, diversification, as the third condition, was much debated, and centered on the industry that De Beers and the Diamond Corporation knew best: diamond production and processing by classification for sale. Finally, administrative co-ordination was Oppenheimer's major bequest to the restructured industry, when financial and technical services were centralized on the model of the gold mining industry.

The aim of this search for monopoly control was twofold: to raise prices for a luxury good in such a way as to maintain confidence throughout the long production, wholesale, manufacturing, and retail chain, especially where it functioned on short-term credit; and secondly, to maximize the profits of the core of integrated corporations in order to service their heavy debt liabilities and pay high dividends.

Payment of dividends is a very crude measure of success in this long-term strategy. But in terms of investors' rewards from retained profits between 1889 and the 1940s, the South African group of diamond mines had clearly been successful on the rising trend of diamond prices by returning some £80.5 million to shareholders.[8] By comparison, the 'outside' companies in Angola, the Congo, and West Africa were relative newcomers, returning a more modest £11.6 million on a shorter time-scale. There were marked differences between companies: and dividends as a percentage of shareholders' equity were high for Premier and the Angola concessions at 204 per cent and 75.5 per cent respectively, because of their low capital base, and rather poor for CDM at 7.2 per cent, because of restricted output under quota agreements. On the whole, De Beers pulled up the South African group to a return of 17 per cent over a period of half a century—perhaps higher, if earlier returns for New Jagersfontein

---

[8] BT, 11/2726, Bliss report, 1944.

were known—compared with 19.3 per cent to outside companies' shareholders, including colonial governments.

It was ironic, therefore, that the historically dominant structure of the South African mines had to be used to restrain production at home during crises, in order to keep the contractual goodwill of much smaller enterprises in colonial states in Central and West Africa and to placate the South African government as legislator and as a rival producer of alluvial diamonds.

While acknowledging Chandler's emphasis on the market and entrepreneurial talent, compared with legislation, taxation, and 'public policy', for case studies of American industrial firms, it would be unsafe to minimize the role of government and administration in the kind of industrial enclaves established around the rush for minerals in southern and other parts of Africa. Such enclaves were too important in underdeveloped societies to escape political monitoring and intervention, mainly for fiscal and social ends.[9] Moreover, the companies engaged in diamond production by the 1930s were of international importance for other reasons; and this change was recognized in wartime in ways which emphasized the utility of monopoly control, rather than real or imagined dangers to particular national sectors such as alluvial diggers or a weak producer squeezed by monopoly priorities.

There was, too, growing interest from other public watchdogs and academics concerned or fascinated by the spectacle of a mining house with multinational influence over diamond markets. The Brookings Institution, which investigated the question of economic and political control of minerals during the war attributed the success of the cartel which became 'a full-fledged world monopoly' simply to the ownership of stock by De Beers with power to appoint the chairman of the Diamond Corporation.[10] And this approach through analysis of share ownership rather than sales contracts has been followed by other investigators. The diamond industry is seen as a corporate octopus regulating supply and always maintaining a 'sellers' market', but allowing secondary markets for 'surplus' in Amsterdam and Antwerp (or India, Israel, and Singapore). Much the same reasoning was served up by E. A. G. Robinson and C. W. Guillebaud, who found that the original monopoly constructed by De Beers in the 1890s 'with complete control over price [sic]' expanded

---

[9] For a different form of expropriation by the colonial state and reduction of royalties paid to government in Northern Nigeria see Bill Freund, *Capital and Labour in the Nigerian Tin Mines*, (London, 1981).

[10] C. K. Leith, J. W. Furness, Cleona Lewis, *World Minerals and World Peace* (Washington, 1943), 126–30.

as a simple continuum, unchanged by new discoveries, the vagaries of market demand, wars, and slumps.[11]

The historian must reject such simple summaries of a dynamic and complex process. It is useful to recall that so much of the initiative for financing concentration in the 1880s, building up the merchant combine in the 1890s, and reconstructing in the 1930s came from London and not from Kimberley. Dominance by shareholding through a producer company's investments was a precarious insurance without the co-operation of the wholesalers. In the end, after many years of discussion about a 'buying and selling company' by De Beers' directors, the move for reconstruction came from a faction within the diamond syndicate. The new syndicate offered a share in outside purchases to the Union producers as a way of imposing greater discipline on world production and convincing the South African government that further 'controls' were not required. Reconstruction as the Diamond Corporation was both a defensive and offensive measure which resulted in some producers being controlled through ownership and others by contract. The South African government eventually opted to become part of the Producers' Association, and it has stayed there, though some outside producers (Congo Zaire) have opted out of the looser contractual network. The fact that by 1938 De Beers owned the Diamond Corporation has tended to overshadow the importance of Barnatos and Dunkelsbuhlers, who helped to finance it and transferred their expertise to the Diamond Trading Company.

In short, it was the London merchants who moved in on the producers, led first by Porges's men and later by Oppenheimer in Anglo, playing an ambiguous role on several fronts as merchant, producer, and politician.

Was De Beers, therefore, a multinational enterprise by the period of reconstruction in the 1930s? On the general criteria advanced as ownership and control of extractive or manufacturing industries in more than one country, probably it was not.[12] For most of the period, De Beers was essentially a South African firm with an 'arm's-length' relationship with the marketing combine. The distance was emphasized after 1902, as a result of a different interpretation of the company's centre of operations by the British Inland Revenue. At most, there was a minor move towards integration through joint financing with Barnato Bros. for purchases of South West diamonds before and during the First World War.

---

[11] E. A. G. Robinson and C. W. Guillebaud, *Monopoly* (Cambridge, 1943), 49–54.
[12] See the valuable discussions in the collection of essays edited by Peter Hertner and Geoffrey Jones (eds.), *Multinationals: Theory and History* (London, 1986).

Some light is thrown on the importance of reconstruction, however, by more recent theory. If international firms arise 'to internalise transaction costs in arm's-length markets', then the whole merger of De Beers with the syndicate can be regarded as a way of sharing the funding for holding buffer stocks, and the Diamond Corporation emerged as a multinational brokerage and a special case. In addition, the producer was given access to inside knowledge within the marketing agency (as Rhodes had once wished). And such an organization decreased the risk of defection by less integrated, contractual clients among the outside producers. But such 'internalization' was not a static mode and expanded to include even a government producer. Otherwise, much of the theory of transaction costs does not apply, being drawn from manufacturing examples.[13]

The theory, in its current state, leaves out of account too the influence of government on the enterprise. In the case of the diamond industry, both world wars were periods when the British government superseded the South Africans and took charge of the 'single channel' at the distribution end in ways which enhanced the power of the monopoly, and recognized that the diamond was much more than a luxury good, as a hard currency earner and an industrial mineral in short supply in qualities required by manufacturers. Little was done, it is true, to protect the diamond companies from the legal suit brought against them under the Sherman Anti-Trust Act. But this failed and left the wartime monopoly intact at the beginning of a new phase of expanded sales in the diamond trade after 1945, and increased industrial use as America began to stockpile both through the Diamond Trading Company and Industrial Distributors Ltd. South Africa under the Smuts government accepted British policies, while extracting high taxes from the De Beers group, which emerged from the war fully in command of the South African diamond mines; while the corporation disposed of stocks at unprecedented levels in what has become a 'luxury-utilitarian' industry with the patronage of governments possessing sources of supply or enjoying returns from the services associated with wholesaling, manufacture, and retail of diamonds. There were some very visible hands of politicians and administrators in the diamond industry, as well as the forces of the market.

For it had been Hertzog who proclaimed the essential interdependence of diamonds and the state, during the legislative attack on syndicate control in 1925. Afrikaner attitudes changed in the 1930s, as the state joined

---

[13] Ibid. for the suggestive essay by Stephen Nicolas, 'The Theory of Multinational Enterprise as a Transactional Mode', 64–79. But note the intriguing suggestion by Mira Wilkins, who stands the problem on its head by positing overseas mining companies as part of banking multinational enterprise, 80–95 (which makes Rothschilds the real multinational?).

the combine. From the 1940s, British and South African governments appreciated the monopoly organization of the diamond industry and its location in their commercial capitals for much the same reasons: it served the fiscal and the strategic interests of governments for the industry to be organized in that way. Since the 1940s, South Africa ranks third or fourth in world diamond production and in proven reserves, but low in percentage terms at 20 per cent and 5.7 per cent.[14] There is widespread diversification of sources among new producers and the cutting industry has found new centres. In these circumstances, analysts of the trade and its corporation have had difficulty in classifying something so protean. Godehard Lenzen called it 'an incomplete collective monopoly'; and Timothy Green regards the whole Central Selling Organisation as a 'producers' co-operative'.[15] (If so, ownership by producers is very narrow.) But the core of the organization is a multinational brokerage financed originally for the purposes of stockpiling. The brokerage has expanded financing and technical services and contractual agreements outside South Africa, even where nationalization has taken place, as in Angola; and it is well placed to deal with minor states such as Botswana and middle-ranking ones such as Australia, not because such producers share in a 'co-operative', but because their governments approve the economic rationality of this way of marketing such a special commodity.

[14] W. C. J. Van Rensburg, *Strategic Minerals: Major Mineral Exporting Regions of the World*, vol. 1 (Brookfield, New Jersey, 1986).

[15] Lenzen, 191; Green, 137.

Appendix

TABLE A.1. De Beers Consolidated Mines: production, 1890–1930

Years (to 31 March)	Loads hauled and washed ('000)				Total loads ('000)	Index (1890 = 100)	Diamonds recovered (mt. cts. '000)	Index (1890 = 100)
	De Beers & Kimberley	Wesselton	Bultfontein	Dutoitspan				
1890	3,443.5				3,443.5	100	1,489.0	100
1891	4,007.8				4,007.8	116	2,074.0	139
(to 30 June)								
1892	6,577.7				5,262.1a	153	2,492.8a	167
1893	5,198.8	1,641.0b			5,198.8	151	2,288.9	154
1894	5,576.9	1,185.0b			5,576.9	162	2,369.7	159
1895	5,380.5	1,459.0b			5,380.5	156	2,500.1	168
1896	5,295.1	1,714.0b			5,295.1	154	2,426.1	163
1897	5,527.8	271.7			5,799.5	160	2,842.9	191
1898	6,592.4	1,838.7			8,431.1	242	2,867.2	193
1899	6,816.7	3,695.5			10,512.2	305	2,917.6	196
1900	6,195.7	1,717.1			7,912.8	230	1,254.1	84
1901	4,434.3	3,089.5	148.0		7,671.8	223	2,512.9	169
1902	4,024.4	3,684.3	373.2		8,081.9	235	2,078.9	140
1903	4,932.4	3,977.1	636.3		9,545.8	277	2,305.2	155
1904	4,842.0	4,045.2	944.1	63.0	9,903.3	288	2,114.6	142
1905	4,866.0	4,100.8	1,217.2	377.3	10,561.3	307	1,994.8	134

1906	4,373.4	4,369.8	2,724.6	2,302.7	13,770.5	400	1,955.7	131
1907	3,571.4	3,995.8	4,048.5	4,021.0	11,615.7	337	2,116.7	142
1908	2,339.6	3,243.8	2,595.5	2,284.0	10,462.9	304	1,512.3	102
1909	1,893.0	3,651.7	2,787.3	nil	8,332.0	242	1,857.9	125
1910	2,239.7	3,841.9	3,917.5	1,797.7	11,794.8	343	2,294.1	154
1911	1,675.5	3,845.2	4,323.6	5,115.0	14,959.7	434	1,975.3	133
1912	702.2	4,593.7	4,360.2	4,564.5	14,225.6	413	2,016.0	135
1913	771.2	4,369.4	4,409.9	4,821.0	14,371.5	417	2,167.4	146
1914	75.8	4,456.9	4,349.4	4,926.2	13,808.3	401	1,957.2	131
1915		436.6	471.4	544.3	1,452.3	42	193.0	13
1916		928.5	924.9	108.5	1,961.9	57	607.0	41
1917		3,483.4	3,853.9	2,092.9	9,432.2	274	1,548.6	104
1918		3,871.0	4,188.1	4,378.8	12,437.9	361	1,598.7	107
1919		2,692.3	2,892.0	2,456.3	8,040.6	234	1,120.8	75
1920		3,574.0	4,272.2	3,689.0	11,535.2	335	1,406.9	94
1921		1,677.7	1,605.4	1,692.1	4,975.2	144	599.6	40
1922		nil	nil	nil				
1923		973.6	273.7c	nil	1,247.3	36	314.0	21
1924		2,103.8	2,376.1	490.4	4,970.3	144	1,152.8	77
1925		3,194.0	2,718.8	1,155.3	7,068.1	205	1,052.6	70
1926		3,171.5	3,094.1	2,135.8	8,401.4	244	1,071.8	72
1927		3,242.2	3,307.5	3,286.3	9,836.0	285	1,133.4	76

Table A.1 (*cont.*):

Years (to 31 March)	Loads hauled and washed ('000)				Total loads ('000)	Index (1890 = 100)	Diamonds recovered (mt. cts. '000)	Index (1890 = 100)
	De Beers & Kimberley	Wesselton	Bultfontein	Dutoitspan				
1928		3,241.5	3,259.9	3,275.2	9,776.6	284	1,142.1	76
1929		3,240.2	3,067.3	3,206.5	9,514.0	276	1,116.5	75
1930		3,220.7	3,252.1	3,226.9	9,699.7	282	1,144.7	77

[a] Adjusted for twelve months, Wesselton excluded from total.
[b] Five million loads hauled and washed under lease by Henry A. Ward excluded from total.
[c] Ground washed only.

Source: DBCM, *Annual Reports* (1890–1930). Small amount from tailings omitted.

TABLE A.2. *De Beers Consolidated Mines: sales and working costs; profitability ratios, 1889–1945*

Financial years	Sales on diamond account	Administration, distribution	Mining costs (stores, labour)	Profit on sales (%; 1890 = 100)[a]	Profit on capital employed (%)[b]	Profit on all capital (%)[c]	Post-tax profit on all capital (%)
1889	34	47	39	45.2	16.0	6.2	6.2
1890	100[d]	100[e]	100[f]	49.8	15.6	15.1	11.9
1891	125	104	93	52.4	20.3	18.8	14.8
1892	119	108	107	50.3	21.6	15.8	15.8
1893	122	115[g]	94	61.8	21.4	20.1	20.1
1894	106	107	99	56.8	17.0	16.1	16.1
1895	117	101	107	57.9	19.1	17.4	17.4
1896	120	105	91	66.9	23.1	21.3	21.3
1897	141	132	101	65.3	25.9	21.9	21.9
1898	138	146	120	61.9	28.1	23.6	23.6
1899	153	155	132	61.7	33.4	27.8	27.8
1900	78	391[h]	69	49.0	10.3	9.2	9.2
1901	175	252[h]	131	62.7	32.8	29.2	29.2
1902	177	175[h]	131	61.5	35.4	28.4	28.4
1903	198	190	142[i]	55.8	37.4	28.9	28.9
1904	186	217	159[i]	52.1	33.3	26.0	26.0
1905	181	186	183[i]	51.4	30.7	25.0	19.5

Table A.2 (*cont.*):

Financial years	Sales on diamond account	Administration, distribution	Mining costs (stores, labour)	Profit on sales (%; 1890 = 100)[a]	Profit on capital employed (%)[b]	Profit on all capital (%)[c]	Post-tax profit on all capital (%)
1906	202	164	221[i]	46.5	34.5	26.1	20.0
1907	244	207	298[i]	46.9	45.2	36.4	30.0
1908	126	167	170	36.6	15.4	14.4	9.8
1909	116	158	150	39.3	13.3	12.3	8.6
1910	204	159	213	54.6	41.7	33.1	30.3
1911	187	169	201	46.4	39.9	28.8	19.3
1912	207	224	179	51.5	49.7	33.6	27.3
1913	238	219	183	56.9	49.1	32.8	27.4
1914	194	232	197	53.0	43.2	27.7	23.4
1915	21	142	20	−61.9	−4.7	0.6	0.6
1916	81	148	39	61.8	22.1	13.5	10.5
1917	175	248	114	65.2	49.5	24.9	21.5
1918	164	233	129	62.9	46.7	23.2	19.9
1919	221	256	153	65.5	81.1	30.9	26.8
1920	256	628[i]	197	63.5	85.7	32.6	28.2
1921	87	487[i]	195	−0.8	−0.3	4.1	2.6
1922	15	212	78	−136.0	−0.01	−2.9	−5.0

notes on p. 386

1923	106	241	95	59.7	30.5	16.6	14.7
1924	130	297	179	41.3	28.9	15.0	12.0
1925	126	343	157	45.3	29.7	19.3	16.0
1926	158	325	120	65.5	65.9	26.2	21.8
1927	163	363	130	63.4	68.9	25.3	20.8
1928	125	331	118	56.7	38.6	17.4	13.9
1929	123	354	121	54.5	33.7	16.1	12.8
1930	124	324	113	58.0	34.4	18.2	14.9
1931	26	377	88	(loss)	(loss)	1.9	1.9
1932	12	121	52	(loss)	(loss)	0.02	0.02
1933	11	203	17	(loss)	2.9	2.9	2.9
1934	34	151	27	58.0	13.0	7.1	7.1
1935	58	246	43	60.0	31.0	23.0	22.0
1936	85	143	44	75.0	48.0	33.0	30.0
1937	96	98	81	65.0	37.0	30.0	28.0
1938	25	132	80	(loss)	(loss)	5.2	5.2
1939	40	165	75	18.2	5.9	7.7	7.7
1940	58	222	45	60.4	17.0	10.5	9.2
1941	67	199	14	82.0	28.0	19.9	15.5
1942	99	197	17	88.0	25.0	21.0	16.5
1943	173	195	41	87.0	37.0	23.8	15.5
1944	175	172	100	75.0	23.0	16.7	10.9
1945	305	210	118	83.0	91.0	37.0	23.0

Table A.2 (*cont.*):

[a] After administration and mining costs and depreciation, but before interest, rents, investment earnings, and taxes: Trading Profit.

[b] Trading Profit

Capital employed (fixed assets + current assets – current liabilities $\times 100$ over 1

[c] $\dfrac{\text{Trading Profit} + \text{investment earnings before interest and tax} \times 100}{1}$

Capital employed and investments

[d] $1890 = 100 = £2,641,700$

[e] $1890 = 100 = £70,400$

[f] $1890 = 100 = £1,012,200$. Costs include compounds, but not replacement of machinery. The index for 1892 is calculated on the basis of 12 months from returns for 15 months.

[g] Including cost of exhibits at Kimberley and Chicago exhibitions.

[h] Including charges arising from the siege of Kimberley.

[i] Including recruitment charges.

[j] Including special donations for public relief and to universities and increases in directors' fees and head office salaries.

Source: DBCM, *Annual Reports* (1889–1945).

TABLE A.3. *Premier (Transvaal) Diamond Mining Company: production, yields, costs, 1903–1920*

Year ending 31 October	Carats found (m.)	Yield per load (mt. cts.)	Value per carat (s.)	Index (1903 = 100)	Cost per carat (s.)	Index (1903 = 100)	Labour charges[a] (£)	Proportion of mine costs (%)	Black wages[b] (s. d.)
1903	101,839	1.324	26.99	100	3.47	100	n/a	n/a	n/a
1904	769,534	0.819	22.5	83	3.22	93	n/a	n/a	n/a
1905	868,078[c]	0.625	22.9	85	5.26	152	n/a	n/a	n/a
1906	923,607	0.309	27.7	103	11.25	324	n/a	n/a	n/a
1907	1,940,108	0.297	17.6	65	7.89	227	596,033	77.7	n/a
1908	2,133,955	0.265	14.4	53	6.99	201	557,596	79.9	2 10.6
1909	1,921,785	0.256	12.2	45	7.62	220	518,165	74.6	2 10.6
1910	2,202,739	0.236	13.6	50	8.67	250	656,605	72.0 (74.5)[d]	2 10.0
1911	1,821,258	0.219	15.7	58	9.9	285	615,539	71.0 (75.7)	2 8.6
1912	2,045,314	0.211	19.6	73	11.37	328	786,917	70.3 (77.0)	2 11.2
1913	2,163,887	0.207	21.6	80	12.35	356	873,032	72.9 (78.0)	3 0.1
1914	1,455,354	0.189	17.3	64	13.18	380	653,434	72.1	3 0.7
1915	no operations						—	—	—
1916	431,083	0.274	22.1	83	9.62	277	138,326	74.4	2 9.3
1917	930,470	0.189	25.7	95	11.76	339	394,572	76.6	3 0.8
1918	874,157	0.182	27.5	102	12.22	352	382,748	75.7	3 2.8

Table A.3 (*cont.*):

Year ending 31 October	Carats found (m.)	Yield per load (mt. cts.)	Value per carat (s.)	Index (1903 = 100)	Cost per carat (s.)	Index (1903 = 100)	Labour charges[a] (£)	Proportion of mine costs (%)	Black wages[b] (s. d.)
1919	836,180	0.185	46.9	174	15.62	450	410,629	72.7	31.2
1920	842,325	0.181	49.8	185	17.77	512	455,153	71.1	33.2

[a] Black and white workers.
[b] Average daily rates including piecework and overtime without provision of food.
[c] Including the 'Cullinan' stone of 3,105 mt. cts.
[d] % in brackets include extraordinary recruiting costs.

Source: Premier, *Directors' Reports* (1903–21).

TABLE A.4. *Premier (Transvaal) Diamond Mining Company: sales, profits, costs, 1903–1930*

Years (to 31 October)	Diamond sales: trading profit (£'000)	Profit as percentage of sales (%)	Return on capital employed[a] (%)	Post-tax profit on capital employed (%)	Index Sales[b]	General charges[c]	Mining costs[d]
1903	101.8	74.0	40.0	40.0	15.3	15.5	22.3
1904	667.8	77.0	78.5	78.5	100	100.0	100
1905	623.2	62.6	198.9	116.0	112	192.0	184
1906	673.5	52.7	213.3	95.9	144	188.0	419
1907	865.9	50.8	169.9	109.9	194	138.0	619
1908	790.1e	51.4	129.2	111.1	173	97.0	563
1909	438.9e	37.4	94.9	67.7	132	77.0	561
1910	541.1	36.2	121.9	55.7	169	86.0	736
1911	531.5	37.0	70.4	38.1	162	69.0	700
1912	841.0	41.9	134.7	70.0	226	89.0	903
1913	1,003.2	42.9	163.5	80.8	263	268.0f	967
1914	302.5	24.0	36.3	27.6	142	99.0	732
1915	–17.4	(loss)	–22.3	–6.0	2.6	80.0	nil
1916	271.2	56.9	64.4	16.3	53.7	37.0	150
1917	651.0	54.0	150.0	45.4	135	66.0	415
1918	665.5	55.0	187.7	74.8	136	65.0	408
1919	1,310.3	66.8	384.1	171.0	221	171.0	456
1920	1,364.4	65.0	208.6	86.4	237	169.0	516
1921	56.3	18.5	60.1	41.8	50.7	43.9	271
1922	23.0	9.0	n/a	n/a	29	n/a	133

Table A.4 (*cont.*):

Years (to 31 October)	Diamond sales: trading profit (£'000)	Profit as percentage of sales (%)	Return on capital employed^a (%)	Post-tax profit on capital employed (%)	Index		
					Sales^b	General charges^c	Mining costs^d
1923	994.1	74.2	g	g	154	99.0	238
1924	557.9	54.3	g	g	118.6	140.0	321
1925	796.3	62.7	562.7^h	178.7	146.7	102.5	341
1926	822.5	56.5	480.1^h	159.8	168.2	82.8	478
1927	320.2	33.6^i	195.7^h	135.7	109.8	n/a	362.7^j
1928	356.8	40.6	223^h	89.0	101.4	n/a	341
1929	312.5	33.6	208.3^h	78.3	107.4	n/a	355
1930	38.5	5.6	25.7^h	14.6	79.2	n/a	372

a $\dfrac{\text{Trading Profit}}{\text{Fixed and Current Assets} - \text{Current Liabilities}} \times \dfrac{100}{1}$

b 1904 = 100 (£866,030).
c 1904 = 100 (£50,700).
d 1904 = 100 (£123,800).
e After share of loss on resales through the diamond syndicate.
f Including pension arrears.
g Liabilities exceed assets.
h Little trading capital and use of government funds.
i Deliveries for 8 months only.
j Rise in charges and costs attributed to 'quantity of ground treated'. General administration charges are not specified in the accounts from 1927, and the base index for 1904 has been combined for general charges and costs.

Source: Premier, *Directors' Reports* (1903–30).

TABLE A.5. *Revenues from diamond mining, 1910–1945*

Financial years	Profits, tax; income tax[a] (£'000)	Special contribution	Registration fees; export duty:[b] (£'000)	Share of profits[c] (£'000)	Total Union diamond revenues (£'000)	Ordinary Union revenues (%)	State alluvial mines: to revenue account (£'000)[d]
1910/11	230.9		27.8	175.6	434.3	3.0	
1911/12	436.0		39.4	333.2	808.6	5.7	
1912/13	391.9		45.5	428.6	866.0	6.1	
1913/14	486.1		48.2	476.9	1,011.2	8.0	
1914/15	290.9		13.3	126.9	431.1	3.9	
1915/16	5.9		9.9	130.8	146.6	1.1	
1916/17	150.1		172.6	304.4	627.1	4.2	
1917/18	372.2		219.2	355.3	946.7	5.9	
1918/19	388.2		340.1	402.0	1,130.3	6.2	
1919/20	593.3		1,331.5	879.5	2,804.3	12.1	
1920/21	538.8		810.5	799.8	2,149.1	8.3	
1921/22	115.6		142.6	54.2	312.4	1.3	
1922/23	−65.5[e]		587.8	14.2	536.5	2.4	
1923/24	201.2		723.4	602.1	1,526.7	6.3	
1924/25	295.6		727.9	339.6	1,363.1	5.4	
1925/26	319.1		874.9	479.3	1,673.3	6.2	
1926/27	532.3		1,186.7	459.2	2,178.2	7.6	
1927/28	511.6		1,218.6	205.5	1,935.7	6.4	

Table A.5 (*cont.*):

Financial years	Profits, tax; income tax[a] (£'000)	Special contribution	Registration fees; export duty:[b] (£'000)	Share of profits[c] (£'000)	Total Union diamond revenues (£'000)	Ordinary Union revenues (%)	State alluvial mines: to revenue account (£'000)[d]
1928/29	417.4		1,153.9	231.8	2,256.1	7.4	453
1929/30	409.5		783.6	170.0	1,831.1	6.0	468
1930/31	325.8		345.0	9.3	918.1	3.2	238
1931/32	19.2		214.8		402.0	1.4	168
1932/33	0.5		123.6		285.1	1.0	161
1933/34	42.7		143.1		323.8	0.9	138
1934/35	20.6		209.5		376.1	0.9	146
1935/36	6.2		176.2	36.2	372.6	0.9	154
1936/37	25.3		270.2	98.3	560.8	1.3	167
1937/38	16.4		237.8		437.2	1.1	183
1938/39	227.7		108.4	7.0	534.1	1.1	191
1939/40	10.9		137.0	0.6	341.5	0.5	192
1940/41	73.1	39.4	65.3	10.5	382.5	0.5	194
1941/42	94.7	50.4	149.1	118.5	625.7	0.6	212.7
1942/43	185.1	90.6	162.7	5.2	701.0	0.6	257.4
1943/44	399.0	265.1	416.0	2.0	1,761.0	1.4	679
1944/45	860.5	764.9	406.5	0.5	2,407.0	1.8	375

[a] Profits tax of 10%, 1910–17; income tax including dividend tax from 1917/18. Small amounts of employers' and company taxes in the provinces excluded. Revenues for 1910/11 are for 10 months.

[b] Registration fees, 1910–18; export duties from 1916/17.

[c] From Premier (Transvaal) DMC.

[d] This new source has been included in the general total for Union diamond mining taxation. In addition to this source, some £8.5 million was paid from state alluvial earnings into the Union's Loan Account over the period from 1928/9 to 1944/5. Revenue from diamond mining exceeded revenue from gold mining in the 3 fiscal years 1918/19, 1919/20, 1920/1, and in the 5 years 1925/6 to 1929/30. From 1933/4, gold revenues rose steeply to 33% of ordinary Union revenues: Katzen, 56–7.

[e] A refund of dividend tax.

Sources: Union of South Africa, *Reports of the Controller and Auditor-General* (1918–39); Department of Mines, *Annual Reports* (1910–39); Leo Katzen, *Gold and the South African Economy: The Influence of the Gold Mining Industry on Business Cycles and Economic Growth in South Africa, 1886–1961* (Cape Town, 1964), table 14; *Official Year Book of the Union of South Africa* (Pretoria, 1916–46).

TABLE A.6. *Diamond production, sales, and revenue, South West Africa 1909/10–1939*

Year	Diamonds produced (cts.)		Diamonds sold (cts.)	Price per ct. (s.)	Total value (£)	Revenue 'mining' (£)[a]	% of ordinary revenues
1909/10	560,977		560,977	28.83	836,000		
1910/11	798,865		798,865	26.77	1,069,000		
1911/12	816,296		816,296	25.60	1,045,000		
1912/13	969,955		902,157	29.36	1,324,500		
1913/14	1,570,000		1,294,727	42.01	2,698,600		
1913/14 (April–July)	438,980		438,980				
1914 (August to British occupation)	74,078	and	57,808[b]	40.00	1,563,322[c]		
			283,873[b]	112.00	415,074		
1915 (Pomona October–December)	13,409		13,409	50.70	34,033		
1916	144,920		144,920	45.30	325,224	58,394[d]	
1917	364,761		364,761	45.90	834,314	201,019[e]	
1918	372,139		372,139	57.00	1,060,887	363,471	
1919	462,180		460,180	93.39	2,204,326	475,000[f]	
1920	606,424		230,751	138.56	1,599,849	367,308	57.0
1921	171,321		121,557	81.03	492,513	1,201,382	75.0
1922	144,156		297,600	53.17	791,211	547,419	62.8
1923	433,229		495,675	66.80	1,656,700	591,385	69.2
1924	492,696		449,846	54.43	1,224,441	459,941	54.2

1925	515,860	56.52	693,864	1,961,408	278,302	42.7
1926	683,801	56.42	726,808	2,050,688	352,252	46.8
1927	723,877	56.15	577,371	1,620,862	240,569	27.1
1928	508,142	49.25	564,383	1,389,864	48,885	7.1
1929	597,189	60.69	533,101	1,617,698	94,937	12.6
1930	415,047	59.62	214,036	640,253	115,551	14.9
1931	71,532	58.18	103,131	300,000	41,354	6.6
1932	17,944	95.30	44,313	211,170	76,690	14.4
1933	2,374	126.98	9,113	57,860	10,348	2.7
1934	4,126	34.84	257,813	449,167	44,761	10.2
1935	128,463	85.10	126,306	537,408	58,723	11.7
1936	184,916	99.30	184,426	915,695	71,601	12.1
1937	196,802	119.06	184,863	1,100,492	111,017	15.8
1938	154,846	152.32	37,258	283,754	105,369	12.4
1939	36,410	111.99	48,405	271,040	41,045	5.6

[a] 'Royalties, Profits and Leases', mainly from the diamond industry. Revenue is for fiscal years.
[b] Unsold surplus from 1912/13, 1913/14.
[c] Estimated in official returns.
[d] Paid during 1918/19.
[e] Paid during 1919/20.
[f] Estimate.

Sources: Official Year Books of the Union of South Africa (Pretoria, 1920–40); *Reports of the Controller and Auditor-General* (Pretoria, 1920–45); CAD, MNW 914.

TABLE A.7. *Consolidated Diamond Mines of South West Africa: sales and working costs, profitability ratios, 1920–1930*

Year	Sales on diamond account	Administration, distribution	Mining (stores, labour, services)	Trading profit
1920				
(12 months)	100[a]	100[b]	100[c]	100[d]
1921	31	82	52	21
1922	41	79	20	57
1923	111	92	99	133
1924	84	86	154	57
1925	139	115	196	127
1926	143	96	278	91
1927	113	96	238	61
1928	96	106	216	43
1929	117	112	258	55
1930	46	97	188	− 32

	Profit on sales (%)[e]	Profit on capital employed[f](%)	Profit on all capital[g](%)	Post-tax profit on all capital (%)
1920	63.3	21.0	18.8	7.1
1921	40.2	4.3	3.3	− 0.1
1922	80.0	11.8	7.5	0.5
1923	69.6	26.1	22.8	5.8
1924	39.1	11.3	10.2	3.5
1925	53.0	23.5	17.2	5.3
1926	36.9	16.5	13.6	6.6
1927	31.2	10.9	12.4	8.0
1928	25.9	7.9	9.6	5.7
1929	27.6	8.9	11.6	7.9
1930	− 36.0	− 5.8	4.1	4.0

[a] Index 1920 = 100 = £1,266,806 (for 12 months). The first accounts are for 15 months from 1 October 1919.

[b] Index 1920 = 100 = £31,087 (for 12 months). Including directors' remuneration.

[c] Index 1920 = 100 = £401,597 (for 12 months).

[d] Index 1920 = 100 = £733,900 (for 12 months). Net profit on diamond sales before other income, interest, or depreciation.

[e] After administration, mining costs, and depreciation, and before interest.

f Profit on sales

Capital employed (fixed assets + current assets − current liabilities × 100

1

g Profit on sales plus investment earnings, before interest and tax × 100

Capital employed plus investments   1

Source: CDM, *Annual Reports and Accounts,* [1902–30].

TABLE A.8. *Union of South Africa: diamond production and sales, 1911–1945*
(Index 1917 = 100)

Years	Mines				Alluvial			
	Production	Sales	Value realized	Price per mt. ct.	Production	Sales	Value realized	Price per mt. ct.
1911	175	n/a	152	71.6	73	n/a	71	97.6
1912	180	n/a	167	81.3	101	n/a	96	94.6
1913	182	n/a	213	91.2	113	n/a	108	95.5
1914	98	n/a	121	83.6	79	n/a	55	70.3
1915	0.08	n/a	21	102.2	53	n/a	38	70.5
1916	80	n/a	83	87.7	92	n/a	91	99.3
1917	100[a]	100[b]	100[c]	100[d]	100[e]	100[f]	100[g]	100[h]
1918	88	112	122	109.3	78	78	93	118.1
1919	87	109	207	189.9	115	115	263	229.6
1920	85	69	154	222.9	121	121	233	192.2
1921	24	17	25	144.5	81	81	86	106.0
1922	16	45	47	104.6	109	109	130	120.2
1923	64	102	118	116.0	130	130	159	122.3
1924	77	76	90	117.3	153	153	206	134.9
1925	78	103	132	128.1	127	127	183	143.7
1926	86	103	136	131.6	428	430	382	88.8
1927	86	85	110	129.6	1,234	1,234	595	48.2
1928	81	99	100	101.2	1,126	759	572	75.3
1929	82	73	109	149.9	728	755	659	87.0
1930	81	43	59	137.2	489	475	275	58.6
1931	53	37	24	64.0	345	317	145	45.5
1932	11	16	7	46.3	260	271	110	40.8
1933	0.5	7	9	122.5	261	257	136	52.7
1934	0.2	37	26	71.1	229	220	110	50.0
1935	10	89	36	40.7	214	178	104	56.5
1936	12	35	44	123.4	151	151	94	60.9
1937	30	32	58	180.6	110	116	78	64.7

Table A.8 (*cont.*):

Years	Mines				Alluvial			
	Produc- tion	Sales	Value realized	Price per mt. ct.	Produc- tion	Sales	Value realized	Price per mt. ct.
1938	35	15	16	105.6	138	94	49	51.0
1939	39	15	21	146.5	86	100	73	72.0
1940	13	43	34	78.9	92	79	72	83.8
1941	0.04	22	38	174.8	84	83	96	109.3
1942	0.02	21	30	142.0	63	89	114	123.0
1943	3	8	29	374.4	116	237	329	134.5
1944	20	16	38	235.3	203	183	296	143.5
1945	32	38	94	248.9	183	205	372	181.6

[a] 100 = 2,718,912 mt. cts.
[b] 100 = 2,292,442 mt. cts.
[c] 100 = £5,129,130.
[d] 100 = 44.75s.
[e] 100 = 187,845 mt. cts.
[f] 100 = 187,845 mt. cts.
[g] 100 = £1,041,776.
[h] 100 = 110.92s.

The quantities of mine stones are not given in the published data, 1911–16. Values sold for those years have been calculated from sales of alluvial stones and total values sold. It would seem that very little alluvial production was held back by producers.
n/a = not available.

Sources: Department of Mines, *Annual Reports* (Pretoria, 1912–1946); Government Mining Engineer, *Annual Reports* (Pretoria, 1912–1946).

TABLE A.9. *World diamond production, 1900–1946*

Years	Gem material and industrial diamonds ('000 mt. cts.)	Index (1900 = 100)	Industrial diamonds (%)
1900	2,144	100	40
1901	3,081	144	41
1902	2,787	130	39
1903	3,056	143	41
1904	3,983	186	40
1905	3,669	171	44
1906	4,436	207	45
1907	5,441	254	46
1908	4,431	207	45
1909	5,989	279	45

Years	Gem material and industrial diamonds ('000 mt. cts.)	Index (1900 = 100)	Industrial diamonds (%)
1910	6,318	295	46
1911	5,991	279	43
1912	6,188	289	43
1913	6,696	313	44
1914	5,393	252	40
1915	1,123	52	27
1916	2,860	133	36
1917	3,698	172	42
1918	3,407	159	44
1919	3,633	169	41
1920	3,838	179	41
1921	2,033	95	43
1922	1,417	66	42
1923	3,269	152	38
1924	3,902	182	44
1925	4,341	202	48
1926	5,797	270	53
1927	7,435	347	52
1928	7,697	359	53
1929	7,439	347	57
1930	7,528	351	70
1931	7,106	331	77
1932	6,116	285	83
1933	4,033	188	82
1934	6,782	316	81
1935	6,838	319	82
1936	8,258	385	81
1937	9,614	448	79
1938	11,620	542	82
1939	12,499	583	84
1940	13,016	607	85
1941	9,211	430	83
1942	9,587	447	83
1943	8,694	406	80
1944	11,764	549	83
1945	14,384	671	85
1946	10,135	473	79

Source: Henry P. Chandler, *Industrial Diamonds: A Materials Survey* (Washington DC, 1964), table 22. Estimates of the production of industrial diamonds before

Table A.9 (*cont.*):

about 1925 must be regarded as very approximate. Production figures from the US Bureau of Mines take no account of sales or stocks held back.

TABLE A.10. *Prices declared and realized for South African mine and alluvial diamonds, 1884–1945*

Years	Price per metric carat (*s.*)	Index	Index adjusted against United Kingdom Wholesale Price Indices
		1913 = 100	*1913 = 100*
1884	24.16	56.8	58
1885	19.88	46.8	51
1886	21.78	51.2	59
1887	22.96	54.0	64
1888	20.40	48.0	55
1889	28.45	66.9	75
1890	32.37	76.1	86
1891	24.98	58.7	64
1892	25.05	58.9	68
1893	26.99	63.5	75
1894	23.75	55.8	70
1895	25.68	60.4	77
1896	25.44	59.8	79
1897	24.90	58.6	76
1898	25.44	59.8	75
1899	29.44	69.2	88
1900	35.53	83.6	97
1901	37.83	89.0	107
1902	39.72	93.5	112
1903	39.57	93.1	112
1904	37.32	87.8	105
1905	38.04	89.5	107
1906	45.88	107.9	124
1907	39.12	92.0	101
1908	21.02	49.5	56
1909	25.10	59.0	66
1910	29.57	69.5	75
1911	34.10	80.2	85
1912	39.10	92.0	93
1913	42.50	100.0	100

Years	Price per metric carat (*s.*)	Index	Index adjusted against United Kingdom Wholesale Price Indices
		1929 = 100	*1929 = 100*
1914	39.2	48.5	67
1915	51.5	63.7	72
1916	44.5	55.1	48
1917	49.8	61.6	42
1918	53.3	65.9	40
1919	98.5	121.9	67
1920	113.9	140.9	63
1921	79.5	98.4	68
1922	61.2	75.7	65
1923	59.8	74.0	64
1924	66.2	81.9	67
1925	66.7	82.5	71
1926	69.0	85.4	79
1927	55.6	68.8	66
1928	60.1	74.4	72
1929	80.8	100.0	100
1930	62.6	77.5	88
1931	37.6	46.5	60
1932	35.1	43.4	58
1933	57.6	71.3	95
1934	39.5	48.9	63
1935	24.8	30.7	39
1936	58.7	72.6	88
1937	79.4	98.3	102
1938	51.0	63.1	71
1939	71.1	87.9	98
1940	44.0	54.5	45
1941	90.0	111.4	83
1942	83.6	103.5	74
1943	158.0	195.5	137
1944	140.6	174.0	119
1945	139.0	172.0	115

Sources: British South Africa, *Annual Statements of the Trade and Shipping of the Colonies and Territories forming the South African Customs Union*; Cape of Good Hope, *Statistical Register* (1890–1905); Department of Mines, *Annual Report* (Pretoria, 1912–1946). Before 1897, declared quantities and values of diamond exports do not include small amounts of alluvial production from the Transvaal or the Free State, though production from Free State mines passed

Table A.10 (*cont.*):

through Kimberley and Cape Town. From 1897, these quantities and values are included in Cape and Union customs returns. From 1906, Department of Mines records of sales have been preferred, because not all diamonds produced and sold were exported in the late 1920s and 1930s, after the establishment of a cutting industry. Later customs quantities and values do not include, for example, sales of Namaqualand state alluvial diamonds. South West African sales were not included in Union exports, and have been excluded from the above. The wholesale prices are taken from B. R. Mitchell, *European Historical Statistics, 1750–1975*, 2nd edn. (London, 1981), 772 with all the reservations made for such a long series which 'splices' a number of indices.

LIST OF SOURCES USED

ARCHIVES AND PRIVATE COLLECTIONS

Archives Nationales, Paris. 65 AQ, 1079. Compagnie française des mines de diamant du Cap, 1880–87; F^{12} 7104–6 [Cape Colony and Union of South Africa].

Baker Library, Harvard Business School. Mining Company Reports.

Barlow Rand Limited, Sandton, Johannesburg [BRA]; Archives of Herman Eckstein and Company [HE]; Wernher, Beit and Company [WB].

Bodleian Library, Oxford [Bod.]. Milner Papers; Harcourt Papers.

Cape Archives, Cape Town. Griqualand West [GLW] 1871–80.

Charter Consolidated Ltd., London. Data Retrieval Unit (unclassified papers); annual reports of mining companies; financial statements.

Consolidated Goldfields PLC, London. Gold Fields of South Africa, Ltd., Minute Books.

De Beers Consolidated Mines Ltd., Kimberley Archive [DBCA]. (For a description of holdings see inventories by Moonyean Buys below.)

Green Library, Stanford University. Despatches from United States Consuls in Cape Town, 1800–1906.

Hoover Institution for War and Peace, Stanford University. W. L. Honnold MS.

Kimberley Public Library. Paton Papers; Company Documents; newspapers and directories.

McGregor Museum, Kimberley. F. S. P. Stow papers.

N. M. Rothschild and Sons, London [RAL]. Letter Copy Books; South African Various; Private Letters Sundry; Sundry Correspondence received; Rothschild Brothers, Paris; Information Books.

Public Record Office, London [PRO]. Board of Trade 11 [Miscellaneous]; 31 [Dissolved Companies]; Colonial Office 107; 109; 461 [Griqualand West]; 551 [South Africa]; 532 [Dominions]; 687 [Trade]; 852 [Economic]; 96 [Gold Coast]; 111 [British Guiana]; 267 [Sierra Leone]; Customs 4/88–94 [Imports]; Dominions Office 35; FO 382 [War Trade Advisory Committee]; 551 [Contraband]; 368 [Commercial]; 371 [Political]; 438 [War].

Rhodes House Library, Oxford [RH]. Rhodes Papers, MSS Africa s. 227, s. 228, and Telegrams; Hildersham Hall Collection, MSS Africa s. 1647; MSS Africa, t 1, t 5, t 6, t 14; W. R. Quinan papers, MSS Africa s. 123–8; Central Mining and Investment Corporation, MSS Brit. Emp. s. 412 [and uncatalogued ledgers of mining companies]; Molteno Papers, I, II; T. W. Baxter, 'Yrs C. J. Rhodes:

The Letters of an Imperialist'. MS [transcripts]; R. Fenton, MSS Afr s. 138; Society for the Propagation of the Gospel. Orange Free State Mission, *Quarterly Papers*.

State Archives, Central Archives Depot [CAD], Pretoria. Mines and Industries [MNW, and MNW (unnumbered)]; Treasury [TES]; Native Affairs [NTS].

PRINTED PRIMARY SOURCES

British Parliamentary Papers [PP]:

C. 508, 1872. *Further Correspondence respecting Affairs of the Cape of Good Hope.*
C. 732, 1873. *Further Correspondence respecting Affairs of the Cape of Good Hope.*
C. 1342, 1875. *Correspondence relating to the Colonies and States of South Africa*, Part 1, *Cape of Good Hope and Griqualand West.*C. 1348, 1875. *Correspondence relating to Griqualand West.*
C. 2220, 1879. *Further correspondence respecting the Affairs of South Africa.*
Cd. 7707, 1914. *Dominions Royal Commission. Minutes of Evidence.*

Cape of Good Hope, Parliamentary Papers [CPP]:

(see the *Index to the Annexures and Printed Papers of House of Assembly 1854–1897* (Cape Town, 1899)). Used particularly for Reports by Inspectors of Mines; Blue Books on Native Affairs; Reports on Convict Stations; Reports on Vooruitzigt Estate; Reports of Commissions and Select Committees on the diamond mines, the diamond trade, the compound system, labour, the Mining Boards, the Detective Department. Kimberley Municipality and water supply, and the administration of Griqualand West.
Correspondence Relating to the Transfer of Certain Interests and Concessions in the South West African Protectorate to the South West Africa Consolidated Diamond Company, Limited. A 1-20.

Acts of Parliament.

Census, 1891 (Cape Town, 1892); *Census, 1904* (Cape Town, 1905).
Statistical Register of the Cape of Good Hope, (Cape Town, 1881–1908).
The Statute Law of Griqualand West, comprising Government Notices, Proclamations, and Ordinances together with an Appendix containing the Regulations Promulgated and Enacted from the Date of the Annexation of the Province as British Territory to the Date of its Annexation to the Cape Colony, (Cape Town, 1882).
Reports of Cases Decided in the High Court of Griqualand West, 2 vols., 1882–3, 1883–4 (Cape Town, 1884, 1885).

Index and Digest of Cases Decided in the High Court of Griqualand, vols. 1–5, 1882–9 (Cape Town, 1890).

Colonial Office Confidential Prints [COCP]:

African 83 (1875); 83A (1875); *Cape* 61 (1875); 76, 78 (1875); *African* 89 (1876); 96 (1876); 105 (1876); 108 (1876); 112 (1876); 147, 154, 162 (1878); 203–4 (1877–9); 215 (1880); *Africa South* 757 (1905); 1033 (1913); 1042 (1914); 1064 (1918).

Colony of British Guiana, *Reports on Administration* (Georgetown, 1928).

Colony of Victoria, *Acts, Orders in Council, Notices, and Mining Board Bye-Laws Relating to the Gold Fields* (Melbourne, 1874).

Mining Companies:

Consolidated Diamond Mines of South-West Africa, Ltd., *Annual Reports and Accounts*, 1920–46.

De Beers Consolidated Mines Ltd., *Annual Reports*, 1889–1946.

De Beers Mining Company, Ltd., *Annual Reports*, 1882–8.

New Jagersfontein Mining and Exploration Company Ltd., *Annual Reports*, 1932–9.

Premier (Transvaal) Diamond Mining Co. Ltd., *Directors' Reports*, 1903–39.

Transvaal Chamber of Mines, *Annual Reports*, 1889–1945.

South Africa (Union and Republic):

Annual Statements of the Trade and Shipping of the Union of South Africa and of Southern and Northern Rhodesia (Cape Town, 1911–46).

Assembly Debates (Cape Town, 1920–45).

Correspondence between the Secretary of State for the Colonies and the Governors-General on the subject of the Mandate for South-West Africa and the Peace Conditions, UG No. 44 (Cape Town, 1919).

Department of Customs and Excise, *British South Africa: Annual Statements of the Trade and Shipping of the Union of South Africa and of Southern and Northern Rhodesia* (Cape Town, 1911–46).

Department of Mines, *The Mineral Resources of the Union of South Africa* (Pretoria, 1939).

—— *Annual Reports; Reports of the Government Mining Engineer* (Pretoria, 1901–50).

Memorandum on the Country Known as German South-West Africa Compiled from such Information as is Presently Available to the Government of the Union of South Africa (Pretoria, 1915).

Report of the Commission on the Economic and Financial Relations between the Union of South Africa and the Mandated Territory of South West Africa, UG No. 16 (Pretoria, 1935).

Report of the Commission of Inquiry into the Diamond Industry of the Republic of South Africa and the Territory of South West Africa (Pretoria, RP 85/1973).

Reports of the Controller and Auditor-General, (Pretoria, 1912–1945).

Senate Debates, (Cape Town, 1920–1945).

Senate Select Committees, *Public Accounts, First and Second Reports (Diamond Cutting Agreement)*, SC 3B-'28; SC 1A-'32.

State Mining Commission, 1916–17, UG No. 6, (Pretoria, 1917).

Territory of South West Africa, *Reports of the Administrator* (Windhoek, 1921–1946).

P. W. THIRION, 'Commission of inquiry into alleged irregularities and misapplication of property in representative authorities and the central authority of South West Africa. Eighth interim report: Control by the State over prospecting and mining for, and disposing of, minerals in South West Africa', (TS, 1985).

United States:

US Congress, *Annual Report of the Bureau of Statistics on the Commerce and Navigation of the United States* (Washington, 1878).

US Department of Commerce, *Statistical Abstract of the United States* (Washington, 1889–1940).

US Law Reports, *Fifth Decennial Digest*, 1936–46, vol. 32 (New York, 1947).

DIRECTORIES, GUIDES, NEWSPAPERS, JOURNALS

BUYS, MOONYEAN, *Archives of Companies on the Diamond Fields of Southern Africa, 1878–1889, Absorbed in the Big Amalgamation* (DBCM, 1979).

—— *Archives of the General Manager 1888–ca 1949 and Department* (DBCM, 1981).

—— *Archives of the Kimberley Board of Directors, 1880–ca 1965* (DBCM, 1981).

—— *Archives of Public Bodies, 1874–ca 1900, Instituted for the Order and Good Government of the Four Kimberley Mines* (DBCM, 1980).

—— *Landlords of the Kimberley Diamond Fields 1870–1889* (DBCM, 1980).

—— *Records of Kimberley Public Institutions, 1882–1976, in the De Beers Archives* (DBCM, 1980).

—— *De Beers' Administrative Records Pertaining to The Rhodes Fruit Farms Limited, 1899–1937* (DBCM, 1982).

Cape Times Law Reports, vol. 1 (Cape Town, 1892).

Dictionary of South African Biography, vols. 1–4 (Pretoria, 1968–80).

GOLDMANN, C. S., *South African Mines; Their Position, Results and Developments: Together with an Account of Diamonds, Land, Finance, and Kindred Concerns*, 2 vols. (Johannesburg, 1895–6).

JULIEN, A., 'A Bibliography of the Diamond Fields of South Africa', *Economic Geology*, 4 (1909), 453–69.

NOBLE, JOHN, *Official Handbook: History, Productions, and Resources of the Cape of Good Hope* (Cape Town, 1886).

Official Year Book of the Union of South Africa (Pretoria, 1916–50).

PEELE, ROBERT, *Mining Engineers' Handbook* (New York, 1918).

South African Who's Who (Social and Business) (Cape Town, 1913–39).

Use of contemporary newspapers ranged from occasional references (from archival clippings) to systematic survey of valuable primary sources. The following have been most frequently referred to in the text:

The African World (London).

The Argus Annual and Trades Directory (1889, 1892).

Die Bürger (Johannesburg, 1927).

The Cape Argus.

The Cape Times.

The Daily Independent.

The Diamond Field (Kimberley).

The Diamond Fields Advertiser and Commercial Guide (Kimberley).

The Diamond News (Kimberley).

The Economist.

The General Directory of South Africa, 1890–1.

Griqualand West Government Gazette.

Kelly's Post Office Directories (London).

The Mining Gazette (Kimberley).

The Mining Journal (London).

The Mining Magazine and Review (London).

The Rand Daily Mail (Johannesburg).

South Africa (London).

South African Mining Manual, ed. W. R. Skinner (London).

South West Africa Government Gazette (Windhoek).

The Star (Johannesburg, 1927).

Trade and Business Directory (Kimberley, 1898–9).

Transvaal Gazette (Johannesburg, 1903).

Turner's Kimberley, Old De Beers, Dutoitspan, Bultfontein and Barkly Directory and Guide (Kimberley, 1878).

Turner's Griqualand West Directory and guide to the Diamond Fields (Grahamstown, 1884).

PRINTED SECONDARY SOURCES

ALGAR, F., *The Diamond Fields: With Notes on the Cape Colony and Natal* (London, 1872).

ARNDT, E. H. D., *Banking and Currency Development in South Africa* (Cape Town, 1928).

ATKINSON, C. E., and SCOTT, A., *A Short History of Diamond Cutting* (London, 1888).

ATMORE, ANTHONY, and SANDERS, PETER, 'Sotho Arms and Ammunition in the Nineteenth Century', *Journal of African History*, 12/4 (1971), 535–44.

BABE, J. L., *The South African Diamond Fields* (New York, 1872).

BALFOUR, IAN, *Evolution of the Central Selling Organisation for Diamonds* (London, n.d.).

BARRON, CAROLINE M., *The Parish of St. Andrew Holborn* (London, 1979).

BAUER M., *Precious Stones* (London, 1904).

BEER, G. L., *African Questions at the Paris Peace Conference* (New York, 1923).

BEIT, SIR ALFRED, *The Will and the Way* (London, 1957).

BLEY, HELMUT, *South-West Africa under German Rule, 1894–1914* (London, 1971).

Board for the Protection of Mining Interests, *Our Diamond Industry* (Griqualand West, 1885).

BOUTAN E., *Le diamant* (Paris, 1886).

BOYLE, F., *To the Cape for Diamonds: A Story of Digging Experiences in South Africa* (London, 1873).

BURLEY, K. H., (untitled review), in *Business History*, 6/1 (1964), 72.

CARTWRIGHT, A. P., *The Corner House* (London, 1965).

—— *Diamonds and Clay* (Cape Town, 1977).

—— *The Dynamite Company: The Story of African Explosives and Chemical Industries Limited* (Johannesburg, 1964).

—— *Gold Paved the Way* (London, 1967).

CATTELLE, W. R., *The Diamond* (New York, 1911).

CHANDLER, A. D., *Strategy and Structure: Chapters in the History of the American Industrial Enterprise* (Cambridge, Mass., 1962).

CHANDLER, HENRY P., *Industrial Diamonds: A Materials Survey* (Washington DC, 1964).

CHAPMAN, S. D., 'Rhodes and the City of London: Another View of Imperialism', *Historical Journal*, 28/3 (1985), 647–66.

CHILVERS H. A., *The Story of De Beers* (London, 1939).

CLARENCE-SMITH, GERVASE, *The Third Portuguese Empire 1825–1975: A Study in Economic Imperialism* (Manchester, 1975).

CLARK, C. M. H. (ed.), *Select Documents in Australian History 1851–1900* (Sydney, 1955).

COCKRAM, GAIL-MARYSE, *South West African Mandate* (Cape Town, 1976).

COHEN, L., *Reminiscences of Kimberley* (London, 1911).

COLVIN, I., *Life of Jameson* (London, 1922).

DAVENPORT, T. R. H., *South Africa: A Modern History*, 3rd edn. (Basingstoke, 1987).

DAVIES, R. H., *Capital, State and White Labour in South Africa, 1900–1960* (Brighton, 1979).

DAVIS, RALPH (untitled review), *Business History Review* 45/1 (1977), 258.

DEAN, FRANS VAN, *Het kartel in de internationale diamanthandel* (Antwerp, 1953).

DE CRESPIGNY, ANTHONY, and SCHRIRE, ROBERT (eds.), *The Government and Politics of South Africa* (Cape Town, 1978).

DE KIEWIET, C. W., *The Imperial Factor in South Africa* (Cambridge, 1937).

DELIUS, PETER, 'Migrant Labour and the Pedi, 1840-80', in Shula Marks and Anthony Atmore (eds.), *Economy and Society in Pre-Industrial Africa*, 293-312.

DEMUTH, JEAN, *Der Diamantenmarkt mit besonderer Berücksichtigung der deutsch-südwestafrikanischen Ausbeute* (Karlsruhe, 1912).

DENOON, S. J. N., *A Grand Illusion* (London, 1973).

DOXEY, G. V., *The Industrial Colour Bar in South Africa* (Cape Town, 1961).

DUMETT, RAYMOND, 'Africa's Strategic Minerals during the Second World War', *Journal of African History*, 26/3 (1985), 381-408.

DUMINY, A. H., and GUEST, W. R. (eds.), *Fitzpatrick South African Politician: Selected Papers, 1888-1905* (Johannesburg, 1976).

EMDEN, PAUL, *Randlords* (London, 1935).

EMMANUEL, H., *Diamonds and Precious Stones* (London, 1865).

ETHERINGTON, NORMAN A., 'Labour Supply and the Genesis of the South African Confederation in the 1870s', *Journal of African History*, 20/2 (1979), 235-53.

FITZPATRICK, P., *South African Memories* (London, 1932).

FLINT, JOHN, *Cecil Rhodes* (London, 1976).

'Fossor', *Twelve Months in the South African Diamond Fields* (London, 1872).

FRANKEL, S. H., *Capital Investment in Africa: Its Course and Effects* (London, 1938).

—— *Investment and the Return to Equity Capital in the South African Gold Mining Industry 1887-1965: An International Comparison* (London, 1967).

FREUND, BILL, *Capital and Labour in The Nigerian Tin Mines* (London, 1981).

GALBRAITH, JOHN S., *Crown and Charter: The Early Days of the British South Africa Company* (Los Angeles, 1974).

GREEN, TIMOTHY, *The World of Diamonds* (London, 1981).

GREENHALGH, PETER, *West African Diamonds 1919-1983: An Economic History* (Manchester, 1985).

GREGORY, THEODORE, *Ernest Oppenheimer and the Economic Development of Southern Africa* (Cape Town, 1962).

—— 'The History of the Diamond Syndicate,' (MS, DBCA, 1964).

HAHLO, H. R., 'The Great South-West African Diamond Case,' *South African Law Journal*, 76/2 (1959), 151-86.

—— and KHAN, ELLISON, *The Union of South Africa: The Development of its Laws and Constitution* (London, 1960).

HANCOCK, W. K., *Smuts: The Sanguine Years, 1870-1919* (Cambridge, 1962).

HARRIS, D., *Pioneer, Soldier and Politician* (London, 1931).

HEERTJE, H., *De Diamantbewergers van Amstderdam* (Amsterdam, 1936).

HENRY, J. A., *The First Hundred Years of the Standard Bank* London, 1963).

HERMANN, L., *A History of the Jews in South Africa* (Cape Town, 1935).

History of the Standard Bank of South Africa Ltd., 1862-1913 (Glasgow, 1914).

HERTNER, PETER, and JONES, GEOFFREY (eds.), *Multinationals: Theory and History* (London, 1986).

HOBSBAWM, E. J., *Labouring Men: Studies in the History of Labour* (London, 1964).

HOCKING, ANTHONY, *Oppenheimer and Son* (Johannesburg, 1973).

HORNSBY, A. H., *The South African Diamond Fields* (Chicago, 1874).

HOUGHTON, D. HOBART, and DAGUT, JENIFER (eds.), *Source Material on the South African Economy*, vol. 1, 1860–1899 (Cape Town, 1972).

HUMBOLDT-DACHROEDEN, WILHELM VON, *Die deutsche diamantenpolitik* (Jena, 1915).

INNES, DUNCAN, *Anglo: Anglo American and the Rise of Modern South Africa* (Johannesburg, 1984).

JESSUP, EDWARD, *Ernest Oppenehimer: A Study in Power* (London, 1979).

JOEL, STANHOPE, *Ace of Diamonds* (London, 1958).

JÖHLINGER, OTTO, *Die Diamanten Südwestafrickas* (Leipzig, 1914).

JOUBERT, S. P., 'Alluvial Diamond-Diggers in South Africa', *South African Journal of Industries* (September 1921), 702–12.

KELLAWAY, P., 'Black Responses to an Industrialising Economy: "Labour Shortage" and "Native Policy" in Griqualand West, 1870–1890', (MS, Conference on South African Labour History, University of the Witwatersrand, 1976).

KATZEN, LEO, *Gold and the South African Economy: The Influence of the Gold Mining Industry on Business Cycles and Economic Growth in South Africa, 1886–1961* (Cape Town, 1964).

KIDD, C. A., *CAST in Namaqualand* (London, 1983).

KIMBLE, JUDY, 'Labour Migration in Basutoland *c.* 1870–1885', in Shula Marks and Richard Rathbone (eds.), *Industrialisation and Social Change in South Africa*.

KNIGHT, JOHN and STEVENSON, HEATHER, 'The Williamson Diamond Mine, De Beers and the Colonial Office: A Case-Study in the Quest for Control', *Journal of Modern African Studies*, 24/3 (1966), 423–45.

KUBICEK, ROBERT, V., *Economic Imperialism in Theory and Practice: The Case of South African Gold Mining Finance, 1886–1914* (Durham NC, 1979).

LANNING, GREG, with Marti Mueller, *Africa Undermined: Mining Companies and the Underdevelopment of Africa* (Harmondsworth, 1979).

LAUNAY, L. DE, *Les diamants du Cap* (Paris, 1897).

LEHMANN, OLGA, *Hans Merensky ein deutscher Pionier in Südafrika* (Göttingen, 1965).

LEHRFELDT, R. A., 'The Shift System on the Witwatersrand Mines', *Economic Journal*, 21 (1911), 223–31.

LEITH, C. K., FURNESS J. W., and LEWIS, CLEONA., *World Minerals and World Peace* (Washington DC, 1943).

LENZEN, GODEHARD, *The History of Diamond Production and the Diamond Trade* (London, 1970).

LEVY A. B., *Private Corporations and their Control*, 2 vols. (London, 1950).

LEVY, HERMAN, *Monopoly and Competition: A study in English Industrial Organisation* (New York, 1977).

LEWSEN, PHYLLIS (ed.), *Selections from the Correspondence of J. X. Merriman, 1870-1890* (Cape Town, 1960).

LINDLEY, A. F., *Adamantia: The Truth about the South African Diamond Fields* (London, 1873).

LOCKHART, J. G., and WOODHOUSE, C. M., *Rhodes* (London, 1963).

London and South African Exploration Company Limited, *Statement Shewing the Position of the London and South African Exploration Company Limited, in Respect of their Property as Affected by Legislation and by the Action of the Executive Government, the Mining Boards and the Claimholders, between the Years 1871 and 1890 Inclusive* (Cape Town, 1890).

MABIN, ALAN, and CONRADIE, BARBARA, (eds.), *The Confidence of the Whole Country: Standard Bank Reports on Economic Conditions in Southern Africa 1865-1902* (Johannesburg, 1987).

MCCRACKEN, J. L., *The Cape Parliament, 1854-1910* (Oxford, 1967).

MACMILLAN, M., *Sir Henry Barkly: Mediator and Moderator, 1815-1898* (Cape Town, 1970).

MARKS, SHULA, and ATMORE, ANTHONY (eds.), *Economy and Society in Pre-industrial South Africa* (London, 1980).

—— and RATHBONE, RICHARD (eds.), *Industrialisation and Social Change in South Africa* (London, 1982).

MARTIN, JOHN, 'Group Administration in the Gold Mining Industry of the Witwatersrand', *Economic Journal*, 3 (1929), 356-452.

MATTHEWS, J. W., *Incwadi Yami, or Twenty Years' Personal Experience in South Africa* (London, 1887).

MAWBY A., 'Capital, Government and Politics in the Transvaal: A Revision and a Reversion', *Historical Journal*, 17/2 (1974), 387-415.

MILIBAND, RALPH, *The State in Capitalist Society* (New York, 1969).

MITCHELL B. R., *European Historical Statistics, 1750-1975*, 2nd edn. (London, 1981).

MORRELL W. P., *The Gold Rushes* (London, 1968).

MURRAY, COLIN, *Families Divided: The Impact of Migrant Labour in Lesotho* (Cambridge, 1981).

NATHAN, MANFRED, *The Gold Law of the Transvaal and the Orange Free State*, 5th edn. (Johannesburg, 1934).

NEWBURY, COLIN, 'Out of the Pit: The Capital Accumulation of Cecil Rhodes', *Journal of Imperial and Commonwealth History*, 10/1 (1981), 25-43.

—— 'Technology, Capital and Consolidation: The Performance of De Beers Mining Company Limited, 1880-1889', *Business History Review*, 61/1 (1987), 1-42.

—— 'The Origins and Function of the London Diamond Syndicate, 1889-1914', *Business History*, 29/1 (1987), 7-26.

NEWBURY, COLIN, 'Spoils of War: Sub-imperial Collaboration in South West Africa and New Guinea, 1914–1920', *Journal of Imperial and Commonwealth History*, 16/3 (1988), 86–106.

OPPENHEIMER, E., and WILLIAMS, ALPHEUS, *Diamond Deposits of German South West Africa* (Kimberley, 1914).

OPPENHEIMER, H., 'The Diamond Industry', *Transactions of the Seventh Commonwealth Mining and Metallurgical Congress* (Johannesburg, 1961).

PAYTON, CHARLES A., *The Diamond Diggings of South Africa: A Personal and Practical Account* (London, 1872).

PERRINGS, C., 'The Production Process, Industrial Labour Strategies and Worker Responses in the Southern African Gold Mining Industry', *Journal of African History*, 18/1 (1977), 129–35.

PHIMISTER, I. R., 'Rhodes, Rhodesia and the Rand', *Journal of Southern African Studies*, 1/1 (1974), 74–90.

RANGER, TERENCE, 'Faction Fighting, Race Consciousness and Worker Consciousness: A Note on the Jagersfontein Riots of 1914', *South African Labour Bulletin*, 4/5 (1978), 66–74.

RANSOME, STAFFORD, *The Engineer in South Africa* (London, 1903).

REUNERT, THEODORE, *Diamonds and Gold in South Africa* (Cape Town, 1893).

—— 'Diamond Mining at the Cape', in J. Noble (ed.), *Official Handbook: History, Productions, and Resources of the Cape of Good Hope* (Cape Town, 1886), 177–219.

RICHARDSON, PETER, 'Nobels and the Australian Mining Industry, 1907–1925', *Business History*, 26/2 (1984), 156–92.

ROBERTS, BRIAN, *The Diamond Magnates* (London, 1972).

—— *Kimberley: Turbulent City* (Cape Town, 1976).

ROBERTSON, MARIAN, *Diamond Fever, South African Diamond History, 1866–1969* (Cape Town, 1974).

ROBINSON, E. A. G., and GUILLEBAUD, C. W., *Monopoly* (Cambridge, 1943).

ROHRBACH, PAUL, *Dernburg und die Südwestafrikaner; Diamantenfrage, Selbstvervaltung, Landeshilfe* (Berlin, 1911).

ROTBERG, ROBERT, *The Founder: Cecil Rhodes and the Pursuit of Power* (New York, 1988).

SARON, GUSTAV and HOTZ, LOUIS, *The Jews in South Africa: A History* (Cape Town, 1955).

SCHUMANN, C. G. W., *Structural Changes and Business Cycles in South Africa 1806–1936* (London, 1938).

SHILLINGTON, KEVIN, 'The Impact of the Diamond Discoveries on the Kimberley Hinterland: Class Formation, Colonialism and Resistance among the Tlhaping of Griqualand West in the 1870s', in Shula Marks and Richard Rathbone (eds.), *Industrialisation and Social Change in South Africa*, 99–118.

SHIPLEY, ROBERT M., 'The Diamond Syndicates and their Successors', *Gems and Gemology*, 6/9 (1949), 199–206.

SIMOND, PHILLIDA BROOKE (ed.), *John Blades Currey, 1850 to 1900* (Johannesburg, 1987).

SMALBERGER, J. M., 'IDB and the Mining Compound System in the 1880s', *South African Journal of Economics*, 42/4 (1974), 398–414.

—— 'The Role of the Diamond-Mining Industry in the Development of the Pass-Law system in South Africa', *International Journal of African Historical Studies*, 9/3 (1976), 419–34.

STOKES, RALPH S. G., *Mines and Minerals of the British Empire* (London, 1908).

SUTTON, I. B., 'The Diggers' Revolt in Griqualand West, 1875', *International Journal of African Historical Studies*, 12/1 (1979), 40–61.

SZENBERG, MICHAEL, *The Economics of the Israeli Diamond Industry* (New York, 1971),

THOMPSON, L. M., and WILSON, M. (eds.), *The Oxford History of South Africa*, 2 vols. (Oxford, 1969, 1971).

TURRELL, R., 'The 1875 Black Flag Revolt on the Kimberley Diamond Fields', *Journal of Southern African Studies*, 7/2 (1981), 194–235.

—— 'Kimberley: Labour and Compounds, 1871–1888', in Shula Marks and Richard Rathbone (eds.), *Industrialisation and Social Change in South Africa*, 45–76.

—— 'Rhodes, De Beers, and Monopoly', *Journal of Imperial and Commonwealth History*, 10/3 (1982), 311–43.

—— 'Sir Frederic Philipson Stow: The Unknown Diamond Magnate', *Business History*, 28/1 (1986), 62–79.

—— *Capital and Labour on the Kimberley Diamond Fields, 1871–1890* (Cambridge, 1987).

VAN DER HORST, S. T., *Native Labour in South Africa* (Cape Town, 1941).

VAN HELTEN, JEAN-JACQUES, La France et l'or des Boers: Some Aspects of French Investment in South Africa between 1890 and 1914', *African Affairs*, 84 (1985).

VAN ONSELEN, C., *Chibaro: African Mine Labour in Southern Rhodesia* (London, 1976).

VAN RENSBURG, W. C. J., *Strategic Minerals: Major Mineral Exporting Regions of the World*, vol. 1 (Brookfield, New Jersey, 1986).

VAN WAGENEN, T. F., *International Mining Law* (New York, 1918).

VON STRANDMANN, HARTMUT POGGE (ed.), *Walther Rathenau Industrialist, Banker, Intellectual, and Politician: Notes and Diaries 1907–1922* (Oxford, 1985).

WAGNER P. A., *The Diamond Fields of South Africa* (Johannesburg, 1914).

WALKER, ERIC A. (ed.), *The Cambridge History of the British Empire*, vol. 8, *South Africa, Rhodesia and the High Commission Territories* (Cambridge, 1963).

—— *A History of Southern Africa*, 3rd edn., (London, 1957).

WARWICK, PETER, *Black People and the South African War, 1899–1902* (Cambridge, 1983).

WHEATCROFT, GEOFFREY, *The Randlords: The Men who Made South Africa* (London, 1985).

WILLIAMS, A. F., *Some Dreams Come True* (Cape Town, 1948).

List of Sources Used

WILLIAMS, GARDNER, F., 'The Diamond Mines of South Africa', *Transactions of the American Institute of Mining Engineers*, 15 (1887), 392–417.

—— *The Diamond Mines of South Africa: Some Account of their Rise and Development* (New York, 1902).

WILSON, A. J., *The Life and Times of Sir Alfred Chester Beatty* (London, 1985).

WILSON, FRANCIS, *Labour in the South African Gold Mines, 1911–1969* (Cambridge, 1972).

WORGER, WILLIAM, 'Workers as Criminals: The Rule of Law in Early Kimberley, 1870–1885', in Frederick Cooper (ed.), *Struggle for the City: Migrant Labor, Capital, and the State in Urban Africa* (Beverly Hills, Calif., 1983).

—— *South Africa's City of Diamonds: Mine Workers and Monopoly Capitalism in Kimberley, 1867–1895* (New Haven and London, 1987).

WRIGHT, H. M. (ed.), *Sir James Rose Innes: Selected Correspondence* (Cape Town, 1972).

YUDELMAN, DAVID, *The Emergence of Modern South Africa: State, Capital, and the Incorporation of Organised Labor on the South African Gold Fields, 1902–1939* (Westport, Conn., and London, 1983).

—— and JEEVES, ALAN, 'New Labour Frontiers for Old: Black Migrants to the South African Gold Mines, 1920–85', *Journal of Southern African Studies*, 13/1 (1986), 101–24.

THESES

ARONHEIM, W. A., 'The Development of Diamond Industry and Trade in Peace and War', M. Social Science thesis (New York, 1943).

BENNETT, ANNE E., 'The West Ridgeway Committee: Its Role and Significance in Relation to Political Developments in the Transvaal, 1905–7, M.Phil. thesis (Oxford, 1984).

PURKIS, A. J., 'The Politics, Capital and Labour of Railway-Building in the Cape Colony, 1870–1885', D.Phil. thesis (Oxford, 1978).

SIEBÖRGER, R. F., 'The Recruitment and Organisation of African Labour for the Kimberley Diamond Mines, 1871–1888', MA thesis (Rhodes University, 1975).

SUTTON, I. B., 'The 1878 rebellion in Griqualand West and Adjacent Territories', Ph.D. thesis (London, 1975).

TURRELL, R. V., 'Capital, Class and Monopoly: The Kimberley Diamond Fields, 1871–1889', Ph.D. thesis (London, 1982).

WILBURN, K. E., 'The Climax of Railway Competition in South Africa, 1886–1889', D.Phil. thesis (Oxford, 1982).

INDEX